D1294921

The U.S. Mint and Coinage

"The First Mint," a painting by Edwin Lamazure made under the direction of Frank Stewart. These were the first buildings erected for public use by the new Congress.

The U.S. Mint and Coinage

An Illustrated History
From 1776 to the Present

Don Taxay

Foreword by Gilroy Roberts

ARCO PUBLISHING COMPANY, INC.
New York

OTHER BOOKS BY DON TAXAY

Counterfeit, Mis-Struck, and Unofficial U.S. Coins

Illustrated History of U.S. Commemorative Coinage

Published by ARCO PUBLISHING COMPANY, Inc.
219 Park Avenue South, New York, N.Y. 10003

Second Printing, 1969

Library of Congress Catalog Card Number 66-18413

Standard Book Number 668-01125-4

Printed in the United States of America

Book designed by Fred Honig

To my good friend

ERIC P. NEWMAN

whose researches in American Colonial numismatics
have been an enduring inspiration.

Foreword

READING DON TAXAY'S MANUSCRIPT took me back nearly thirty years, to when I first entered the fortress-like Mint building in Philadelphia, to report as an understudy to the Engraver, John Sinnock.

In retrospect it seems but a short time ago that I first passed through the heavy iron double doors to the ornate marble-tiled lobby, with its massive pillars arching to the ceiling, and the colorful murals—allegories of early minting processes being performed by children, a style and decor more reminiscent of a bygone era. Even then it was being overtaken by our changing times, though it still had strength and pride.

On the second floor I found the door that had "Engraver" in faded gold letters on the frosted glass panel. This was the "inner sanctum," a part of the Mint that was held with something akin to awe by the other departments.

Here were kept the closely guarded master dies and hubs for our U.S. coinage, the original portraits and designs in steel that were so familiar as everyday coins. Here was performed the difficult and somewhat mysterious art of shaping into tool steel the intricate designs and inscriptions that are later to be impressed into other metals as coins and medallions. And it was here that I would be initiated into the secrets of a craft whose beginnings are obscured in antiquity.

The high-ceilinged room, the oaken bracket on the wall that once held loaded rifles for defense, the heavy laminated-wood engravers' benches and tools, worn and polished by the hands of men, all spoke in mute eloquence of those, now gone, who had left their mark. The ghosts of the past crowded in; noted engravers had worked here, and trod these floors. The files of memoranda and letters, the vigorous pen strokes now fading with age—these reached back even

vii

to earlier mints and gave hints of the personalities of the people whose spirit still seemed to pervade the surroundings.

These recollections brought to mind the great traditions of the Mint's past.

Fortunately all of this fascinating story, all the significant parts that the Mint and its people played in the affairs of our country will not be left to moulder in dusty archives or remain hidden in cans of microfilm. All of us who share an interest in our nation's coinage, from its faltering beginnings up to the present, are indebted to Don Taxay. He has done a monumental work of research and reconstruction. Available documents have been introduced and revitalized by Mr. Taxay's own knowledgeable observations. The daily problems, achievements, ambitions and disappointments of our early Mint officials, their sometimes humorous, sometimes generous, and often petty, but very human personalities are convincingly portrayed.

Without doubt, *The U.S. Mint and Coinage* is the most complete and authoritative treatise on the subject ever written, and is certain to become a prime reference source for numismatists, historians and students interested in our coinage and the part it played in the affairs of the nation.

Gilroy Roberts
Chief Engraver of the United States Mint (1948–1964)

Preface

THE HISTORY of our federal coinage, from its uncertain beginnings in 1776 up to the present day, is not simply a numismatic chronicle, but a kaleidescope of economics, politics, art, biography and technology. While the present volume attempts to cover each of these aspects, certain subordinate topics—the branch mints, medallions and commemorative coinage—have necessarily been omitted. The exclusion of the first two will, I think, be self-explanatory. The third might have been treated as a supplement, but will be published serially at a later date.

A few basic reference sources have not been footnoted, and are as follows: 1) The published proceedings of Congress: *The Journals of the Continental Congress, 1775–1789; The Debates and Proceedings of Congress, 1789–1824; The Register of Debates in Congress, 1825–1833; The Congressional Globe, 1833–1873; The Congressional Record, 1874–.* 2) Correspondence from the letter files of the Director of the Mint, National Archives. 3) Correspondence of the Commission of Fine Arts, National Archives (this is the sole reference source for chapters 28 to 31).

I would like to acknowledge the generous assistance I have received in preparing this manuscript. In particular, I wish to thank the retired chief engraver of the Mint, Gilroy Roberts, for gracing the work with his excellent foreword; Mr. Roberts, Professor Julian P. Boyd, Eric P. Newman, Walter Breen, Robert W. Julian and Richard Miller for critically reading the text in whole or part and furnishing many valuable suggestions; Raymond Williamson for providing a microfilm of certain dispatch papers; Howard K. Weinman for furnishing copies of his father's correspondence; Mrs. Margo Russell of *Coin World* and Henry

Cadwalader, Executive Director of the Historical Society of Pennsylvania, for reprint rights, Dr. Sarah Elizabeth Freeman for supplying data on certain specimens in the Johns Hopkins University collection; Louis Werner and Aaron Feldman for lending me out-of-print works; and my assistant Mrs. Karin Martin and secretary Glenda Palmer for typing up certain sections of the manuscript. I should also like to thank the following persons, staffs and institutions, for making available various historical documents: Dr. Neil Franklin, Dr. Hope Holdcamper, Mr. Buford Rowland and Miss Jane Smith of the National Archives in Washington; the manuscript division of the Library of Congress; the curatorial and library staffs of the American Numismatic Society; Mr. Barney Chesnick and Mrs. Lillian Tonkin of the Library Company of Philadelphia; Miss Shirley Beresford of the New York Historical Society; and the manuscript divisions of the Historical Society of Pennsylvania, the American Philosophical Society Library, and the American Antiquarian Society. I am deeply indebted to Mrs. Jessie Harley of the Assay Office of Birmingham, England, for spending so much time on my behalf in locating pertinent Matthew Boulton papers.

Last but not least, I am grateful to Fred Honig, editor of Arco Publishing Company, for his great care and patience in dealing with a frequently difficult manuscript.

Illustrated material has been reproduced through the courtesy of the Chase Manhattan Bank, the National Archives, the American Numismatic Society, Whitman Publishing Co., New Netherlands Coin Co., the New York Historical Society, Library Company of Philadelphia, American Philosophical Society Library, Johns Hopkins University, *Coin World*, Mrs. Laura G. Fraser, the late Anthony De Francisci, Gilroy Roberts, Eric P. Newman, Harry J. Forman, Lester Merkin, and Empire Coin Co.

D. T.

Contents

Part IV
THE THIRD PHILADELPHIA MINT

PART I

ATTEMPTS TO ESTABLISH A PERMANENT MINT

CHAPTER 1

The 1776 Continental Currency Coinage

IT IS CUSTOMARY for emerging nations to establish mints, not only to regulate their coinage, but as an act of sovereignty. In our own country there were even weightier reasons. The coinage, like the Continental paper currency, was intended to help finance the Revolution by enlisting the loyalty of private resources; a certain proportion of specie was also required to support the Congress notes.

The first issue of Continental paper currency was authorized on June 22, 1775.[1] The notes were paid out in large quantities, had no backing, and could be redeemed only at some indefinite future date—if and when America won its independence. In January 1776, it was declared treason to refuse the currency or otherwise discourage its circulation. This fiat, however, did little to increase public confidence, and on February 17, the *Pennsylvania Evening Post* warned:

> "Should the Colonists conduct the war with prudence and success, loans of money may, perhaps, be negotiated among foreigners, and even in England, on easy terms; a Contraband trade will enrich some of our merchants, and bring in gold and silver; the procurement of these precious metals is an object of the utmost Consequence; a certain proportion will be requisite to give credit to our paper currency."

For almost a year and a half, the "continentals" passed at close to par. Their stability, however, was largely an illusion. With coins rapidly disappearing from circulation, the *real* value of the paper lay in its purchasing power, and by the

---

[1] The May 10, 1775 date appearing on the earliest Continental Currency refers to the session of Congress that opened on that day.

spring of 1776 this had already begun to dwindle because of foreign trade restrictions and the widespread hoarding of goods.

Like an aspiring alchemist, Congress sought to transmute its printed paper into gold and silver. All that it needed was a philosopher's stone, in this instance nothing more than a popular faith in the Continental treasury, and a willingness to receive its notes on par with specie. Instead, people hoarded their coins and raised the price of commodities, which, in effect, depreciated the notes. Congress then attempted to fix a ceiling on goods but it only provoked further hoarding and a slackening of trade.

The growing distress of the colonists was reflected in a letter of March 7, 1776 to the Committee of Inspection and Observation for the City and Liberties of Philadelphia. The author, who signed his letter "Luke the Physician," suggested the following remedy: [2]

". . . if the establishment of a mint were added where the plate with which many families abound could be fitted for ready exchange with foreigners for commodities of which the most opulent will soon be in want, I flatter myself the salutary consequences would soon become sensible to everyone."

Copies of the letter were ordered printed, and the proposal for a Mint was rendered even more timely by an urgent communication from General Schuyler to General Washington, which was published two days later. Schuyler wrote:

"I have this moment received a letter from General Wooster, of the 1st instant. He says not a word relative to Quebeck; complains of a want of specie, and indeed, not without reason, as he is greatly distressed, the Canadians absolutely refusing to take our paper money. . . . The difficulty of procuring specie is such, that I fear the most fatal consequences from the want of it in Canada."

Despite such appeals, no remedial action seems to have been taken by Congress. On April 4, the *Post* quoted from a report of William Adcock, President of the Committee of Privates, to the Committee of Inspection of the City and Liberties of Philadelphia:

". . . while every mode of introducing gold and silver is totally cut off, and we stand in need of so many articles which must be procured by paying in specie, we are in danger of a scarcity of such articles, but also of having our currency depreciated; as it will be very difficult if not impossible to support its credit without introducing real cash into the country nearly in the same proportions to the sum we are obliged to strike."

Shortly after the War, Thomas Jefferson, in a letter to his young Dutch friend, G. K. van Hogendorp,[3] mentioned the early need of the Continental Congress for "a general coin, acknowledged and accepted everywhere," but tantalizingly omitted to say whether Congress had ever struck such a coin.

Since no reference to a mint or coinage during the year 1776 can be found among the papers of the old government, orthodox historians have assumed that neither one existed. The 1776 "Continental Currency" coins, which are familiar to every numismatist, have thus remained generally unknown or been repudiated as a private issue.[4]

---

[2] *American Archives*, edited by Peter Force, Fourth Series, Vol. 5, Washington 1837-53. Also, Eric P. Newman, "The Continental Dollar of 1776 Meets Its Maker," *The Numismatist*, July 1959.
[3] See under May 4, 1784; *The Papers of Thomas Jefferson*, Vol. 7, edited by Julian P. Boyd, Princeton University Press, 1950—.
[4] See for example: Neil Carothers, *Fractional Money*, John Wiley & Sons, 1930.

The designs on the Continental Currency coinage are derived from the Congress notes of February 17, 1776. The obverse legends read:

CONTINENTAL CURRENCY 1776 and FUGIO (i.e., I, Time, Fly) MIND YOUR BUSINESS.

At the upper left, the sun's rays strike a sundial, illustrating the monition. The reverse shows a perpetual chain, arranged in a circle, each link inscribed with the name of a colony. In the center, the legend reads:

AMERICAN CONGRESS: WE ARE ONE.

Only three Continental Currency coins are known in silver and a dozen or so in brass, some of these being quite worn. The pewter specimens are considerably less rare and often found in mint condition or with no more wear than they might have received as keepsakes. Four obverse and two reverse dies were used to strike the coins, and where specimens of more than one metal are known from the same die combination, the order of emission is brass, silver, and pewter, respectively.

Eric P. Newman, the eminent numismatic historian, has offered weighty evidence to prove the official status of these coins.[5] His principal arguments are 1) that the suspension of the $1 Congress note from July 1776 through the penultimate currency emission of September 26, 1778 implies that Congress intended to issue a substitute in coin; and 2) that the New York engraver Elisha Gallaudet, whose initials appear on one obverse die of the Continental Currency coinage, apparently produced the cuts used to print fractional Continental paper currency. Newman concludes that the coinage was official (although in the pattern stage), that the pewter pieces may have been struck for official consideration because of the unavailability of silver in sufficient quantities, and that the brass impressions are trials.[6]

Nevertheless, several perplexing questions remain, as for example: By whom were the Continental Currency coins struck, and by what authority?[7] Did they actually circulate? Why are there no contemporary records? Although conclusive answers have not been found, the writer would like to offer some additional citations which may throw light on this fascinating subject.

Up to May 9, 1776 all of the issues of Continental paper currency included a $1 note, but with the July 22 issue this denomination was dropped. Newman assigned the period between these two dates as the logical one in which the Mint project may have crystallized. It is significant, therefore, that between the last week of June and the first week of July, newspapers in many eastern cities reported the following news item from Holt's *New York Journal or the General Advertiser:* [8]

> We hear it is proposed, that after three months, the currency of all Copper Coin made of bad metal, or wanting in weight, is to be totally suppressed, and that the rest is to pass at the rate of 15 for an eighth part of a dollar. And if it shall appear that there is not a sufficiency for common use, that it will be all called in, and a new impression struck of Continental Copper Coin, of a larger size; twelve of which is to pass for an eighth of a dollar, after which no other Coppers are to pass current.

---

[5] Eric P. Newman, "The 1776 Continental Currency Coinage," *The Coin Collector's Journal,* July 1952; "The Continental Dollar of 1776 Meets its Maker," *The Numismatist,* July 1959.

[6] That is, in the sense of patterns, not die trials.

[7] The twin olive-leaf edge design, though similar to that on the 1783 patterns of Robert Morris, is not identical as formerly believed.

[8] The date of the *Journal's* article is June 27, 1776. It may also be significant that the news emanated from New York (were Gallaudet lived) rather than from Philadelphia.

The word "proposed" as used here is unfortunately ambiguous. If we take it to mean "intended," then it would probably refer to Congress, with the implication that an ordinance had been passed. But if it is understood to mean "suggested" or "put forth," it cannot refer to Congress as a body, but only to a committee or to an individual. In this sense, it would imply that a bill had been prepared for submission, though not necessarily acted upon.

The writer is inclined to accept this second interpretation. It seems probable, however, in view of the suspension of the Continental $1 note, that a more comprehensive Mint bill was contemplated. Such a bill was indeed passed by Congress, but not until February 20, 1777. The Continental Currency coins may thus have been struck in anticipation of the bill's passage, or to stimulate further interest in it.

The information given in Holt's *Journal* is important for several reasons. First of all, it would have been illogical to strike a copper coin of unfamiliar size unless the dies were also intended for some other purpose. Secondly, this purpose may have been to strike silver dollar-sized coins which were sorely needed for trade as well as to stabilize the faltering paper currency.

Benjamin Franklin, who was intimately connected with treasury affairs, and whose advice was sought by Congress on almost every important question, later suggested that the dies used to strike national medals "be usefully employed in striking copper money, or in some cases silver." [9] The striking of copper coins from silver dollar dies would have been even more logical, and could explain the absence of any denomination on the pieces.

Let us examine the value suggested to Congress for its copper coin. Twelve coppers were to pass for a Spanish "bit," or twelve-and-a-half one-hundredths (one eighth) of a dollar. This is nothing less than decimal money-arithmetic expressed through the Spanish system of eighths. For convenience, the coppers were reckoned in terms of an intermediate silver coin, preventing the rate from being precisely expressed as one hundred to the dollar. However, in making change, the fraction would have been dropped.

It is significant that Congress, at this time, was considering a decimal copper coinage. Decimal reckoning had never previously been applied to the problems of American currency. The Spanish dollar, or eight-reales piece, served as the money unit, and other coins were valued in relation to it and to its fractions. In accounting, the cumbrous English system of pounds, shillings and pence prevailed, at various ratios to the dollar.

It is well known that in 1784 Thomas Jefferson urged the adoption of a coinage based on decimal divisions of a dollar, despite the opposition of Robert Morris. Jefferson's influence on our coinage, however, began considerably before this time. On April 19, 1776 a Congressional committee of seven persons was appointed "to examine and ascertain the value of the several species of Gold and Silver Coins, current in these colonies, and the proportions they ought to bear to Spanish milled dollars." In the report which the committee submitted on May 22, the values of the current foreign coins were expressed in whole numbers and common fractions. This report was tabled, and recommitted on July 24 when Jefferson was added to the committee. Shortly afterwards, Jefferson submitted a report of his own which, though similar to the

---

[9] Letter of Benjamin Franklin to John Jay, May 10, 1785; Joseph F. Loubat, *The Medallic History of the United States of America, 1776-1876.* 1881.

previous one, expressed the values of each of the foreign coins in decimals.[10] It is thus possible that Congress was planning an entire system of decimal currency at the very time it laid the foundations of our independence.

According to Holt's *Journal*, the Congress Mint might begin operations after three months. If the general project matured on schedule, the Continental Currency coins would have been struck around October 1776. Significantly, the *London Chronicle* of December 24 reported the following quotation in an "Extract of a Letter from an Officer of the 64th Regiment, in York-island, to his Friend in Town: [11]

"The Congress have established a Mint at Philadelphia, where they coin copper and silver pieces about the size of half a crown: In silver go for twelve shillings, in copper for fourteen pence."

It may be observed that "York Island" was an English colloquial name for Manhattan, and that the 64th British Regiment was at this time occupying New York. The officer's statements are pertinent for the most part, but it is evident that he was writing from hearsay. For example, the Congress coins were nearly as large in diameter as the old British crown, though appreciably lighter.[12]

The reference to copper coins is less strange since the terms "copper" and "brass" were often used interchangeably.[13]

The rate of twelve shillings for a Congress dollar could well reflect the depreciation of paper currency in and around New York after its occupation by the British.[14] Fourteen pence for a Congress "copper," however, is impossible, and may be a confused rendering of "fourteen coppers to the shilling."

Despite such ambiguities, the letter establishes certain facts which can only be explained at their face value. First, that coins attributed to the Continental Congress were being struck at Philadelphia; secondly, that both the silver and "copper" impressions were of large, presumably equal size; and lastly, that at least some of these pieces had entered circulation. Allowing two months for the letter to have reached England, we can assume that its observations were made sometime in October 1776, which would suit our chronology to perfection.

There is, however, good reason to believe that the Continental Currency coins were only intended as patterns, and that those entering circulation did so unofficially. For one thing, the issue of brass coins would have been contrary to the intention of Congress, which was to suppress the circulation of base coppers. For another, the establishment of a mint could hardly have passed unnoticed. Next to military affairs, Continental finance was the subject of the day. It was discussed at length in newspapers and magazines, and it is clear that the authors had no knowledge of a federal mint. Even the diarist William Smith, who was a friend of many members of Congress and a keen

---

[10] *The Papers of Thomas Jefferson*, Vol. 1, Boyd.

[11] This extract was reprinted without comment, under the date of December 21, in the October 1891 *American Journal of Numismatics*. It appears to be the only contemporary acknowledgement of the Continental Currency coins.

[12] Newman gives the average weight of the three surviving silver impressions at 378 grains, which is about 15% less than that of the George II English crown.

[13] However, the writer has seen an impression from the Continental Congress dies on a small copper planchet, possibly a button blank. This may be a die trial.

[14] On November 18, 1776 the Tory-controlled *New York Gazette & Weekly Mercury* reported that "The people in New Jersey, sensible of the precarious Worth of the Continental Bills, are endeavoring to purchase with them any Commodities of a *material* and *durable* nature. Iron, for instance, instead of 28s. per Hundred, when paid in Congress Notes, is valued at the Rate of 56s."

We hear it is propoſed, that after three months, the currency of all Copper Coin made of bad metal, or wanting in weight, is to be totally ſuppreſſed, and that the reſt is to paſs at the rate of 15 for an eighth part of a dollar. And if it ſhall appear that there is not a ſufficiency for common uſe, that it will be all called in, and a new impreſſion ſtruck of Continental Copper Coin, of a larger ſize; twelve of which is to paſs for an eight of a dollar, after which no other Coppers are to paſs current. (Mr. Holt's Journal.)

The Congreſs have eſtabliſhed a Mint at Philadelphia, where they coin copper and ſilver pieces about the ſize of half a crown: In ſilver go for twelve ſhillings, in copper for fourteen pence.

Continental Currency pattern for a dollar. **Below:** clipping from the "Constitutional Gazette," June 29, 1776 and the "London Chronicle," December 24, 1776. *New York Historical Society.*

observer of Continental finance, seems not to have known about the coinage.[15]

The earliest known reference to the pewter Continental Currency coins appears in the February 9, 1786 edition of Richard Watson's *Chemical Essays*, published in London.[16] Watson, a professor at the University of Cambridge, compared the pieces to "the leaden money which was struck at Vienna when that city was beseiged by the Turks," and he estimated that the composition of the pewter consisted of twelve parts tin to one part lead. The comparison, however, should not be taken too seriously, for there is no evidence that the pewter "dollars" were intended for any other purpose than to revive Congressional interest in the Mint. That they succeeded seems obvious, for on February 20, 1777 Congress resolved:

"That as much Gold and Silver bullion as can be procured in these States be purchased and paid for in continental currency or loan Certificates payable in specie with Interest at four per cent per annum at the expiration of three years next after the termination of the present war, and that the bullion so purchased be coined into money, of such value and denominations as shall hereafter be ordered by Congress.

"That any persons who will bring gold and silver to the mint may have it coined on their own account.

"That a quantity of Copper be purchased and coined into pence and half pence, each penny to weigh half an ounce Avoirdupoize and be in value equal to one seventy-second part of a Dollar."

The half-ounce standard proposed for the American penny is of considerable interest. At the rate of 7000 troy grains to the pound avoirdupois, the penny would have weighed 218.75 grains, which is close indeed to the 224 grain average Newman quotes for the surviving brass impressions. Thus, despite the change in reckoning, the standard may have been the same as intended for the "Continental Copper Coin of a larger size." In any event, the brass impressions emerge at the penny standard, and perhaps as patterns for the only penny ever authorized by the American government!

By January 1777, the Continental paper currency had begun to depreciate throughout New England, defeating the purpose for which the Mint ordinance was intended. On the 6th, the Tory-controlled *New York Gazette* announced:

> The congress bills are now no longer passable in Philadelphia itself, but upon such terms as shew that the purchasers only mean to traffic them a little further to the southward, where likewise we hear the people look upon them very shily.
>
> The people of New England in general, and of Connecticut in particular, are in extreme distress on account of the scarcity and consequent high price of provisions and necessaries of all kinds. Trade is in a manner entirely stopped; and they have no intercourse in a commercial way but by barter. Those who have gold and silver, and even coppers, carefully hoard them, lest they should be forced out of their hands for the vile continental currency, a cartload of which they know in a little time would not purchase a single dollar. A piece of coin is scarcely to be seen in the whole country, and especially since the Act of the Connecticut assembly in October last, which made the continental bills a legal tender, for the express purpose of getting all the specie into the hands of some leading men.

Congress was caught in a vicious circle. Although its paper could not succeed without an extensive backing in specie, the very instability of the notes

---

[15] *Historical Memoirs of William Smith,* edited by William H. W. Sabine, N.Y., 1956.

[16] Eric P. Newman, "The 1776 Continental Currency Coinage," *The Coin Collector's Journal,* July 1952.

drove silver and gold coins from circulation in accordance with Gresham's law. For the same reason, no owner of bullion would have brought it to the Mint for exchange in paper currency. The first attempt to establish a Mint at Philadelphia had failed, and it was not until 1781, two years after the emission of the "continentals" had ceased, that Congress resumed its plans for a national coinage.

February 20, 1777 resolution of the Continental Congress for establishing a Mint.
National Archives.

CHAPTER 2

The Proposals of Franklin, Morris and Jefferson

THE CONTINENTAL CURRENCY coinage, with its homely motto, must have appealed to Ben Franklin, for just a few years later he suggested a whole series of coins, each bearing a different proverb. As Minister Plenipotentiary to the Court of France, Franklin began to negotiate unofficially with his friend Edward Brigden, an English coiner who was sympathetic to the American cause.

In September 1779, Brigden sent sample planchets to Franklin via Edmond Genet,[1] and on October 2, Franklin replied from Passy, France, to Bridgen as follows:[2]

Dear Sir: I received your favor of the 17th past, and the two samples of copper are since come to hand. The metal seems to be very good, and the price reasonable, but I have not yet received the orders necessary to justify my making the purchase proposed. There has indeed been an intention to strike copper coin, that may not only be useful as small change, but serve other purposes.

Instead of repeating continually upon every half-penny the dull story that everybody knows (and what it would have been no loss to mankind if nobody had ever known), that George the Third is King of Great Britain, France, and Ireland, etc., etc., to put on one side, some important proverb of Solomon, some pious moral, prudential or economic precept, the frequent inculcation of which, by seeing it every time one receives a piece of money, might make an impression upon the

[1] Eric P. Newman, "Poor Richard's Mottoes for Coins," *The Numismatist*, Dec. 1956.
[2] Ibid; also, *The Works of Benjamin Franklin*, Vol. 8, edited by Jared Sparks, Hilliard Gray, and Co., 1840.

mind, especially of young persons, and tend to regulate their conduct: such as, on some, The Fear of the Lord is the beginning of Wisdom; on others, He that by the plough would thrive, himself must either hold or drive; on others, Keep thy shop, and thy shop will keep thee; on others, A penny saved is a penny got; on others, He that buys what he has no need of, will soon be forced to sell his necessaries; on others, Early to bed and early to rise, will make a man healthy, wealthy, and wise; and so on, to a great variety.

The other side, it was proposed to fill with good designs, drawn and engraved by the best artists in France, of all the different species of barbarity with which the English have carried on the war in America, expressing every abominable circumstance of their cruelty and inhumanity that figures can express, to make an impression upon the minds of posterity as strong and durable as that on the copper. This resolution has been a long time forborne; but the late burning of defenceless towns in Connecticut, on the flimsy pretence that the people fired from behind their houses, when it is known to have been premeditated and ordered from England, will probably give the finishing provocation, and may occasion a vast demand for your metal.

I thank you for your kind wishes respecting my health. I return them most cordially fourfold unto your own bosom.

Although Franklin continued, for some years, to promote his and Brigden's plan, it was eventually forgotten amidst new efforts to establish a federal Mint.[3]

* * *

The early finances of the Continental Congress were managed by several autonomous departments consisting of the Commissioners of the Chambers of Accounts, an Auditor-General, a Treasurer, a Paymaster-General, a Treasurer of Loans, and an advisory body called the Board of Treasury. The last of these soon developed into a pugnacious group, whose hostile relations with other bodies of Congress reached a climax in 1780.

In June of that year, Francis Hopkinson, the Treasurer of Loans, submitted a bill for "Sundry Devices, Drawings, Mottos, &c, for the public use" which included designs for the Continental Currency.[4] The bill was approved by Congress and forwarded to the Board of Treasury for payment. After using every possible subterfuge to delay settlement, the Board finally refused to acknowledge Hopkinson's claim on the ground that he had failed to produce the vouchers on which the Government had ordered the work. The fact that the designs had been supplied by Hopkinson and employed by Congress was unworthy of consideration. The controversy resulted in Hopkinson's resignation, and an investigation of the Treasury Board in which the latter was charged with neglect of duty, indolence, malattention to the public interest, incapacity and partiality. The investigating committee recommended that the members of the Board be dismissed, and that Congress place the Treasury Department under the direction of a single officer.

There were also more important reasons for considering this recommendation. The nation was bankrupt, and large numbers of soldiers were deserting for lack of pay and provisions. In desperation, Congress turned to Robert Morris of Philadelphia. Morris, an unusually able merchant, had already obtained for Congress some of its most crucial loans. In June 1780, he helped organize the Bank of Pennsylvania to raise funds for the purchase of military

---

[3] Nevertheless, Franklin's idea of the mottoes survived: cf. Robert Morris' (1785?) design for a gold crown, the 1787 Fugio cent, and the Mint patterns of 1792.

[4] George E. Hastings, *Life and Works of Francis Hopkinson*. University of Chicago Press, 1926.

supplies. In February 1781, he was appointed Superintendent of Finance by unanimous vote, replacing the old Board of Treasury. When Morris took up his duties in May, his most immediate objective was to found a National Bank as fiscal agent of the Treasury. The idea had previously been introduced by Alexander Hamilton who wished to annex a mint to the establishment.

Hamilton presented his banking plan in an anonymous and undated letter which was probably addressed to Robert Morris [5] between December 1779 and March 1780. Writing to Congressman James Duane, on September 3, 1780, Hamilton enlarged upon the subject. He thought that plate and bullion should be accepted in the sale of bank subscriptions, and thereafter, if necessary, coined. Apparently contemplating a seignorage, he wrote: "The bank may be allowed to purchase plate and bullion and coin money allowing the government a part of the profit."

On April 30, 1781 Hamilton submitted a detailed report to Morris, who nevertheless laid a different plan before Congress on May 17. Morris did not annex a mint to his national bank, for he would soon propose the former as an independent establishment. On May 24, two days before the Morris plan was adopted by Congress, William Barton, a Philadelphia attorney, submitted a scheme of his own [6] which more closely followed Hamilton's thought. As Barton devoted considerable attention to the subject of a mint, his remarks are, in part, quoted below:

"Let a *mint* be established under the direction of Congress, where all bullion and plate deposited at the Bank, that may become forfeited thereto, should be *coined* agreeable to the sterling standard; and after making the necessary deduction, for defraying the expense of the coinage, (which should be fixed) and for too great alloy, the residue to be paid into the bank.

"The charges of all *other* bullion and plate, coined at the mint, to be borne by the bank; so that every person bringing bullion or plate to be coined, shall receive an equal weight in coin, deducting only for base alloy. For in proportion as the circulating medium of specie is increased, will the demand for it, at the bank be lessened; and, consequently, the company will be enabled to employ a greater part of their capital, for their joint emolument. It is evident, that as much *less* than *five per cent* as the bank pays for coinage, *so* much will they be gainers thereby, exclusive of other advantages."

Barton suggested that the widespread practice of melting down coins for plate be prohibited by law. Anticipating the Constitution, he said that Congress alone should have the right to coin money.

❋   ❋   ❋

On June 28, 1781 John Bradford informed the President of Congress, Samuel Huntington, of a large quantity of pure copper in storage at Boston.[7]

Sir . . I Beg leave to mention to your Excellency that we have a very large quantity of rough Copper laying in the Stores upwards of two years. It has always been supposed that it was sent with a design to mix with other metals for the purpose of Casting Brass Cannon. It is a sort of Copper in so rough a State, as has

---

[5] The identity of the addressee has inspired considerable debate among historians; see *The Papers of Alexander Hamilton*, Vol. 2, edited by Harold C. Syrett. Columbia University Press, 1961—.
[6] *Observations on the Nature and Use of Paper-Credit*, private printing.
[7] *Papers of the Continental Congress and the Constitutional Convention*, Record Group 360, No. 78, IV, National Archives.

not been seen among us. I have had the Opinion of several of our most ingenious artisans respecting the quality of it, who all were of the same Sentiment, that it was scarcely worth the freight, but two days ago I had an Essay made by Mr. Dudley, and we find it to be the purest Copper. He melted down about two pounds into three ingots, and we find no dross among it. Mr. Dudley assured me he can Roll it into Sheets of any thickness, and Can either harden or Soften it. We find it to be very malleable. He tells me that if Congress shou'd see meet to Strike of a parcel of Coppers for a Currency he Can make the Apparatus and go through the whole process. This gentleman comes to America highly recommended as a warm friend to our cause and being possessed of a most uncommon extensive Genius. A Doctor Pei— who was his patron left London with him to come over via France in Order to bring over some arts unknown to us, but the Doctor was advertised and a large reward offered to stop him from taking Mr. Dudley out of the kingdom, but they just escaped being taken. The Character of both those Gentlemen are known to my son as being acquainted with them ten months in France. The Doctor is waiting a favorable Opportunity to get to America. Mr. Dudley has already given such proofs of his ingenuity that ———— him as an important acquisition to this infant nation, and I hope he will meet with encouragement. I have the honour etc.

Morris, evidently impressed by Bradford's comments, wrote to Dudley on July 16, inviting him to Philadelphia. Dudley arrived on or before the 10th of November, just a month after the defeat of Cornwallis at Yorktown. Much of the remaining story can be found in the diary of Robert Morris: [8]

> *Nov. 10th.* Ordered some money on application of Mr. Dudley to pay his expenses.
> *Nov. 12th.* Sent for Mr. Dudley to consult him respecting the quantity of Alloy Silver will bear without being discoloured, he says he can put 6 drops into an ounce. Desired him to assay some Spanish Dollars and French Crowns, in order to know the quantity of pure Silver in each.
> *Nov. 16th.* Mr. Dudley assayed a number of Crowns and dollars for our information respecting the Mint.
> *1782. Jan. 2d.* Mr. Benjamin Dudley applied for money to pay his Board which I directed to be paid by Mr. Swanwick, this gentleman is detained at the public expense as a person absolutely necessary in the Mint, which I hope soon to see established. My propositions on that subject are to be submitted to Congress as soon as I can get the proper assays made on Silver coins &c.

On January 4, Congress appointed a committee consisting of Samuel Osgood, Edmund Randolph and Thomas Bee to ascertain the value and weights at which all foreign coins should be received in taxes by the Treasurer of the United States. The committee reported three days later, passing the responsibility to Morris who was instructed by Congress to prepare and report a table of rates for the commoner foreign coins in circulation. Morris seized the opportunity to present a comprehensive coinage plan, the details of which had been devised by his assistant (though no relation) Gouverneur Morris. The Superintendent reported on January 15,[9] advocating a silver standard. Morris believed that silver, because of its smaller value, was less susceptible than gold to fraudulent practices.[10] Although he recognized the greater portability of gold, he considered the advantage unimportant because it would "always be in our Power to carry a Paper Circulation to every proper Extent." Morris esti-

---

[8] The original document is in the Library of Congress; also see *Historical Magazine*, Jan. 1867; and George G. Evans, *Illustrated History of the United States Mint*, 1885.
[9] *The Papers of Thomas Jefferson*, Vol. 7, Boyd.
[10] Morris was probably thinking of the current influx of lightweight and mutilated gold coins.

mated that the average market ratio between gold and silver was 14½ to 1. He suggested the adoption of a small seignorage to prevent the exportation of coins,[11] as well as to defray the expense of the Mint. He argued that coins should be valued as money distinct from their value as a commodity, and that it was natural and proper for citizens to pay a charge for it just as they did to have plate fashioned.

In order to understand the coinage plan devised by Gouverneur Morris, it is necessary, first, to consider the peculiar state of American finance at this time. The coin shortage had gradually abated, and towards the end of the war there was more specie circulating than ever before. The most numerous coins were the Spanish milled dollars. These were exported from Havana and the West Indies, and outnumbered all other forms of specie by three or four to one.[12] Gold currency consisted largely of French louis', which poured into America by the millions through loans to Congress and from the allied fleets and armies. Portuguese, Spanish, and English gold coins likewise worked their way into the heart of the country, where they circulated in a variety of mutilated forms. Some were holed, and others diminished, particularly those that had passed behind the British lines at New York.[13] The Spanish silver coins were often cut into rough fractions, and passed as halves, quarters and eighths. For smaller transactions, people used the British halfpence and French sous'.

At the same time, each colony had its own currency system and reckoned the various coins at different rates. For example, a Spanish dollar was worth five Georgia shillings, six of Virginia and the New England states, eight of New York and North Carolina, and seven shillings and sixpence in the currencies of all the other states except South Carolina where it was valued at thirty-two shillings and sixpence.

In creating a unified currency, one could proceed in either of two ways. The first was to devise a system for converting the different Colonial rates, the second to abolish the diversity and begin anew.

Robert Morris and Gouverneur Morris favored the first alternative. The latter thus selected for his money unit the largest common divisor by which the currencies of the several states (excepting South Carolina, where the figure was too abberant to conform neatly with the scheme) could be converted without the use of a fraction. This divisor was 1/1440 part of the Spanish dollar, equal to 1/1600 part of the British crown. Morris selected as the value of his tiny unit one fourth grain fine silver. He said that it was not necessary for the unit to be represented by a coin, so long as its value was precisely known.

Morris proposed the issue of the following denominations: [14]

---

[11] From ancient times up to the sixteenth century, the relative market value of gold to silver generally ranged between 10 and 12 to 1. However, with the discovery and working of rich silver mines at Potosi, the proportion gradually widened. Fluctuations in the relative value of the two metals posed a constant problem since nations coined at a fixed standard. The fluctuations continually overvalued the coins of one metal relative to the other, making it profitable to trade the former for the latter.

[12] François Jean Chastellux, *Travels in North America, 1780-82,* printed for G. G. J. & J. Robinson, London, 1787.

[13] The mutilations were popularly known as "Robertsons" because of the large number attributed to James Robertson, the British military Governor of New York.

[14] In a letter dated April 30, 1783 Gouverneur Morris mentioned to William Hemsley the possibility, also, of coining gold at the rate of 6664 units per hundred grains fine bullion. See *The Papers of Thomas Jefferson,* Vol. 7, Boyd.

Mark	1000 units	250 Grains fine silver	20 Grains copper alloy
Quint	500 units	125 Grains fine silver	10 Grains copper alloy
Cent	100 units	25 Grains fine silver	2 Grains copper alloy
Eight	8 units —Pure copper (Weight not given)		
Five	5 units —Pure copper (Weight not given)		

Now let us see how the Morris plan would have actually worked. Since the Spanish dollar was equal to 1440 units, we can calculate the unit value of the shilling in each of the colonial currencies by dividing 1440 by the number of shillings equal to the dollar.

Number of shillings equal to the dollar.	Number of units equal to the shilling.[15]
5	288
6	240
7½	192
8	180

The Morris plan was not only ingenious, but the most cumbersome scheme for coinage ever devised by Man. It seems to have been received with little enthusiasm, and (Robert) Morris, sensing the reaction, left it to trail unobtrusively in the wake of his plan for establishing a Mint. In his report to Congress, he had written:

> Shortly after my Appointment finding that there was a considerable Quantity of Public Copper at Boston I ordered it round to this Place. It has arrived safely and will when coined amount to a considerable Sum. The necessary Machinery of a Mint can be easily made and there are Persons who can perform the whole Business.
>
> If Congress are of Opinion with me that it will be proper to Coin Money I will immediately obey their Orders and establish a Mint. And I think I can say with Safety that no better moment could be chosen for the Purpose than the present.

On January 18, Morris noted in his diary: "I went to Mr. Govr Morris's Lodging to examine the plan we had agreed on, and which we had drawn up respecting the Establishment of a Mint, we made some alterations and amendments to my satisfaction and from a belief that this is a necessary and salutary measure. I have ordered it copied to be sent into Congress."

On January 26, Morris recorded: "Dudley applied for money to pay his Lodgings &c. I ordered Mr. Swanwick to supply him with fifty dollars, informed him that the Plan of a Mint is before Congress, and when passed, that he shall be directly employed, if not agreed to by Congress, I shall compensate him for his time &c."

The Morris Plan seemed assured on February 21 when Congress approved the establishment of the Mint, and directed the Superintendent to prepare and report "a plan for establishing and conducting same." On the 26th, Dudley presented Morris with a rough draft of the proposed Mint building, and on the 28th, with a proposition from Samuel Wheeler, a country smith who wished to manufacture screws for the coining presses, rollers and other machinery for the institution. Dudley suggested, as a possible site in Philadelphia, an unoccupied building on Fourth Street near Vine, which had previously served as the Dutch Reformed Church. The Masons' Lodge and a group of buildings on the east side of South Seventh Street were also considered.

---

[15] In South Carolina, 48 units equaled thirteen pence.

Notwithstanding the instructions of Congress that he merely report a plan for the Mint, Morris now engaged Dudley in the actual construction of coining apparatus. In his diary, Morris noted:

March 22d. Mr. Dudley and Mr. Wheeler came and brought with them some Models of the Screws and Rollers necessary for the Mint. I found Mr. Wheeler entertained some doubts respecting one of these Machines which Mr. Dudley insists will answer the purposes and says he will be responsible for it. I agreed with Mr. Wheeler that he should perform the work; and, as neither he nor I could judge the value that ought to be paid for it, he is to perform the same agreeable to Mr. Dudley's directions, and when finished, we are to have it valued by some Honest Men, judges of such work, he mentioned Philip Syng, Edwd Duffield, William Rush and _____ all of whom I believe are good judges and very honest men, therefore I readily agreed to this proposition. And I desired Mr. Dudley to consult Mr. Rittenhouse and Francis Hopkinson Esquire, as to the Machine or Wheel in dispute, and let me have their opinion.

March 23d. Mr. Dudley called to inform me that Mr. Rittenhouse & Mr. Hopkinson agree to his plan of the Machine &c.

April 12th. Mr. Dudley wants a horse to go up to Mr. Wheelers &c.

May 20th. Mr. Dudley wrote me a Letter this day and wanted money. I directed Mr. Swanwick to supply him, and then desired him to view the Masons' Lodge to see if it would Answer for a Mint, which he thinks it will, I desired him to go up to Mr. Wheelers to see how he goes on with the Rollers &c.

June 17th. Mr. Dudley applied for money to pay his Bill. I directed Mr. Swanwick to supply him.

June 18th. Issued a warrant in favor of B. Dudley £7.11.6.

July 15th. Mr. B. Dudley applied for money, he is very uneasy for want of employment, and the Mint in which he is to be employed and for which I have engaged him goes on so slowly that I am also uneasy at having this gentleman on pay and no work for him. He offered to go and assist Mr. Byers to establish the Brass Cannon Foundry at Springfield. I advised to make that proposal to Genl. Lincoln and inform me the result tomorrow.

July 16th. Mr. B. Dudley to whom I gave an order on Mr. Swanwick for fifty dollars, and desired him to seek after Mr. Wheeler to know whether the Rollers &c. are ready for him to go to work on rolling the copper for the Mint.

August 22d. Mr. Saml. Wheeler who made the Rollers for the Mint, applies for money. I had a good deal of conversation with this ingenious gentleman.

August 26th. Mr. Dudley called and pressed very much to be set at work.

Sept. 4th. Mr. Wheeler for money. I desired him to leave his claim with Mr. McCall Secretary in this office, and I will enable the discharge of his notes in the Bank when due.

Novr. 8th. Mr. Dudley applies for the amount of his Bill for Lodgings and Diet &c. and I directed Mr. Swanwick to pay him, but am very uneasy that the Mint is not going on.

As of December, Morris, without authority, had been employing men for over eight months to construct a mint. On the 12th, he apologized to Congress for the delay, and proposed that, in the interim, new rates be established for the various foreign coins in circulation. Congress seems not to have caught on, and the Superintendent returned to his plan for a *fait accompli.*

Under his instruction dies were forged by the Philadelphia blacksmith and machinist John Jacob Eckfeldt and sunk by a Mr. Du Bois. Statements in the expense books of the old government [16] tell us that on February 8, 1783, Jacob Eckfield (sic.) was paid $5.18 for dies; on March 21, Dudley was paid $75.24 for "preparing a Mint"; on April 17 John Swanwick was paid $22.42 for dies;

---

[16] Sylvester S. Crosby, *Early Coins of America,* 1875.

and on May 5, A. Dubois was paid $72.00 "for sinking, casehardening, &c. four Pair of Dies for the Public Mint."

Swanwick was a business partner of Robert Morris, and the payment recorded on April 17 was apparently a reimbursement for bills drawn against the former.

On April 2, 1783 Morris noted in his diary that Dudley had delivered to him "A piece of Silver Coin, being the first that has been struck as an American Coin." [17]

On the 16th, and again the following day, Morris urged Dudley to furnish him with patterns of the other denominations which he might lay before Congress "to Establish a Mint." Dudley complied on the 22nd, by sending "Several Pieces of Money as patterns of the intended American Coins." A day later, Morris enclosed the coins in a letter to Congress, requesting that he be allowed to explain his plan for a Mint, and to select a committee to report on the subject.

A solitary mark, two quints, and two cents are all that survive of the Morris pattern coinage. The mark and the first quint were discovered in a secret drawer in the desk of Charles Thomson, Secretary of the Continental Congress, and were probably among the coins sent to Jefferson by Robert Morris on May 1, 1784 with the request that they be delivered to Thomson. Morris' letter, however, would suggest that the Superintendent was also enclosing copper coins of eight and five units.[18]

> . . In this Letter you will find enclosed my original Letter to Congress of the twenty third of April 1783, together with the Specimens of a Coin[age] there mentioned. These you will be so kind as to deliver to the Secretary of Congress after you have done with them and as the Reasoning on such Subjects is facilitated by a Reference to visible Objects let us take the largest of these Silver Coins as the Money *Unit* divisible into a thousand Parts each containing ¼ of a Grain of pure Silver, and worth about two thirds of a Dollar viz: 4/2 Virginia Money. The smallest Copper Piece is worth one Farthing Virginia Money . . .

An independent reference to the copper 5-unit piece appears in the diary of Samuel Curwen, who on March 15, 1784 received a specimen from Judge Josiah Bartlett.

The diary of Robert Morris tells us that on July 5, Dudley urged Morris, apparently without success, to purchase a coining press which was on sale in New York.

Just one month later Congress requested Morris to submit "an Estimate of the expence which will attend the establishment of a mint, including Buildings, Tools, Salaries to officers, &cc." The encouragement, however, was momentary, and no further action appears to have been taken until the following year,

---

[17] It is evident from this statement that Morris did not regard the Continental Currency coinage as an authorized issue. His own patterns, however, were equally unauthorized, and in no way more deserving of the *primo genitus* distinction.

[18] *The Papers of Thomas Jefferson*, Vol. 7, Boyd. All of the known Nova Constellatio patterns, except for one specimen of the cent with plain instead of leaved edge, repose in the Johns Hopkins University collection. The alternate cent is in the possession of Eric P. Newman. It is a testimony to Dudley's workmanship that these pieces have perfect weights, excepting only the quint with a variant reverse, about which nothing is known.

The Nova Constellatio copper coins of 1783 and 1785 were struck in Birmingham, England upon order of Gouverneur Morris. They represent a private venture. See Eric P. Newman, "The Source of the Nova Constellatio Coppers," *The Numismatic Scrapbook Magazine*, Jan. 1960.

Patterns dated 1783 for a coinage proposed by Superintendent of Finance, Robert Morris.
From top down: cent, quint, quint (alternate reverse), mark. *Johns Hopkins University.*

when the Morris plan was referred to a new committee which included Thomas Jefferson.

During this period, hope for the completion of the Mint slowly dwindled because, as Morris had written earlier, "like so many other important matters" the business was "retarded by the tediousness of the States in supplying the Continental Treasury." [19] Morris' disappointment over the failure is evident from his final notes on the subject:

> *August 19th.* I sent for Mr. Benjamin Dudley, and informed him of my doubts about the establishment of a Mint, and desired him to think of some employment in private service, in which I am willing to assist him all in my power. I told him to make out an account for the services he had performed for the public, and submit at the Treasury office for inspection and settlement.
>
> *August 30th.* Mr. Dudley brought the dies for Coining in the American Mint.
>
> *Sept. 3d.* Mr. Dudley applies for money for his expenses which I agree to supply, but urge his going into private business.
>
> *Sept. 4th.* Mr. Dudley for money which is granted.
>
> *Nov. 21st.* Mr. Dudley applies for money. He says he was at half a guinea a week and his expenses borne when he left Boston to come about the Mint, and he thinks the public ought to make that good to him. I desired him to write me and will state his claims to Congress.

The settlement of Dudley's account is recorded in scattered references, the last on January 7, 1784.

❉ ❉ ❉

After the end of the war and the long austerity imposed by trade restrictions, people grew extravagant and purchased all sorts of "foreign fripparies," as they were called. Local merchants, unable to remit goods for goods,[20] except on ruinous terms, exported specie. The result was another coin shortage.

In June 1783, Jefferson was elected to Congress and subsequently served as chairman of a currency committee. Here he learned of Morris' coinage plan, but was unable to obtain the original report which, by this time, had been lost.[21] Having, however, seen an exegesis of it in a letter from Gouverneur Morris to William Hemsley,[22] Jefferson sketched his own ideas on the subject, and forwarded them to Robert Morris.

Jefferson's genius for clarity and simplicity, his sound understanding of money-arithmetic, and his sympathy with the common man are all in evidence here. He criticized the Morris plan as being "defective in two of the three requisites of a money Unit." First,

"It is inconvenient in its application to the ordinary money transactions. 10,000 dollars will require 8 figures to express them, to wit, 14,400,000. A horse or bullock of 80 dollars value will require a notation of six figures, to wit 115,200 units. As a money of account this will be laborious even when facilitated by the aid of decimal arithmetic. As a common measure of the value of property it will be too minute to be comprehended by the people. The French

---

[19] Letter of Robert Morris to the Rev. William Gordon, July 25, 1782. *Historical Magazine,* January 1867. Between August 26, 1780 and March 16, 1781 Congress had made three specie requisitions upon the states, amounting to more than ten million dollars.

[20] The exchange of commodities, in lieu of money, was a common practice among merchants during the eighteenth century.

[21] Letter of Thomas Jefferson to Robert Morris, April 26, 1784, *The Papers of Thomas Jefferson,* Vol. 7, Boyd.

[22] Ibid, Vol. 6; see under date of April 30, 1783.

are subjected to very laborious calculations, the livre being their ordinary money of account, and this but between the 1/5 & 1/6 of a dollar. But what will be our labours should our money of account be 1/1440 of a dollar?" And secondly,

"It is neither equal nor near to any of the known coins in value."

Ultimately, the only justification for the Morris plan lay in its facility to convert the currencies of the diverse Colonial systems. Jefferson laid the ax to the root of the plan when he observed that "as our object is to get rid of those currencies, the advantage derived from this coincidence will soon be past." He proposed an alternate decimal system, in which the unit was a dollar, equal to the Spanish milled dollar, or Piece of Eight.

"The unit or dollar is a known coin and the most familiar of all to the mind of the people. It is already adopted from South to North, has identified our currency and therefore happily offers itself as an Unit already introduced. Our public debt, our requisitions and their apportionments have given it actual and long possession of the place of Unit. The course of our commerce too will bring us more of this than of any other foreign coin, and therefore renders it more worthy of attention. I know of no Unit which can be proposed in competition with the dollar, but the pound: But what is the pound? 1547 grains of fine silver in Georgia: 1289 grains in Virginia, Connecticut, Rhode Island, Massachusetts and New Hampshire; 1031¼ grains in Maryland, Delaware, Pennsylvania and New Jersey; 966¾ grains in North Carolina and New York.

"Which of these shall we adopt? To which State give that preeminence of which all are so jealous? And on which impose the difficulties of a new estimate for their coin, their cattle and other commodities. Or shall we hang the pound sterling as a common badge about all their necks? This contains 1718¾ grains of pure silver. It is difficult to familiarise a new coin to a people. It is more difficult to familiarise them to a new coin with an old name. Happily the Dollar is familiar to them all, and is already as much referred to for a measure of value as their respective State pounds."

Jefferson suggested the issue of a gold ten-dollar piece, a unit, or silver dollar, a half dollar, double tenth, tenth, twentieth, and copper hundredth. He pointed out that each of these denominations was similar to a coin already circulating, the gold piece to the Portuguese half-joe and the British double guinea, the silver dollar and its fractions to the Piece of Eight with its bits, and the copper hundredth to the English halfpenny.

Morris argued that decimal reckoning based on the dollar did not always express English farthings without a remainder, and would therefore inconvenience the merchant. Since Morris himself was a merchant, this small disadvantage appeared critical. To Jefferson, however, it was more than offset by the other advantages of the system. He felt, besides, that people could never be led to compute generally with the Morris unit. Jefferson also rejected the view that a copper two-hundredth piece was needed for the transactions of the poorer classes. Although Congress upheld Morris on this point, time abundantly proved the wisdom of Jefferson's view.

Despite the prodding of both Morris and Jefferson, the subject of a Mint was not resumed for more than a year.

On May 10, 1785 John Jay submitted to Congress the proposals "of Mr. (Solomon) Simson who sustains the Character of a Whig Citizen and an honest man" for establishing a Mint.[23] Jay added that "the subject appears to me of sufficient public Importance to merit the Attention of Congress and this Paper if committed may possibly be the means of putting that Business into proper Train."

Simson's paper can no longer be found in the Archives and we are left without knowledge of its contents. Nevertheless, it seems to have goaded Congress into action, for only three days later a "Grand Committee," consisting of thirteen members including James Monroe, submitted a new report on the Mint. The report began with a recapitulation of the Morris Plan. It then stated its objections, saying that the plan introduced "a Coin unlike in Value to anything now in Use. It departs from the national mode of keeping Accounts, and tends to preserve inconvenient Prejudices. Whence it must prevent national Uniformity in Accounts; a thing greatly to be desired."

The committee then offered Jefferson's plan, with several modifications. It reduced the largest coin to five dollars, replaced the double tenth by a quarter dollar, and added a copper piece of one two-hundredths of a dollar. The silver dollar was to contain 362 grains fine silver, and the copper one-hundredth to weigh 131 grains.

In favor of the plan, the committee urged "that a Dollar, the proposed Unit, has long been in general Use. Its value is familiar. This accords with the national mode of keeping Accounts, and may in times produce the happy effect of Uniformity in counting money throughout the Union."

A silver standard was preferable because "Sundry advantages would arise to us from a system by which silver might become the prevailing money. This would operate as a bounty to draw it from our neighbors by whom it is not sufficiently esteemed.[24] Silver is not exported so easily as gold and it is a more useful metal."

The committee agreed that the coins should be valued on their face slightly above the price of bullion in order to defray the expense of the Mint and discourage melting. It fixed the ratio between gold and silver at 15 to 1, and the alloy at one twelfth the total weight of each coin.

Appended to the original of this report is an alternate version of the Morris plan. The date of its composition is unknown, although it would seem to post-date the letter of April 30, 1783 from Gouverneur Morris to William Hemsley. The following denominations are given:

Gold crown	188 grains fine	10,000 units
Gold ———	94 grains fine	5,000 units
Silver dollar	260 grains fine	1,000 units
Silver ———	104 grains fine	400 units
Silver ———	52 grains fine	200 units
Silver bit	26 grains fine	100 units
Copper ———	—— grains fine	5 units
Copper ———	—— grains fine	4 units

Morris did not suggest names for all his values, and of those mentioned, he added: "they, like all other names, are arbitrary, and better may perhaps be

---

[23] *Papers of the Continental Congress and the Constitutional Convention*, Record Group 360, No. 80, I, National Archives.

[24] The committee, however, did not actually contemplate a monometallic standard. Indeed, a gold coinage was necessary for payments abroad if the balance of silver was to be favorable to the United States.

substituted. The word crown occurred from the following idea of an impression for the gold coin—An Indian, his right foot on a crown, a bow in his left-hand, in his right hand thirteen arrows; and the inscription Manus inimica Tyrannis . . ."

Top: sketch accompanying May 13, 1785 Congressional report. **Bottom:** pattern coin, illustrating designs suggested by Robert Morris.

Also enclosed with the Grand Committee report is a sketch of a proposed design consisting of thirteen stars surrounded by a gloriole, the word CONFEDERATIO, and the date 1785.[25] Two very rare copper coins (probably patterns) exist which show on one side the Confederatio design, and on the other the device for the gold crown, with the alternate legends INIMICA TYRANNIS AMERICA(NA). These pieces are punch-related to the Nova Constellatio coppers, and were thus probably made by Wyon at the instance of Gouverneur Morris. It is not known, however, whether they were intended for official or private issue.[26]

On July 6, 1785 Congress unanimously passed the plan of the Grand Committee, resolving:

1) That the money unit of the United States be the dollar.
2) That the smallest coin be of copper, of which 200 shall pass for one dollar.
3) That the several pieces shall increase in a decimal ratio.

During 1784, the seat of the Government had been moved to New York, and Robert Morris resigned as Superintendent of Finance. The office was returned to the Board of Treasury which, on April 8, 1786, presented three

---

[25] Walter Breen and Lynn Glaser, "Miss Liberty's American Debut," *Numismatic Journal,* Nov. 1961; also, Lynn Glaser, "Art in American Coinage," *The Numismatic Scrapbook Magazine,* Sept. 1962.

[26] Sometime prior to 1787, all of the Wyon dies for striking "American" coins were brought to this country, and found their way into the private New York mint known as Machin's Mill.

elaborate reports to Congress, each suggesting different weights for the unit in gold and silver, as well as different ratios.[27] The Board also proposed a coining charge of two per cent on silver, and one half per cent on gold, but neglected to calculate these figures into the ratios. Their several conclusions were as follows:

	Silver Dollar	Gold Dollar	Coin Ratio	Mint Ratio (Reconstructed)
	Fine Grains	Fine Grains		
#1	375.64	24.6268	1:15.256	1:15.47
#2	350.09	23.79	1:14.749	1:14.97
#3	521.73	34.782	1:15	1:15.22

On August 8, Congress fixed the unit at 375.64 grains of pure silver or 24.6268 grains pure gold. The following denominations were proposed:

Gold Eagle ($10)	to contain 246 268/1000 grs. pure gold
Half Eagle ($5)	to contain 123 134/1000 grs. pure gold
Silver Dollar	to contain 375 64/100 grs. pure silver
Half Dollar	to contain 187 82/100 grs. pure silver
Double Dime	to contain 75 128/1000 grs. pure silver
Dime:	to contain 37 564/1000 grs. pure silver
Cent:	2¼ pounds copper avoirdupois to equal 100 cents (157.5 grains)
Mill:	. . . .

The Eagle and the Half Eagle were to "be stamped with the impression of the American Eagle," but no other devices were specified. Congress also resolved "that the board of treasury report a draft of an Ordinance for the establishment of a Mint."

On August 22, while the Board was still preparing its report, William Barton submitted a plan of his own to Congress.[28] Barton proposed, as a first step, the coinage of $40,000 in pence and half pence, the sum to be repeated annually for a period of ten years. The coppers would be reckoned at 90 and 180 to the Spanish dollar (that is, 12 and 24 to a shilling Pennsylvania currency), and weigh 174 and 87 grains respectively. Barton estimated that the copper coinage would yield an annual profit of $10,000, and defray the expense of coining annually (from the second year on) $150,000 in silver and $250,000 in gold.

The plan provided for the issue of a five-dollar gold piece, and silver coins of five shillings, or two thirds of a dollar (to weigh 278 14/20 grains and be 11/12ths fine), and two-and-a-half shillings.

Barton's plan suffered from two fundamental defects. First it preserved the undesirable system of reckoning in pounds and shillings from a dollar unit, and secondly, it laid the yoke of Pennsylvania rates on every other state.

On September 20, the Board introduced a Mint bill which provided for the offices of an Assay Master, Master Coiner, and Paymaster, or Treasurer. Con-

---

[27] David K. Watson, *History of American Coinage*, G. P. Putnam's Sons, 1899.
[28] Barton's ideas were ignored by the Board of Treasury, and the only record of them appears in the April 1788 issue of *Columbian Magazine*.

gress resumed consideration of the bill on October 16, when it was read for a third time and passed.

Under the new ordinance, bullion received from depositors would be coined within ten days. The Mint was to coin gold and silver bullion at 11/12ths or .916 2/3 fine, charging respectively $209.77 and $13.777 the troy pound, or what amounted to a seignorage of about two per cent. In a rather daring measure, Congress permitted its copper coins to be paid to the Government in sums of up to five per cent of all dues. State-franchised coppers, though not a legal tender, were allowed to pass at the rate of one cent per 157½ grains. The circulation of foreign copper coins was to be prohibited after September 1, 1787.

The ordinance was not the first passed by Congress to establish a mint, and like the earlier legislation it was soon forgotten. Moreover, when the Constitution was ratified in June 1788, it repealed certain provisions of the Ordinance conceived under the Articles of Confederation. Whereas the Ordinance had regulated the copper coins struck by the states, and granted a small, quasi-tender status to its own coppers, the Constitution stipulated that "No State shall coin money, emit bills of credit, make anything but gold and silver coin a tender in payment of debts." New legislation was thus required, but a growing opposition in Congress to the establishment of a Mint delayed the matter for several years. The opponents of the Mint believed that the nation could subsist on the gold and silver coins in circulation, and that it should contract for its copper money. Some members evidently preferred to contract for all our coins rather than incur the expense of a Mint. For several years, various promoters lobbied with members of Congress, while the fate of American coinage hung in the balance.

CHAPTER 3

Experiments in Contract Coinage

WE HAVE SEEN that as early as 1779, Franklin attempted to interest Congress in a foreign contract coinage. For several years, he continued to promote the idea, and on December 24, 1782 he wrote, from Passy, to Secretary of Foreign Affairs Robert Livingston: [1]

> The commissioners have joined in a letter to you, recommending the consideration of a proposal from Mr. Brigden relating to copper coin. With this you have a copy of that proposal and a sample of the copper. If it should be accepted I conceive the weight and value of the pieces (charge of coinage deducted) should be such that they be aliquot parts of a Spanish dollar. By the copy enclosed of an old letter of mine to Mr. Brigden you will see the ideas I had of the additional utility such a coinage might be of in communicating instruction.

Unfortunately for Franklin and his coinage plan, Robert Morris, who dominated the finances of Congress, was dedicated to the establishment of a Mint. Early in 1784, however, when Morris announced his intention to resign, reconsideration of a contract coinage seems to have resumed almost immediately.

In a letter to Jefferson, dated May 12, 1784 Francis Hopkinson expressed his fears at such a prospect, at the same time confiding his aspiration to direct a mint at Philadelphia.[2] Hopkinson's views seem to have made a deep impression on Jefferson, who, a few years later, repeated them to Congress almost verbatim. Hopkinson wrote:

---

[1] *The Revolutionary Diplomatic Correspondence of the United States,* Vol. 6, edited by Francis Wharton, Government Printing Office, 1889; also, Eric P. Newman, "Poor Richard's Mottoes for Coins," *The Numismatist,* Dec. 1956.
[2] George E. Hastings, *Life and Works of Francis Hopkinson.* University of Chicago Press, 1926.

. . It appears by your letter that Congress have again taken up the idea of a public Mint. I beg leave to mention to you that I have long had it in Contemplation to sollicit the super-Intendency of this Department should it ever be established. Mr. Morris marked out this Station for me when he first formed the Idea of striking metal Coin for the U. States. My Gim-crack Abilities and I flatter myself my Integrity and Attention would be of Service in the Department—but my whole Scheme would fail unless this Mint should be carried on in or near this City. The Business of the Admiralty Department takes up but little of my Time, and it's Emoluments (£500 pr. An) which is the whole of my Income, you may easily suppose to be insufficient for the Support and Education of so large a Family as I have in Charge. What with the Depredations of the Enemy and my little Capital which lies entranced in the Monuments of the public Funds, I have given up all hope of leaving my Family any thing of Importance at my Death; but my earnest Desire is to be enabled to leave them well educated; to do which I must procure in some Line or other, a more liberal Income than £500 pr. An. This I cannot do in the way of Trade; my office as Judge prohibits it—at least not openly— but there will be no Inconsistence, in my holding such a Department under Congress. I promise myself your friendly Advice and Interest in this Matter. You are the only person to whom I have ever mentioned this Business, except Mr. Morris, who in Truth first brought the object into my view; and who I am sure, will exert his Influence to the Extent in my Behalf. I shall wait your Opinion, and follow your advice. I have heard it suggested that Congress intended to have their Money coined in Europe. I can hardly believe this. Innumerable are the objections. It is one of the Acts of sovereignty. Shall we depend on another Nation for this? Are we not able of ourselves? May we not in the Course of Events be at War with that Nation, and will they not have it in their power to play Tricks with our Money to the greatest Advantage &c. &c. &c.

[We have a Machine here already constructed by Mr. Dudley for the Purpose by Order of Mr. Morris.] [3] Sudden Changes may be necessary in the Coinage which cannot be effected in Time at so great a distance. An Importation may be lost at Sea, which would greatly distress us (altho' Insured) and in Time of War there will be no Possibility of conducting this Business in this Way.

Hopkinson evidently spoke with Jefferson a short time after writing the above, for on the 21st the latter wrote to James Monroe: [4]

Hopkinson tells me he had mentioned in his letter to me that the office of Director or master of the mint would be acceptable. He was therefore uneasy when I told him that I had left a request with a friend to open my letters. But I satisfied him perfectly on that head, and that you would render him any service which the duties of your situation would permit. He is a man of genius, gentility, & great merit, & at the same time poor & the father of a numerous family. He holds a little office here, more reputable than profitable, for he can but barely live. He is as capable of the office as any man I know & the appointment would give general pleasure because he is generally esteemed.

We recall that on May 13, 1785 a committee report had recommended Jefferson's coinage plan in preference to that of Robert Morris. The committee stressed the particular need to begin striking copper coins, saying that the entire expense of a Mint would not amount to the $30,000 lost annually through the importation of base, counterfeit English halfpence.

The most immediate effect of this report was an influx of propositions for supplying a contract copper coinage. On July 16, 1785 James Bowdoin, the Governor of Massachusetts, presented to Congress the proposals of a Swedish

---

[3] This sentence was deleted by Hopkinson.
[4] George E. Hastings, *Life and Works of Francis Hopkinson;* also, *The Papers of Thomas Jefferson,* Vol. 7, Boyd.

ship's captain named Frederick Walden.[5] Walden offered to furnish the Government with up to £100,000 of copper halfpence and farthings, the obligation to be paid in equal parts per annum over a period of ten years. The designs he enclosed may still be found among the records of the Continental Congress.

On August 18, 1785 the proposals of Edward Brigden and Walter Mould were referred to the Board of Treasury. Mould later contracted to coin coppers for the state of New Jersey.

On October 25, the proposal of Marinus Willet was likewise referred to the Board, and on December 22, a memorial was presented by Peter Allaire a "Native and Citizen of New York."

In March 1786, the Board of Treasury was reorganized, and Colonel William Duer appointed secretary. The reader may recall that the Board, in its earlier term, had exerted a baleful influence over Congress. With Duer's advent, this influence at once became deplorable. A money-mad opportunist, he promptly organized a group of friends to assist him in syphoning a profit from contracts of all kinds, and in particular through the sale of land tracts in the middle west. His labors were crowned by a luxurious mansion in New York City, where, it is said, guests were regaled with more than fifteen different kinds of after-dinner wine.

When Duer took office, several different bids for a contract copper coinage had already been submitted to the Board of Treasury. He at once endorsed the idea, and, on April 8, the Board announced its intention to report upon the various propositions whenever Congress would select its specie unit.

In the meantime new propositions were submitted. Late in 1786, Joseph Hopkins, a stockholder in the Connecticut "Company for Coining Coppers"[6] offered to strike up to fifty thousand pounds of coppers for the Government. For every "Hundred, Gross Weight, of good malleable Copper of suitable fineness" the Government would provide, Hopkins promised to deliver "fifty weight of Copper well coined." Just imagine, Hopkins not only wanted to make a good profit, but avoid doing the most difficult part of the work!

A much more attractive proposal was offered, on March 23, 1787 by Matthias Ogden.[7] As a member of the Legislative Council of New Jersey, Ogden had successfully promoted a bill, during the previous year, to provide his state with a contract copper coinage. He was also the bondsman for Thomas Goadsby and Albion Cox, two of the three men with whom the state contracted. Now, with these men as his associates, Ogden agreed to strike three hundred tons of coppers at federal standard, paying Congress fifteen percent of the coins for the privilege. The proposal was well conceived in every way. It not only relieved Congress of all responsibility, but offered it an immediate profit on the operation. Moreover, Ogden promised that: "In 14 days we can begin the work. Everything necessary is already prepar'd and before any Company on this Continent (if there are any adequate to it) can Erect works and a sufficient

---

[5] Letter of James Bowdoin to Richard Henry Lee, President of Congress. *Papers of the Continental Congress and the Constitutional Convention*, Record Group 360, No. 65, II, National Archives.

[6] A private firm which supplied Connecticut with a contract coinage (see Silvester Crosby, *Early Coins of America*, 1875). The proposal can be found in the *Papers of the Continental Congress and Constitutional Convention*, Record Group 360, No. 139, II, National Archives.

[7] Ibid.

Establishment to carry the Contract into Effect, we can nearly finish it and we add with Confidence with better Execution."

On April 9, 1787 the Board of Treasury outlined five proposals for a copper contract coinage. Three of these demanded payment on delivery in specie or good bills, and were rejected because of the "embarrassments of the Public Finances." The remaining two were submitted to a committee of Congress for further consideration.

One of these two proposals was that of Matthias Ogden. The other was offered by James Jarvis, a member of Duer's elite, who was empowered to trade in land tracts and securities for the Board of Treasury. In the same month that the Board first suggested a contract coinage, Jarvis became partner in the Connecticut "Company for Coining Coppers." He offered Congress a ten per cent premium for the privilege of coining its coppers. Payment was to be made on delivery, in government obligations which ran up to twenty years, at an interest rate of six per cent per annum. On April 20, Congress advised the Board of Treasury to accept the proposals of Jarvis providing he meet Ogden's premium of fifteen per cent. Jarvis agreed, suggesting that the premium be applied to the weight of the coins. The idea was rejected, and on the following day the Board of Treasury contracted with him for the coinage of three hundred tons of copper at the 157½ grain standard.

The purpose of the coinage was expressed as follows:
"That the whole of the foresaid loan shall be sacredly appropriated and applied to the reduction of the domestic debt of the United States and the premium thereon toward the payment of the foreign debt."

Finally, on May 8, Congress authorized the Board of Treasury to dispose of its stock of copper "as they shall judge most for the Interest of the U.S."

What is most intriguing about this whole business is the fact that it was a hoax, and that Duer had already given 12,809 pounds of government copper to Jarvis on January 16, nearly four months before Congress even agreed on a contract coinage. Jarvis' proposal is dated November 1, 1786 [8] and nowhere mentions the ten per cent premium clause later represented as being a part of it. The draft, in fact, which Jarvis sent Duer on the previous October 16,[9] states that "The loan must be an established and solid sum; and not subject to any deduction by Congress, or any body, acting under their authority."

It would appear that Jarvis was informed of Ogden's late proposal, in the light of which he reconsidered his own terms. To offset the burden of the premium, Duer permitted Jarvis to pay the fifteen per cent as an additional forty-five tons of copper coin. For his solicitude, however, Duer demanded a fee of ten thousand dollars. The terms of this arrangement later became a source of dispute between the two men, and on November 1, 1790 Jarvis wrote to two of Duer's associates, presenting his own version: [10]

It is with reluctance that anything is said by me on the subject of the copper contract; and if in it I impeach Mr. D in any respect, I have the resolution to know that my assertions are true & that he cannot presume to deny them!

Mr. D saw my proposals, *if accepted* would give me the power of great benefit,

---

[8] Ibid.
[9] *William Duer Papers*, New York Historical Society collection.
[10] Letter of James Jarvis to Andrew Craigie and Melancton Smith. *Andrew Craigie Papers*, American Antiquarian Society. Jarvis had given Duer a promissory note for the amount, and the latter apparently palmed it off on Craigie and Smith.

and therefore demanded a share in the business, & which I consented to, provided he would pledge himself to be at least dormant & secret with respect to people out of doors—there were many reasons to instigate these conditions—I knew Mr. D. was engaged in a sort of treaty with others; and tho I did not want his assistance, I wished him not interested against me—from Mr. D.'s official situation, he must necessarily know all applications made to the Board of Treasury—Whether this was in the interest of the United States I shall not presume to determine!

Mr. D had ever said that it was not proper for him to enter into written engagements, and that in all events he would confide in my honor to pay him in the event of my contract, his proportion of advantage.

It is but justice to Mr. D. to acknowledge that in no stage of my application did he interfere, after the understanding between us, nor can he be chargeable with planning and arranging in any respect but in drafting the contract, which the Board of treasury order'd him to do at his own home, in conjunction with myself—for this purpose we met, when the first article he proposed was a *private one* to engage to pay him for value rec'd ten thousand specie dollars and which he demanded as *sine qua non*.

Mr. D. will remember that at this proposal, I proposed to leave his house, declaring that rather than comply with his demand I would resign all pretensions to the contract, and inform the board that some recent objections had arisen in my mind to engaging in the business & I assured him that no treatment of his, should tempt me to betray him to them.

Finding me obstinate, he declared that he had no intention of demanding *any* thing of me, should the contract not succeed; but that as some person was concerned with him *who could not be mentioned,* it was necessary to have some sort of evidence of the amount he was to receive; and that he would rather the sum should be *defined,* than *contingent* and proposed the paper in existence, to which I agreed, on his *re-pledging* himself that it should only operate in case of success.

According to his original contract of May 12, 1787 Jarvis agreed to furnish the Government with three hundred and forty-five tons of copper. By the terms of a second contract, signed on the same date, Jarvis purchased 71,174½ pounds of copper from the Board of Treasury. The sum was to be repaid in federal coppers by August 31, 1788. In addition to the original 12,809 pounds of copper, however, the only delivery chargeable to Jarvis which Duer recorded was for 19,195 pounds, on May 14.[11]

On contracting with Congress, Jarvis entered into a bond of $20,000 "to indemnify the United States against any damages which might result from a breach" on his part. He obligated himself to manufacture and deliver at New York over thirty million cents, according to the following schedule:

25 tons by December 1, 1787
25 tons by March 15, 1788
50 tons by August 31, 1788
100 tons by August 31, 1789
100 tons by May 11, 1790

On April 26, Congress ordered the Board of Treasury to furnish several devices for the cents and on May 11, these were submitted by a committee consisting of Samuel Osgood, Walter Livingston and Arthur Lee. It was not until July 6, however, that a sufficient quorum was present in Congress to proceed with the business. On that date Congress deferred to the choice of William Pierce, John Kean, and Samuel Holten, resolving:

---

[11] Letter of March 4, 1791 from Nicholas Eveleigh, Comptroller of the Treasury, to William Duer, *William Duer Papers*, New York Historical Society collection.

that the board of Treasury direct the contractor for the copper coinage, to stamp on one side of each piece the following device, viz. thirteen circles linked together, a small circle in the middle with the words, "American Congress" flowing round it: and in the center of that circle, the words "WE ARE ONE.";

On the opposite side of the same piece the following device to be stamped, viz a Dial with the hours expressed on the face of it; a meridian Sun above; on one side of which, is to be the word "fugio," and on the other, the Year in figures "1787." Below the Dial, the words "mind your business."

This design, which was almost identical to that on the 1776 Congress coins, was then amended to show: "thirteen circles linked together, a small circle in the middle with the words, [UNITED STATES] round it: and in the center the words "WE ARE ONE."

It is a curious fact that at the time Jarvis contracted to lend the Government over three hundred thousand dollars in coppers, he was without any means to do so. On November 12, he sailed for Amsterdam [12] in the hope of enlisting financial support. Failing in this, he proceeded to England to see the famous Birmingham contract coiner, Matthew Boulton.

❋   ❋   ❋

Before continuing our story, we must go back a few years to an exhibition held at the Paris Mint by Jean Pierre Droz. Droz was a coiner and an inventor, as well as one of the finest engravers in his line in Europe. In 1786, he exhibited an improved coining press, featuring a segmented die-collar for impressing the planchet simultaneously on its edge and sides. The collar was made up of six parts which joined at the moment of impact, then separated, allowing the planchets to be fed and replaced mechanically. Droz, hoping for a lucrative position at the Paris Mint, struck off some pattern *écus* of Louis XVI, one of

---

[12] *New York Daily Advertiser,* Nov. 12, 1787.

Impressions from pattern dies for the Fugio cent, illustrating coinage bill before and after amendment. These impressions were made in the 1860's when the dies were discovered in Connecticut.

which he presented to De Calonne, the French Finance Minister. Among those who witnessed the exhibition were Thomas Jefferson, then resident minister at Paris, and Matthew Boulton. Both men were favorably impressed, and on December 23, Jefferson wrote to Francis Hopkinson: [13]

> Have they connected you with our mint? My friend Monroe promised me he would take care for you in that. Or perhaps the establishment of that at New York may have been incompatible with your residence in Philadelphia.
>
> A person here has invented a method of coining the French écu of six livres, so as to strike both faces and the edge at one stroke, and makes a coin as beautiful as a medal. No country has ever yet produced such a coin. They are cheaper too. As yet, he has only made a few to show the perfection of his manner. I am endeavoring to procure one to send to Congress as a model for their coinage. They will consider whether, on establishing a new mint, it will not be worth while to buy his machines, if he will furnish them. . . .

Jefferson conveyed his sentiments to Droz through their mutual friend Ferdinand Grand, a French banker. On December 28, Jefferson wrote to Grand: "It will be in good time if I receive the crowns to-day, tomorrow, or even the next day."

On January 9, 1787 Jefferson, having received gold and silver patterns from Droz (and evidently anticipating further specimens of copper) wrote to John Jay: [14]

> Observing by the proceedings of Congress that they are about to establish a coinage, I think it my duty to inform them, that a Swiss, of the name of Drost,[15] established here, has invented a method of striking the two faces and the edge of a coin at one stroke. By this and other simplifications of the process of coinage he is enabled to coin from 25000 to 30000 pieces a day, with the assistance of only two persons, the pieces of metal being first prepared. I send you by Colo. Franks three coins of gold, silver and copper, which you will perceive to be perfect medals, and I can assure you from having seen him coin many, that every piece is as perfect as these. There has certainly never yet been seen any coin, in any country, comparable to this. The best workmen in this way acknolege that his is like a new art. Coin should always be made in the highest perfection possible because it is a great guard against the danger of false coinage. This man would be willing to furnish his implements to Congress, and if they please, he will go over and instruct a person to carry on the work: nor do I believe he would ask anything unreasonable. It would be very desirable that in the institution of a new coinage, we could set out on so perfect a plan as this, and the more so, as while the work is so exquisitely done, it is done cheaper . . .

In a letter of January 16 (apparently) to Ferdinand Grand,[16] Droz apologized for being unable to furnish any more pattern coins. Political forces had frustrated the attempt to promote his inventions in France, and the artist now looked forward hopefully to American patronage. His letter, in translation, reads:

> I have the honor to inform you that I am unable to make the gold pieces for which you asked, as I have heard it is no longer permitted to do so without running the risk of displeasing the Government, orders having been received on this subject. Would you be so kind as to inform Mr. Jefferson that it is also not possible to have

---

[13] *The Papers of Thomas Jefferson*, Vol. 10, Boyd.

[14] Sylvester Crosby, "The Cents of 1793," *American Journal of Numismatics*, January, 1897.

[15] This mis-spelling recurs in the diplomatic dispatches.

[16] *Papers of the Continental Congress and the Constitutional Convention*, Record Group 360, No. 107, I, National Archives. The transcript of this letter erroneously states that it is addressed to Jefferson.

the pieces for which he asked nor possible to make any more for the moment before having received further authorization.

I have not as yet had the time to work on the memorandum which you kindly requested of me relative to the manufacture of the coins. I am more than ever resolved to accept offers which might be advantageous to me and even go abroad. So, my dear Sir, if Congress will make a reasonable offer I will in turn establish all the machinery necessary in order to strike the most beautiful coins, which, perhaps, have hitherto existed, and also with much less expense. I believe it would be sufficient to prepare an estimate of what these machines will cost, which could be made here and then sent to America. With regard to the coining of specie, it is much more difficult to determine a fair price. All I can do is assure you that they will be struck at a price below what they cost here. Anyway, I will take care of the machines, the coins and the engraving at a price agreed upon, though not the casting and the alloying of the gold and silver metals. It will be enough, if I am entrusted with the establishment of the machinery, the rolling of the copper, the adjustment of the planchets, and the actual coinage. Soon I will try to have a memorandum and I shall have the honor to bring this to you and at the same time to confer with you and I remain with respect sir &c.

The letter was forwarded to Jefferson who, on February 1, wrote to Jay:

. . . I had the honor of informing you of an improvement in the art of coinage made here by one Drost, and of sending you by Colo. Franks a specimen of his execution in gold and silver. I expected to have sent also a coin of copper. The enclosed note from Drost will explain the reason why this was not sent. It will let you see also that he may be employed; as I suppose he is not so certain as he was of being engaged here. Mr. Grand, who knows him, gives me reason to believe he may be engaged reasonably. Congress will decide whether it be worth their attention . . .

Unfortunately for Droz, the Board of Treasury was at this time negotiating with Jarvis, and the possibility of a federal mint, with full capabilities, was best ignored. In the meantime, Droz accepted an offer to join Boulton and Watt at their private mint at Soho, Birmingham.

Ironically, it was only a few months later that Jarvis arrived from Holland with the intention of subcontracting with Boulton for the Fugio coinage. On February 24, 1788 Jarvis wrote to Boulton: [17]

Sir! The nature of my contract with the United-States of America, involves with it the necessity of delivering the copper-coin into the treasury of the United-States, by certain instalments; and at each delivery, the Commissioners of the treasury are to give me their official obligation for the amount, calculating the coin of a certain established rate per Ct.

These obligations are redeemable within a fixed period, and bear an interest of Six percentum per annum, as per a special law of Congress, in this behalf made.

One hundred tons of the coin should be delivered by the first day of September next; one hundred tons within twelve months from that period; and the last delivery within a year following.

An advance will be required of the first one hundred tons to be paid for on the first day of September 1789. This advance will be a leading principle in any contract that I make and for which satisfactory security will be given.

If you are willing to meet me on this ground, I fancy from the conversation that has already passed between us, that no insurmountable difference of price will arise; and that an adequate compensation can be agreed on, for an impressing apparatus, as well as for the original dies to be made by Monsr. Droz.

From the nature of my contract with the United-States, I am willing that any engagements entered into between you and myself, should be examined by, and executed before, the American Minister here. In order that a candid, unreserved,

---

[17] *Matthew Boulton Papers,* Assay Office of Birmingham, England.

and explanatory conversation may take place between us, I propose, that we meet at my lodgings, as soon as may be convenient to you.

I am at your Service this day till 2 oclock and at any time you may be pleased to appoint on monday, tuesday, or wednesday, and remain etc.

Apparently not very much was accomplished at the meeting owing to the inability of Jarvis to provide Boulton with security. On March 8, a week before his second delivery of cents was due, Jarvis again wrote to Boulton:

Sir! Since the conversation that passed between us, before Mr. Matthews, I have reflected on a mode of Security to you, in case you are willing to make the one hundred tons advance of blanks, which may be acceptable to you *in all events.* I think it not amiss to submit it to your consideration yet. I propose to authorize you or your Attorney, *by virtue of my contract,* to make the delivery of the 100 Tons of coin, to the Commissioners of the treasury of the United States of America and to receive from them the payment, in the manner I am to receive it.

2nd. In addition to the price that I shall be agreed on you shall be put into possession of 50 Pct. on the amt. of the 100 Tons, as a security to you for my ful-filling the contract I will make with you, and which shall contain the following articles, namely

1st. The 100 tons shall be estimated at _____ Pct. and be paid for on the 1st. day of September 1789, with interest.

2nd. 250 Tons in addition, shall be contracted for to be delivered at Stipulated periods, but not any part before September next; and to vary or be governed in price, by the price of copper—the difference between the price of copper and the blanks, to be ascertained.

3rd. The payment of the 250 tons shall be by good bills on Paris or Amsterdam, at my option which, at three usances, and on delivery of the blanks at Bristol, or any other port agreed on.

4th. The expence that may accrue in consequence of the delivery of the first one hundred tons either for commissions to the Agent, or that shall be deemed necessary, in case of some persons going out shall be allowed, and paid by me.

I have to observe that no security be more valid in itself than what I offer, as the whole United States of Ama. gurantee [sic] me.—The fifty Pct. on the amt. to be received over and above the payment, will be a valuable indemnity, in case of failure on my part, either of the payment, or purchase of the residue of 250 tons.

I am ready to convince you by my documents, that what I offer is in my power and am Sir! etc.

Boulton's reply has not been located, and the next letter we see is from Jarvis on the 13th.

Sir! The night before last, about eleven oclock, yours of the 11th inst. was given me, and tho' I had determined to reply yesterday morning I was nevertheless pre-vented. -

The proposition I made you with respect to the necessary 250 tons, to be paid for by bills on Paris or Amsterdam, you have understood perfectly well as it relates to good accepted bills; but this part of the contract should not be deliverable untill after September next, and indeed not before the funds are ready to represent the quantity as far as 350 tons, the 50 per Ct. would be the security.

The 50 per Ct. would be paid thus, if the amount of the 100 tons is £ 10,000 on the delivery of that quantity, you should be put into possession of £ 15,000 of the payment I am to receive.

Suppose I was to pay you £ 5000, either in money, or satisfactory bills. Would you supply the 100 tons, and receive for security of payment of the remaining £ 5000, what I am to receive from the treasury? I am etc.

Considering the depreciated state of Continental Congress obligations, we can understand Boulton's insistence on security. His reply (undated on the fair copy), hints a growing impatience—though not yet so much to dissuade him from further negotiations.

Sir: I have been so much hurried with various engagements for some days past that I could not find time to answer your favr. of the 13th Inst. Youl observe in all which hath passed between us that I decline putting my property into the possession of the Great Mogul, the Emperor of the turks or of Germany or any other potentate whose Will is the law. I must own I should feel the security you propose of putting me into possistion [sic] of my portion of the paymt. you are to receive from your States is dissatisfactory as of under any of the forementd. predicaments & therefore dont let us talk of it.

If its agreeable to you to go upon the other plan I will endeavor to execute your Command as much to your satisfaction as it is my power but I must be upon a Certainty in regard to paymt. Otherwise I may be saddled with a large quantity of Manufactured Blanks wch. are not applicable to any other purpose than to return to the Melting furnace as old Copper.

I propose to set out within these 2 Hours to Birmgh. where I should be happy to receive your commands or to see you when ever your affairs bring you into that neighborhood [remainder missing]

Sometime before May 21, representatives of Jarvis delivered a token offering of 8,968 pounds of Fugio cents (slightly less than 400,000 coins) to the Treasurer of the United States.

It is not known with certainty where these coins were struck. Contemporary newspapers generally credited New York, but this may be due to the fact that it was the temporary residence of Congress, and the site for the proposed federal Mint. Seventy years later, a pair of Fugio cent dies were found in a New Haven store where Jarvis' father-in-law, Samuel Broome, had once operated a mint. Broome was subcontractor for the Connecticut state coinage, but whether the New Haven mint was used to make Connecticut coppers, Fugio cents, or both (which would have been illegal under the state contract), has never been determined. It is significant, however, that Jarvis never accounted for all of the Government copper, and that the fabric and striking peculiarities of the two coinages are similar.

On May 21, the Board of Treasury reported on Jarvis' delivery. Ignoring the fact that Jarvis had already defaulted his contract, the Board advised Congress to revalue the coins "to be struck" by him. They observed that the rate on coppers had fallen considerably, and that it would probably be impossible to circulate the Fugio coins as cents. Moreover, a high seignorage would invite counterfeiting.

The Board presented a bill to revalue the cent at 209 98/100 grains (making the Fugios three-quarter cent pieces), and provide for the issue of cents and half cents at the new standard. On July 16, the bill was endorsed by a committee of Congress. The status of the copper contract was then taken up by a committee of five which seems to have reported unfavorably. By August 4, however, this report was mysteriously missing.

When Jarvis left England, on June 20, he had not yet come to terms with Boulton. There is an undated draft of a conditional contract between the two men in which Boulton agreed to furnish Jarvis with one hundred and fifty tons of copper coins, a press and six pair of dies "as soon as Mr. J. acceeds to the price herein mentioned & gives B. such a security for the payments as may be satisfactory to him." This arrangement, however, was not completed.[18]

Back in New York, Jarvis visited Congress on August 21, only to learn that

---

[18] It may have been this paper that led Dickinson, in his *Matthew Boulton*, to assert that Boulton had furnished the United States with a copper coinage in 1788.

a committee had reported unfavorably on his contract the previous day. On the 23rd, he submitted a lengthy appeal: [19]

Gentlemen: Since my personal respects to you of Thursday, it appears an incumbent duty to the Public as well as to myself to state the reasons, why the deliveries of my Contract heretofore due have not been regularly made: and to endeavor to prove that no real injury has arisen in consequence of my delay to the Public. Should I be so fortunate as to clear up these two points to the satisfaction of Congress, I flatter myself they will extend a liberal and generous conduct to me; and will rather accept of a beneficial accommodation, than pursue any measures which may not only materially injure me, but eventually tend to the disadvantage of the Public.

When my propositions were first made, three Years were required to complete the Business and as it appeared not ineligible to Congress, that Honorable Body authorized the Commissioners of the Treasury to proceed accordingly.

It was ever understood that the idea of procuring a sufficiency of Copper in the Country, within the proposed period was a fallacy too notorious to be attended to; [20] and that therefore it would be necessary to Import it from Europe: this had not only been part of the plan on which my first calculations were founded but my declared intention to many of the Honorable Members of Congress, as well as to your Honble Board.

To effect this purpose, it was my wish to obtain as much time for the first deliveries as possible, which I presume your Board may very well remember, but which you thought proper should be confined to the periods stipulated as per Contract.

Not being able to accomplish my object as to the first periods it became a duty to guard myself as to the manner of each separate delivery, and to gain as much time for the larger part as possible. Impressed with these ideas, you will not be surprised at my stipulations for each delivery in the manner I did as separate Contracts. Several months elapsed from the time I signed the Contract, until Official directions were given to me, as to impression, weight &c after which I hastened to Europe to complete my Arrangements. It will be needless to observe that my Interest urged me to finish the Business as speedily as possible, in order to possess myself of my proposed advantage; with this view the moment of my Arrival was embraced by me, and tho' I had founded myself as to the obligations I had to receive from the United States and from which the necessary Monies for my operation were to arise, there were yet difficulties to encounter of a different nature.

In order to inspire the necessary confidence to entitle me to my Bonds, obtainable only by some one, or more of my deliveries, it became necessary to explain candidly my relative situation with the United States by exhibiting my Contract or to give Security for the performance of this new trust.

The former mode was *felo de se* to my object, as the first delivery was already due; and the second within three Months would become so—this difficulty tho' forseen, was unavoidable, and did not admit of any remedy, unless by indulgence of Congress. The great object of my pursuit now demands a compliance with the latter, namely security for the performance of any engagements that were necessary with respect to payment. This circumstance was not so embarrassing as productive of delay: and finally the third delivery would nearly become due, before a sufficient quantity of Copper could be delivered me, to answer my engagements in America. In this state I found myself as to time, before any substantial, and satisfactory arrangements could be made so as to make it prudent for me to return to America.

I now present myself to Congress thro' the medium of your Honorable Board, and request they will consider the foregoing facts as my apology for want of punctuality and that they will have the goodness to infer from what I have

---

[19] *Papers of the Continental Congress and the Constitutional Convention,* Record Group 360, No. 149, II, National Archives.
[20] Compare this with Ogden's original proposal.

already said, compared with what follows, as favorably as the nature of the case will admit.

On my Arrival in England I found there were propositions to the Government of that Country for a new Copper Coinage *by Contract* and that the proposed value, proportioned to the faederal Coin would be as 32 to 44 or nearly; beside that, the execution by a new invented apparatus, was far superior to anything that could be executed by the former mode of Coining.

In this comparative view of the English and American Copper Coins, it was obvious that we should experience every possible disadvantage of depreciation, together with the burthen of immense Imports of spurious Coin, as an Article of Commerce, and that of course, the object of consuming part of the Domestic Debt, with the Faederal Copper Coin would be in a great measure defeated.

It was not impossible from any distant situation to represent in time, the inconveniences that would arise to the United States, by circulating the faederal Coin at the value that had been determined on previously to my departure. On this occasion I can aver with the strictest attention to truth, that I experienced the greatest anxiety, as I neither then, or ever had intended the Coin contracted for as an advantage *merely* to myself; but on the contrary had ever proposed benefit to the Public for the privilege I had obtained, as will appear by the Premium of 15 p Cent.

Thus far I have stated the honest and real causes of my want of puctuality, and have exhibited to view consequences that would have arisen to the Public had my deliveries been regular by which it is plainly demonstrated that the community have not only not been injured but have actually avoided great loss and inconvenience.

It now remains to inform your Honble Board that I have made such Arrangements in Europe, as to enable me to ascertain the periods of my deliveries and to execute the Coin in such stile as will not only be reputable to myself but as must facilitate the circulation, if some attention is paid to the relative value of Copper.

Should the Honorable Committee of Congress allow me to present myself before them I doubt not but I shall be able to remove from their mind any impressions to my disadvantage. I am etc.

The appeal was in vain. On September 16, Congress voided the copper contract, and two weeks later a committee, appointed to inquire fully into the department of finance, reported:

There are . . two contracts made by the Board of Treasury with James Jarvis, the one for coining three hundred tons of copper of the Federal standard, to be loaned to the United States, together with an additional quantity of forty five tons which he was to pay as a premium to the U.S. for the privilege of coining; no part of this contract has been fulfilled. A particular statement of this business so far as relates to the three hundred tons, has lately been reported to Congress. *It does not appear to your committee, that the Board were authorized to contract for the privilege of coining 45 Tons, as a premium exclusive of the 300 mentioned in the Act of Congress.*

The other contract with said Jarvis is for the sale of a quantity of Copper amounting as per account to 71,174 pounds; this the said Jarvis has received at the stipulated price of Eleven pence farthing sterling per pound, which he contracted to pay in copper coin of the federal standard on or before the last day of August 1788, now past; of which but a small part has been received. The remainder, it is presumed, the Board of Treasury will take effectual measures to recover as soon as possible.

The "presumption," however, proved presumptuous, for Jarvis soon returned to Europe, and, with his father-in-law Samuel Broome, began a new promotion to establish a subsidiary of Boulton's Albion Mill at Paris.

Duer, for obvious reasons, allowed the matter to rest, and no further action was taken until 1791, when Secretary of the Treasury Hamilton sued Jarvis for breach of contract. The case was tried in the New York Supreme Court, and on February 24, 1791 a judgment of 20,000 Spanish milled dollars, plus damages, was made against Jarvis.[21]

On March 4, the Comptroller of the Treasury, Nicholas Eveleigh, wrote to Duer: [22]

> Sir: It seems that an action has been commenced against Mr. James Jarvis of New York by directions from the late Board of Treasury for a breach of Covenant. It also appears by a letter which I have lately received from Colonel Troup who has had management of the suit, that a Judgement is filed up against Jarvis for 20,000 dollars, being the penalty of the Bond, which he and others gave to indemnify the United States against any damages which might result to them from a breach of his Contract of the 12th of May 1787.
>
> It being necessary however to furnish the United States Attorney with the evidences of our Claim against Mr. Jarvis, I have hitherto searched the Treasury office, without being able to discover, any documents which can be regarded as conclusive, with respect to the quantity of Copper delivered to him. It is true, that the Contract in question alludes to 12,809 lbs. of crude Copper delivered to Jarvis on the 16th of January 1787—And there is a receipt of his in the Contract Book which proves the delivery of a further quantity of 19,195 lbs. on the 14th day of May following—But as the Board of Treasury had stipulated to furnish Jarvis with Thirty seven Tons of crude Copper, I cannot bring myself to believe that the two parcels, above mentioned, form the whole quantity for which he is accountable. I have therefore to request sir; that you will as soon as possible, afford me some further light on the subject.
>
> I must once more solicit your attention to the absolute necessity for your coming forward yourself or sending on your accounts by the first safe conveyance. I am etc.

Whether or not on Duer's testimony, Jarvis was finally charged for the entire 71,174½ pounds. The auditor's voucher book, under October 17, 1791 [23] debits Jarvis $14,828.01 for this amount, from which is subtracted $3,985.77 for the delivery of 8,968 pounds of Fugio cents. Eveleigh computed that Jarvis owed the Government $10,842.24, but no part of this amount was ever collected.

In the meantime, the ill-fated Fugio cents were playing out their last hand. During mid-1787, the New York rate on coppers had fallen to 62½ cents a hundred, or little more than a half cent each! The Government, unable to circulate the Fugios at their face value, held them intact until July 7, 1789 when it found a buyer in the Broadway merchant Royal Flint,[24] another speculator and friend of Duer's. Flint purchased the coins at face value, but on credit, apparently with the idea of circulating them out of state. His project, however, was almost immediately terminated by a severe panic which broke out as an accumulative effect of the immense number of coppers being poured into circulation by various private coiners. The panic began in New York, but quickly spread throughout the Eastern seaboard, and Flint was caught without an outlet for his near four hundred thousand Fugio cents. He had repaid the Government for only a third of the coins when, on January 29, 1792 he was taken away by the Sheriff.[25]

---

[21] New York Supreme Court, Parchment Roll 103-H-10.

[22] *William Duer Papers,* New York Historical Society collection.

[23] General Accounting Office, Auditor's report No. 1671 National Archives.

[24] General Accounts of receipts of the Board of Treasury, July 1-Sept. 12, 1789, p. 286. National Archives.

[25] Minute Books of the Supreme Court of New York.

CHAPTER 4

More About Contract Coinage

ONE WOULD THINK that the Fugio cent fiasco would have dampened the ardor of those favoring a contract coinage. Nevertheless, it was not long before certain members of Congress began a new liaison, this time with a young entrepreneur from Charleston, South Carolina.

John Hinkley Mitchell had gone to England to complete his education, and met Boulton through his mother's family at Birmingham. Mitchell had originally hoped to supply his home state with a copper coinage, but after the adoption of the Constitution, he turned his eye toward a federal contract.

During September 1789, Mitchell journeyed to New York where he apparently received some encouragement from President Washington. On October 9, while en route back to Charleston, Mitchell wrote to Boulton: [1]

Dear Sir, Being just arrived from New York—the seat of Government of the United States—and having had a conference with Genl. Washington, the President of the United States, respecting a general Coinage for the Union—I have to request of you as a favor that you will be so obliging as to favor me with the rates you could furnish two hundred thousand pounds, one-third copper, one third silver, one-third gold coin, payable in the coin of Great Britain, as I have the preference of supplying Congress with their first Coinage. I think we can do it on as good terms as any person whatever. The amount of the Coinage will be shipped to London before the delivery of the new Coinage. I beg you to be very plain and explicit, which I have not time to be, as I am this moment arrived and the vessel for London leaves this place this moment, but very next will explain myself more fully, I beg of you to mention particularly every circumstance about

---

[1] *The Mitchell-Boulton Correspondence 1787-1792*, edited by C. B. Mitchell. Princeton University Press, 1931. The originals of these papers are likewise in the Assay Office of Birmingham.

39

furnishing the above sum. With my best compts to Miss Boulton and Mr. and Mrs. Matthews, I remain etc.

[P.S.] The money must be all made in two years before this date. If your terms suit I shall ship you on the first information two thousand barrels of rice and a quantity of indigo.

On the following day, Mitchell posted another letter to Boulton, similar in content to the above.

Boulton replied on November 25, giving a lengthy account of his operations and expenses. He offered to furnish Mitchell with any quantity of coppers at 14 pence per pound, adding:

It will also be necessary that you (in Conjunction with General Washington or such persons as may be appointed) fix upon a proper Device & proper inscription. I saw a design for an American Half penny with a Sun Dial on one side with a Motto, mind your Business—& on the other a Chain with 13 Links.

This device is easily copied by a moderate Artist, but if there was on one side the Head of General Washington or a beautiful Female Figure representing in proper attributes the 13 United States, it would not only be a handsome piece of Money but it would be more difficult to copy, particularly if an inscription was struck upon the Edge, as there is no Artist in England capable of doing that, or engraving such a Figure as the Britannia which my Artist hath nearly finished for the intended British Coinage, but the Dies being not yet hardened, I cannot send one at present. However you will see by those I have sent the stile of Workmanship.

It is the interest of America to attend to the principles mentioned in the paper I have sent you herewith, & by leaving but little temptation for Counterfeiters, & throwing many difficulties in their Way, is the only sure means of preventing great quantities of counterfeit half-pence from being sent from Europe to America.

I cannot help advising you to be perfectly explicit with General Washington, or such members of the Congress as you may have the honor of conversing with; there is no doubt but they will make you a proper allowance for your trouble; and if you think proper to mention my Name, I refer them to Dr. Franklyn whom I have had the pleasure & the honor of being acquainted with for 30 years past.

It will be necessary that you lose not a moment in this business & that it be brought to a conclusion as soon as possible that I may arrange my own time & Business properly, for besides the British Copper Coinage, I am now in treaty with some other European States for the conduct of the whole of their Coinage, but I am determined not to undertake more than I can do; however I am willing to contract for the whole quantity you mention & execute within the time.

I can equally excel in the Gold & Silver Coin, but I have not or calculated at what price I can do it, however I can positively say that I can make it a much finer Coin, & at a much lower price than any other State in Europe hath yet done. I am obliged to set out to London tomorrow & fear I must delay entering into the Gold & Silver Coin untill my return which will be about the 6th Decemr. & then you may depend upon hearing from me distinctly on that Subject.

Please to take a Copy for yourself of my Paper upon Copper Coinage & then present it also some of my Specimens, & my most respectful Complts. to the truly great & honble. General Washington. . . .

I recommend an Elegant figure to represent the United States by any Dress or Attributes that may be thought proper, perhaps it might be approved if she held fast in one hand 13 Arrows—& for the Reverse, suppose there was a Chain of round links with the Arms of the 13 Provinces in the 13 Links. This I submit to the President or Members of the Congress, but I advise at all events that all your Money, both of gold & Silver & Copper be struck in Collars like those I have sent you, by which they will be perfectly struck round & of equal Diameter, & without which they be neither round nor of equal diameter. Nor will the inscription be distinct or well defined. As to the inscription round the edge, it may be in Letters indented or in relief, the latter will be rather the neatest.

On March 14, after receiving Boulton's samples, Mitchell replied:

Dear Sir, Your favor of the 25th Novr. 1789 has not until this moment come to hand owing to the uncommon long passage of the ship which brought it, having been out fourteen weeks from London, the contents of which and the Specimen Coins shall be immediately laid before Congress, and hope it will meet with their approbation, as the present new Government is an efficient one and able to carry on and be punctual to an engagement of the kind. There is a paper in your letter which you several times refer me to I have not received. I suppose it was not sent through mistake. Your terms shall be sent to Congress to-morrow, and in the course of a fortnight will proceed on myself to see if I cannot bring the business to a conclusion. People of all denominations are anxious for a Copper Coinage as there is not a halfpenny in circulation in the United States,[2] nor no less a piece than one-sixteenth of a dollar, which passes for four pence sterling. Rice sells here at ten shillings, indigo from one to three shillings per hundred. You shall hear from me particularly as soon as Congress is made acquainted with your terms. In the meantime I shall be glad to receive such further instructions as you may be pleased to give me. As I have a number of friends in Congress who have promised me their interest and support in this business I am in hopes shall be able to settle it to our satisfaction.

But as I am in a manner but a third person in this business, it will be necessary to know what regard I am to expect—for my trouble—when the money is exchanged for the coin, as I cannot expect anything from Congress. As I am certain to have the preference and the whole management of contracting for coin of the United States, will be glad if you will inform me by the first opportunity what you will allow me for every thousand pounds paid you for the new coin at the rate you have mentioned and I hope shall soon receive your terms respecting gold and silver coins also. Congress has been offered a considerable loan in Holland—out of which they propose paying for the coinage to be paid on the shipping of the coin. Public faith is fully restored in America under our new Government and the establishment of a National Bank is under contemplation in Congress which will be of great use to the mercantile interests—and I hope that before a long period our country will make a conspicuous figure among the nations of the world.

If you think proper to ship any articles of the Birmingham manufacture here I shall be very happy to sell them on commission for you, or if you would send me an assortment of them to the amount of 1200 or 1500 £. I would take them on my own account and send you the returns in rice and indigo on the return of the vessel which may bring the goods. Merchandises in general sell well here, particularly hardware, and if you are inclinable to try some of your articles I make no doubt I shall render you satisfaction as I shall be extremely happy to form a connection with you which I am sure will be attended with mutual advantages.

With my best compliments etc.

The chances for Mitchell obtaining his contract now seemed most favorable. Boulton's coins had been unanimously acclaimed, and at the opening of the second session of Congress, January 8, 1790 Washington urged: "Uniformity in the currency, weights and measures of the United States, is an object of great importance and will, I am persuaded, be duly attended to."

On January 15, the House complied, requesting Secretary of State Thomas Jefferson to prepare and report a plan. Meanwhile, on April 7, Representative Tucker of South Carolina laid Mitchell's proposals before the House which, in turn, referred them to Jefferson. Although Mitchell offered the proposals and specimen coins in his own name, Jefferson at once recognized Droz's workmanship. On April 14, he reported to Congress: [3]

---

[2] That is, they were anxious for a uniform copper coinage. The lack of coppers in circulation was due not to any shortage, but to the excess, and consequent panic, that put Royal Flint out of business.

[3] The report was read in the House the following day. See *American State Papers*, Finance, Vol. I; also, *The Papers of Thomas Jefferson*, Vol. 16, Boyd.

The Secretary of State has before been apprised from other sources of information, of the great improvements made by this Undertaker in sundry Arts: he is acquainted with the Artist who invented the method of striking the edge and both faces of the Coin at one blow; he has seen his process, and Coins, and sent to the former Congress some specimens of them, with certain offers from him, before he entered into the service of the present Undertaker (which Specimens he takes the liberty of now submitting to the inspection of the House as proofs of the superiority of this method of Coinage in Gold and Silver, as well as Copper:)

He is therefore of Opinion,

That the Undertaker, aided by that Artist, and by his own excellent Machines, is truly in a condition to furnish Coin in a state of higher perfection, than has ever yet been issued by any Nation: That perfection in the engraving is among the greatest Safeguards against Counterfeits, because Engravers of the first Class are few, and elevated by their rank in their Art, far above the base and dangerous business of counterfeiting: That the perfection of Coins will indeed disappear, after they are for some time worn among other pieces, and especially where the figures are rather faintly relieved as on those of this Artist; yet their high finishing, while new, is not less a Guard against Counterfeits; because these, if carried to any extent, must be ushered into circulation new also, and consequently may be compared with genuine Coins in the same state: That, therefore whenever the United States shall be disposed to have a Coin of their own, it will be desirable to aim at this kind of perfection. That, this cannot be better effected than by availing themselves, if possible, of the Services of the Undertaker and of this Artist, whose excellent Methods and Machines are said to have abridged as well as perfected the operations of Coinage. These Operations, however, and their expense being new and unknown here, he is unable to say whether, instead of the larger Copper Coin, the Legislature might not prefer a lighter one of Billon, or mixed Metal, as is practised with convenience by several other Nations: a Specimen of which kind of Coinage is submitted to their Inspection.

But the propositions under consideration suppose that the Work is to be carried on in a foreign Country, and that the implements are to remain the property of the Undertaker; which conditions, in his opinion, render them inadmissible, for these reasons.

Coinage is peculiarly an Attribute of Sovereignty. To transfer its exercise into another Country, is to submit it to another Sovereign.

Its transportation across the Ocean, besides the ordinary dangers of the Sea, would expose it to acts of piracy by the crews to whom it would be confided, as well as by others apprised of its Passage.

In time of War it would offer to the enterprizes of an enemy what have been emphatically called the Sinews of War.

If the War were with the Nation within whose Territory the Coinage is, the first Act of War or Reprisal might be to arrest this Operation with the implements and Materials coined and uncoined, to be used at their discretion.

The Reputation and Principles of the present Undertaker are Safeguards against the abuses of a Coinage carried on in a foreign Country, where no Checks could be provided by the proper Sovereign, no Regulations established, no Police, no Guard exercised, in short none of the numerous Cautions hitherto thought essential at every Mint; but in hands less entitled to confidence, these will become dangers. We may be secured indeed, by proper experiments as to the purity of the Coin delivered us according to Contract, but we cannot be secured against that which, though less pure, shall be struck in the genuine Die, and protected against the vigilance of Government, 'till it shall have entered into Circulation.

We lose the Opportunity of calling in and recoining the clipped Money in circulation, or we double our risks by a double transportation.

We lose in like manner, the resource of coining up our Household plate in the instant of great distress.

We lose the means of forming Artists to continue the Works, when the common Accidents of a Mortality shall have deprived us of those who began them.

In fine, the carrying on a Coinage in a foreign Country, as far as the Secretary knows, is without example, and general example is weighty Authority.

He is therefore of opinion on the whole,

That a Mint, whenever established, should be established at home; That the Superiority, the Merit, and Means of the Undertaker will suggest him as the proper person to be engaged in the establishment and conduct of a Mint on a scale which, relinquishing nothing in the perfection of the Coin, shall be duly proportioned to our purposes.

And in the meanwhile, he is of opinion, the present proposals should be declined.

Although Mitchell had boasted the encouragement of President Washington, the latter, as Professor Boyd observes, wholly endorsed Jefferson's view. On April 12, just two days before Jefferson delivered his report, the President noted in his diary: [4]

"The Secretary of State submitted the draught of a Report to me, which he was about to make to the House of Representatives in Congress consequent of a letter and other Papers which had been referred to him on the subject of coinage,—which report appeared to me to be sensible and proper."

---

[4] *The Diaries of George Washington,* Vol. 4, edited by John C. Fitzpatrick, Houghton Mifflin Co., 1925.

CHAPTER 5

Toward Final Legislation

UPON RECEIVING Jefferson's report, the House directed the Secretary of the Treasury (Alexander Hamilton) to "prepare, and report . . . a proper plan or plans for the establishment of a national Mint."

In the meantime, Jefferson was preparing his report on coinage, weights and measures. He proposed as the unit in silver, the weight of a cubic inch of rain water which he called an ounce. This was equal to 376 grains.

On June 12, 1790 Jefferson submitted a draft of his report to Hamilton who was then preparing his own report on the Mint. Jefferson expressed the hope that Hamilton could "accomodate his plan of a mint to the very small alteration of the money unit proposed." Hamilton replied on the 16th: [1]

> Mr. Hamilton presents his Compliments to Mr. Jefferson. He has perused with much satisfaction the draft of his report on the subject of weights and measures. There is no view which Mr. H has yet taken of the matter which stands opposed to the alteration of the money-unit as at present contemplated by the regulations of Congress either in the way suggested in the report or in that mentioned in the note of yesterday. And there are certainly strong reasons to render a correspondency desirable. The idea of a general standard among nations, as in the proposal of the Bishop D'Autun seems full of convenience & order.

Jefferson reported to Congress on July 4.[2] Hamilton did not submit his own plan until January, and in the interim, Congress pursued other possibilities. First of all, there was John Hinkley Mitchell who had begun a new promotion to import Boulton's machinery and establish a subsidiary of the Soho Mint in

---

[1] *The Papers of Alexander Hamilton*, Vol. 6, Syrett.
[2] *The Papers of Thomas Jefferson*, Vol. 16, Boyd. The report was presented by the Speaker of the House on July 13.

America. Mitchell was evidently inspired by Jefferson's statement that whenever a Mint should be established, it would be proper to engage the "Undertaker" whom Mitchell represented. Although Jefferson had Droz in mind, Mitchell's plan seems to have won a number of votaries. On May 10, 1790 he wrote to Boulton:

Dear Sir: In conformity to my promise, I have taken the earliest opportunity of sending you the Report of the Secretary of State on your proposals, which you will observe are unfavorable. I received them two days ago from a member of Congress, who says the elegance of your coinage is admitted and admired by everyone. They wish much for the establishment of one of your coining machines in America, as a coinage is much wanted indeed. If you thought it practicable to establish one of your machines here, you may be assured we shall get the conducting of the whole of the coinage business in this country. You will be best able to judge of whether it will suit you.

If you have not thought of doing it, if you will send me your terms and conditions particularly specified, they shall be immediately settled and nothing shall be wanting in my power that can be done for your interest.

You will much oblige me by an answer on this business as soon as possible, and I hope you will make it suit you to make them such proposals as will not be declined.

With my best compliments etc.

Mitchell wrote again on July 20:

Dear Sir: Your much esteemed favour of the 4th May ult. with the enclosure per New York packet I received two days ago and am happy to hear of the health and welfare of yourself and family. You have no doubt ere this received the report of the Secretary which I am sorry was so unfavorable.

I received a letter a few days ago from the Speaker of the House, who wishes much for your opinion respecting the establishment of a mint in America. They are all very much in favour of your new method of coining. A late New York paper pronounces your coin to be far superior to any ever coined in the world. You will be best able to judge whether it even would be practicable to set one of your machines in this country under the sanction of Government. You desire me in your letter to make inquiry after a Mr. Jarvis, which I have accordingly done and find that he had contracted with the old Congress under the old Constitution to furnish them with a certain sum in copper coin within a certain limited time but he not being able to fulfill the contract, it of course became nonvalid and at present there is no contract subsisting between Congress and any person whatever relative to coining . . .[3]

In the course of a letter dated October 8, 1790 Mitchell informed Boulton that "the members of Congress from this State are all here during the recess of the House and have begged of me to write you if it was possible to fall on any plan to establish a mint in America but am just this moment going to the country."

Then there was Boulton himself, who appears to have been eager to shake off Mitchell and establish his own contacts in America. This much at least can be inferred from the letter of David Hartley, an English statesman and inventor, to Thomas Jefferson, dated December 1, 1790:[4]

---

[3] On May 4, 1790 Boulton had written to Mitchell: "A Mr. Jarvis (who was in London at the time you were there) said He had a patent from Congress and a Contract for making all their Money in America; But it is not in his power to do what they want, and ought to have. I have not heard of Him lately. Pray learn what He hath done, or is about doing, as I hear He is expected every day in England."

[4] *Matthew Boulton Papers*, Assay Office of Birmingham, England.

Dear Sir, I have lately had some conversation with Mr. Boulton of Soho near Birmingham relative to a proposed new coinage of the Copper money of this Country for which he is at present in negotiation with the British Ministry. Upon this Occasion he has shewn to me from the Charlestown Gazette of April 14 1790 the report which you have presented to Congress upon a similar Point in your States by which I find that he or his friend Mr. Mitchell has had similar Negotiation with you. Mr. Boulton is a very excellent Mechanic & has many excellent Artists in his Employ & wd. I don't doubt execute such an Undertaking to his own honour & to the satisfaction of your Country. The same Apparatus may serve in the first instance for both Countries. It has cost a very large sum of money to Mr. Boulton. I conceive that his views & yours are not at all inconsistent, but perfectly coincident.

By the first Part of your Report you approve of Mr. Boulton as the Undertaker. But you object to a foreign dependance for the supply of your Coinage. This Objection seems for the reasons assigned to be very forceful and decisive. The right of sovereignty in Coinage is most essential in Gold & Silver. But it is not so essential in Copper. Copper is not esteemed in the Country as Coin. It is only esteemed as a convenient merchandise of Exchange. Several companies in this Country coin for themss. medals in Copper as pence & half pence & give and receive them in the intercourse of Payments. I understand that Mr. Boulton's Proposition to you is upon similar Ground to this. He proposes as Manufacturer & Merchant to supply your Country in this first Instance with your Copper money, but he has not the most distant view that the sovereign Mint for Gold & Silver in your States should be established at his Soho. He proposes merely in this first Instance that he should supply you with the merchandise of the Copper Money which you may want for immediate use & that he should execute this by means of the Apparatus which he has provided for such purposes in this Country. After that he proposes to transfer all his Apparatus to your Country if you chuse to become purchaser & in the meantime in the Course of the proposed Coinage for you he will be very ready to instruct any workman from the United States who shall be sent him by public Authority, in the arts & use of his mint, so that even your first copper Coinage may be executed by the handcraft of your own countrymen. His Mint is fundamentally improved in all the most essential points wh. upon the completion of the first essay & necessary instructions will be transplanted for ever after for the adoption & use of the sovereign power of your Country.

Mr. Boulton will transmit his proposals specifically by the next mail subsequent to the date of this letter wh. I have taken the Liberty of addressing to you because I think it a point of justice which is due to an eminent Manufacturer as & much more so in consideration of his universal & approved Character for liberality & honor in all his mercantile transactions. I shall only add to the one personal motive for myself wh. is to take this Opportunity wh. incidentally offers itself of reviving to your recollection the name & memory of an old friend & fellow labourer with yourself in the common cause of peace & friendship between two Countries. I am etc.

What a tantalizing offer to be pitted against a principle! Not for nothing did Jefferson remark a few months later, that his position on the copper coinage had "wavered between difficulties."

* * *

We have observed that Jefferson, albeit ambiguously, advised Congress to engage Droz as superintendent of the Mint. On April 23, 1790, nine days after he had reported to the House, Jefferson wrote to the French banker, Ferdinand Grand: [5]

Dear Sir, You may remember that we were together at the Hotel de la Monnoye,[6]

---

[5] Sylvester Crosby, "The Cents of 1793," *American Journal of Numismatics,* Jan. 1897.
[6] i.e., the Paris Mint.

to see Mr. Drost strike coins in his new manner, and that you were so kind as to speak with him afterwards on the subject of his coming to America. We are now in a condition to establish a mint, and should be desirous of engaging him in it. I suppose him to be at present in the service of Watts [sic] and Boulton, the latter of whom you may remember to have been present with us at the Monnoye. I know of no means of communicating our dispositions to Drost so effectually as through your friendly agency, and therefore take the liberty of asking you to write to him, to know what emoluments he receives from Watts and Boulton, and whether he would be willing to come to us for the same? If he will, you may give him an expectation, but without absolute engagement, that we will call for him immediately, and that with himself, we may probably take and pay him for all the implements of coinage he may have, suited to our purpose. If he asks higher terms, he will naturally tell you so, and what they are; and we must reserve the right to consider them. In either case, I will ask your answer as soon as possible. I need not observe to you, that this negotiation should be known to nobody but yourself, Drost and Mr. Short . . .

At the time Jefferson wrote, Droz seems to have already left Boulton & Watt. According to Watt, Droz had promised Boulton a new method of multiplying dies, which he did not possess.[7] Moreover, the segment collar was "found to be difficult of execution, and subject to wear very soon when in use, and in short very unfit for an extensive coinage." Watt recorded that several of Droz' contrivances had to be redesigned by Boulton and his assistants, and that the artist was "of a troublesome disposition." Droz, "after being liberally paid," was thus dismissed, and we next hear of him in London, when Grand, on August 28, 1790 wrote to Jefferson: [8]

. . . Upon receipt of your first letter I sent a copy to Mr. Droz, in London. He is a decent fellow who does not understand and does not know anything but his profession, so that in order to speed up a slow correspondence and also to obtain for you the reply which you are waiting for more promptly, I decided to combine his opinion with mine to establish a draft of an agreement as enclosed; I am even more willing to do it since he said that he leaves it entirely up to me as I have explained to Mr. Short when I transmitted the letters to him. Even though Mr. Droz is not concerned with him, I have reason to believe that he prefers to establish a mint in his own way than to work for one which has the faults of the old method which is so difficult to uproot, as he has experienced here. Therefore, I do not doubt that if, in some way or other, you offer him an honest living, he will prefer it to the offers that are being made to him by several places, especially by Spain.

Jefferson received this letter on November 23, transmitting it the next day to Hamilton. As of December, the latter had not yet submitted his plan for a Mint, and on the 8th Washington gently reminded Congress, saying: "The establishment of the militia, of a mint, of standards of weights and measures, of the Post-office and post roads, are subjects which (I presume) you will resume of course, and which are abundantly urged by their own importance."

In a letter of December 29, Jefferson suggested to Hamilton the possibility of a billon minor coinage: [9]

Th: Jefferson . . . incloses to the Secretary of the Treasury a report of a committee of the National assembly of France, on the subject of Billon, containing

---

[7] H. W. Dickinson, *Matthew Boulton.* Cambridge University Press, 1937.
[8] *The Papers of Thomas Jefferson,* Library of Congress collection. The original of this letter is in French.
[9] *The Papers of Thomas Jefferson,* Vol. 16, Boyd.

more particular information as to that species of coin than he had before met with. If the metal be so mixed as to make it of ⅛ of the intrinsic value of the standard silver coin of the U.S. the Cent of billon will be a little smaller than the present 16ths of dollars, & consequently be more convenient than a Copper cent. This he submits to the better judgement of the Secretary of the Treasury & hopes he will consider the liberty taken as an advance towards unreserved communications for reciprocal benefit.

On January 28, 1791 Hamilton submitted to the House his famous report on the Mint.[10] He observed that the Spanish dollar, by successive diminutions of its weight and fineness, had depreciated by five percent.[11] This, he said, was the reason why a mint was necessary. No nation should allow the property value of its citizens to fluctuate with the fluctuations of a foreign mint and the regulations of a foreign sovereign. A national mint would remedy this situation, arrest the importation of base coin, and put an end to the unequal rates of exchange and dissimilar currencies of the several states.

The first topic which Hamilton introduced was the "unit," and he began by presenting two popular and conflicting economic views. To determine what *ought to be* the unit, one had only to know, in point of usage, what it actually was. Although the unit of account was the British pound, that of the currency was the Spanish dollar. But if the dollar were chosen and given a superior legal tender status, the issue of gold coins, each being equal to a certain number of dollars, would make the unit a matter of form rather than substance. Gold was therefore the logical choice. It was, besides, more stable and less an article of merchandise than silver had become through trade with the East Indies and China. Lastly, it seemed illogical to give preference to the least valuable of the two metals.

Having presented both sides of the argument, Hamilton suggested that the unit not be annexed preferentially to either metal, as this would tend to destroy the office and character of the other, to diminish its utility, and reduce it to mere merchandise. Moreover, a monometallic standard would produce too scant a circulation for the nation's requirements. Hamilton considered these disadvantages a greater evil than occasional adjustments in the ratio of the two metals.

He said that the ratio between gold and silver in the colonies had slowly depreciated from 15.6:1 to 15:1. This, however, was opportune because it now approximated the world ratio, and especially that of the market to which U.S. specie was principally exported.

He recommended a fineness of eleven twelfths. This was the gold standard of Portugal, England, France and Spain, and it would permit their joes, guineas, louis' and doubloons to be recoined at the Mint without refining. Gold, he thought, should be alloyed with silver and copper to make coins neither too white nor too red.

Hamilton favored a coining charge of one-half per cent, but said that the depositor should, in this case, receive an immediate exchange of coins for bullion.

The unit was to contain 24¾ grains pure gold or 371¼ grains pure silver, equal, when alloyed, to 27 grains standard gold or 405 grains standard silver.

---

[10] For an account of the sources and development of Hamilton's report, see *The Papers of Alexander Hamilton,* Vol. 7, Syrett.

[11] At this time, the Spanish dollar was coined at 374⅞ grains fine silver, with one grain tolerance.

The way in which Hamilton arrived at this new valuation is very interesting.

He began by having a number of Spanish dollars assayed. The assay that Dudley had performed for Robert Morris in 1782 disclosed an average fine weight of 373 grains. Hamilton's assay, however, showed a mean of only 371 grains. To be on the safe side, Hamilton adopted the value paid out on the Spanish dollars in fine gold by merchants, which was 24¾ grains per coin. By multiplying this figure fifteen times he arrived at a fine weight of 371¼ grains for the American dollar, which was obviously low. The error was fundamental. The Spanish dollar in mint condition weighed 420 grains, and at its *actual* fineness of about .893 contained nearly 375 grains of silver. By the time it had worked its way to America, however, it was worn and the attrition increased as it continued to circulate.

Merchants received the coin at its *actual,* not its *original* weight since they were paying for it in fine gold. Hamilton, following their example, based the fine weight of the new American dollar on that of a worn Spanish one. Although such a relation might have been justified for domestic use, it overvalued the silver dollar for purposes of export.

Hamilton nevertheless defended his unit, saying:

> The Secretary of the Department of State, in his report to the House of Representatives, on the subject of establishing a uniformity in the weights, measures, and coins of the United States, has proposed that the weight of the dollar should correspond with the unit of weight. This was done on the supposition that it would require but a very small addition to the quantity of metal which the dollar, independently of the object he had in view, ought to contain; in which he was guided by the resolution of the 8th of August, 1786, fixing the dollar at 375 grains and 64 hundredths of a grain.
>
> Taking this as the proper standard of the dollar, a small alteration for the sake of incorporating so systematic an idea, would appear desirable. But, if the principles which have been reasoned from, in this report, are just, the execution of that idea becomes more difficult. It would certainly not be advisable to make, on that account, so considerable a change in the money unit, as would be produced by the addition of five grains of silver to the proper weight of the dollar, without a proportional augmentation of its relative value; and to make such an augmentation would be to abandon the advantage of preserving the identity of the dollar, or to speak more accurately, of having the proposed one received and considered as a mere substitute for the present.

Although Jefferson agreed generally with Hamilton's report, he rejected the low weight proposed for the silver dollar. ". . . I very much doubt a right now to change the value and especially to lessen it," [12] he wrote to Hamilton on January 24, 1791. "It would lead to so easy a mode of paying off their debts. Besides, the parties injured by this reduction of the value would have so much matter to urge in support of the first point of fixation. Should it be thought, however, that Congress may reduce the value of the dollar, I should be for adopting for our unit, instead of the dollar, either one ounce of pure silver, or one ounce of standard silver, so as to keep the unit of money a part of the system of measures, weights and coins."

Senator Thomas Benton, among others, later charged that Hamilton overvalued silver in relation to gold. This is untrue. The Hamburg quotations,[13]

---

[12] "International Monetary Conference, 1878, Report and Proceedings," pgs. 708-09, *Senate Exec. Doc. No. 58, 45th Congress, 3rd Session;* also, *The Papers of Alexander Hamilton,* Vol. 7, Syrett.
[13] Ibid.

which are considered the most accurate prior to 1833, indicate an average ratio of 15.08 to 1 for 1790-92. But Hamilton did not realize that the value of silver was declining, and that within a decade the ratio would be hovering around 15.3 to 1.

Hamilton suggested the following denominations:

"One gold piece equal in weight and value to ten units or dollars.

"One gold piece, equal to a tenth part of the former and which shall be a unit or dollar.

"One silver piece, which shall also be a unit or dollar.

"One silver piece, which shall be, in weight and value, one tenth part of a silver unit or dollar.

"One copper piece, which shall be of value of a hundredth part of a dollar.

"One copper piece, which shall be half the value of the former."

Although the gold dollar was redundant, Hamilton included it to physically express the unit in both metals. He wished, however, to limit its circulation to fifty thousand pieces. Like Robert Morris, Hamilton believed that a half cent was necessary to restrain the minimum price of goods.

He suggested that the dollar be known also as the "unit," and its tenth part as simply a "tenth." The largest gold piece might be called an "eagle." The appellation, he admitted, was not very expressive, but he could think of nothing better. Hamilton recommended a 264-grain cent which would have discouraged the most ardent contract coiner. He said that he would have liked to unite a small proportion of silver with the copper in order to lessen the bulk of the cents, but such a measure would encourage counterfeiters to simulate the plug by a mixture of base metals.

Devices, he observed, should be made "vehicles of useful impressions . . . emblematic, but without losing sight of simplicity." The fewer the sharp points and angles, the less would be the effects of attrition.

Hamilton was in favor of abolishing foreign coins from circulation as soon as they could be adequately replaced. Although this might be done after a year, he was willing to grant an additional one or two years to the circulation of Portuguese, English and French gold coins, and the silver coins of Spain. Even after this time, the Spanish dollars might continue to pass at the value of their fine silver.

Hamilton provided for the offices of director, assay master, master coiner, cashier, auditor, and as many clerks or assistants, and workmen as required, plus a porter. He estimated that the annual expense of a Mint would average between fifteen and twenty thousand dollars. Assays were to be conducted on a certain number of reserved pieces taken from every fifteen pounds of gold, with a "tolerance," or "remedy" (i.e., the maximum deviation permitted by law), of forty grains fine gold for every standard pound examined.

On the whole, Hamilton's report was an elaboration of principles founded by Jefferson and modified by the 1786 Grand Committee. Bi-metallism would eventually prove undesirable, but Hamilton's arguments were sound in their own time and context. For one thing, there were only four banks in existence with a limited note emission. For another, fiduciary coinage was unfamiliar, and a single standard meant *literally* the coining of only one metal. Hamilton's weight for the silver dollar was, of course, erroneous, and his rigid decimal system, omitting any denomination between the dollar and the tenth, absurd.

The measure ostensibly required fewer coins than Jefferson had proposed, but in the practice of making change, it called for many more. Hamilton's only non-decimal denomination, the half cent, was to prove cumbersome and unpopular. Moreover, Hamilton, like the earlier Grand Committee, failed to provide the Mint with a melter and refiner. He had copied the roster of European mints, without realizing that they did not refine their own bullion.

On February 7, 1791 Hamilton's proposals were submitted to a Senate committee which included Robert Morris. Morris reported favorably for the committee on March 1, and on the 3rd, Congress resolved:

> That a mint shall be established under such regulations as shall be directed by law.
>
> That the President of the United States be, and he is hereby authorized to cause to be engaged, such principal artists as shall be necessary to carry the preceding resolution into effect, and to stipulate the terms and conditions of their service, and also to cause to be procured such apparatus as shall be requisite for the same purpose.

✿　　✿　　✿

The passage of a Mint Act, without specific provisions, did little to discourage entrepreneurs. In April 1791, Mitchell wrote to Hamilton with the intention of promoting Boulton's machinery. Receiving no reply, Mitchell then wrote to Washington, who advised him that Jefferson was in charge of the Mint. On September 23, Mitchell finally wrote to Jefferson, inquiring "what Assistance is now wanted towards the Establishment of the Mint as I have it in my power to furnish one of the most Compleat Machines that has ever been invented." [14] Mitchell still fancied himself as Boulton's agent, though it is difficult to understand how he expected to deceive Jefferson.

On April 25, 1791 Jefferson wrote to the American minister at Paris, William Short: [15]

> . . . I enclose you a copy of Mr. Grand's note to me, stating the conditions on which Drost would come, and also a letter from the Secretary of the Treasury, his ideas as to those terms, with which I agree. We leave to your agency the engaging and sending Mr. Drost as soon as possible, and to your discretion to fix the terms, rendering the allowance for expenses certain, which his first proposition leaves uncertain. Subsistence here costs about one third of what it does in Paris, to a housekeeper. In a lodging house, the highest price for a room and board is a dollar a day, for the master, and half that for their servant. These facts may enable you to settle the article of expenses reasonably. If Mr. Drost undertakes assaying, I should much rather confide it to him, than to any other person who can be sent. It is the most confidential operation in the whole business of coining. We should expect him to instruct a native in it. I think too, he should be obliged to continue longer than a year, if it should be necessary for qualifying others to continue his operations. It is not important that he be here till November or December, but extremely desirable then. He may come as much sooner as he pleases. . . .

Short replied on June 26: [16]

> . . . I have seen Mr. Drost. He is now engaged in contending with other artists for the engraving of the new money to be struck here—of course he could not engage immediately to go to America—the question however will be decided in fifteen

[14] *Miscellaneous letters received*, Record Group 59, National Archives.
[15] *The Writings of Thomas Jefferson*, Vol. 8, edited by Andrew A. Lipscomb and Albert E. Bergh, Thomas Jefferson Memorial Association, 1905.
[16] *Diplomatic Dispatches*, State Department Instructions, Record Group 59 (as are the following letters from Short to Jefferson), National Archives.

days & I doubt whether he will succeed as his rivals and judges are both academicians. Should he not succeed he will undertake the business on the terms sent to you, and of which you returned me a copy. He says it will be indispensable to have the presses made here, & that it will be best to have the other instruments also as it will be more economical & as they may be made at the same time as the presses. He says they cannot be finished before the winter, & that he could not go until the spring; but that in the mean time he could send directions for erecting the necessary buildings so that no delay would ensue. He would recommend the having four presses made here but says two may suffice for the present—they will cost about 22,000# each. I hope you will instruct me with respect to the number you would chuse. He hopes that if he should succeed in the struggle he is engaged in here that he might still find time to go to America for the purpose you wish— or if not he thinks that he could have a mint erected & established there by having the proper instruments made here & giving the proper directions to a person he could send from hence. He is to give me his answer with respect to his going in fifteen days. I hope he will agree to undertake the voyage as I do not see from your letter that I am to engage another in the case of his refusal. He tells me he does not understand the business of assaying but that it is so simple an art that he will undertake to make himself master of it if he should go, & will instruct in it any person you may designate, not chusing to meddle with the operation practically himself on account of the delicacy of the subject. I am particularly happy that he undertakes this part of the business, as your letter & the copy of that of the Secy. of the Treasury to you left me in doubt whether I was to send another person for this purpose & on what terms. On the whole I think you may count on M. Drost for the next spring, but you shall hear further from me on the subject very soon.

Short wrote again on July 20:

. . . Drost has not succeeded in his competition for the place of engraver general of the mint here—it is given to Dupré. I saw Drost two days ago & he seemed non [now?] determined to go to America. He observes that it is indispensible to have two *balanciers* at least made here—he even desired to have four made, but as I apprehend that you did not count on such an operation, from the length of time it will take to make them, I shall insist on the smallest number possible. He found it impossible to have these machines executed in England without the assistance of workmen whom he was obliged to send for from Paris. Of course I suppose them within the meaning of the Secretary's expression—*difficult of execution*. Drost says they will cost about 22,000# each & that they cannot be finished before the next winter. He offers to have them executed by employing workmen in detail & charging their salaries to the U.S. or to contract to furnish them at a stipulated price—this latter mode will be preferred as being the best in all cases for a government. The other instruments he tells me will be inconsiderable. He is to decide finally in two or three days whether he will go or not & I have little doubt of his going. In that case he will not embark before the next spring because the instruments cannot be finished sooner. . . . Drost wishes that you would send him the intended devices of the money to be struck—he says he would engrave one of the dyes here which he seems to speak of as a means of shewing his talents in that way, perhaps with a view to being employed by the U.S. as the engraver of their money.

In a letter dated August 24, Short wrote that Droz, upon final consideration, had decided not to undertake assaying.

Jefferson had received the first of these three letters when he replied to Short on August 29:

. . . You observe, that if Drost does not come, you have not been authorized to engage another. If he does not come, there will probably be one engaged here. If he comes, I shall think him a safe hand to send the diplomatic dye by, as also all the dyes of our medals, which may be used here for striking off what shall be wanting hereafter. But I would not have them trusted at sea, but from April to October inclusive. Should you not send them by Drost, Havre will be the best route. I have not spoken with the Secretary of the Treasury yet, on the subject of the presses, but believe you may safely consider two presses as sufficient for us, and agree for no more without a further request.

Jefferson wrote again, on November 24:

You mention that Drost wishes the devices of our money to be sent to him, that he may engrave them there. This cannot be done, because not yet decided on. The devices will be fixed by the law which shall establish the mint . . .

❋   ❋   ❋

In the meantime another promotion was afoot. Jefferson, who would have vetoed the scheme, was scrupulously avoided, and it was not until two years later that he learned the details from Thomas Digges.[17] Digges wrote from Birmingham, the hub of counterfeiting and private coining in England. His first letter, dated March 10, 1793 reads in part as follows:

Since my letter to you by Wm Pearce the double loom maker and the original inventor of Arkwright's first weaving and spinning machinery, I have not had occasion to write, nor would I have likely done it before my embarkation for America. But as indeed not to do so from having accidentally seen a Birmingham production of one of the American Cents, the intended coin of America & the 1/100th part of the Dollar [would be wrong]. Knowing it had been determined in Congress to have all their money minted in the States, I made it my business to seek out and inform myself all I could about this Cent coinage here and of the Artists and Merchts engaged about them.—I first apply'd to Messrs. W. & Alexr Walker (who have a partner Mr. Thos. Ketland in Phila), and they shewed me the specimens . . . sent herewith & afterwards gave them to me. They said it was merely a speculation or trial to obtain the orders for making the intended Cents here which induced them to the attempt in 1791 and that some hundred wt or so had been sent to America and given to the President & other public gentn; But that on the determination of Congress to mint their own money, their scheme here had fallen thro'. They were close and secret as to who the diesinker was, where coined & . . . but upon further inquiry I found Messrs Walker had ordered them to be done at Mr. Obediah Westwood's (a considerable maker of those kinds of money), and that his die sinker Mr. Jno Gregory Hancock (one of the first in this place tho' with Character of a dissapated man) and a prentice lad Jno Jordan very clever in that line, had executed them, & still hold the dies. This lad Jordan has two years of His time (to serve) wishes much to go to America, but I suppose his time would be worth 200 £. The face likeness on both are the same die and a good likeness of the President, tho the Eagles and motto are different—The likeness was taken from a large medal struck at Phila.[18]

Digges' letter of April 6, 1792 to Thomas Pinckney, the American Minister in London, is also pertinent. Digges writes:

. . . Since these my communications with MB and MW,[19] and my last letters

---

[17] R. W. Julian, "The Digges Letters," *Seaby's Coin and Medal Bulletin*, Oct.-Nov. 1962. Digges was born in America but lived his adult years in England where he conducted a shipping business. He was a warm friend of the American cause.

[18] The "large medal" seems to be the "Washington before Boston" (1786), though this was actually made at Paris and is not the exact prototype. See W. S. Baker, *Medallic Portraits of Washington,* published by Robert M. Lindsay, 1885; reprinted with annotations by George Fuld, Krause Publications, 1965. The remainder of the letter describes the excellence of Boulton's mint machinery. Boulton's press was "not worked in the old way, but the metal is put into a kind of copper & drops out into a bag . . ." Jefferson sent Digges' letter to the Director of the Mint, David Rittenhouse, and in the same year an automatic feed and ejecting device was introduced on the Mint's presses.

[19] Mr. Boulton and Mr. Watt.

to you, I have found out a variety of money coining practices here, highly disgrace
ful, I think, to the Parties, to the Country and its laws; and in the instances I shal
mention likely to do infinite mischief to the vast circulation of Spanish silver ii
the United States.

As early as 1791 they began with the American Copper *Cent* only upon readin₁
the resolve of Congress to have such a money and the getting over a print of th
American Eagle. There were three different sorts of those cents made here (th
samples of two of which I forwarded for your perusal in Mr. Jefferson's Book) [20] al
with the President's head, not a bad likeness, & tolerably well executed—I fin
however this was merely an attempt of some artists here to induce Congress to giv
Birmingham the order for coinage of their copper money.

The three coins designed by Hancock and struck by Westwood are un
doubtedly the 1791 large and small eagle Washington cents and the simila
1792 "cent" (in gold, silver and copper).[21]

Although Walkers' plan failed, Congress had far from relinquished th
idea of contract coinage. In fact it was giving so much attention to Boulton'
proposals that Jefferson, with the assistance of Thomas Paine, prepared
counter-offensive. In a letter to Jefferson, dated September 15, 1788 Pain
had written of being requested by a Mr. Le Conteulx "to examine the construc
tion of the Albion Steam Mills erected by Boulton and Watt." [22]

During his subsequent visit to the Soho factory, Paine learned about th
Jarvis contract and the lucrative business of coining copper. On September 2£
1790 he wrote to Jefferson: "Coining is a new business in America. Those, wh
have proposed contracts, knew, either of themselves, or from those who wer
to execute, what they were doing; but they supposed Congress to know nothin
of the matter. Accident and a turn for mechanics have thrown me into a knowl
edge of their plans and the profits they expected to make."

After commenting on the general inconvenience of copper coins, Paine ad
vocated a remarkable plan for a fiduciary copper coinage:

> If in America we were to coin silver as low as the twentieth part of a dolla₂
> which would be pieces of five cents, the occasion for coppers would be very muc
> diminished; and such pieces would be nearly of the size of the French silver si
> sous. I think the policy is in favor of keeping as much silver coin as we can i'
> the country; and this is one of my motives for excluding copper as much as possibl₄
>
> Some denomination under the five cent pieces would still be necessary—but a
> the occasions would be diminished, a- small quantity would be sufficient. It ½
> convenience only, that ought to be considered with respect to copper coinag₄
> and not money or riches. It was going on this last idea, instead of the first on
> that entangled the former Congress and the Several States. They attempted to d
> what no other nation ever thought of doing, and which is impossible to do—tha
> of exalting copper into national wealth. Nature has fixed its boundary; and w
> must keep it.
>
> It is therefore something by which to divide the five cent silver pieces, tha
> appears to me the only thing to be considered, with respect to a copper coinag₄
> This may be done either by coining copper cents of the size and intrinsic valu
> they ought to be, which will prevent their being counterfeited, or depreciated

---

[20] Digges had previously sent to Jefferson a coin album containing specimens of Boulton's an
Westwood's work.

[21] There is also a fourth Washington piece designed by Hancock, which, from letter-punch rel
tionship, appears to have been made after the others. This is the "Roman Head" cent. From th
imperial conception of the bust, however, it seems likely that the issue was intended for "collect₄
consumption" in England.

[22] *The Complete Writings of Thomas Paine.* Edited by Philip S. Foner, 1905. Reprinted by Citad₄
Press, 1945.

or to coin or stamp small copper pieces, as a sort of treasury notes, or notes of the mint, of the nominal value of one, two and three cents, to be exchanged, if any person chooses to exchange them, at the treasury or the mint, for silver. These will be more durable than paper tickets, and capable of being extended over the continent without the danger of wearing out; and people will not compare the value of them by the metal they contain, but by the obligation to exchange them for silver, if required. To prevent their being counterfeited, they should not be tender for anything above five cents, or more than five in any one payment. As they would be merely for the purpose of dividing the five cents by, and not for the purpose of supplying the place of silver coin in large quantities, the mint or the treasury should always exchange them to any amount, though the amount can never be much at any one time.

To give these notes the opportunity of getting into circulation faster, nor in greater quantities than the occasions for them require, the mint should not issue them in payment, but have them in readiness for merchants, shopkeepers, &c. to fetch away by tale, in exchange for silver or gold. This used to be the way the copper coinage at the tower of London got into circulation; every shopkeeper knew where to go to get ten or twenty shillings worth.

Paine observed that the seignorage would be "equal to the first year's expense in establishing a mint." He said that copper could be reasonably obtained from the West Indies where there was an abundance of old boiler stills and worn-out utensils the planters had no means of melting up.

Jefferson did not reply to this letter until July 29, 1791 when he wrote to Paine: [23]

Your observations on the subject of a copper coinage have satisfied my mind on that subject, which I confess had wavered before between difficulties. As a different plan is under consideration,[24] & will be taken up at their meeting, I think to watch the proper moment, & publish your observations (except the Notes which contain facts relative to particular persons which I presume you would dislike to see published,[25] & which are not necessary to establish the main object), adding your name, because it will attract attention & give weight to the publication. As this cannot take place under four months, there is time for you to forbid me, if it should be disagreeable to you to have the observations published, which however I hope it will not be. . . .

On October 9, Short informed Jefferson that Boulton had tried unsuccessfully to secure a contract with the French Assembly. "I have learned lately," the letter continues, "that Drost & he differed [;] they speak ill of each other & Bolton particularly of Drost's Machine although Drost says it is used by him (Bolton) in the copper he has struck. Drost assures me he shall be ready to go the next spring. I find him exceedingly dilatory."

It was probably some time during October that Jefferson arranged for the publication of Paine's observations. Paine had condemned not only contract coinage, but the contractors as well. Boulton's strongest argument was the perfection and economy of his coinage, but Jefferson weakened this position by promising the services of Droz. Indeed, with Droz as coiner, engraver, superintendent and general factotum, Boulton must have seemed a splendid superfluity. We can thus imagine Jefferson's chagrin upon reading Short's letter of October 14:

Dear Sir: Drost called on me yesterday and after some hesitation told me that

---

[23] *The Writings of Thomas Jefferson*, Vol. 8, Lipscomb and Bergh.
[24] i.e. Boulton's.
[25] Unfortunately these notes have not been located.

several circumstances had taken place in his private affairs which rendered it necessary that he should decline going to America. I was as you may readily conceive much astonished at such an announcement & the more so as two days before he had repeated to me what he had before told me twenty times that he should be ready to go out in the Spring. I suppose now that the fact is that he has never been absolutely decided in his own mind & for that reason always delayed on various pretexts forming the Contract. Hitherto when I have pushed him, which was very often, to lose no time in executing the machines which were to be made here, he always answered that he had several articles to complete first, but that he had already begun the models & other necessary preliminaries & would certainly be ready as soon as the season would permit his undertaking the Voyage. On my observing to him that his conduct appeared to me far from delicate, that I had written to you as authorized by him that you might count on his going and that it was probable arrangements would have been taken in consequence thereof he seemed somewhat hurt, & said that if I learned from you that, that was the case that he would consent to go,—whether this was mainly a palliative or not I cannot say—he said however that he would write me a Letter today conformably thereto. Should it be received before the departure of this letter it shall be forwarded to you. He went further and said that he should continue to have two balanciers made on his own Account and that if you insisted on his going he would yield them to the U.S. & set out.—It would be unsafe however I fear to count on him. He has intention at present of treating the French Revolution in a series of medals & thinks he shall soon make a large fortune by this means. Should his speculation fail he may be more disposed to go to America; unless indeed his declining it at present proceeds from a consciousness that his Machine will not answer for striking Money although perfect for striking Medals—This as I have informed you is insisted upon by Dupre the Engraver here & by Bolton (sic) also.—so long as Drost shewed an intention of going to establish a Mint on that principle & on the condition of not being paid until the work was executed, it was not allowed to doubt of his own conviction at least, but I own since his declining it in this abrupt manner it is impossible not to expect some uncertainty. Mr. Gautier of the House of Grand had told me that Drost could not be depended on he feared for such an undertaking, & that at any rate it would be necessary to deal with him with much caution—he had collected this opinion from Bolton & his friends. I mentioned the circumstances to Mr. Grand who said he did not know Drost well enough to answer for him, but advised me to mention to him what had come to my knowledge with respect to his machine having not answered at Birmingham. I did it & Drost expressed his thanks to me for this Opportunity of explaining to me his difference with Bolton—he showed me many papers & among the rest an Arbitration & an agreement in consequence thereof by which Bolton was to pay him a certain sum of money for his time—all this did not prove the success of his Machine & I had only his word that it was made use of by Bolton & Bolton's denial of it. However as you had directed me to employ him as he was to be paid only after the work was compleated I determined to prosecute the measure, & particularly as he then said if I had any doubts about his ability to execute the engagement he was willing it should stop there & as Mr. Grand seemed to think that under those circumstances there would be no risk in treating with him. I sent you in my last a Copy of Bolton's proposals for striking the copper coin of this country. It will be perhaps found well to contract with him for striking the same for the U.S. as that must be the most pressing, the Gold & Silver of other countries having course with us. He will strike the Copper at Birmingham at a very low rate, or will make an establishment for it in the U.S. Drost tells me that whilst he was in England, Bolton was in treaty for that purpose either with the U.S. or some Citizen thereof. I shall let him know through Mr. Gautier that Drost does not go to America so that he may make overtures directly to you for establishing a Mint in America on the principle proposed in his memorial sent you. Viz., for a given sum or for striking at Birmingham and furnishing by Contract the copper coin of which the U.S. may have immediate need—should you persist however in preferring Drost & he binds himself by the Letter mentioned above then you will be so good as to give me your orders thereon. It will be necessary at the same time to give some idea of the extent to which this undertaking is to be carried that Drost may know how many balanciers & what other instruments may be requisite. He thinks nine or ten will be necessary, being the smallest number of the several hotels de monnoye in France.

I am exceedingly sorry for this disappointment & the delay which will ensue in consequence thereof, in a business so interesting to the credit & dignity of the U.S. as the having their own coin. I should be particularly so at Drost's not going if his conduct did not inspire some doubts with respect to the plan which he proposes, & which as yet has not been reduced to real practice in the Coinage of large sums of money as far as we know of. . . .

On the following day, Short wrote that Droz had proposed sending another person to America in his place.

The situation could hardly have been more confused. For a year and a half, Jefferson had openly opposed contract coinage, and after having won considerable support in Congress he was now faced with the loss of Droz. It was, of course, several weeks before Jefferson received Short's letter, and in the meantime he had arranged for the publication of Paine's observations condemning contract coinage. President Washington was probably cued to Jefferson's plan, for on October 25 he reminded Congress:

"The disorders in the existing currency, and especially the scarcity of small change—a scarcity so peculiarly distressing to the poorer classes, strongly recommend the carrying into immediate effect, the resolution already entered into concerning the establishment of a mint. Measures have been taken, pursuant to that resolution, for procuring some of the necessary artists together with the requisite apparatus."

In compliance with Washington's request, the Senate, on October 31, appointed a committee under Robert Morris to consider the subject of a Mint and report a bill if they thought proper. Paine's observations appeared in the *National Gazette* on November 17, and were republished, the same month, in the *American Museum*.[26] With Congress hopefully enlightened, Morris, on December 21, introduced his comprehensive bill.[27]

The debate began in the Senate on January 9, 1792 and centered around the devices proposed for the coins. The bill provided:

That, upon said coins, respectively, there shall be the following devices and legends, namely: Upon one side of each of the said coins there shall be an impression or representation of the head of the President of the United States for the time being, with an inscription which shall express the initial or first letter of his Christian or first name, and his surname at length, the succession of the Presidency numerically, and the year of the coinage; and upon the reverse of each of the gold and silver coins there shall be the figure or representation of an eagle, with this inscription, "UNITED STATES OF AMERICA" and upon the reverse of each of the copper coins, there shall be an inscription which shall express the denomination of the piece, namely cent, or half cent, as the case may require.

Sometime before December 1791, Morris had already engaged artists to prepare patterns for a half dollar and cent. The die beds were forged and hardened by John Harper who owned a saw manufactory at the corner of Sixth and Cherry Streets in Philadelphia. The devices were engraved by

---

[26] Foner states erroneously that Paine's observations were published only in the *Gazette*.

[27] Thus, by a queer twist of fate, Morris became the author of a Mint bill that was essentially the same as one he had previously opposed.

From l. to r. 1791 pattern cents made by Obediah Westwood from dies by John Hancock, an 1792 half dollar by Peter Getz.

twenty-three-year-old Peter Getz, a self-taught silver and goldsmith from Lancaster, whom Barton described as "remarkable for the extraordinary accuracy, elegance and beauty of the workmanship he executed." [28] Getz is said to have aspired for the position of Mint engraver, and to have been patronized by Washington himself. Robert "Bob" Birch [29] supervised Getz's work on the dies and sunk the punches for the date and legends.

Getz and Birch produced a single obverse and two reverse dies, with large and small eagles. The devices closely follow those on the 1791 Westwood Hancock patterns, which evidently served Getz as models. Years later, in fact Adam Eckfeldt, who supervised part of the coining, became confused between the two issues and attributed the Hancock patterns to Getz. [30]

The Getz variety with the large heraldic reverse was apparently the first executed. Getz copied the 1792 Hancock pattern, and ended up without sufficient room for the legend. Only one specimen, in silver, is known with this reverse, struck after the die had been cancelled. In the second reverse the eagle is considerably reduced. Its wings are inverted, and border fifteen stars. The device is copied from Hancock's 1791 small eagle cent.

The half dollars were struck in December 1791, in the cellar of Harper'

---

[28] William Barton, *Memoirs of the Life of David Rittenhouse*, Edward Parker Publ., 1813.

[29] Birch had evidently come to America from England after the Revolution. On November 25 1784 he advertised his work in the *New York Packet* as follows:

"Likenesses (simply imitative of the originals) are painted in crayons, at one guinea each; with elegant oval gilt frames included.

"Seals and Copperplates, Cyphers, Crests, Toys, Trifles, &c. Engraved.

"Hair Devices set in Rings, Lockets, &c. Watches Repaired: And any wheel, Arbor, Pevot, Spring Cock, Slide, Figure-piece, verge, &c. made new and fitted. Watch glasses fitted at one shilling each, and a quantity to be sold cheap for ready cash. Any curious Punch or Instrument made in steel, iron brass, &c. By B. Birch, from London." Birch gave his address as "Mr. Stites's, No. 17 Queen St." John Stites was a merchant and importer specializing in dry goods.

[30] *Historical Magazine*, September 1861, pp. 277-8. The story was given by the Mint's former melter and refiner J. R. McClintock, but the source was obviously his friend Adam Eckfeldt.

saw factory, and distributed to members of the Senate when the Morris bill was reported on the 21st. An amendment, to place on the reverse of the silver coins conjoined links and united hands, and on the reverse of the copper coins a female figure of justice with the legend "To all their due," was defeated. The bill passed the Senate on January 12.

In the meantime, additional copper patterns were struck in the old coach house on Sixth Street near Chestnut, directly opposite Carpenter Street. Adam Eckfeldt, a subsequent officer of the Mint, built the screw press that was employed, and superintended the coinage. It seems probable, considering the weight of these copper pieces, that they were intended as cents, there being, however, no time to engrave an appropriate reverse die.[31]

The "cents" were distributed in the House of Representatives where they provoked a storm of criticism because of the "monarchical" effigy of the president's head. Washington himself seems to have disapproved of the device, for Snowden relates: [32]

"It is a well-ascertained fact that Washington did not favor the proposition to place his likeness upon the coins of the United States. It is even said, that when several specimens of that description were exhibited to him, for inspection and approbation, he indignantly ordered the dies to be destroyed; and expressed his desire that there should be placed on the coins an ideal head of Liberty."

Whether or not the entire story is true, a motion was introduced in the House, on March 24, to strike out the tenth section from the words "Or representation" to "Presidency numerically," and insert instead the words "Emblematic of Liberty." In support of this motion Republican John Page said that it had been "a practice in monarchies to exhibit the figures or heads of their kings upon their coins, either to hand down in the ignorant ages in which the practice was introduced, a kind of chronological account of their kings, or to show to whom the coin belonged. We have all read," he added, "that the Jews paid tribute to the Romans, by means of a coin on which was the head of their Caesar. Now as we have no occasion for this aid to history, nor any pretence to call the money of the United States the money of our Presidents, there can be no sort of necessity for adopting the idea of the Senate. I second the motion, therefore, for the amendment proposed; and the more readily because I am certain it will be more agreeable to the Citizens of the United States, to see the head of Liberty on their coin, than the heads of Presidents. However well pleased they might be with the head of the great man now their President, they may have no great reason to be pleased with some of his successors; as to him, they have his busts, his pictures everywhere; historians are daily celebrating his fame, and Congress have voted him a monument. A further compliment they need not pay him, especially when it may be said, that no Republic has paid such a compliment to their Chief Magistrate, and when indeed it would be viewed as a stamp of Royalty on our coins, would wound the feelings of many friends, and gratify our enemies."

Representative Hugh Williamson observed that while even Julius Caesar

---

[31] Walter Breen, "The United States Patterns of 1792," *The Coin Collector's Journal*, March-April 1954. Breen notes that the weights of both the silver and copper Getz patterns, while varying considerably because of Harper's primitive rollers, average close to the 208 and 264 grains prescribed by the Morris bill for the half dollar and cent.

[32] James Ross Snowden, *Washington and National Medals*, 1861.

wanted to have his effigy on a coin, he "only ventured to cause thereon the figure of an elephant."

Then Samuel Livermore rose and answered Page and Williamson with an uncommon degree of humor. He said it was incomprehensible to him how the President's head on our coins could affect the liberty of the people. The President was a very good symbol of liberty, but what an emblematical figure might be, he could not tell. A ghost, was said to be in the shape of the sound of a drum, and so might liberty for all he knew.

The amendment was nevertheless carried by a large majority. On the 26th, the bill passed in the House and was sent to the Senate which promptly rejected the amendment. The bill was then returned to the House where debate resumed with unusual warmth.

Samuel Livermore said he could not conceive it possible that any friend of the President—"that great and good man"—would have refused to pay every tribute and respect which was justly due to him.

"We now have a favorable opportunity of complimenting him without any shadow of flattery and without expense. But instead of this, what is proposed? An emblematical figure of Liberty. But what is this Liberty which some appear to be so fond of? I have no idea of such a Liberty as appears to possess the minds of such gentlemen. It is little better than the liberty of savages—a relinquishment of all law that contradicts or thwarts their passions or desires. My idea of Liberty is that which arises from law and justice, which secures every man his proper and social rights. Some gentlemen may think a bear broke loose from his chain a fit emblem of Liberty; others may devise a different emblem; but I cannot conceive that any of them would be applicable to the situation of the United States, which justly boasts of being always free. If any idea of an emblem is necessary, I think it might be applied to the head of the President of the United States. The present occasion affords the best opportunity of doing honour to the man we love; instead of which, we offer him an affront. I cannot reconcile this conduct to propriety or consistency; for while it is proposed to raise a monument to the memory of the President, which will cost fifty thousand guineas, a proposition to honor him in a more effectual manner, and in a way which will be satisfactory to the people, without public expense, and with perfect security to their liberties, is objected to." He concluded with the hope that the House would recede from its amendment.

Representative Mercer replied that a rule might be advantageously adopted in the House such as that in the British House of Commons which did not permit the King's name to be mentioned in debate. He said that placing the President's head on our coin could not be justly considered as honoring him, since Nero, Caligula and Heliogabalus (Elagabalus) had enjoyed this distinction. Several other members spoke with severity and sarcasm against Livermore's statements and the conduct of the Senate in rejecting the amendment.

Finally Mr. Page stood up and delivered an impassioned speech which concluded the debate. He said: "I am sorry to find that some gentlemen endeavored to ridicule Republican cautions. I think it both indelicate and inconsistent with their situations, as well as highly impolitic. I confess that, as long as the people are sensible of the blessings of liberty, and have their eyes open to watch encroachment, they will not be enslaved; but if they should overshut them, or become inattentive to their interests and the true principles of a free

Government, they like other nations, might lose their liberties. It is the duty of the members of the House to keep the eyes of their constituents open, and to watch over their liberties. It is therefore unbecoming a member to treat with levity and to ridicule any sentiment which had that tendency. For my part, I think it the peculiar duty of the Representative of a free people to put them upon their guard against anything which could possibly endanger their liberties. With this view I warn my constituents of the danger, not merely of imitating the flattery and almost idolatrous practice of Monarchies with respect to the honor paid to their Kings, by impressing their images and names on their coins, but I wish to add as few incentives as possible to competition for the President's place. I warn my Country against the cabals, the corruption and animosities, which might be excited by the intrigues of ambitious men, animated with the hope of handing their names down to the latest ages on the medals of their country. But this indiscriminate honor is unworthy of the President's acceptance. A Nero, a Caligula, a Heliogabalus, it has been observed, may enjoy it as well as a Trajan. To apply it to the present Chief Magistrate, alone, would be less exceptionable. But this would be highly improper for if he should pass an act for this purpose, it might blast his reputation. I am of the opinion that the Senate knew his delicacy would not permit him to pass such a one. They have therefore extended the compliment to all his successors. We are under obligations to the great man now our President; but a lover of liberty and friend to the rights of man, would be cautious how he showed his sense of that obligation. As a friend to the President, I am unwilling to offer him a compliment which, if accepted, might damn his reputation. Were I in his place, I would cut off my hand rather than it should sign the act as it now stands. Were I his greatest enemy, I should wish him to pass it as it was passed by the Senate. Sir, I am as much his friend as the member from New Hampshire [Mr. Livermore] and have shown, at proper times and places, that I was so. I am too sensible of the honor our President has acquired to suppose that an unbecoming compliment can in any degree contribute to its increase. I hope, therefore, the amendment which the House has made will not be receded from."

The question then being put to a vote, the amendment was retained.

The following day, the Senate announced its concurrence, and on April 2, the long awaited "Act establishing a Mint and regulating the coins of the United States" was enacted.

It is proper to conclude this chapter with a letter written by James Madison, on March 28, 1792 to Henry Lee, the Governor of Virginia: [33]

> My dear Sir:—The mint bill sent from the Senate passed the House of Rp. yesterday—It was disliked and voted against by some as it stands, because it does not establish any systematic proportion of alloy, conforming to the arbitrary one of the last and basest edition of the Spanish dollar, but by most, on account of the expense which is estimated at about thirty thousand annually, and the additional weight of influence it throws into the preponderating scale. In the course of the bill a small circumstance happened worthy of notice, as an index of political biasses —The Senate had proposed in the Bill that on one side of the coin should be stamped the head of the Prest. for the time being—This was attacked in the House of Rps as a feature of Monarchy, and an amendment agreed to establishing an emblematic figure of Liberty—On the return of the Bill to the Senate the amend-

---

[33] David K. Watson, *History of American Coinage*, G. P. Putnam's Sons, 1899.

ment was instantly disagreed to, and the Bill sent back to the H of Rps—The question was viewed on acct. of the rapidity & decision of the Senate as more serious than at first. It was agitated with some fervor and the first vote of the House confirmed by a large majority—The Senate perceiving the temper and afraid of losing the Bill, as well as unwilling to appeal in such controversy to the public criticism, departed from their habitual perseverance and acceded to the alteration proposed . . .

PART II

THE FIRST PHILADELPHIA MINT

CHAPTER 6

The Birth of the Mint

THE ACT OF APRIL 2, 1792 was the first of three comprehensive laws relating to the Mint and regulating its coinage.

Section 1 located the Mint, for the time being, at the seat of the Government (then Philadelphia), and provided for a Director, assayer, chief coiner, engraver and treasurer. No reference was made to the office of melter and refiner.

Section 2 authorized the Director to employ as many subordinate workmen as necessary, subject to the approval of the President.

Section 3 enumerated the duties of each of the offices.

Section 4 required that every officer and clerk take an oath to faithfully and diligently perform his duties.

Section 5 provided that the assayer, chief coiner, and treasurer each post a bond of ten thousand dollars, with one or more sureties, to the satisfaction of the Secretary of the Treasury.

Section 6 authorized the salaries of the respective officers. The Director was to receive two thousand dollars per annum, the chief coiner and assayer fifteen hundred dollars each, and the engraver and treasurer twelve hundred dollars each.

Section 7 directed the Mint to render quarterly accounts for settlement at the Treasury, and submit an annual report of its business to Congress.

Section 8 authorized the construction of buildings for the Mint. The expenses were to be defrayed from the seignorage on coining, and from available treasury funds.

Section 9 authorized the issue of the following United States coins:

Metal	Denomination	Value	Weight in Grains		Fineness
			Fine	Standard	
Gold	Eagle	$10	247½	270	.916⅔
	Half Eagle	$5	123¾	135	.916⅔
	Quarter Eagle	$2½	61⅞	67.5	.916⅔
Silver	Dollar or Unit	$1	371¼	416	.892⅖
	Half Dollar	50¢	185⅝	208	.892⅖
	Quarter Dollar	25¢	92¹³⁄₁₆	104	.892⅖
	Disme (pronounced dime)	10¢	37⅛	41⅗	.892⅖
	Half Disme	5¢	18⁹⁄₁₆	20⅘	.892⅖
Copper	Cent	1¢	264	264	1.000
	Half Cent	½¢	132	132	1.000

In selecting their denominations, Congress wisely ignored Hamilton's rigid decimal scheme. They added five coins that Hamilton did not suggest, and omitted the gold dollar.

Section 10 required that one side of each of the coins show "an impression emblematic of liberty, with an inscription of the word Liberty, and the year of the coinage; and upon the reverse of each of the gold and silver coins there shall be the figure or representation of an eagle, with this inscription, 'UNITED STATES OF AMERICA' and upon the reverse of each of the copper coins, there shall be an inscription which shall express the denomination of the piece, namely cent or half cent, as the case may require."

Section 11 provided for bi-metallism at a ratio of fifteen to one.

Sections 12 and 13 prescribed the fineness of the gold and silver coins. Gold was to be coined at 11/12ths fine, and alloyed with silver and copper, the silver not to exceed fifty percent. The fineness of the silver coins was fixed at 1485/1664ths, with an alloy of pure copper.

Section 14 allowed persons to bring gold and silver bullion to the Mint, and have it coined free of charge. With the approval of the Director, and for a fee of one-half percent, the depositor could request an immediate exchange of coins for bullion. The Mint was to receive a bullion fund for this purpose.

Section 15 instructed the Mint to coin all deposits, if demanded, in the order submitted. This provision not only offset the advantage of the deposit fee, but made its rationale absurd. It cost the Mint little more to refine a large quantity of bullion than a small one, and the refining of deposits in the aggregate would have resulted in considerable savings. Instead, the Mint had to return to the depositor his exact metal, remelting, rolling and cutting the scrap several times. The only deposits that could normally be combined were those purchased outright by the Mint through an immediate exchange for coin; and in each instance, the depositor was mulcted a fee "as an indemnification for the Mint for the time . . . required" and for the "advance!"

Section 16 made the gold and silver coins of the United States legal tender for all debts, "those of full weight according to their respective values . . . and those of less than full weight at values proportional to their respective weights."

This section should have provided for the recall of diminished coin. Instead, following European tradition, it left it up to merchants and ordinary citizens to weigh and calculate the value of every coin they received.

Copper coins were not legal tender, and thus could be refused by banks, shopkeepers and private individuals.

Section 17 made it the duty of the Mint's officers to preserve the legal weights and standards of the coinage, and to use only copper of good quality in the cents and half cents.

Section 18 authorized the treasurer of the Mint to select at random, and from different deliveries, three or more coins of both gold and silver, to be assayed once a year under the inspection of the Chief Justice, the Secretary and Comptroller of the Treasury, the Secretary of State, and the Attorney General, or under the inspection of any three of them, in the presence of the Director, assayer and chief coiner of the Mint. A tolerance [1] of 1/144 part in the fine weight of the coins was permitted.

Section 19 fixed the death penalty for any Mint employee who debased the coinage for profit or other fraudulent purpose, or who embezzled any sum in coins or bullion left in his control.

Section 20 made it a misdemeanor to pay or receive in payment any copper coins except those of the United States.

* * *

On May 8, Congress belatedly authorized the purchase of up to 150 tons of copper for the Mint. The Act also provided that after six months from the time $50,000 worth of cents and half cents had been issued, the Treasurer of the U.S. was to annul, by proclamation in at least two gazettes or newspapers, the circulation of all other copper coins. This provision tacitly repealed Section 20 of the original Mint Act, and extended an indefinite lease to privately issued coppers. In fact, from this time on, the federal cent and half cent, which were not legal tender, enjoyed no more prestige than the English halfpence, foreign and domestic counterfeits, and miscellaneous tokens, all of which circulated freely, regardless of weight or intrinsic worth. Theoretically this situation should have ended in 1799 when the issue of cents and half cents reached $50,000. But despite two reminders by the Director of the Mint, no proclamation was ever issued, and the motley coppers circulated for some forty years afterwards.[2]

The original Mint Act also failed to provide for gradually withdrawing the foreign gold and silver coins from circulation. Congress finally acted on February 9, 1793 by repealing the legal tender status of all foreign specie except for the gold coins of Great Britain, Portugal, France, Spain and the Spanish dominions, and the silver coins of France and Spain. After three years the only foreign coin to remain current would be the Spanish dollar.

* * *

Had Francis Hopkinson still been living, he probably would have become the first Director of the Philadelphia Mint. Instead, on April 14, 1792 Washington gave the commission to David Rittenhouse, the foremost American scientist, and a man universally esteemed for his selfless character.

In 1751, at the age of nineteen, Rittenhouse had opened an instrument shop on his father's farm where he established a reputation for the fineness

---

[1] i.e. the maximum disparity allowed by law. This was originally known as the "remedy", but is now called the "tolerance."

[2] On April 9, 1803, Secretary of the Treasury Gallatin wrote to Jefferson that $50,000 in coppers had been paid into the Treasury as of March 31, 1800, but that the proclamation was "forgotten." Jefferson, in reply, asked that no action be taken until the middle or end of the following month. He said that if the Mint were abolished, the exclusion of other copper coins would be inconvenient. Despite this correspondence, the proclamation was never issued.

of his work, especially in clock-making. Although entirely self-educated, he quickly mastered an English translation of Newton's *Principia* and other scientific works, studying so intensely as to permanently injure his health. In 1756, he constructed an astronomical observatory with the first telescope in America. In 1763 he was selected by William Penn and Lord Baltimore to arbitrate the famous Mason-Dixon line, and in 1767 he built the first of his celebrated orreries. He is credited also with inventing the metallic thermometer and the collimating telescope, solving the problem of Archimedes, and independently discovering fluxions.[3] During the war, Rittenhouse was elected to Congress, and served on the Committee of Safety, ultimately becoming its president. Afterwards he was appointed professor of astronomy at the University of Pennsylvania.

At the time of his appointment to the Mint, Rittenhouse was sixty and in failing health. For several weeks, he continued to decline the office though, characteristically, he at once entered upon its duties. Thus encouraged, Washington, through the agencies of Jefferson and Hamilton, urged him to accept, and finally, on July 1, 1792 Rittenhouse took the oath of Director. He held office for three years, managing the Mint with zeal and dedication. Dr. Rush, subsequently treasurer of the Mint, recounts[4] how Rittenhouse often paid from his own pocket an expenditure he thought might incur criticism. Apropos, Barton tells a touching anecdote of how Rittenhouse was once offered an elegant but rather expensive pair of balances by Peter Getz who had hopefully fashioned them for the Mint. Anxious to reward the young man's labor, the Director purchased the balances for himself, and subsequently obtained a less expensive pair for the Mint. It appears, however, that Rittenhouse later presented the Getz balances to the Mint, for they are mentioned by Crosby as having been there.[5]

Immediately after his appointment (on April 14), Rittenhouse was asked to select a lot on which to erect the Mint building. He chose as a tentative site the property of Frederick Hailer, which was situated on the east side of North Seventh St. (Nos. 37 and 39), with a contiguous lot at 631 Filbert St., Philadelphia. At the time of its purchase, the site was occupied by a vacant old distillery, and frame tenement building.

On June 9, Jefferson wrote to Washington:[6]

Th. Jefferson, with his respects to the President, incloses him a letter from Mr. Rittenhouse on the subject of procuring a house for the mint. Mr. Rittenhouse thinks the house on 7th Street can be bought for £ 1600. It is probable that none can be rented under £ 150 and this sum will pay the interest and sink the principal of £ 1600 in 15 years. The outhouses will save the necessity of new erections, and there is a horse mill, which will save the building one for the rolling mill; so that on the whole Thomas J. concurs in opinion with Mr. Rittenhouse that it will be better to buy this house; and submits the same to the President. A plan for the ground and building is inclosed.

Mr. Rittenhouse thinks the appointment of a Chief coiner & Engraver

---

[3] i.e., differential calculus.
[4] Dr. Benjamin Rush, *An Eulogium Intended to Perpetuate the Memory of David Rittenhouse,* Printed by J. Ormrod & Conrad, 1796; also William Barton, *Memoirs of the Life of David Rittenhouse,* 1813.
[5] Sylvester S. Crosby, *Early Coins of America,* 1875.
[6] The following correspondences between Washington, Jefferson, and Rittenhouse are found in the Library of Congress collection. Other sources are cited appropriately.

(in one office) necessary to prepare the proper machines for coining copper. He thinks Voigt perfectly equal to the duties of the coiner. He is no engraver himself, and it is therefore proposed that he shall consider the cost of engraving dies as a charge to be deducted from his salary of 1500 Doll.[7] He has not been consulted on this point. He is willing to accept the appointment, and retire from it of course on the arrival of any successor whom we shall import from abroad.

On June 14, Jefferson wrote to the U.S. minister in England, Thomas Pinckney,[8] regarding the need to obtain "artists" [9] for the Mint.

Sir, The U.S. being now about to establish a Mint, it becomes necessary to ask your assistance in procuring persons to carry on some parts of it; and to enable you to give it, you must be apprised of some facts.

Congress, some time ago, authorized the President to take measures for procuring some artists from any place where they were to be had. It was known that a Mr. Drost, a Swiss, had made an improvement in the method of coining, and some specimens of his coinage were exhibited here, which were superior to anything we had ever seen. Mr. Short was, therefore, authorized to engage Drost to come over, to erect the proper machinery, & instruct persons to go on with the coinage; and as he supposed this would require about a year, we agreed to give him a thousand louis a year and his expenses. The agreement was made, two coining mills, or screws, were ordered by him; but in the end, he declined coming. We have reason to believe he was drawn off by the English East India Company, and that he is now at work for them in England. Mr. Bolton had also made a proposition to coin for us in England, which was declined. Since this, the act has been passed for establishing our mint, which authorizes, among other things, the employment of an Assayer at 1500 D. a year, the chief coiner at the same, and an engraver at 1200 D., but it admits of the employment of one person both as Engraver and chief coiner; this we expect may be done, as we presume that any engraver, who had been used to work for a coinage must be well enough acquainted with all the operations of coinage to direct them; and it is an economy worth attention, if we can have the services performed by one officer instead of two; in which case it is proposed to give him the salary of the Chief coiner, that is to say 1500 D. a year. I am therefore to request that you will endeavor, on your arrival in Europe, to engage and send us an Assayer, of approved skill, and of well attested integrity, and a Chief coiner & Engraver, in one person, if possible, acquainted with all the improvements in coining and particularly those of Drost and Boulton. Their salaries commence from the day of their sailing for America. If Drost be in England, I think he will feel himself under some obligation to aid you in procuring persons. How far Boulton will do it seems uncertain. You will doubtless make what use you can of the good dispositions of either of these or of any other person. Should you find it impracticable to procure an Engraver capable of performing the functions of Chief-coiner also, we must be content that you engage separate characters. Let these persons bring with them all the implements necessary for carrying on the business, except such as you should think too bulky & easily made here. It would be proper therefore that they should consult you as to the necessary implements & their prices that they may act under your control. The method of your paying for these implements and making reasonable advances to the workmen shall be the subject of another letter, after the President shall have decided thereon. It should be a part of the agreement of these people that they will faithfully instruct all persons in their art, whom we shall put under them for that purpose. Your contract with them may be made for any term not exceeding four years. I have the honor, etc.

P.S.—Should you not be able to procure persons of eminent qualifications for

---

[7] On January 1, 1793, Henry Voigt was paid $875 salary to cover the period from June 1 to December 31, 1792. This means that no deductions were made for the engraving of dies, and that Voigt must have paid the artists out of his own pocket. It also explains the absence of any warrants by the Mint for payment to engravers during 1792-93.

[8] Sylvester Crosby, "The Cents of 1793," *American Journal of Numismatics*, Jan. 1897.

[9] i.e., skilled craftsmen.

their business in England, it will be proper to open a correspondence with Mr. Morris on the subject and see whether he cannot get such from France. Next to obtaining the ablest artists, a very important circumstance is to send them to us as soon as possible.

Evidently the postscript was added after Jefferson had consulted with Washington. On the 15th, the President advised: [10]

Dear Sir: When Artizans are imported, and criticism is at Work, the inducement is greater to obtain those who are really skillful: for this reason, if Mr. Pinckney should not readily meet with those who are unequivocally such; or, if there is a chance of getting better in France than in England, I think it would be well to instruct him to corrispond [sic] with Mr. Morris on this Subject with view to obtain the best. I should be mortified to import men not more understanding in the business of Assaying, Engraving and Coining than those who are already among us. Yours etc.

On June 17, Washington wrote to Jefferson: [11]

"The Attorney General will, I presume, draw the Deed for the Lot for the Mint. The purchase of it, I approve of."

In a letter to Washington, on July 9, Rittenhouse announced his decision to accept the Directorship, and his selection of Henry Voigt as chief coiner pro tem.[12]

Sir: Tho' a long continued state of ill health has left me little relish for the usual pursuits of Interest and Ambition, I am extremely sensible of the honor you have done me by appointing me, unsolicited, Director of the Mint. Having by the advice of friends [13] determined to accept that office, for the present, I think it my duty to give every assistance in my power to the business, and have taken the oath of office required by law.

On consulting with the Secretary of State I find that some of the Officers for the mint are still expected from Europe. This will occasion further delay, at least as to going generally into coining. But as small money is very much wanted we think proper, in the mean time, if your Excellency approves of it, to Coin some Copper Cents & Half Cents, and likewise small Silver, at least Dimes and Half Dimes. I have purchased on account of the United States, a House & Lot which I hope will be found convenient for the Mint, but considerable alterations must be made, and some small new buildings erected. I have likewise engaged Mr. Voigt to act as Coiner, and he has several workmen now employed in making the necessary engines and preparing the Dies. A quantity of copper will be wanted, perhaps 15 Tons might be sufficient, and measures for procuring it ought to be immediately taken, and for these several purposes some money will be required.

I shall be happy in receiving your Excellency's approbation of these preparatory steps, together with such further directions as you may think proper to give. I am etc.

Washington forwarded the letter to Jefferson, asking him to draft a reply.

---

[10] *The Writings of George Washington*, Vol. 32, Fitzpatrick.

[11] Ibid. In his *History of the First United States Mint,* Stewart quotes a letter of June 9 from Washington to Jefferson (in reply to Jefferson's letter of the same date) concerning the Mint. This is omitted here as Professor Boyd is doubtful of its authenticity. No text of the letter can be found either as a retained file copy in the Washington papers or as a recipient's copy in the Jefferson papers. Moreover, Washington's two letters of June 15 and 17, 1792 (see above) seem to be replying to Jefferson's letter of June 9. Adding all these things together, not to mention the text itself (particularly the allusion to "the lots and houses"), and considering the large number of skillful forgeries of Washington letters made during the 19th century, it is difficult to give this letter full credence.

[12] R. W. Julian, "The Patterns of 1792," *The Numismatic Scrapbook Magazine,* July 1962.

[13] i.e. Jefferson and Hamilton.

Jefferson furnished two different forms, of which the President chose the more detailed, changing only spelling and punctuation. Still on the same day he replied to Rittenhouse:[14]

> Having had under consideration the letter of the Director of the Mint of this day's date, I hereby declare my approbation of the purchase he has made of the house and lot for the Mint, of the employment of Mr. Voigt as Coiner; of the Procuring fifteen tons of Copper, and proceeding to coin the Cents and Half Cents of Copper, and Dismes and Half Dismes of Silver; and I leave to his discretion to have such alterations and additions made to the buildings purchased, as he shall find necessary; satisfied that under his orders no expense will be incurred which reason and necessity will not justify. And I desire that he will make out an Estimate of the sums of money which will be wanting, in order to enable the Treasury to make arrangements for furnishing them with convenience. Given under my hand this 9th day of July, 1792.

On July 10, Rittenhouse sent Washington an estimate of $10,000. The Director said that $4,266⅔ was needed to purchase the property, $933⅓ for repairs, workmen's wages, etc., and $4,800 for fifteen tons of copper at 16¢ a pound. Later in the same day, Washington issued a warrant on the Treasury for the full amount.

✦ ✦ ✦

There is much evidence, direct and indirect, concerning the 1792 pattern coinage. We might begin by quoting B. L. C. Wailes, who visited the Mint in 1829, and afterwards recorded: [15]

"Mr. Eckfeldt, one of the Superintendents (the second in grade) is an artist & has been in the Mint from its first establishment. [He] made the first dye used in it."

The die referred to is almost certainly the obverse for the 1792 disme. Not only is this the one 1792 die that cannot be attributed to other hands, but its portrait is almost identical to that on the 1793 half cent, for which Eckfeldt is said to have claimed credit.[16] In lot 2021 of his October 20-24, 1863 auction catalogue, coin dealer W. Elliot Woodward described an uncirculated 1793 half cent as follows:

"A peculiar interest attaches to this coin. Nearly sixty years since it was presented to a gentleman, by Mr. Adam Eckfeldt, as a specimen of his work, and has remained in the possession of the person referred to within a few days."

Since Wailes mentions a *single* die, it is probable that the reverse of the disme should be assigned to Robert Birch. Stylistically, the eagle is similar to that on the half disme designed by Birch.

Only a few patterns were struck for the 1792 disme, Washington preferring to begin with the coinage of half dismes. The dismes were apparently made on or before July 13, for on that day Jefferson recorded in his household account book: [17]

"rec'd from the mint 1500 half dimes of the new coinage."

[14] Frank Stewart, *History of the First United States Mint.*
[15] *A View of Philadelphia in 1829, Selections from the Journal of B. L. C. Wailes of Natchez* [Miss.], edited by John Hebron Moore, Pennsylvania Magazine, July 1954.
[16] Walter Breen, "The United States Patterns of 1792," *The Coin Collector's Journal,* April-March, 1954.
[17] *The Papers of Thomas Jefferson,* Library of Congress collection.

Details of this historic issue are provided by a memorandum of Dr. Jonas McClintock, which is now in the possession of Walter Breen.[18]

"On one side—a Head—1792 Lib. Par. of Science & Industry—on the other side—An Eagle flying—Half Disme—United States of America—

"In conversation with Mr. Adam Eckfeldt today at the Mint, he informed me that the Half Dismes above described were struck at the request of Gen. Washington to the extent of One Hundred Dollars which sum he deposited in Bullion or Specie for the purpose—Mr. E. thinks that Gen. W. distributed them as presents—some were sent to Europe but the greater number of them he believes, were given to acquaintances in Virginia—No more of them were coined except those for Gen. W.—they were never designed as Currency—the Mint was not at the time fully ready for going into operation—the coining Machinery was in the cellar of Mr. Harper's, saw maker at the Corner of Cherry and 6th Streets, at which place these pieces were struck—

"April 9, 1844. J Mc"

Although Eckfeldt was slightly off on the number of half dismes struck, his memory otherwise appears remarkably undimmed.

The dies for the half disme were engraved by Robert "Bob" Birch who, fortunately for historians, left his name on another, stylistically similar coin— the 1792 large cent. According to an old tradition, the portraits on both coins represent Martha Washington, copied in profile from Trumbull's painting.

✻　　✻　　✻

The Mint site was deeded to the United States on July 18, 1792 and work began the following day.

Although Voigt was only employed on a temporary basis, he was a skilled operational mechanic and, like Rittenhouse, a well known watch maker. A year earlier he had assisted John Fitch in building the engine and fittings for the first American steamboat, the performance of which was attested to by a committee that included Rittenhouse. Voigt superintended the demolition of the old stillhouse as well as the construction of new buildings for the Mint and, in the absence of Rittenhouse, hired and paid the workmen, purchased supplies, and served as general factotum.

The work was faithfully recorded in Voigt's account book, and constitutes the first record ever kept of operations at the Philadelphia Mint.

> 1792, July 19.—The following men began to work at taking down the still house. To Saturday the 21:
>
> | | |
> |---|---|
> | John Maul | 3 days |
> | Jno. Christian Glouse | 3 do. |
> | John Keyser | 2 do. |
> | Nicolas Sinderling | 2 do. |
> | John Biting | 1½ do. |
> | Matthias Sumer | 1 do. |
>
> 21.—8 carpenters at work this day taking down the still-house frame.

On July 30, the first mortar sand was hauled by Baltis Clymer, and the following day, at about ten a.m., Rittenhouse laid the foundation stone. To cele-

---

[18] This letter was discovered by Edward B. Haden, and published in the letters-to-the-editor column of *The Numismatist*, May 1943; the "J Mc" was correctly identified by Charles McSorley in the same column of *The Numismatist*, July 1943; the letter itself was illustrated for the first time by Walter Breen in the April 20, 1962 edition of *Coin World*, p. 82.

brate the occasion, the Director sold off some of the distillery junk for a dollar, and purchased punch for the workmen.

By Saturday, August 25, the foundation and walls had been completed and were ready for the superstructure, and on the same afternoon the framework was raised. Thereafter the work advanced so rapidly that by September 7, the building was ready for the installation of a furnace, bellows and other internal features.[19]

Four days later, Voigt made the first purchase of copper, amounting to six pounds, at the cost of one shilling and three pence to the pound.

The Mint began with only one very small screw press which had been built by Adam Eckfeldt. Two larger presses were sent from abroad by Droz, and arrived on Friday, September 21. On the 25th it was recorded that "Flude began, after breakfast, trimming the heavy press."

In his annual address to Congress, on November 6, 1792 Washington described progress at the Mint, and called attention to its first emission of coins: ". . . in execution of the authority given by the Legislature, measures have been taken for engaging some artists from abroad to aid in the establishment of our Mint; others have been employed at home. Provision has been made of the requisite buildings, and these are now putting into proper condition for the purposes of the establishment. There has also been a small beginning in the coinage of half dismes; the want of small coins in circulation calling the first attention to them."

In Jefferson's draft of the above, there is reference also to the coinage of cents.[20] These would have been the first "Birch" cents, probably, as Julian suggests, the variety with G.W.P.[t] (George Washington President) in the reverse legend. Only one trial impression survives, and it may well be that Washington rejected the issue because of the personal allusion.

It appears that as early as May, 1791 Washington had decided to give the supervision of the Mint to Jefferson [21] though, logically, it had no connection with the State Department. The President made no formal assignment, however, until October 20, when he wrote to Jefferson:

. . . The Post Office (as a branch of Revenue) was annexed to the Treasury in the time of Mr. Osgood; and when Colo. Pickering was appointed thereto, he was informed as I find by my letter to him dated the 29th. of August 1791, that he was to consider it in that light. If from relationship, or usage in similar cases (for I have made no enquiry into the matter, having been closely employed since you mentioned the thing to me, in reading papers from the War Office) the Mint does not appertain to the Department of the Treasury I am more inclined to add it to that of State than to multiply the duties of the other.

In November 1792, the Mint acquired three of its original balances from Adam Eckfeldt. It is recorded that on November 22, Voigt paid John Bringhurst nineteen cents for hauling one of these to the Mint, and that on the 28th a porter was given twenty-five cents for fetching two smaller balances, likewise from Eckfeldt's place. Eckfeldt also brought to the Mint his own lathe for the purpose of turning dies.

---

[19] The larger brick building, which fronted on Seventh St., was not completed until a few months later. Between the two buildings, a frame mill house was built, and on the Filbert St. lot, a wooden stable.

[20] R. W. Julian, "The Patterns of 1792," *The Numismatic Scrapbook Magazine*, June 1962.

[21] See John Mitchell's letter to Jefferson, Sept. 23, 1791; *Misc. Letters Received*, Record Group 59, National Archives.

On September 3, 1792, and for several weeks thereafter, the Mint advertised in *Dunlap's Daily Advertiser*, offering to pay the highest price for old copper. These purchases, however, proved insufficient, and on November 28, 1792 Jefferson wrote from Philadelphia to President Washington:

> Sir, The rise in the price of copper, & difficulty of obtaining it from other quarters, has induced the Director of the Mint (as I had the honor of mentioning to you yesterday) to turn his attention to Sweden as the country from which according to his information it may be obtained on the best terms. He wishes that some means could be adopted of importing same on the public account. There is so little direct commerce between this country & Sweden that we shall be obliged to resort to some intermediate port & I have imagined that (our resident in Holland being absent) our Minister in London could be the best person to confide the business to for the present occasion. You will see by mr. Rittenhouse's letter inclosed that he proposes an importation of 30. or 40. tons from Sweden at present, the former quantity by his estimate will cost between nine & ten thousand dollars. If you approve of this mode & quantun of supply, a bill from the Treasury of 10,000 Dol. on the Holland bankers payable to mr. Pinckney shall be desired to adopt the best means he can of having 30. tons of copper shipped from Sweden for the Mint.—I also inclose the Director's letter of yesterday asking a supply of 5000. D. for the current purposes of the mint, & I have the honor to be etc.

On the following day, Washington's secretary, Tobias Lear, replied to Jefferson:

> By the President's command T. Lear has the honor to inform the Secretary of State, that a bill for ten thousand dollars will be drawn by the Treasury of the US on our Holland Bankers payable to Mr. Pinckney, for the purposes of obtaining Copper for the Mint. The President, however, suggests, that it would not perhaps be best to confine Mr. Pinckney strictly to Sweden for the purchase of the Copper, but to leave it to his discretion to obtain it where it can be had on the most advantageous terms, after calling his attention to Sweden, for the reason mentioned in the letter from the Director of the Mint to the Secretary of State.

Despite the shortage of copper, experiments to determine a proper cent were resumed before the end of the year.

An entry dated December 17, 1792 in Voigt's account book reads: "Struck off a few pieces of copper coin." The identity of these, the first coins actually struck at the Mint, is revealed in a letter from Jefferson to Washington, written the following day: [22]

> Th. Jefferson has the honor to send the President two cents made on Voigt's plan by putting a silver plug worth ¾ of a cent into a copper worth ¼ cent.
> Mr. Rittenhouse is about to make a few by mixing the same plug by fusion with the same quantity of copper. He will then make [one] of copper alone of the same size, & lastly he will make the real cent as ordered by Congress, 4 times as big. Specimens of these several ways of making the cent may be delivered to the Committee of Congress now having the subject before them.

Rittenhouse apparently wanted to give Congress the benefit of every possibility. "Voigt's plan" had already been anticipated and rejected by Hamilton in his 1791 report. The mixed-metal, or billon, cent was, of course, Jefferson's idea, and the small copper cent would represent a fiduciary coin such as Thomas Paine suggested. All of these essays were struck from the same pair of dies, engraved by Henry Voigt.[23]

---

[22] David K. Watson, *History of American Coinage*. G. P. Putnam's Sons, 1899.

[23] The "Voigt" attribution is inescapable when one compares the style to that of the 1793 chain cent dies which Voigt is known to have engraved. All show the same general crudeness and faint relief that characterize an untrained hand.

The larger "real cent" was struck from a new pair of dies engraved by Birch, and bore the artist's name upon the obverse.

The House committee, to which these pieces were sent, had been appointed on November 30 to report a bill amending the weight of the copper coinage. The bill was introduced in Congress on December 31,[24] and enacted on January 14, 1793. It reduced the weight of the cent to 208 grains, and that of the half cent proportionately. It also deprived Americans of the possibility of having a Martha Washington copper coinage.

The last 1792 pattern we shall discuss is, in many ways, the most interesting of the group. It is the beautiful copper coin with an eagle standing on a half globe. Judd, following the 18th edition of *The Standard Catalogue of United States Coins*, attributes the piece to Droz, and calls it a pattern for a half eagle.[25] In his introduction, however, he admits that nothing is known of its origin.

It is true that Droz, anticipating American employment, once offered to engrave dies for the Mint. However, when the Mint Act was finally passed, and designs were selected by Congress, the artist had already stepped out of the picture. Had Droz actually prepared dies, or been given a commission to do so, there should be some reference to the fact among the diplomatic dispatches. That there is not, is sufficient reason to assign the "eagle on globe" pattern to a local artist.

The superior style and distinctive letter punches eliminate Birch and Eckfeldt (and, of course, Voigt), but could very well reflect the hand of Joseph Wright. Moreover, since Jefferson selected Wright to engrave dies for the Henry Lee medal, it is natural to suppose that the artist would have been similarly employed in something touching the Secretary's interest and duty so much more deeply.

The eagle-on-globe piece is uncomfortably large for a half eagle, though it would serve nicely as an essay for a quarter dollar. That the Mint was indeed planning an early quarter dollar coinage—from dies by Joseph Wright—is revealed in a memorandum of one Moid Wetherill, written September 11, 1793: [26]

"Joseph Wright being very ill and not expecting to recover requested the subscriber to make a memorandum as follows:

"That the said Joseph Wright had presented an account against the United States for cutting a medal amount fifty Guineas.

"Two Essays of a Quarter Dollar, cut by direction of David Rittenhouse, Esqr. and presented to him (broke in hardening) value about 40 Guineas."

By "cutting" a medal and essays of a quarter dollar, Wright was, of course, referring to the dies. The allusion to the quarter-dollar dies breaking is significant because of the heavy die cracks on the reverse of one of the eagle-on-globe pieces.

---

[24] During the House debate on this bill, the subject of a device "emblematic of Liberty" was again raised. Elias Hewitt Boudinot remarked that all the artists who submitted designs differed in their conception of Liberty. He moved an amendment to substitute the head of Columbus for that of Liberty, calling the House's attention to the importance of Columbus to America. After some debate, the amendment was voted on and lost.

[25] Dr. J. Hewitt Judd, *United States Pattern, Experimental and Trial Pieces*, 3rd edition, Whitman Publishing Co., 1965.

[26] Statement of account of Joseph Stretch (administrator of the estate of Joseph Wright), January 13, 1795, *Miscellaneous Treasury Accounts*, Microfilm Publication M235, reel 19, National Archives.

Patterns for coinage, struck during 1792 after passage of the Mint Act. **Left:** half disme by Robert Birch, disme by Adam Eckfeldt (reverse by Birch?), silver-center cent by Henry Voigt; **right:** cents by Robert Birch; **bottom:** quarter dollar (die trial with wide rim) by Joseph Wright.

Additional evidence is furnished by artist William Dunlap, a contemporary of Wright: [27]

> He [Wright] was a modeller in clay and practised die-sinking, which last gained him the appointment, shortly before his death, of die-sinker to the Mint. (I have before me a design for a cent, made by Mr. Wright, and dated 1792. It represents an eagle standing on the half of a globe, and holding in its beak a shield with the thirteen stripes. The reverse has been drawn on the same piece of paper, and afterwards cut out.)

The author of an article on Wright in the *Dictionary of American Biography* remarked with apparent disappointment that no such coin was known. The reason is obvious. In the first place, Dunlap was wrong about the denomination, an eagle design being eligible only for a gold or silver U.S. coin, and then for the reverse, not the obverse side. Secondly, if Wright's heraldic eagle design had been used, it would have been cut out to make an initial transfer impression.[28]

The other design, which Wright removed, may have been for the obverse of the coin, or for an alternate reverse. In any event, we can say that Wright prepared quarter dollar dies for the Mint, that he preferred his eagles to stand upon a half globe, and that one 1792 pattern (otherwise unattributed) qualifies on both counts. Equally important, and in the writer's opinion conclusive, is the fact that the 1793 Liberty Cap cents, which suggest the same hand, are attributable to the brief period when Wright was evidently employed by the Mint.

✿   ✿   ✿

We may recall that in 1790, Matthew Boulton laid a very tempting proposal before Jefferson. Boulton had offered to furnish Congress with his best machines, instruct American workmen in his elegant mode of coining, and in the meantime contract for a copper coinage. His proposals were rejected, in part at least, because of the anticipated employment of Droz. When the latter finally declined coming, Boulton resumed his overtures, this time through the agency of his friend Ralph Mather.

In a letter to Boulton dated July 18, 1792 Mather wrote: [29]

> ". . . I have particularly noted your directions & will punctually observe them, especially in regard to the Engines for *Coining*."

Soon afterwards Mather embarked for America, carrying with him Boulton's proposals and sample coins.[30] Jefferson submitted the coins to Washington on November 16, recommending them as superior to "anything we can do here," and justifying "our wish to set our mint going on that plan."

Three days later, Mather wrote to Boulton:

> Sir: It having been heretofore your wish to form a correspondence with the Congress, and being recommended through my father & Mr. Jefferson, I have presumed to give him your terms as herewith instant you *guarded*, as you will

---

[27] William Dunlap, *A History of the Rise and Progress of the Arts of Design in the United States,* 1834; reprinted with additions by Frank W. Bayley and Charles E. Goodspeed, C.E. Goodspeed & Co., 1918.

[28] This will be explained in the next chapter.

[29] *Matthew Boulton Papers,* Assay Office of Birmingham, England.

[30] According to a letter from Mather to Boulton, dated March 20, 1801 these were specimens of Boulton's contract halfpence.

observe in the copy. Mr. Jefferson was highly *pleased* both with the *Coin* and with the *terms* proposed. The latter he thought *very reasonable* as a *temporary* accommodation. It was not against the coinage in England, he said, but the perpetuity of it to which he could not give his consent. He likewise observed that it were equal with them to pay money. I understand that the American Ambassador is commissioned to treat in England already about the same subject. The coinage is to be laid before *a committee,* and I hope you will hear of some offers made by them agreeable with your wishes. Mr. Rittenhouse is appointed director of the Mint. Some dies are already made for the purpose of coinage . . .

On February 4, 1793 Mather wrote to Boulton:

Having wrote you the 19th Novr. particularly, there appears nothing material to communicate, as Mr. Jefferson informs me that *till* they receive letters from their Ambassador, nothing decisive could be effected, the mint department having commissioned *that* gentleman to treat with *you.* Mr. Washington is highly pleased with your samples.

In the end, Boulton's proposals were rejected, leaving the Mint to make its own way into the world. That it was not an easy way, we shall now see.

CHAPTER 7

The First Mint and Its Operations

"The time of work and Labour in the Mint, shall be understood by all employed therein, to be Eleven Hours in each Day—and shall from the 10th of November, begin at 6 o'clock in the morning and continue till 7 o'clock in the Evening allowing from 8 to 9 o'clock for Breakfast, and from 1 till 2 o'clock for Dinner"—From the Mint's rules and regulations for 1795.

ON DECEMBER 3, 1828 MINT DIRECTOR SAMUEL MOORE wrote a lengthy report to Representative John Sergeant, enclosing a drawing of the Mint plot, and describing the location of its various operations. This document, which has never been published, enables us to reconstruct a faithful and comprehensive plan of the first Philadelphia Mint.

On July 18, 1792 Director David Rittenhouse purchased two lots for the Mint. The main lot (A) fronted on Seventh Street between Market and Arch, at what is now known as Nos. 37 and 39 No. Seventh St. It was not quite thirty-seven feet wide and extended back about one-hundred-and-twenty feet. The other lot (B) faced Sugar Alley at 631 Filbert Street, and was contiguous, in the rear, with the first. It was seventeen feet wide and twenty feet deep.[1]

On October 4, 1794, a third lot (C), located on the other side of Bone Alley, was purchased from William Hamilton. It likewise faced Sugar Alley, measuring twenty feet, six inches in width, and eighty-eight feet in depth. Its address

---

[1] The measurements given here reflect the disposition of the lots on Moore's diagram. Technically, the 7th St. lot ended at the point where it was intersected by the Filbert St. lot. (see Stewart, pgs. 136-140.)

was 629 Filbert St. These three lots constitute the entire property owned by the first Philadelphia Mint.

In June 1805, the Mint leased a neighboring lot (5) from Jacob Cromley, and on December 13, another lot (E), from Robert Griffith. The latter was leased, after 1810, from Samuel Yorke, and at no time did the Mint pay more than sixty dollars annually. In 1827, the Yorke lot was offered for public sale, and purchased for the Mint's benefit by Adam Eckfeldt, who continued to rent out the property at the same rate. With the acquisition of the Cromley and Griffith lots, it became possible to erect gates at both ends of Bone Alley, preventing further intrusion into the Mint property.

The largest of the Mint's principal buildings was a double house, built of brick three stories high.[2] It fronted on Seventh Street, covered the width of the lot, and extended back just thirty-three feet. In its basement were the vaults of the Mint, and on the first floor the deposit and weighing rooms, as well as the press room where the gold coins were struck. The second floor was appropriated to the various offices excepting that of the assayer. The assay furnace and the office of the assayer (which apparently doubled for his parting laboratory) were situated on the top floor, an unpleasant arrangement due to the diffusion of fumes from the nitric acid. To go from one floor to another, it was necessary to walk a dark, winding stairway in which a tallow lamp was kept burning throughout the day.

Beyond this building was a small paved yard (2), and then a frame house which contained the horse mill for driving the rolling machines. The rear of the mill house was adjoined by a two-story brick building, the first built by the Mint in 1792. Here, on the first floor, the Mint kept its rolling and drawing machines, and on the upper level its smelting furnace. In January 1816, the mill house, together with this adjoining building, caught fire. The former was completely destroyed and afterward replaced by a substantial brick building.[3] These two houses were again adjoined, apparently by an overhead bridge, and considered a single unit. The seven foot division between the two can be reckoned on the diagram from the point where the structure narrows. A ten horse-power steam engine was installed in the basement of the new building, and its first and second floors evidently held the rolling and drawing machines and one of the planchet cutters. The milling machine and the screw-driven planchet cutters were probably in the farther building, which had no basement and was only one-and-a-half stories high. After 1816, all of the Mint's smelting operations were carried on elsewhere, a fact of which Stewart was unaware.

The small lot (B), which we have called 631 Filbert St., contained a small, rudely constructed frame building which, until 1816, served as the stable. Evidently the horses had to share their quarters with an arrester,[4] which was used to grind up the "sweeps"[5] prior to refining. Afterwards the stable served as a repository for all the Mint's coined and uncoined copper.

The far lot (C) held four buildings. Facing Sugar Alley was a frail, two-story

---

[2] Moore's report gives the impression that this building was formerly a dwelling house which had been converted for the Mint's use. This is incorrect. Rittenhouse's expense report of March 25, 1793 indicates that the original dwelling house was removed, and a brick building erected in its place.

[3] Apparently the farther building was not completely rebuilt, for Stewart found planchets in it dating from 1792.

[4] Frank Stewart, *History of the First United States Mint*, p. 147.

[5] The collective name for worn out crucibles, dipping cups and miscellaneous refuse refined by the Mint to extract traces of gold and silver.

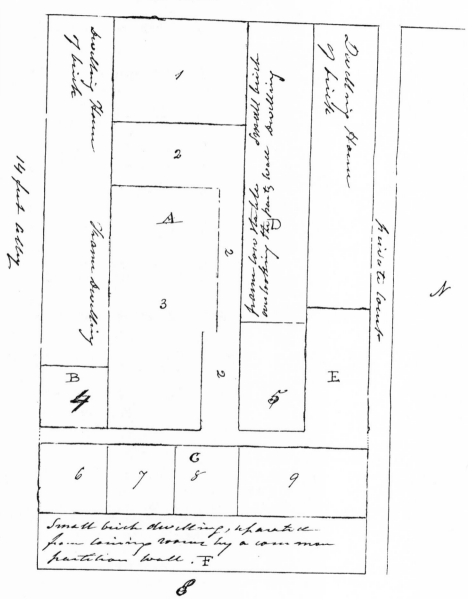

Diagram of the Mint plot. Drawing was made in 1828. *National Archives.*

frame house (6), and immediately behind this, a small, dilapidated two-story brick building (7). The lower levels of each of these contained press rooms, the first for striking most of the Mint's silver coins, the second for striking coppers. This designation, however, was made in 1828, and it appears that in earlier years copper was coined in the first of the two buildings. The upper level of each contained shops where the machinery was made and repaired. Behind these were a smith shop (8), and a coal house (9), both very rough frame buildings.

After 1816, all of the Mint's furnaces, except that for assaying, were situated in the two-story brick building on the Cromley lot. The refining furnace was located in the cellar, which was so cramped that the contingent operations were often delayed. The contiguous Yorke lot had no building on it, and appears to have been leased in order to close off Bone Alley. The lot was employed as a woodyard.

A large furnace which the Mint completed in September 1794 was located in the Commons at the north end of Sixth Street. The furnace occupied a frame house, on leased ground, and probably was not used after the Cromley lot was rented.

Until 1816, the Mint derived its power entirely from men and horses.[6] Such, apparently, was not the original intention, for on January 12, 1798 Henry Voigt wrote to Director Boudinot:[7]

> The Mint work was originally constructed for a steam Engine, to be the impelling power for the mill work, in case it was found that Dollars should be made; it was no error of the Director [i.e. Rittenhouse] that horses were employed, they only were protemporary till it should be found more convenient to erect a steam Engine; for he knew perfectly well, that horses were insufficient to make Dollars to advantage; but towards the time when Dollars were to be struck, he was fearful of the expenses; because too much fault had already been found with the expenses that had been; and therefore he declined. For all the calumny against the mint, there is nevertheless as much work done therein, as in any one in the world, in proportion to the power therein applied; those who have seen Mints in Europe will testify the truth thereof [except he be a prejudicial Englishman] [8] . . .

Four contemporary accounts of our earliest Mint operations are known, though none are even vaguely comprehensive. The remarks made in 1794 by James Davy, a self-styled efficiency expert, and the recollections in 1893 of engineer George Escol Sellers have been chronicled more than once. B. L. C. Wailes' (1829) description of the self-loading coining press was first published in *Pennsylvania Magazine*, July 1954. Another important document, and the only one touching upon assaying methods, is the report of Mint Director Samuel Moore to Congress, January 22, 1831. For the rest, the writer has had to content himself with collecting fragments and arranging them to show a reasonably complete picture.

The operations of a Mint can be divided under three heads: first, the preparation of dies; secondly, the smelting and standardizing of the metal; and lastly, the making and stamping of the planchets. The period under our immediate observation is 1793 to 1816.

---

[6] Except during its construction when oxen were also employed.

[7] James L. Whitehead, "Federal Archives in Philadelphia," *Pennsylvania Magazine*, April 1938. This letter was supposed to have been accessioned by the National Archives in Washington, but it has not been found there.

[8] The bracketed words were crossed out. Voigt was probably referring to James Callender (see Chapter 5).

Preparation of Dies

One of the serious problems that faced the new Mint was obtaining good steel from which to forge its dies. If the metal were too fine it over-hardened under pressure and became susceptible to cracks and other flaws. On the other hand, steel with too coarse a grain often shattered during the hardening process or acquired fissures when used in the multiplying press. If the die were to survive, even temporarily, it had to be forged from a steel of medium fineness, and exhibit a uniform texture when washed with nitric acid to dissolve "pins" of iron and other irregularities in its composition.

Although the preparation of dies, in its entirety, devolved by law upon the engraver, the initial forging and turning was done by the coining department. The steel arrived at the Mint in cast bars. These were cut into short sections which were then annealed by being heated in an iron pot of charcoal and allowed to cool slowly. Each section was turned to a cylindrical shape and given a neck at one end. The surface of the neck, i.e., the die face, was smoothed down with a dead-smooth file until no spots or patches remained, and lapped with a fine cutting oilstone or very fine emery until perfect. The engraver covered the face with a thin layer of transfer wax and laid upon it, face down, a drawing of the head or eagle intended for the coin. He then carefully rubbed the design with a smooth instrument or burnisher, impressing each line into the wax. The impression was finally gone over with a chisel and graver which cut the design into the steel. As the engraver worked, he occasionally took impressions from the unfinished die, probably in soft wax or clay. This original die,[9] when completed, contained only the device, or central part of the design, and was never used to strike coins.[10] Its function was to raise a hub (i.e., a duplicate of itself in relief), which could sink a number of intaglio working dies.

The original die, with its face lubricated (to prevent rusting) was hardened by the following process. It was first heated to a bright cherry red, a delicate operation since excessive heat would cause even good-quality steel to shatter. The die was then immersed in a large cistern of cold water and swished back and forth to cool. Ideally, the die issued a bubbling or hissing sound, but sometimes it "piped" or "sung," indicating the presence of a crack.

When all the noise had ceased, the die was removed from the water. It was now, however, not only hard but very brittle, and so it was tempered in another vessel of water which was slowly boiled. When heated throughout, the die appeared almost deep blue. It was then removed and allowed to cool slowly, after which it was ready to raise a hub.

The hub blank was given a conical face to facilitate the displacement of metal during striking, and then annealed. The original die was fixed as the upper stake of a large screw press,[11] with the hub blank as the lower one. The die was then brought down with great force upon the blank, depressing its surface all around the device. Just as today, the blank had to be struck several times, with successive annealings, in order to fully bring up the relief.

---

[9] Today, we use the term "master die."

[10] Because of extensive retouching in the working die, it is sometimes difficult to ascertain the use of master dies. The 1793 Liberty Cap cents are the first U.S. coins to which they can be definitely assigned. From 1796, however, master dies are readily discerned in all denominations of United States coins.

[11] Called a multiplying press when used for this purpose.

Any hand-finishing more easily executed in relief was done on the hub, which was thereafter hardened and used to sink working dies. The remainder of the design was now added, the stars, numerals and letters by individual punches, the wreath (at first) by means of a graver.[12]

It might be asked why the Mint should adopt such a cumbrous method, instead of sinking complete master dies to begin with. The use of incomplete master dies and hubs, prior to 1836, has been attributed to an insufficient force in the screw press to raise and sink the border elements in a steel blank. While it is true that force diffuses as it spreads outward from the center of impact, the explanation is still inapplicable for the reason that the Mint used a manually operated screw press to multiply hubs and dies long after 1836. The use of incomplete matrices must therefore have been to preserve the life of the master die.

We may observe that a great many early coins with stars, lettering, etc., at the border, show peripheral die breaks. In other coins, the principal line of stress is from the center outward. These two characteristic die-breaks, the peripheral and the radial, are well known to all collectors of early die varieties. Since die breakage was a serious problem to the Mint, it would have been expedient to leave the punching of stars, letters and numerals for the working die, which was more expendable than the master matrix.

SMELTING OPERATIONS
Assaying

The output of the Mint, except for copper coins, depended entirely on the size of its deposits. There was no fund with which to purchase bullion, and when deposits were lean, the institution was idle.

Deposits of gold and silver were brought to the receiving room on the main floor of the Seventh Street building. Often the bullion took the form of ingots, but it was not uncommon for the Mint to receive nuggets, grains, foreign coins, jewelry, and plate. Whatever the form, it invariably contained an alloy of other metals, and sometimes traces of non-metallic substances. For this reason it was necessary to refine the metal, and the assay was really just that, although in a very small way. Let us take, for example, a deposit of gold.

The bullion was received by one of the treasurer's clerks and brought to the weighing room where it was weighed by the assayer (or an assistant) in the presence of the depositor. The depositor was given a receipt for the bullion by weight, the value not having yet been determined. The deposits were now taken to the assaying room on the third floor. Deposits of foreign coins of well established character were usually valued according to their known fineness and only occasionally assayed. For other deposits, an assay was performed as follows:

The assayer scraped a small sample piece, or "test," from each ingot or separate mass of bullion. The test was trimmed to a prescribed weight,

---

[12] However, the individual leaves and berries may have been placed in the die with punches. Reporting to a Congressional committee in January 1795, Mint engraver Robert Scot said that it took four or five days to cut each original die for the cent, and six to eight days for that of the dollar. After a hub had been raised, it was a matter of one or two more days to complete a working die. He added that this estimate depended on the success of the hardening and transfer processes.

Mint of the United States.

Treasurer's Office,
Oct 1st 1795

Gold Bullion.
No. 17

I acknowledge to have received from *John Vaughan of Philadelphia, merchant* gold bullion, weighing *two hundred and fifteen* ounces, pennyweights, and *twelve* grains, to be assayed and coined, and for which, according to the value of standard gold therein contained, gold coins of the United States are to be delivered to the said *John Vaughan* agreeably to law and the usage of the mint.

Nicholas Way
Treasurer.

Ounces.	dwts.	grs.
Gross weight 215		12

Deposit receipt made out to John Vaughan and signed by Nicholas Way, treasurer of the Mint. *National Archives.*

probably about 12 grains, and placed within a cone of thin lead sheets. The cone was then pressed into a ball, and deposited in a bone-ash cupel.[13]

The cupel was placed under a tunnel-shaped wrought iron muffle within the assay furnace, and heated by a charcoal fire. From time to time the assayer peeked through a small hole in the door of the furnace to follow the progress of the cupellation.

As the cupel became red hot, the base metals in the gold rapidly oxidized and, trickling out, were absorbed by the porous cupel. In this process, the lead covering served a dual purpose. First, it formed a very liquid oxide which washed away the oxides of the other base metals. Secondly, it prevented a portion of the silver from volatilizing from the direct contact of the heat.

When the cupellation was complete, the assay piece remained as a small lustrous bead, mostly of gold, but containing also a small amount of silver. The bead was then reweighed, and from the difference between the old and new weights the assayer calculated the loss in base metal.

Because of the inevitable loss of a minute quantity of silver by absorption into the cupel, and variations in the condition of the muffle, the assay admitted a liability to error of about one half per cent. To reduce this liability as far as possible, a "proof" piece of determinate standard, and near the fineness of the other, was cupelled at the same time. Any discrepancy found in the "proof" thus furnished a basis for correction which was applied to the assay sample.

Considerable difficulty existed in measuring high temperatures, and only an experienced assayer could successfully regulate the assay furnace. It was essential to maintain the requisite temperature (about 4000°F.), for if it fell too low, cupellation would cease, and if the heat became too intense, the silver would melt and be lost with the base metals.

The second part of the assay process, which was to separate the silver from the gold, was called "quartation" or "parting". This consisted of boiling the assay piece in nitric acid,[14] which dissolved the silver but left the gold intact. Since the gold would normally protect the silver from dissolution, the assayer first added silver to the mass until the proportion of gold was reduced to one fourth part. To do this he first determined the approximate proportion between the two metals by means of a specific gravity test.

After the metallic mass had been properly alloyed (quarted), it was annealed, flattened, reannealed, reduced in a small rolling mill to a plate, and finally rolled spirally into a "cornet." This cornet was placed in a small glass mattrass or parting glass which was shaped like a truncated cone. Nitric acid was then added in a weight proportional to the silver of three to two.

The mattrass was heated for about ten minutes in a bed of hot sand. When the effervescence had ceased entirely, the assayer decanted the silver-imbued nitric acid (silver nitrate). This boiling operation was twice repeated, each time with a fresh supply of acid in less quantity but of greater strength than previously. When the third solution had been decanted, the gold was gathered up and washed with boiling distilled water to remove any traces of the solution or silver which adhered to it. The assayer did not use a stronger solution at the beginning because it would have disunited the gold and reduced

---

[13] A small paste dish made from the ash of animal bones. The Mint kept a stockpile of these bones in the narrow passageway which divided the site, and which, for its peculiar use, was known as Bone Alley.

[14] To a small extent sulphuric acid was also used at the Mint for this purpose.

it to powder. This way, however, the metal was preserved in the form of small masses which could be easily collected.

Despite its cleaning, the gold now appeared to the assayer in a dull, tarnished state. It was thus reheated in the muffle furnace until red hot. During this operation, the gold contracted and solidified, and when removed and allowed to cool, it was found to possess its full beautiful color. The assay sample was reweighed, and the figure subtracted from its previous weight, giving the proportion of silver. With the assay complete, the treasurer calculated the value of the deposit (making an allowance of one pennyweight in every twelve ounces) and gave the depositor a receipt for the amount.[15]

Each separate mass of the deposit was now stamped with the assayer's seal—a spread eagle—and delivered to the smelting department of the Mint.

Before leaving the assay process, we might pause, with interest, to examine the weights and measures employed by the first Mint. The weights, as we shall later see, were brought from England in 1793 by Albion Cox. They were bell-shaped, with large handles, and contained screw plugs for adjusting. Coins and ignots were weighed in bulk, in pounds, ounces, pennyweights and grains. The pounds, however, were reduced to ounces before the assayer entered the figures in the ledger. This system, in which a pennyweight equalled twenty-four grains, was much more cumbrous than decimal computation based upon the gram.

Fineness was also expressed in the British way, i.e., in carats,[16] of which twenty-four equalled full purity. The carat was divided into four carat-grains (no relation to troy grains) and sub-divided into eighths. The smallest fraction which could thus be expressed was $\frac{1}{768}$ part.

Refining

If a deposit were excessively pure, the melter and refiner added to it a measured quantity of alloy. Inferior deposits were melted in a large cupel in the melting furnace.[17] Since the melted alloy was now more than could be absorbed by the cupel, it collected loosely over the gold where it was blown off by a bellows and removed.

As in the assay, cupellation was followed by parting. Here, however, the masses of silvery gold were melted in lead crucibles and poured into a large vessel of cold water where the metal formed flakes, or granules. As the molten metal was poured, it was diffused by quickly stirring the water in a circular motion with a long stick. The purpose of this operation was to expose as much as possible of the metal to the acid during parting.

The resultant granules were boiled in nitric acid in a large vessel, about seven inches wide at the bottom, a foot high, and having a one- or two-inch aperture at the top. The vessels were placed in water-filled copper pans, which were supported on trivets and heated over a flame. At first the heat had to be applied very slowly to prevent the as yet unsaturated acid from overflowing. If the heat became too intense, the melter and refiner carefully poured cold

---

[15] The assaying of a silver piece was, of course, performed entirely by cupellation, and involved only one calculation to determine the loss of the base metals.

[16] That is, in the physical operations. Otherwise the metric system was used.

[17] Even in its early days, the Mint had as many as seven furnaces, one for the assay, another for refining, a third for melting, plus three for annealing and one for boiling metal.

18th century refining furnace. Reproduced from "An Essay on Coining," an illustrated holograph by Samuel Thompson, Dublin, 1783, American Numismatic Society collection. Letter A indicates muffle, letter B the large cupel. The oxidized base metal can be seen as the dark fluid ring which is channeled into receptacle below.

water against the side of the pan. We can imagine how sometimes, to arrest a sudden rise of the acid, an apprentice must have poured the cold water directly onto the vessel, which thereupon cracked, releasing its contents into the copper pan.

Ideally, the parting glasses were well annealed and free from flaws, but sometimes they may have cracked because of exposure to cold or even when touched by the hand. Perhaps the Mint adopted the traditional safeguard which was to coat the outside of the vessel with a mixture of quicklime, flaked with beer and the whites of eggs, covered by a linen cloth. The cloth was wrapped around the lower part of the vessel and packed with a layer of clay and hair. The upper part remained uncovered, permitting the workman to observe the progress of the parting.

The melter and refiner had now to recover the silver from the nitric acid. This was done by the use of copper, a metal having a greater affinity for nitric acid than does silver. The silver nitrate solution was placed in a copper vessel, causing the copper to slowly dissolve. When the nitric acid had become perfectly saturated, a few fresh drops of acid were added, producing a silver precipitate. Finally, the copper nitrate solution was decanted, and the silver gathered together, washed in boiling distilled water and fused with saltpeter to scorify any particles that might have adhered.

The pure bullion was now standardized, i.e., alloyed in the correct proportions required for coinage, melted in a furnace, and cast in rectangular ingots of about a foot long, one to two-and-a-half inches wide, and a half inch thick. Each ingot was then individually assayed, and any found to be inferior were returned to the furnace. The others were stamped with the melter and refiner's seal—a circle of stars—and delivered to the chief coiner under whose supervision the metal was rolled, punched out and finally stamped with an impression.

As we recall, Congress resolved to coin its silver at a fineness of 1485/1664. The assayer Albion Cox complained that the fraction was cumbersome to work with, and that so great an alloy would prevent a proper rolling of the strips from which the planchets were punched out. To make his case more effective he also told Rittenhouse that the alloy made the coins too black. Cox recommended a diminution of the copper to 10 per cent, which would have changed the gross weight of the silver dollar from 416 to 412½ grains. This, in fact, was precisely what Congress did many years later, but at the time it vehemently opposed any further reduction in the weight of the silver coins. Rittenhouse then proposed that Congress increase the fine silver in the dollar from 371¼ to 374¾ grains. This would have reduced the alloy to one tenth, but increased the fine weight of the silver coins, bringing them closer to their nominal value. Having secured the approval of Jefferson and Hamilton, and anticipating early action by Congress, Rittenhouse began coining at the new standard in October 1794. Congress, however, ignored the matter, and for more than a year the Mint coined its silver at an unauthorized ratio. The most immediate effect of this practice was that depositors of silver had to pay an additional 2½ grains bullion (about 1 per cent extra) for every dollar they received. John Vaughan, a friend of President Washington and one of the Mint's largest depositors, suffered a loss of $2,260 for the reimbursement of which he later petitioned Congress. Director Boudinot, arguing like the good

Philadelphia lawyer he was, said the coins were still within their legal tolerance and Vaughan was therefore not entitled to his claim. The case dragged on until February 11, 1800 when Congress finally granted Vaughan his restitution.[18]

COINING OPERATIONS
Rolling

The alloyed ingots were annealed and then washed; those of gold with dilute nitric acid, those of silver with alum water (as nitric acid corrodes silver), and those of copper with salt water. After being rinsed and wiped clean, they were brought to the rolling room.

The Mint began with only one pair of rollers, but it purchased a second from John Harper on May 23, 1794 and, in early 1795, built a third which was appropriated to the smaller coinage. The rollers used to make strips for the small coins wrought about 7,500 ounces of metal daily, while the machines for large strips rolled twice this amount.

In a letter to Secretary of State Edmund Randolph, in December 1794, an English engineer named James Davy criticized operations at the Mint,[19] and in particular that of rolling. He said that the metal ingots should be rolled cold the first and second times as was done in England. He also maintained that the Mint's rollers were much too small, that they became overheated and thereby injured, and that time was lost waiting for them to cool. His advice, in so far as it was practicable, was evidently adopted, for the Mint's inventory of February 9, 1795 lists two rolling machines "one for hot, one for cold metal."

The rolling mill was run by a team (apparently a pair) of horses which tramped around a capstan in the basement below. The capstan turned a large horizontal gear-wheel which worked an equally large vertical wheel. The latter was connected by a shaft to the lower of the two pig-iron rollers which communicated the motion to the upper roller by means of copper pinions. Davy, in his report, suggested that the pinions were too short. He said they should be from eight to twelve inches long, made of steel, and have their teeth much closer together. The distance between the rollers was regulated by two large screws which turned at the top of either side of the casing, where they connected to the shaft of the upper roller. The rollers themselves, as we have indicated, were in a building adjoining the mill house.

The ingots were probably rolled at least ten times and reannealed after every two or three runs to prevent them from becoming brittle and cracking. By the end of the operation they had been reduced to long ribbons of metal approximating the thickness of the intended planchet.

On June 26, 1798 a pair of planishing rollers, which the Mint had ordered from London, arrived on the packet "Adriana." These were made of highly polished steel, and were operated manually, giving a high gloss to the gold strips.

Because of the crudeness of these early rollers, the gold and silver strips had finally to be equalized in a drawing machine. This consisted of a long

[18] John M. Willem, Jr., "The Case of John Vaughan and the Rittenhouse Dollar," *The Numismatic Scrapbook Magazine*, March 1957.

[19] Frank Stewart, *History of the First United States Mint;* also, Walter Breen, "Davy on Mint Processes in 1794," *The Numismatist*, August 1951.

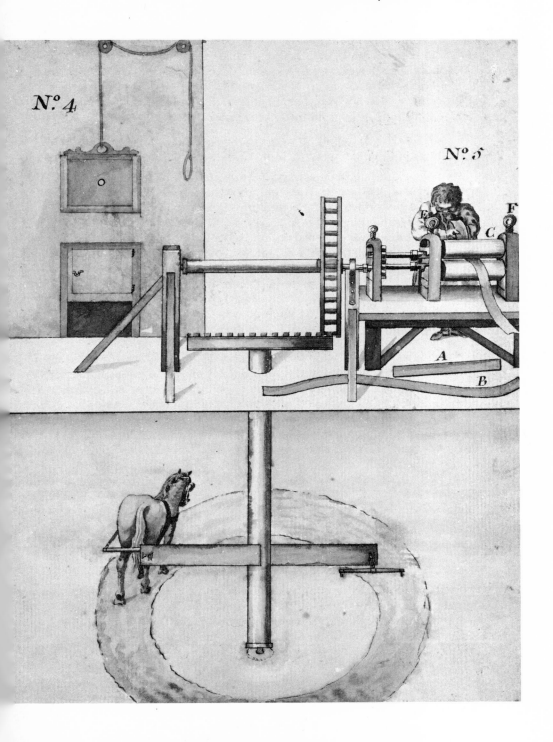

Horse-driven rolling mill, reproduced from "An Essay on Coining." An annealing furnace can be seen at the left.

bench, fixed at one end with a vertical frame. The frame enclosed a series of beveled slots, each the thickness of a particular planchet. A strip was annealed, and one end "pointed", i.e., given a chisel-shape by rollers with flattened spaces on them. It was then lubricated (if gold, by wax; if silver, by grease) and inserted through its particular slot. The chisel-end was locked in a pair of nippers, or "dog," which, being actuated by a crank, drew the strip backwards, allowing it to pass entirely through the board.

Planchet Cutting, or Blanking

After the strips had been washed in hot water to dissolve the lubricant, they were annealed, cut lengthwise, and brought to the planchet cutter which operated on the principle of a screw press. The cup, a circular block of metal with an aperture in the center, was screwed to the foundation. Directly above, a cutting cylinder was fastened to the base of a vertical column which could be moved up and down by rotating the two long arms to which it was attached. The arms were heavily weighted at each end, and could be turned by means of a long handle. The operator placed a strip over the cup, gave the handle of the press a jerk, and watched the punch corkscrew down, pushing a circular blank of metal through the aperture. Each planchet was then annealed and cleaned with Sal Enixum (crude acid Potassium Sulphate), while the perforated strips were returned to the furnace for remelting.

The critical James Davy reported that a child could perform the cutting operation as competently as the man employed. He recommended that the strips be widened, since only two rows of cents could then be cut from each. He said also that the annealed planchets should be allowed to cool slowly in dilute aquafortis (nitric acid) until blackened, then dipped in a stronger solution of the acid, and finally cleaned with oil of vitriol (sulphuric acid). This method would rid the metal of calx, make it brighter, and more faithfully preserve the polish of the dies.

In 1795, there were three planchet cutters at the Mint, each of which required one operator. Together, the machines could punch out from fifteen to eighteen thousand planchets daily.

Milling

The planchets were now weighed, and the "heavies" adjusted with one or two strokes across the face by a file. These crude gashes can still be seen on numerous early coins, much to the regret of collectors. Any planchets lighter than their tolerance permitted were consigned to the furnace.

The remainder were taken to the milling machine where their edges were impressed with a lettered or reeded device, as the case required. This ingenious machine was built on a table and consisted primarily of two parallel bars, one fixed and one movable, each containing half the device. The movable bar was grooved at the top, and slid along a thin rail. The operator placed two planchets between the bars and gave the crank a partial turn. This rotated a cog which worked along the rack, thrusting the movable bar forward sufficiently to entirely rotate the planchets. The distance between the two bars could be adjusted by means of two large screws which held the fixed bar.

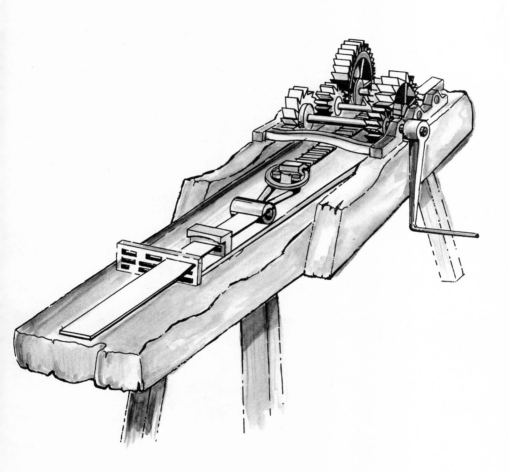

Drawing machine used to equalize strips. From a sketch by the author.

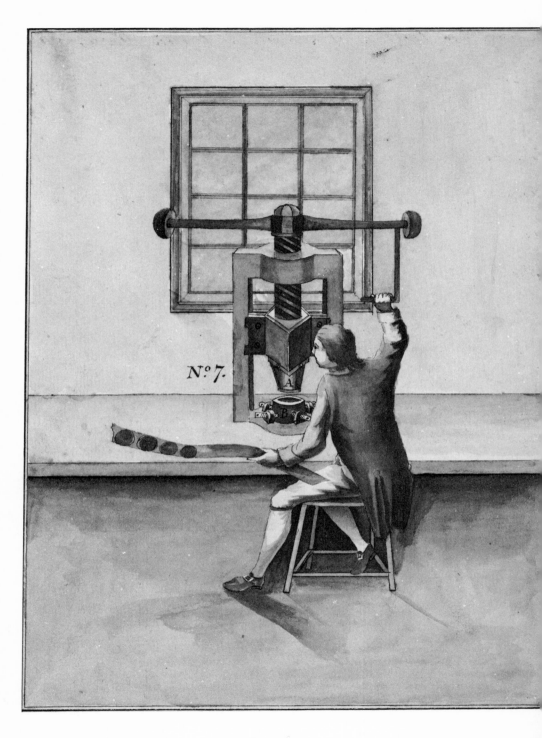

Planchet cutting press, reproduced from "An Essay on Coining."

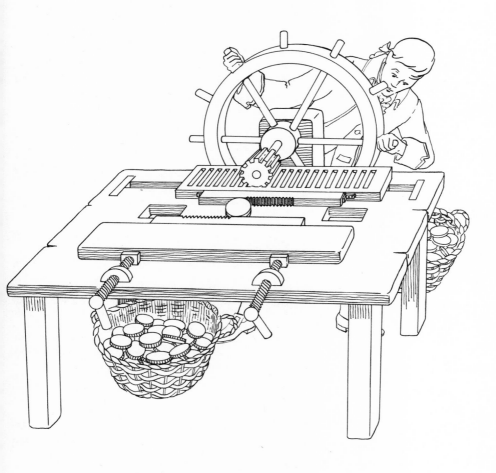

Milling machine, copied with modifications from "An Essay on Coining."

According to Boudinot's report of February 9, 1795 the Mint possessed only one milling machine which was operated by a single hand. The report said that the machine was to have been powered by horses, and that when these were obtained, its production would equal that of the cutting press.[20] In its present state, however, it could mark no more than ten thousand planchets a day.

Stamping

From the milling machine, the planchets were annealed, then taken to the coining presses, which, in February 1795, numbered three "with the improvement of supplying and discharging themselves by machinery." A fourth, for medals and dollars, was completed about three months later.

The coining presses worked by a screw, and were similar to those used for cutting out planchets. The obverse die, of course, replaced the cutting cylinder, while the reverse die was mounted in the cup. In 1793, Adam Eckfeldt invented a device for automatically feeding and ejecting the planchets. This is described in detail in B. L. C. Wailes' 1829 journal, from which we quote:

> "This [the coining press] is a very powerful, ingenious, simple (tho very perfect) piece of machinery. It consists (like the cutting machine) of a very powerful upright screw, to the top of which is affixed a heavy & strong lever worked with great apparent ease by one man at each end, & by which the screw is made to make about one fourth of a revolution & returning instantly to its former position. At the lower end of the screw is affixed the die which gives the impression on the upper side, & immediately under it is the die containing the impression for the reverse of the coin, around which a pair of nippers (which gives the milling or impression on the edges),[21] & by which placing as a rivit in the manner of shears admits the introduction of the coin before & its ejection after it receives the impression. Near the lower end of the Screw stands a tube sufficiently large to admit a considerable number of the coins, one on top of the other, which may be termed the hopper, at the bottom of which is an apparatus sufficiently large to admit the passage of the coin, one at a time. The lower end in the file (or hopper) is struck out with great accuracy by a thin piece of iron made to strike edgewise at each movement of the lever and is conveyed by a channel formed for the purpose & is conveyed directly on & under the dye. The screw is brought down & the *nippers* close with a force that makes the impression. The lever is instantly brought back, the *nippers* open, the stamped coin is struck out of its place & conveyed into a Box by a spout (or conductor) as the Screw rises, and another unstamped coin takes its place, & the Screw comes down again."

The importance of the automatic feed can be inferred from Pistrucci's description of the 19th century London Mint, where every "moneyer" had lost at least one of his finger joints.[22]

Sellers, who as a child lived and played in the vicinity of the first Mint, has also left a graphic description of the stamping operation.[23]

---

[20] It is doubtful whether the Mint, at any time, actually employed a horse mill for this purpose.

[21] The close reeded collar had been introduced only the previous year. Before that time, planchets were reeded in the milling machine, and then struck in an open collar to avoid squashing the edge impression.

[22] Sir John Craig, *The Mint,* Cambridge University Press, 1953.

[23] George Escol Sellers, "Early Engineering Reminiscences," *American Machinist,* May 4, 1893; also, R. H. Williamson, "A Visit to the U.S. Mint in 1812," *The Numismatist,* Jan. 1951.

Screw coining press, reproduced from "An Essay on Coining." At the Philadelphia Mint, planchets were fed by a hopper and, after striking, automatically ejected.

In the rear room, facing on the alley,[24] with a large lowdown window opening into it, a fly press stood, that is a screw-coining press mostly used for striking the old copper cents. Through this window the passersby in going up and down the alley could readily see the bare-armed vigorous men swinging the heavy endweighted balanced lever that drove the screw with sufficient force so that by the momentum of the weighted ends this quick-threaded screw had the power to impress the blank and thus coin each piece. They could see the rebound or recoil of these end weights as they struck a heavy wooden spring beam, driving the lever back to the man that worked it; they could hear the clanking of the chain that checked it at the right point to prevent its striking the man, all framing a picture very likely to leave a lasting impression, and there are no doubt still living many in Philadelphia who can recollect from this brief notice the first mint.

Sellers goes on to relate an incident which happened at the Mint when he was only four years old.

One day in the charge of my elder brother I stood on tip-toe with my nose resting on the iron bar placed across the open window of the coining room to keep out intruders, watching the men swing the levers of the fly press; it must have been about noon, for Mr. Eckfeldt came into the room, watch in hand, and gave the signal to the men who stopped work. Seeing me peering over the bar, he took me by the arms and lifted me over it. Setting me down by the coining press he asked me if I did not want to make a cent, at the same time stopping the men who had put on their jackets to leave the room. He put a blank planchet into my hand, showed me how to drop it in, and where to place my hand to catch it as it came out; the lever and weights were swung, and I caught the penny as we boys called cents, but I at once dropped it. Mr. Eckfeldt laughed and asked me why I dropped it? Because it was hot and I feared it would burn me; he picked it up and handed it to me, then certainly not hot enough to burn; he asked if it was not cold when he gave it to me to drop into the press; he told me to look and see there was no fire, and feel the press that it was cold; he then told me I must keep the cent until I learned what made it hot; then I might, if I liked, spend it for candy.

1816-1832

We have earlier mentioned the steam engine that the Mint installed on June 24, 1816 after a fire consumed the old wooden mill house. The engine, purchased from Oliver Evans, was used to drive the rolling and drawing machines as well as one of the planchet cutters. The drawing machine, hereafter known as the drawing bench, was evidently built in the 1820's on a principle invented by Sir John Barton, deputy comptroller of the Royal Mint. Barton's bench was built in 1816 and adopted by the English authorities towards the end of 1819.[25]

The upright frame of the drawing bench enclosed a single slot, with its inner diameter regulated by two vertical steel cylinders set apart at the required distance. The operator inserted a strip through the cylinders and, by pressing a foot pedal, caused it to be seized by nippers projecting from a small, iron carriage. With another touch of the pedal, a hook in the rear of the carriage dropped between the links of a moving, perpetual chain. The carriage was thus drawn along its track, pulling the strip through the slot. Finally, the strip was released and the carriage unhooked and rolled back by hand to its starting position.

The new planchet cutter worked by the action of a small eccentric wheel

[24] Evidently the room at 629 Filbert Street.
[25] Sir John Craig, *The Mint*.

(a wheel with its axis slightly off-center) on top of the press. The eccentric was encased in a "tire" which projected a rod, and did not rotate with the wheel. As the eccentric turned (driven by a large fly-wheel), its long and short radii passed alternately over the rod, pushing it down and raising it up with great force and rapidity, the cutting edge at the end of the rod punching out a planchet with every stroke. This press is said to have produced up to two hundred and fifty planchets a minute, and was still in working order in 1860, never having required even fifty cents worth of repairs.[26]

---

[26] Illustrations of this type of planchet cutter and an improved drawing bench are shown in the next section.

CHAPTER 8

Members of the First Mint

ON THE WHOLE, THE OFFICERS of the first Mint were men of merit and ability, some of them patriots during the American Revolution. We have already met Rittenhouse and Voigt, and the following sketches will acquaint the reader with the other principals.

Directors

David Rittenhouse, April 1792 to June 1795.

Henry William De Saussure, the second Director of the Mint, was a lawyer of considerable distinction. In 1789, he helped prepare a constitution for South Carolina, and two years later served on the state legislature. In June 1795, while at New York, De Saussure received a commission to head the Mint. Believing himself unqualified, he protested to Hamilton, who reassured him and encouraged him to accept. De Saussure served as Director for only a few months, resigning in October because of the hostility of Congress. Washington expressed his regret at the decision and consulted him respecting the appointment of a successor.

The third Director, Elias Boudinot, was a Revolutionary War patriot and, like his predecessor, a distinguished lawyer. In 1776, Boudinot was appointed Commissary General of Prisoners, and three years later elected a member of the Continental Congress. In 1782, he became president of the Congress, and it was Boudinot's pen which signed the peace treaty with Great Britain. After the adoption of the Constitution he was again elected to Congress, and continued to serve until his appointment, in October 1795, as Director of the

Mint. Boudinot was at first reluctant to accept the Directorship because he lacked a thorough grounding in chemistry. He recommended that Dr. Isaac Smith, a Congressman, be appointed instead. Acting Secretary of State Thomas Pickering consulted Benjamin Rush, the celebrated surgeon and husband of Boudinot's niece, regarding the relative merits of the two men. Rush replied [1] "that in everything connected with philosophy" Smith was decidedly superior to Boudinot. But Pickering preferred Boudinot, and Rush lent him some science textbooks for study.

On September 23, Washington wrote to Pickering: [2]

> . . . For reasons you have assigned, I think it best that Mr. Boudinot should fill the Directorship of the Mint, and request he may be informed so. At the same time, urge him to come forward, if for no other purpose than to arrange matters with the present occupant, and derive from him all the insight into the business, his experience has acquired, and which he promised me he would communicate to his successor. Inclosed is a blank commission for the Successor of Mr. Desaussure, which may take date at the close of his services, according to the arrangement proposed above.

Boudinot retained the Directorship for ten years, after which he retired from public life to pursue literary and philanthropic activities.

Robert Patterson, the fourth Director of the Mint, was professor of mathematics at the University of Pennsylvania when he received his appointment from President Jefferson. On April 27, 1805 Jefferson wrote to Dr. Patterson: [3]

> I have learnt indirectly that Mr. Boudinot will shortly resign the office of Director of the Mint, in that event I should feel very happy in confiding the public interest in that place to you. Will you give me leave to send you the commission in the event of Mr. B's resignation? I pray you consider this as confidential, as what you write me shall be. Accept my friendly salutation.
>
> P.S. I should be sorry to withdraw you from the college; nor do I conceive that this office need do it; it's duties will easily admit your devoting the ordinary college hours to that institution. Indeed it is so possible that the Mint may some time be discontinued that I could not advise a permanent living to be given up for it.

Jefferson wrote to Patterson again on June 13, saying that Boudinot had given his notice, and would resign at the end of the month. Patterson received his commission on July 2, and served as Director of the Mint until July, 1824. During his administration the Mint was partly mechanized through the introduction of steam power.

In tendering his resignation, Patterson warmly recommended his son-in-law, Dr. Samuel Moore, for the appointment of Director. This came as a blow to the Director's son, Robert Maskell Patterson, who likewise aspired for the office. Against the latter's wishes, however, an intervention was sought by Thomas Leiper, father-in-law of the younger Patterson, who solicited a letter of favor from Jefferson.[4] The attempt was abortive, and Moore was appointed in July 1824. Formerly a physician and merchant, Moore served as Director

---

[1] Pickering to Washington, Sept. 18, 1795 *The Papers of George Washington,* Library of Congress collection.

[2] *The Writings of George Washington,* Vol. 34, Fitzpatrick.

[3] Frank Stewart, *History of the First United States Mint.*

[4] Letter of Thomas Leiper to Jefferson, July 14, 1824; letters of Jefferson to Leiper and to President James Monroe July 22; also, letter of Samuel Moore to Thomas Jefferson, September 21, 1824. *The Papers of Thomas Jefferson,* Library of Congress collection.

of the Mint until May 1835. During his term the Mint moved to Chestnut Street, and plans were drawn for the complete mechanization of its operations.

Coiners

Although Voigt received a commission on January 29, 1793, his employment as chief coiner remained on a tentative basis. The search for a more qualified officer continued in France and England, and once again there appears to have been some hope of obtaining Droz, who was rather unhappily situated in Paris. On March 12, however, Thomas Pinckney advised Jefferson that Gouverneur Morris had given up on Droz. Jefferson had not yet received this letter when, on April 20, he wrote to Pinckney: [5]

> We shall be glad to receive the assayer you hope to procure, as soon as possible, for we cannot get one in this country equal to the business in all its parts. With respect to Mr. Drost, we retain the same desire to engage him, but are forced to require an immediate decision, as the officer employed in the interim, and who does tolerably well, will not continue much longer under an uncertainty of permanent employment. I must therefore desire you to press Mr. Morris to bring Drost to an immediate determination; but we place the matter on this ground with him, that if he is not embarked by the first day of July next, we shall give a permanent commission to the present officer, and be free to receive no other.

On December 30, 1793 Jefferson advised President Washington that it would be impossible to obtain from abroad a more able coiner than Henry Voigt.

Adam Eckfeldt, the second chief coiner of the Mint, was the son of John Jacob Eckfeldt who forged dies for Robert Morris in 1783. Snowden remarks that the senior Eckfeldt owned a large smithery which was "celebrated for the manufacture of sickles and trowels, the best of that day," [6] and that Adam, who served as his father's apprentice, was trained to do all kinds of iron work, and possessed a peculiar aptitude for machinery.

Adam Eckfeldt's connection with the Mint probably began in January 1792, when he supervised the striking of the "Getz" Washington head patterns for Robert Morris. From the following year, he was frequently engaged to build machinery, turn and forge dies and do smith work, and from July 1795 he was regarded as a permanent employee. In a Mint payroll dated October 10, 1795 Eckfeldt is listed as "Die Forger and Turner" at the salary of $500 per annum. On January 1, 1796 he was appointed assistant coiner, and his duties as such were very broad. In a letter to Jefferson on October 14, 1806 Director Patterson requested a $200 per annum increase for Eckfeldt who was said to have "the management of the whole coining department." With Voigt's death, in February 1814, Eckfeldt became chief coiner, a position he still occupied when the Mint relocated in 1833.

Assayers

On December 27, 1792 Rittenhouse wrote to Washington: [7]

> Sir: We have begun to assay some of the European coins and shall proceed tomorrow at the mint, if it will be convenient for the President to attend about 12

---

[5] *The Papers of Thomas Jefferson,* Library of Congress collection.
[6] James Ross Snowden, *Washington and National Medals,* 1861.
[7] R. W. Julian, "The Mint in 1792," *The Numismatic Scrapbook Magazine,* April 1962.

o'clock. Should any accident happen before that time to occasion delay I will give you notice.

In the absence of a regular officer, the assay was performed by David Ott, who on January 7, 1793 was paid $24.17 "for assaying coins at the Mint and expenses." On the same day, Rittenhouse wrote to Jefferson that a small source of error had been detected in the assay, too late for correction, and that it would be guarded against in the future. Jefferson transmitted the assay report to the House on January 8, and it no doubt served as a basis for the Act of February 9, 1793 which established the legal value of certain foreign coins.

Apparently Hamilton ran some assays of his own, for on November 25, 1795, a treasury warrant for $27. was made out "in favor of John Shield, assignee of Ephraim Brasher; being for assays made by said Brasher, in the year 1792, for the Mint, on sundry coins of gold and silver, pursuant to instructions from the then Secretary of the Treasury." [8] Ephraim Brasher is better known to numismatists as the maker of a rare gold coin called "Brasher's doubloon."

The first commissioned assayer of the Mint was Albion Cox, a relative of William Cox of Cox, Merle & Co., refiners and bankers of Little Britain. This firm recommended Albion Cox as being the equal of any man in England in assaying gold, silver, copper and lead.

Cox had left America only a few years earlier and was not particularly anxious to return. In 1786, he co-contracted with Thomas Goadsby and Walter Mould to furnish the state of New Jersey with a copper coinage.[9] A breach soon occurred, however, between Cox and Goadsby on the one hand, and Mould on the other, and a new contract was drawn up permitting the latter to coin separately. Mould then brought suit against his former companions but the case was never settled. A year later, Goadsby, together with Samuel Atlee, a member of a private "coin manufactory" in Newburgh, New York, sued Cox who, as a result, was condemned to debtors' prison. Cox escaped and fled to England where, ironically, he was offered the esteemed and lucrative position of assayer for the United States Mint.

On March 8, 1793 Cox was provisionally engaged for a period of three years, and on behalf of the Mint he purchased and brought from England five cases of glassware, assay scales, weights and other equipment necessary for his work.

Pinckney informed Jefferson of the arrangement in a letter written on the 12th: [10]

Mr. *Albion Cox* having been recommended to me to fill the office of Assayer of our Mint I made all the requisite Enquiries concerning his abilities and Integrity and received a satisfactory account of both, but as he has been under misfortunes in America I thought it prudent not to make a final agreement with him unless his Character should bear the Test & Inquiry there as well as in this Country and for this reason you will observe a clause in our Agreement stipulating that it shall be void if not approved by the President. I enclose a copy of his receipt for the Money furnished him in part of Salary and for Articles bought. He had been employed some time in procuring these articles and conceives his salary should commence from the time in which he was so engaged. Though I saw the Equity of the Proposal, yet being limited by my Instructions I told him all I could do would be to state the matter to you.—I believe you must go on with the other Officers you

---

[8] *American State Papers*, Finance, Vol. 1, p. 366, "Estimated expenditures for the year 1796."
[9] Sylvester S. Crosby, *Early Coins of America*.
[10] *Diplomatic Dispatches*, State Dept. Instructions, Record Group 59, National Archives.

have as Mr. Morris thinks he cannot procure Droze, and I cannot obtain others in conformity to my directions.

Jefferson replied on June 4: "Tho' the character of Mr. Albion Cox here was not exactly what we would have wished, yet he will be received if he can give the security required by law."

Cox served as assayer of the Mint until December 1795 when he died suddenly of apoplexy. He was succeeded, on the 12th, by the well known Quaker, Joseph Richardson, who held the appointment for thirty-six years. Interestingly, Richardson was at first uncertain whether to remain at the Mint because of the noxious fumes imparted during the assaying process. He died in March 1831 and was succeeded by his son, John Richardson. The younger Richardson had assisted in the assaying department for about ten years and, according to Director Moore, was highly skilled. Richardson resigned after a year and was succeeded by Jacob R. Eckfeldt, son of the already legendary Adam Eckfeldt.

Melter and Refiners

Under the Act of March 3, 1795 David Ott, who had served as unofficial melter and refiner since the previous November, was appointed on a pro tem basis. A permanent commission, however, was finally given to Joseph Cloud. Cloud was appointed by Washington on January 2, 1797, and served for the remainder of the first Mint.

Engravers

In his Congressional report of February 1795, Elias Boudinot remarked that the chief coiner had been forced to make the Mint's dies until a permanent engraver could be hired. Boudinot's statement obviously does not refer to 1792, which was considered a pre-operational year, but may be understood to cover the early part of 1793.

The 1793 chain cent is an exceedingly crude piece of work and shows the same artistic defects as the 1792 small cent. It can almost certainly be attributed to Voigt. The Droz attribution given by Crosby [11] was purely speculative and can now be rejected.

On March 20, 1793 the *Pennsylvania Gazette* reported: "The American cents (says a letter from Newark) do not answer our expectations. The chain on the reverse is but a bad omen for liberty, and liberty herself appears to be in a fright.—May she not justly cry out in the words of the Apostle 'Alexander the coppersmith hath done me much harm; the Lord reward him according to his works.'" [12]

It may have been such diatribes that led Voigt to assign the cutting of new cent dies to another artist—presumably Adam Eckfeldt. Not only is the modeling of the head and the flowing hair style similar to that on Eckfeldt's 1792 disme, but the reverse is a virtual prototype for his 1793 half cent. Eckfeldt discarded the chain in favor of a wreath design, and placed a trefoil beneath Liberty's head. The new cents were issued from April 9, 1793.

---

[11] Sylvester Crosby, "The Cents of 1793," *American Journal of Numismatics*, Jan. 1897.
[12] A jibe on Alexander Hamilton. Voigt probably got the idea for his chain from the Fugio cent.

As of June, a permanent engraver had not yet been hired for the Mint. Jefferson writing on the 4th to Thomas Pinckney,[13] rejected the proposal of an English artist named Holloway who solicited the office "for life."

> With respect to Mr. Holloway, my former letters will have informed you that the necessity of proceeding in our coinage would admit no longer delay in the appointment of officers; and that for this reason a day was fixed after which even Drost would not be received. The same reason operates more powerfully against Mr. Holloway; the office he desired cannot remain so long unfilled and we shall be obliged to fill it immediately with some one of the officers here, some of whom are pretty good.

Although the word "officers" in the last sentence is ambiguous, we can infer that Jefferson intended to engage an engraver from the talent at hand. It is doubtful that the Secretary, as a man of taste, could have considered Voigt for the position. More likely candidates would have been Joseph Wright or Adam Eckfeldt. Of the two men, Wright was an incomparably better artist, but Eckfeldt's other qualifications would have made him a more economical choice.

While Jefferson and Rittenhouse were still pondering the matter, Eckfeldt engraved the dies from which the first half cents were struck on July 20. Thereafter, he was employed for other purposes, and Joseph Wright was appointed engraver. Wright probably began work at the Mint in August 1793, a few weeks before his death of yellow fever. His appointment is acknowledged by Dunlap, and implied by the letters of Jefferson and Washington. On October 11, Washington wrote to Jefferson: [14] "I have no objection to the Director of the Mint, with your concurrence, chosing an Engraver in place of Mr. Wright." Jefferson, sojourning in Germantown, Pa., wrote in turn to Rittenhouse on November 6: [15] "It has been understood that Mr. Wright our engraver is dead. If this be the fact, will you be so good as to recommend for the office such person as you think best qualified to execute it?" It is thus almost certain that the beautifully designed Liberty Cap cents, which were issued from September 18 on (and which, in modeling, so closely resemble the 1792 eagle-on-globe pattern), were struck from dies engraved by Wright. The Liberty Head is classical; strong and noble, yet delicately modeled and thoroughly feminine. The hair is neatly arranged in soft curls. Behind the bust a liberty cap is held on a pole. The wreath is also more perfectly formed, and the annoying strings of berries have been eliminated.

On November 23, Jefferson wrote to the English-born engraver, Robert Scot: [16]

> Sir, the President of the United States, desiring to avail the Public of your Services as Engraver of the Mint, I have now the honor of inclosing you the commission and of expressing to you the sentiments [of] perfect respect with which, I am etc.

Scot had practised as a watchmaker in England, where he probably engraved the fancy work on numerous watch cases. In the *Pennsylvania Packet* for June 5, 1781 he is advertised as follows: "Robert Scot, late engraver to the State of Virginia, begs to inform the public, that he executes that business in all its

---

[13] *The Papers of Thomas Jefferson,* Library of Congress collection.
[14] Frank Stewart, *History of the First United States Mint.*
[15] Ibid.
[16] *The Papers of Thomas Jefferson,* Library of Congress collection.

branches, at his shop, the west side of Front Street, next door to the corner of Vine Street, Philadelphia."

During the American Revolution, Scot engraved plates for the subsistence money, bills of exchange and office scales used by Robert Morris and, later, the architectural plates for Dobson's Encyclopedia. At the time of his appointment, Scot was already advanced in years and his talents, never marked, show a rapid decline.

His earliest attempt on the silver coinage is described in the *New Hampshire Gazette* for December 2, 1794:

> Some of the dollars now coining at the Mint of the United States have found their way to this town. A correspondent put one into the editor's hands yesterday. Its weight is equal to that of a Spanish dollar, but the metal appears finer. One side bears a *Head*, with flowing tresses, incircled by *Fifteen Stars*, and has the word "LIBERTY" at the top, and the date, 1794, at the bottom. On the reverse, is the *Bald Eagle*, enclosed in an *Olive Branch*, round which are the words "One Dollar, or Unit, Hundred Cents." The *tout ensemble* has a pleasing effect to a connoisseur; but the touches of the graver are too delicate, and there is a want of that boldness of execution which is necessary to durability and currency.

Mint Director De Saussure apparently found the *tout ensemble* less than pleasing for he engaged Gilbert Stuart, the renowned portrait painter, to re-design the Liberty head. Stuart had come to America to paint President Washington, arriving in Philadelphia only the previous November. We learn of the artist's connection with the Mint from Director James Ross Snowden, who, more than a half century later, wrote: [17]

> The head of Liberty on the dollar of 1795 was designed by Stuart, the celebrated portrait painter, at the request of the Director, as we learn from a relation of the family, Stuart facetiously remarking that "Liberty on the other coins had run mad" —referring to the dishevelled hair on the previous coins—"We will bind it up, and thus render her a steady matron."

As most artists work from models, it is tempting to speculate on the possible identity of Stuart's Liberty Head. A single portrait among his collected works, that of Mrs. William Bingham [18] (Ann Willing), whom he first painted in England in 1780, bears a close resemblance, despite the three-quarter view. Interestingly, Stuart began a second portrait of Mrs. Bingham in 1795 (when he probably saw the earlier work), but never completed it.

De Saussure apparently did not even trust Scot to prepare a die from Stuart's drawing, for the expense books of the Mint show that John Eckstein, a Philadelphia artist, was paid thirty dollars on September 9, 1795 for "Two models [i.e. original dies] for dollars." It was probably Eckstein, rather than Stuart, who redesigned the eagle.

Sully has described Eckstein as "a thorough-going drudge in the arts. He could do you a picture in still life—history—landscape—portrait—he could model —cut a head in marble—or anything you please." [19] Eckstein advertised himself

---

[17] James Ross Snowden, *Washington and National Medals*, 1861. The late David Bullowa rejected Snowden's remarks on the ground that the episode is not recorded in any of Stuart's biographies ("Gilbert Stuart and the Silver Dollar", *The Numismatist*, March 1942). It seems unreasonable, however, to insist that a pencil drawing, possibly executed in a few minutes, would necessarily be recorded for posterity.

[18] Mrs. Bingham, a friend of both Washington and Jefferson, was considered the most beautiful, charming and intelligent woman in Philadelphia.

[19] *Diary of William Dunlap*, Vol. 2. Printed for the New York Historical Society, 1930.

as an "historical painter and statuary to the King of Prussia." He is listed in the Philadelphia directories for various intervals between 1796 and 1816.

The first of the new silver dollars were struck in October 1795.[20] During the following year, Scot copied the designs on the other silver and copper denominations, but left his fat and frowsy capped-Liberty to adorn the gold coinage.

A contemporary criticism of our early coins is given in a letter from Carlisle Pollock, a New York City theatre agent, to General Williams of Salem New York.[21] Pollock (despite his claim), had probably not yet seen the new dollar when, on January 26, 1796 he wrote:

> . . . Heaven forbid that future ages should judge of the taste and talents of the present citizens of America by so mean and pitiful a sample of their works. I have seen all the coins already issued, and nothing can be more wretched; an unmeaning fool's-head on one side, and something that resembles a turkey cock on the other. Oh, shame, shame, shame! The Eagle of America mantling the arms of the United States, as you see it on the City Hall, would have been a dignified impression, and on the other side, if the President's head should be too *aristocratic,* a plough and a sheaf of wheat would be better than an Idiot's head with flowing hair, which was intended to designate the head of an Indian squaw. Since I began with this subject, I shall beg leave to mention an error in opinion that prevails with respect to the arms of America, and which the new coin justifies me in stating. In the coins the bald eagle is the representative of America, and is there placed as her arms. This is *not* the case, the arms of America are stripes of blue, red and white on a shield; the blue denotes dominion, the red implies power of force, and the white represents purity. To decorate and embellish the arms, the bald eagle was introduced, as a mantle or supporter to the shield, *but making no part of the arms,* according to the rules of heraldry; no more than the lion and the unicorn make a part of the British arms; they are *supporters* of the arms, but *not the arms themselves* . . .

Pollock's criticism may have reflected general opinion, for beginning the same year, a large heraldic eagle gradually replaced the naked bird on the reverse of the gold and silver coins. Although the heraldic device is also found on some 1795 half eagles, these are known to have been struck from a leftover obverse die the following year.

In November 1794 John Smith Gardner was appointed assistant engraver, and to him are attributed the head punches and wreaths for the 1795 and 1796 Liberty Cap cents, the "small head" half dollars of 1795 and the half cents of 1795-97.[22] The Gardner heads are neat and compact, their hair clipped and showing a short end curl. On the half cents, the size of the head is conspicuously reduced. The last payment recorded to Gardner is on March 31, 1796 for "78 days' work as assistant engraver @ 3.00."

On May 23, 1801 President Jefferson wrote to Mint Director Boudinot: [23]

> I received from a German of the name of Reich some specimens of engraving & a wish to be employed. He is just arrived & in distress. I send them to you by Mr. Leslie that you may judge for yourself whether he may be employed usefully for the public. I have taken the liberty of desiring [him] to present himself to you.

---

[20] Walter Breen, "Silver Coinages of the Philadelphia Mint 1794-1916," *The Coin Collector's Journal,* 1958.

[21] *The Coin Collector's Journal,* February 1877.

[22] Walter Breen, "The United States Minor Coinages 1793-1916," *The Coin Collector's Journal,* May-June 1954; "Silver Coinages of the Philadelphia Mint 1794-1916," *The Coin Collector's Journal,* 1958.

[23] *The Papers of Thomas Jefferson,* Library of Congress collection. Reich had emigrated from Germany as a bondslave, and was enfranchised by Henry Voigt, who employed him to make scales and other fine work.

Boudinot replied on June 16: [24]

> I have been waited on by Mr. Reich and was much pleased with his work; he has been liberated from his servitude by means of one of the officers of the Mint since which I have set him to work on a particular medal to be ascertained of his abilities. I am obliged to use great precaution in regard to employing him in the Mint before I have good evidence of his character.

Although Reich proved himself to be the finest die-sinker in Philadelphia, it was some years before he could secure a permanent position at the Mint. Indeed, on December 24, 1804 John Lithgow wrote to Jefferson: [25]

> I have often lamented the misery and distress in which artists find themselves on their arrival in this country, and therefore I cannot let slip the present occasion of reminding you of Reisch [sic] the Engraver or Dye-sinker—He is acknowledged to be one of the first in his line in the world besides being a man of polite manners, pure morals and an admirer of Republican principles & yet it is with difficulty he can procure a bare existence—The coin of the United States has a wretched appearance after they have been a month in circulation, executed by Scot who has made an independent fortune & who would [not] wish to employ Reisch only from a fear that the excellence of his work would cause him to be supplanted. I have heard it said the other day, that it was a shame there was only one Republican officer in the Mint (Voigt)[26] and that we should have such poor coin while we could command the talents of Reisch and do honour to the Jeffersonian Age. I wish that I had power I think I could provide a remedy for these evils without making the remedy equal to or worse than the disease, which is the only thing that ought to prevent a good man from following the bent of his benevolent intentions. I think Scot might be induced to give him a subordinate Situation—to give him part of the loaf with a view to securing the rest, as we poor people do with our Liberties . . .

Jefferson, inaccessible to flattery, refused to pressure Boudinot, and the situation dragged on until March 25, 1807 when the new Director, Robert Patterson, wrote to the President: [27]

> Our present Engraver, Mr. Scot, though indeed a meritorious and faithful Officer, is yet so far advanced in life, that he cannot very long be expected to continue his labours. In the event of his sickness or death, the business of the Institution would probably be stopped for some time, since few, if any one could be found qualified to supply his place, except Mr. Reich, an artist with whose talents, I presume, you are not unacquainted, and this gentleman, not finding business here sufficient for his support, is I understand, about to remove to Europe. A small salary would, however, retain him in the country, and secure his services to the Mint—And, in truth, the beauty of our coins would be greatly improved by the assistance of his masterly hand.
>
> An assistant Engraver was formerly employed by Mr. Rittenhouse, and by Mr. De Saussure—and with your approbation, Sir, I would immediately employ Mr. Reich in that capacity. He is willing, for the present, to accept of the moderate compensation of Six hundred dollars per annum; and should this gentleman be employed, perhaps more than his salary would be saved to the public, in what is usually expended on the engraving of dies for medals, but which might then be executed by an artist in their own service, with little or no additional expence.

Jefferson immediately consented, and Reich entered the Mint service on April 1. On the following day, Patterson wrote to Jefferson that the artist was "now

---

[24] Frank Stewart, *History of the First United States Mint.*
[25] *The Papers of Thomas Jefferson,* Library of Congress collection.
[26] Lithgow had evidently forgotten about Rush.
[27] Patterson Du Bois, "Our Mint Engravers," *American Journal of Numismatics,* July 1883.

preparing a set of new dies in which some improvements in the devices will be introduced, (adhering, however, strictly to the letter of the law) which it is hoped will meet with public approbation."

The devices were introduced on the half dollar and half eagle. In the following year they were placed on the cent and quarter eagle, and in 1809 on the half cent and dime. The devices vary somewhat for each of the metals. On the gold coins, Liberty wears a loosely fitting cap which folds over behind the head. The eagle, though still heraldic, is more natural and artistic than formerly. On the silver coins, the end of the cap is bent over the top, facing forward, and the eagle's wings are inverted. On the coppers, the head is adorned with a simple Liberty band.

Modern writers, inspired by contemporary appraisals of Reich, have been too generous in their estimation of the artist. The truth is that Reich, though an excellent die-sinker, was only a moderately talented portrait engraver. It was his good fortune, however, to encounter little competition from the aging Scot.

Reich's design for the silver coins was far from an improvement. The reason (according to a Mint tradition still current a half century later) was that the artist had actually portrayed his "fat mistress" in order to make her famous. An alternative version of the story is that the fat mistress belonged to E. Luigi Persico who furnished Reich with the design. This, however, is impossible since the Neapolitan Persico did not arrive in America until 1818.[28] Reich redesigned the head before placing it on the dime, and in 1810 the new device was substituted on the half dollar. Reich's designs are more attractive on the gold and copper coins, although the matronly appearance of Liberty never quite disappears.

Unable to secure an increase in his wages, Reich finally resigned on March 31, 1817, leaving the Mint after exactly ten years. Director Patterson failed to induce Christian Gobrecht to accept the subordinate office, and Scot passed his remaining days without competition. During all this time, Scot had made no attempt to recoup his authority, engraving new original dies only as required. The first instance was in 1813, when he redesigned the obverse of the half eagle. In 1816 he placed a new head on the cent, and in 1821, another on the quarter eagle. From the crudeness of these last designs one suspects that Scot's vision had begun to fail. He died in November 1823, having served the Mint for thirty years.

On December 1, Gobrecht wrote to President Monroe soliciting the position of chief engraver.[29] Gobrecht was an engraver, inventor and mechanic all rolled into one. Among his inventions are the medal-ruling machine (for reproducing relief on a plane surface), a kind of melodion, a talking doll, and the camera lucida. Gobrecht's bid for the Mint engravership failed, and on Adam Eckfeldt's recommendation the appointment was given to William Kneass, a well known engraver of plates for books and banknotes. Kneass succeeded Scot on January 29, 1824.

On December 30, 1824 the Mint paid E. Luigi Persico $80 for "modeling a small medallion head for the silver coins," but this design seems never to have

---

[28] *The New York Historical Society's Dictionary of Artists in America,* George C. Groce and David H. Wallace, Yale University Press, 1937.
[29] *The Papers of Christian Gobrecht,* Historical Society of Pennsylvania collection.

Gold coin designs as typified on the half eagles. **Top:** standing and heraldic eagle types by Robert Scot. **Bottom:** 1808, obverse and reverse designs by John Reich, and 1814 obverse by Robert Scot.

been used.

In 1828, Kneass introduced the raised blank rim and beaded border on the dime, extending these to the half dime and half eagle in 1829, and to other denominations in later years. In 1830 he touched up the half dollar die, attenuating the lower part of the chin and straightening the outline of Liberty's neck. By the following year he had fully developed his ideas on the quarter dollar. Kneass redesigned the Liberty head, making it more graceful and attractive. He introduced smaller punches for the stars, letters and numerals, and deleted the scroll and motto. To accommodate the new designs, the planchet was reduced in diameter and made proportionately thicker. On January 29, Director Moore sent a specimen of the new coin to Secretary of the Treasury Woodbury, who approved the change.

In 1832, Philadelphia artist Titian Peale (son of Charles Wilson Peale) submitted a number of drawings of Liberty heads to the Mint. During the following year, the celebrated artist Thomas Sully also tried his hand as appears from William Dunlap's diary. Under the date of June 22, 1833 Dunlap records: [30] "Sully gave a model to the Manager of ye Mint here for a new Liberty's head but they prefer'd the old one of the half dollar."

Treasurers

The first treasurer of the Mint, Tristam Dalton, resigned on April 23, 1794 and was succeeded by Dr. Nicholas Way. The latter held office only through

---

[30] *Diary of William Dunlap,* Vol. 3, Printed for the New York Historical Society, 1930.

Silver coins and their designers. Half Dollars: 1795, Robert Scot; 1795, John Smith Gardner; 1801, Robert Scot after Gilbert Stuart; 1807 and 1812, John Reich; 1831 quarter dollar, William Kneass.

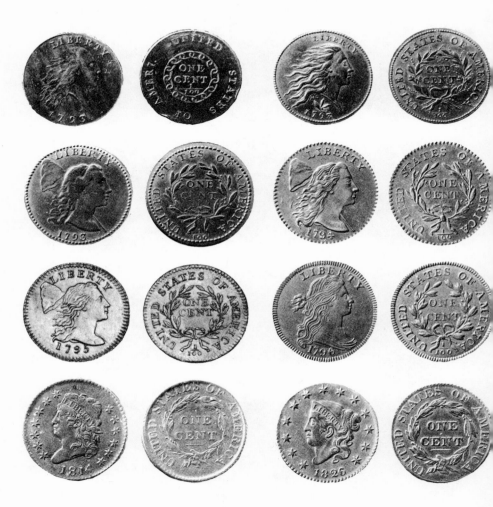

Large cents and their designers. 1793 (chain reverse), Henry Voigt; 1793 (wreath reverse), Adam Eckfeldt; 1793 (liberty cap), Joseph Wright; 1794, Robert Scot; 1795, John Smith Gardner; 1796, Robert Scot after Gilbert Stuart; 1814, John Reich; 1826, Robert Scot.

Top: half cents and their designers. 1793, Adam Eckfeldt; 1794, Robert Scot; 1796, John Smith Gardner; 1804, Robert Scot after Gilbert Stuart; 1809, John Reich. **Bottom:** 1795 cent, made by John Harper to solicit coining contract with the Mint.

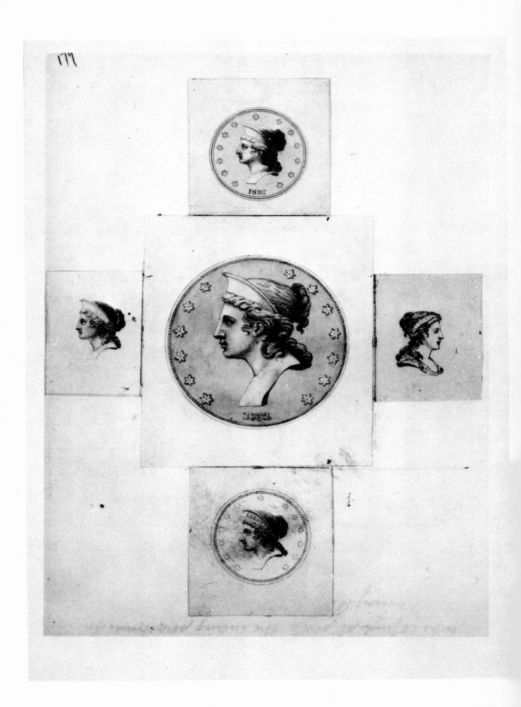

Designs for the obverse of the coinage submitted to the Mint by artist Titian Peale.
American Philosophical Society Library.

August 1797 when, as a member of a citizens' committee appointed to tend yellow fever patients, he himself was stricken and passed away.

The third treasurer was the brilliant and irascible Dr. Benjamin Rush. Rush graduated from Princeton College at the age of fifteen, and nine years later was elected professor of chemistry in the Medical College of Philadelphia. An early advocate of American Independence, it was he who instigated Thomas Paine to write his famous and inflammatory pamphlet *Common Sense.* Rush served as a member of the Continental Congress and was one of the signers of the Declaration of Independence. In April 1777, he was appointed surgeon-general of the American forces and eventually became the most celebrated physician and surgeon of his time.

When David Rittenhouse was about to resign the Directorship, Rush was approached as the most likely successor. In his *Commonplace Book,* he records the incident under the date April 9, 1795: [31]

"This day Tench Coxe [32] called upon me to know whether I would accept the Directorship of the Mint with a salary of £750 a year in the room of Dav. Rittenhouse, who was about to resign. I declined the offer on the steps of my door without deliberating one moment upon it." Rush goes on to explain that the appointment would have interfered with, among other things, his highly lucrative medical practice.

But Rush was soon to repent his decision. Pugnacious by nature, he had made a number of enemies, one of whom, William Cobbett, undertook a series of editorial assaults against the doctor. During the yellow fever epidemic of 1797, when Rush applied his therapy of bloodletting, Cobbett charged him with bleeding to death hundreds of patients. So persistent was Cobbett's attack that Rush's practice became greatly diminished and he was forced to seek additional income. Finally, as Rush himself records: [33]

> To supply the diminution of the resources of my business, my wife's uncle, and my excellent friend, Mr. Boudinot, applied in my behalf to Mr. Adams, then President of the United States, for the office of Treasurer of the Mint, rendered vacant by the death of Dr. Way in the fever of 1797. There were above 40 applications for it. Upon my being nominated by the President, several persons remonstrated with him against my appointment, urging that I was a French Democrat. Even Mrs. Adams was applied to, to use her influence with the President against me. These efforts proved ineffectual to shake the President's determination. "I know (said he) Dr. Rush's principles perfectly. He is no more a French Democrat than I am." When I received the appointment, I waited upon him to thank him. He took me by the hand, and with great kindness said "You have not more pleasure in receiving the office I have given you, than I had in conferring it upon an old Whig."

Within a few years, however, the relationship between Rush and Boudinot had grown so bitter that it threatened to disrupt the business of the Mint.[34] The source of the dispute was William Bradford, former Attorney General under President Washington. Bradford was the brother-in-law of Director

---

[31] *The Autobiography of Benjamin Rush,* edited by George W. Corner, Princeton University Press, 1948.

[32] As this time, Coxe was Commissioner of the Revenue. He had formerly served as Assistant Secretary of the Treasury, succeeding William Duer.

[33] *The Autobiography of Benjamin Rush,* Corner.

[34] Both Butterfield and Stewart allude to this controversy, but neither does justice to the subject. From Stewart's allusion to the "mass of contemporaneous letters and other data in my possession" one would scarcely suppose that his source was the Rush papers in the Library Company of Philadelphia. The letters reproduced here are from that source unless otherwise noted.

Boudinot, and a close friend of Rush. Just before his death, Bradford had torn up a will in which he left most of his estate to his wife. He then signed several promissory notes, including one to Rush, and died intestate. Rush testified that Bradford had acted in sound mind. As the latter's physician, Rush was upheld in court despite the opposition of Boudinot and other members of Bradford' family who tried to force the terms of an earlier will. The case was settled just a few months before Boudinot, with apparent distaste, recommended the appointment of Rush to the Mint. The undercurrent of friction between the two men can be discerned in Boudinot's letter of November 29, 1797. After outlining the duties of the treasurer, Boudinot wrote:

> As the greatest Harmony has hitherto prevailed among the officers of the Mint they cannot but lament the loss of the late excellent Treasurer, by an untimely Death, who had endeared himself to them, by the most friendly & exemplary Conduct, while at the same time they feel their loss so fully made up by the judicious Choice of the President, and the Director takes the greatest pleasure in contemplating that the former Harmony will not be interrupted by the accession by the present Treasurer to their number.

By mid-1800, the breach had perceptibly widened. Boudinot accused Rush of neglecting his work,[35] and asked him to resign. Rush ignored the request and the two men ceased speaking to one another.[36] When Rush proved obstinate, Boudinot himself may have considered resigning, for rumors to this effect were in the air.[37]

The controversy reached a head in 1802, when Boudinot presented Mrs. Rush with a letter accusing her husband of having given false testimony in the Bradford case. Rush, furious, charged Boudinot with using the Mint's iron, tools and workmen for his own purposes, paying his tenant commissions on articles purchased for the Mint, and stealing dung from the stable. On September 10 1802 Rush wrote a menacing letter to Boudinot who, at the time, was visiting a sick relative in Newark, New Jersey:

> Sir, A sense of duty in my present responsible situation has imposed upon me the painful necessity of informing you that I have lately heard of certain practices that have been & in part are still carried on by you in the mint of a very improper nature, & extremely dangerous in this tendency in an institution in which the most scrupulous integrity is expected from all its members.
>
> I need not suggest what is your duty upon this Occasion in order to prevent your Conduct being publicly known. I have hitherto mentioned it, to but one person out of my own family. He is your friend, & concurred with me in the propriety of my giving you this private information of it.
>
> I will receive no letter from you, nor hold any intercourse with you upon this disagreeable business. If you have forgotten the practices alluded to, Mr Nath. Thomas formerly a Clerk in the Mint will furnish you with details of them
> From your old and much injured friend.

Boudinot, on returning to the Mint, read out Rush's letter and asked the officers to testify to his innocence. Fearing a scandal, the assayer Joseph Richardson wrote to both Boudinot and Rush, attempting to reconcile the two men.

---

[35] The charge was probably true, for Rush wrote to Ashton Alexander on Feb. 20, 1798: "The Mint employs a few minutes only of my time 3 or 4 times a week." *The Letters of Benjamin Rush*, Edited by L. H. Butterfield, Princeton University Press, 1951.

[36] Ibid. See the letter of Rush to John Adams, April 5, 1808.

[37] According to a letter of John Adams, September 9, 1800 John Hinkley Mitchell had heard that Boudinot would shortly resign, and was soliciting the Directorship through Secretary of State John Marshall. See *The Works of John Adams*, Vol. 9, edited by Charles Francis Adams, Little, Brown and Co., 1854.

Robert Scot posted a notice to the same effect. Nevertheless, on the 14th, Rush wrote to the other officers:

> Before you subscribe the certificate composed by Mr. Boudinot in favor of the propriety of his conduct as Director of the mint, I think it my duty to state to you that the following particulars are a *part* of the improper practices alluded to in my letter to Mr. Boudinot.
>
> He has paid his tenant, Joseph Pierson, five per cent upon certain purchases made by him for the use of the Mint at a time when they might have been made free of Commissions by one of the clerks of the Mint.
>
> He has taken all of the dung of the stable of the Mint for his own use for several years without crediting the Mint for it. This article has since the year 1793 commanded a higher price, & more ready sale than usual. Should you subscribe to the proposed certificate after this information, I wish you to reflect, how far you may be considered as criminal by the President of the United States, especially as the means for ascertaining its truth, or falsehood are completely within your power. I wish you to know further, that Mr. Thomas will attest that he has more than once mentioned the above articles of complaint and *some others* against Mr. Boudinot in the presence of several of you while he has acted as Clerk of the Mint. Should Mr. Boudinot make retribution in value for what he has taken from the Mint above his salary no further notice shall be taken by me of his conduct. I am etc.
>
> P.S. You are at liberty to shew this letter to Mr. Boudinot.

On the same day, Rush wrote to Joseph Richardson:

> My good friend, I have received your kind letter, & shall always consider it as a mark of a friendly & christian disposition towards the persons to whom it was addressed.
>
> Mr. Boudinot has accused me unjustly & cruelly of having taken the false Affirmation in order to deprive his Daughr. of a part of her husbd. estate. By the remoteness of the *time*, (nearly five years) and the *manner* in which he put his accusation into my hands, he has violated the Obligations of consanguinity, friendship, humanity and Religion. Relying upon the influence in Society which he derives from his uncommon wealth, office and professions of piety, to establish his evidence, he has refused to hear from me a refutation of his charges, and a deference of innocence. This conduct at first surprised and distressed me, for I had been in the habit of believing him to be a religious and honest man, and most sincere friend, for upwards of five & twenty years, but the knowledge I have lately obtained of his character from a number of his transactions with other people (some of which will ere long be made public) has changed my Surprise & distress exclusively into pity. I no longer wonder at his attack upon veracity, for his avarice I have discovered knows no restraints from the laws of God or man. From this statement of facts, you will readily perceive your good offices cannot be effectually empd. to bring abt. an intercourse between us. I do not call upon him to do so, having the means in my power of doing myself justice, and partly from under Boudinot's own hand. From your sincere friend.
>
> P.S. The short & private communication I made to him of his improper practices in the mint, was dictated by a sense of duty, & was advised by one of his friends. His pitiful appeal to the officers of the mint to exculpate him by a certificate instead of boldly confronting his accuser, is a striking proof of weakness and the folly which characterize the conduct of men who are at variance with truth & justice.

In the meantime, Rush's letter to the officers of the Mint had been forwarded ɔ Boudinot, who immediately replied:

> Gentlemen: I received the very extraordinary letter you received from Dr. Rush and forwarded to me by Mr. Eckfeldt. All I think proper, at present, to say upon it is, that it confirms me greatly in my opinion of this unhappy man. I pity him, and consider him as one bent on his own destruction, which he is hastening much faster than I could wish.

When I shall condescend to put myself on a par with him or Mr. Thomas his associate, or trouble myself about any falsehoods, they may think proper to fabricate between them, then indeed I should think my ownself somewhat culpable. I doubt not you feel the same consciousness of perfect integrity, that I do, with regard to all our conduct in the Mint. I hope therefore you will not give yourselves a moment's consideration of his malicious charges. There will, very soon, be an opportunity of fully justifying ourselves.

All I have expected from you, on my part is, that you will declare your knowledge of my conduct according to your nicest sense of truth and honor; and if that will not serve me, I am willing to abide by the Consequences. I am etc.

Sometime in early November, Nathaniel Thomas the former clerk and co-plaintiff against Boudinot, came to the Mint and removed certain papers belonging to the treasurer's department. When an attempt was made to search him, he bolted away, returning, however, the following day with the same papers which he requested be burned. Boudinot presented charges against Thomas to Secretary of the Treasury Dallas, and Rush, on November 30, followed with charges against Boudinot. On the same day, Boudinot sent a lengthy defense of his own conduct to Dallas. The Director enumerated two very minor repairs which had been made by Mint workmen on his carriage and admitted that his watch had been repeatedly regulated by Voigt. Boudinot said also that his farmer had hauled away the Mint's dung because a hostler could not be found who would remove it without charge, and that the same individual had saved the Mint hundreds of dollars by his judicious purchases.

Rush likewise submitted a defense of Thomas, saying that his quondam clerk had removed the papers at his express order. Dallas dismissed the charges against both Boudinot and Thomas but the matter did not end there. Boudinot, with great joy, discovered what appeared to be an irregularity in Rush's books but which turned out to be a mere clerical error. Rush and Thomas then made countercharges against Boudinot, and the controversy continued for months.

On December 9, Rush, in the course of a long and indignant letter, wrote to Boudinot:

> I wait with impatience for the day of your trial when I have no doubt Heaven will appear in favor of my innocence and integrity, and at the same time expose your character to our whole city in the same light that it now appears to the individuals whom you have injured and deceived.

When Boudinot's intention to resign became known, Rush applied for the appointment which, however, had been given already to Robert Patterson. Jefferson wrote to Rush on June 13, 1805 that Patterson had been selected because the office required "the best mathematical talents which could be procured, as well as on account of mechanical execution as the difficulty of the problems constantly occurring in the mixture of metals received and delivered out." Jefferson admitted that this had not always been the ruling consideration in the past but that "we thought it our duty to follow the best examples" (i.e., Newton in England and Rittenhouse in America). Pity poor Rush who had once declined the office, and then lent his own chemistry books to Boudinot upon the latter's appointment!

Rush remained at the Mint until his death in April 1813. He was succeeded in office by his son, James Rush, who served as treasurer until September 1830 During the remaining years of the first Mint, the office was filled by ex-Pennsylvania Governor William Findlay.

CHAPTER 9

Early Impediments

WHEN THE MINT BEGAN OPERATIONS, it lacked not only the necessary machinery but even the tools to build more. The situation was gradually remedied through the skill of Henry Voigt and Adam Eckfeldt who, with the assistance of workmen, forged tools and constructed from theoretical principles the requisite coining apparatus. But progress was very slow. Sometimes the new machines were unable to produce enough force, and at other times they collapsed and had to be rebuilt. Even the materials needed for construction were difficult to obtain, including bar iron and castings. And finally, when sufficient machinery was built, the Mint was found to be too small to conveniently house it all! For the sake of economy the buildings had been constructed on a modest scale, but now the working areas were so congested that operations were hindered and the business of the Mint delayed.

Voigt complained that his vault was too small and very damp, and he apparently declined using it. Instead, he kept the planchets for the different denominations and stages of preparation in individual chests.

Of all the Mint's early machinery, none caused such persistent grief as the rolling mills. There is in the archives a draft of a letter dated September 3, 1796 which illustrates the situation. Although unsigned, the letter appears to be from Voigt to Boudinot. Spelling and punctuation are preserved as in the original.

Some time ago I spoke to you that we have made repeated trials to procure rollers for the Mint, of this Country Manufactory, but not one of them succeeded. The rollers we have cast at Hanover furnace in New Jersey, not one of them proved sound, after considerable work had been bestowed on them; and if they

119

had been sound the Metal being so soft, that they could not have been of any
duration of time, and you for that reason thought proper to send to Europe for
some Rollers, on which we could depend, and gave a description of what temper
those Rollers ought to be to answer our purpose for the Mint. But, Sir, since
that time, I find that the rollers now in use are getting dailey worse than what
could have forseen and find that if we cannot get a new pair of Rollers very soon
the Business of the Mint, will be Stopped for the want of this very material, and
necessary tool—for those we use are so much worn out, that the hard Crust on
them is quite gone in some places, and wair their is yet any hardspots on them, it
only for the worse because, they cannot be kept round, for the soft places will dent
in in Rollings, and the hard ones, remain high, and make the Gold and Silver
which is worked threw them so unevenly that it is impossible to cut planchets, from
the strips rolled, with any degree of Accuracy; Besides those difficulties the
Rollers begin to crack in different places; and am every Moment, under fear of
their breaking to pieces, & I am certain they cannot last nearly that length of time
till those will arrive from Europe, you have sent for, and as I have been informed
that some Rollers are hear in this City imported by a Gentleman for his own use
but as he has received more than what he had sent for, and has no use, for them
all, I have been informed, that this Gentleman will part with a few, but as they
are compleated with fraims to them, he will not part with the Rollers alone, but
the fraims must go along with the Rollers and we cannot object to that, altho our
fraims will not fit those Rollers, the Gentleman has; or those Rollers will not fit
our fraims; and in our present circumstances, it rather would be an inpeedment to
us, if those new Rollers wair without their fraims and other things belonging their
unto because our fraims not fitting as aforesaid, we would be under the immediate
necessity to make a fraime for them, and considering new pattrons [1] for the Casting,
and the difficulty attending to get the Castings done here, as they ought to be
besides the delay, of time to get done, the fraime alone would cost fifty per cent
more then what (I am informed) those Rollers and fraims can be purchased at
To make myself shure of what I have said about those new Rollers in question,
have sent an ingenious machanick to the place, to take a view of them, and ask
the price; and Information I have received threw him; I am able to judge that those
Rollers & fraims are of the best kind; and can be purchased at the price of 400
Dollars [with?] everything belonging theirto—This I think is not out of the way
price. If I had gone their myself he would have asked me an Exorbident price
knowing that it wair wanted for the publick, for that reason I have maid use
of this mode, to keep the Gentleman in the Dark not to get any knowledge about
those Rollers wair to be for the Mint . . .

The rest of the letter is no longer extant. Two days before it was written
however, Voigt had already paid one of the adjusters, Lewis Bitting, $400 to
purchase the rolling apparatus.

One of the Mint's immediate problems was the inability of either Voigt or
Cox to post the bond which would allow them to handle gold and silver. By
December 1793, only cents and half cents had been struck [2] and on the 30th
Jefferson wrote to President Washington: [3]

Sir: I am informed by the Director of the Mint, that an impediment has arisen to
the coinage of the precious Metals which it is my Duty to lay before you.

It will be recollected that, in pursuance of the authority vested in the President
by Congress, to procure Artists from abroad, if necessary, a Mr. Drotz, at Paris
so well known by the superior style of his coinage, was engaged for our Mint; but
that after occasioning to us a considerable delay, he declined coming. That there
upon our Minister at London, according [to] the instructions he had received

---

[1] i.e., patrons or patterns.
[2] Except, of course, for the initial emission of half dimes.
[3] *American State Papers,* Finance, Vol. 1.

endeavored to procure, there, a Chief Coiner and Assayer; that, as to the latter, he succeeded, sending over a Mr. Albion Coxe, for that Office but that he could procure no person, there, more qualified to discharge the duties of Chief Coiner, than might be had here; and therefore did not engage one. The Duties of this last Office, have consequently been hitherto performed, and well performed, by Henry Voight, an artist of the United States; but the law requiring these officers to give a Security in the Sum of 10,000 dollars each, neither is able to do it. The coinage of the precious metal, has therefore been prevented, for sometime past, though, in órder that the Mint might not be entirely idle, the coinage of copper has been going on, the trust in that, at any one point of time being of but small amount.

It now remains to determine how this difficulty is to be got over. If, by discharging these officers, and seeking others, it may well be doubted if any can be found in the United States, equally capable of fulfilling their duties; and to seek them from abroad, would still add to the delay; and if found either at home or abroad, they must still be of the description of artists, whose circumstances & connections rarely enable them to give security in so large a sum. The other alternative would be to lessen the securityship in money, and to confide that it be supplied by the vigilance of the Director, who, leaving as small masses of metal in the hands of the officers, at any one time, as the course of their processes will admit, may reduce the risk to what would not be considerable. . . .

Jefferson left little doubt of which alternative he preferred, and on March 3, 1794 Congress passed a special act reducing the bond of the chief coiner to $5,000, and that of assayer Cox to a mere $1,000. Rittenhouse himself stood surety for Voigt, and Charles Gilchrist for Cox.

As coinage got underway, the problem of early die breakage became acute. Often the original hubs and dies broke during the hardening process or the working dies cracked after taking only a few impressions. In 1794, operations were suspended more than once because of the inability of the engraver to keep pace with the coiner. The breakage seems to have been largely caused by a "very ingenious and complicated" press which applied more pressure than the rather poor grade steel could bear.[4] The press was undoubtedly one of the two sent over by Droz, which had a multiple thread screw for producing a faster, more forceful blow. In January 1795, John Harper advised the adoption of a simpler mechanism, and the more powerful of the two Droz presses was replaced a few months later by a model built by Adam Eckfeldt.

With the new coining press, and greater experience in selecting and hardening steel, die breakage became less of a problem for the Mint.

Another impediment was the shortage of copper, which was needed not only to strike cents and half cents, but also to alloy the gold and silver coins. In the beginning the shortage was so acute that the Mint willingly accepted shipments of copper nails, utensils, foreign tokens and scrap of all kinds. Some of these came from England and Sweden, the rest from domestic firms and individuals, at first mostly from Philadelphia. At best, the quality of these shipments was less than satisfactory, and in October 1795 the only copper in the Mint consisted of clippings which apparently had been over-wrought, and were unfit for rolling into strips.

On June 28, 1796 Voigt, without informing anyone of his purpose, left the Mint in search of copper. Since no one was allowed to leave during working hours, even for meals (which were brought to the men by their families),

---

[4] *Debates and Proceedings of Congress,* H. of R., January 20, 1796.

Voigt's absence was particularly observed by Director Boudinot who, on the same day, posted the following notice:

> The Director has with great regret received Information that one of the principal officers of the Mint has left the public Service without leave, or any notice given of his intended absence, whereby the Business of the Mint has been impeded, and all Responsibility destroyed. One of the Horses belonging to the public has also been used on this occasion, contrary to every Principle of Justice The Director therefore cannot but express his disapprobation of this reprehensible conduct, and insist that it never be repeated, as he cannot again submit to Conduct so ruinous to the Discipline necessary to be kept up in the Mint.

It was not until July 5 that Voigt, in his quaintly inarticulate style, replied:

> I received a letter on my return last Friday, dated June 28 being a copy signed I think in which it appears that the Director of the Mint greatly regretted the absence of one of the principal officers of the Mint who had left the public business without leaf or any notice given of his intended absence—
>
> It is true Sir, that I rather went off in hast, after waiting three days to see the Director of the Mint and could not have that opportunity, tho I confess it was my duty to have obtained leaf first from my Superior, before I went away there fore having transgressed, and am very sorry for it and shall in future not be guilty of such an Offence again and beg pardon for having done so—
>
> But Sir I did not go altogether on my own Account in the Country you will remember, Sir, that I spoke to you concerning good Copper, for Alloying Gold of which Copper I went in serch of and should have got at some, and would have brought some with me, to make the Experiment, If that I could of staid two Day longer, for obtaining it as I found Hands rather scarce to serch for the same contrary to my expectation—The second was on Account of the Copper Clippings & lack of Copper or crude Copper, belonging to the Mint, of which I maid mention to you some time before, Likewise to see weather their was a probability to bring that Copper into fine Copper again [that?] the same might be useful to the Mint again, which I found can be done if the *parties*, who can perform the business can agree with the Director of the Mint—
>
> Thirdly the Rollers in the Mint began to be very defective and none can be obtained without Brass or Copper Moulds, this Sir, is not only a difficult piece of Work to Cast, but required nicity to finish, and power of Action for finishing the Moulds. With [this?] Sir I had laid out for my business for the Mint to perform to see weather these things might be obtained without much difficulty; and have found that all things are to be Obtained altho not without some difficulty, but not so much as I expected. Any further particular Information on those subjects, I am ready to communicate to you Verbally whenever you think proper.
>
> As for the horse I took out of the Mint before the chair [5] has certainly not been to benefit myself by, but as the Horse has been for some time under the Farrior's hands and the Farrior recommended to the Hostler that a Trip of that Kind, would be of Service, to the Horse, by being put to Pasture afterwards, I thought (Altho it being more Expensive to me than going in the stage) to take the horse with me in the Country, and as I had very little more Business for the Horse, when I was at the place of destiny she should have Pasture their for the time I could stay which I did and the horse is much recovered by that means. Nevertheless I con fess I should not have done without leaf first obtained from you, I am certain you will not concider this as done to benefit myself by [the] horse as you are well acquainted that a Horse & Chair to take a trip of 70 Miles, and then let the Horse in Stable at a Tavern & Pasture which amounts to _____ be sides the hire of the Chair. I am etc.

The problem of obtaining good copper was finally solved in April 1797 when the Mint began importing prepared planchets for cents and half cents from

---

[5] i.e., carriage.

Boulton & Watt. The first shipment was pronounced by the Director as "perfect and beautifully polished," and a short time later the Mint disposed of the remainder of its stock of rough copper clippings.

Perhaps nothing reflects the Mint's early economy quite so much as its production of half cents. On April 23, 1795 the Mint received over a thousand pounds of copper Talbot, Allum & Lee tokens.[6] Instead of being melted, the tokens were simply cut down on a planchet cutter and overstruck with half-cent dies. These overstrikes are frequently found among the variety with a plain edge and no pole. In the same year, several hundred "Cents spoiled & Clipt" were cut down and overstruck with half-cent dies, and apparently some also in the following year. In 1797, U.S. half cents were struck over Massachusetts half cents, cut-down large cents and Talbot, Allum & Lee tokens. In 1800, some 5,750 half cents were struck on cut-down planchets of spoiled cents, and the entire half-cent emission of 1802 was made from the same source.

Coining operations could, of course, proceed no faster than those of smelting. One impediment was the lack of a regular melter and refiner. Another was the insistence of Congress that each deposit be wrought in order. This provision cost the Mint a great deal of time and money and in the end benefitted no one.[7] Although the Mint was permitted (with the consent of the depositor) to trade coin for bullion, minus a small charge, the Treasury took no note of this arrangement and refused to appropriate the requisite fund. In the beginning, in fact, the Mint had to endure the entire expense connected with coining, which was considerable when a deposit was more than usually debased. On February 4, 1795 John Vaughn deposited 95,791 ounces of silver bullion, which proved to be 24,000 ounces below coin standard, and cost the Mint over $1,300 to melt and refine. This incident seems to have contributed to the Act of March 3, 1795 which authorized a charge of two cents per ounce on silver deposits and four cents per ounce on gold deposits of less than standard fineness. The Act also permitted the Mint to give preference to standard deposits, and refuse silver in quantities of less than two-hundred ounces or substandard gold of less than twenty ounces.

An annual occurrence which disrupted the Mint as it did everything else in Philadelphia was the visitation of yellow fever. Those who were able moved from the city, and the Mint itself closed its doors during the summer and fall of 1797-99, and again 1802-04. Joseph Wright the engraver, and Joseph Whitehead of the assaying department died of the fever in 1793, and the Mint's treasurer, Dr. Nicholas Way, succumbed in 1797. Elaborate preparations accompanied the closing and reopening of the Mint, as can be observed from the following notice written by Director Boudinot on September 14, 1803.[8]

> The appearance of a malignant Fever in the City again threatens the dispersion of the Citizens, and the probable Shutting up of the Mint—This must take place whenever the Officers of the Mint shall officially certify to the Director, that it is dangerous to the Officers and Workmen to continue the usual work of the Mint. —It will therefore be necessary for the Officers to be prepared for so disagreeable

---

[6] R. W. Julian, "The Copper Coinage of 1795," *The Numismatic Scrapbook Magazine*, Dec. 1964.

[7] In 1797, apparently to ease the strain caused by small deposits, purchases of bullion were made by Joseph Richardson, David Ott, and Nathaniel Thomas (clerk to Benjamin Rush), and then deposited collectively.

[8] This same notice had been posted during the epidemic of the previous year and it is possible to distinguish, under the latter date, the earlier one of August 16, 1802.

an event, that no confusion may take place in case of the necessity of suddenly closing the business—

The following directions must be particularly attended to:

1st. All the accounts of Bullion and Expenses must be closed till the Day of shutting the Mint so that the Ballance due by or from the Mint may be clearly ascertained.—

2d. The Workmen must be all paid off on that day.—

3d. If any of the Officers should want any advances on account of their Salaries, it may be done, provided they do not exceed the portion of the Quarter due to them.—Partial receipts may be taken by the Treasurer on Account.

4th. All the gold and Silver Bullion in the Mint must be coined as far as possible, and every deposit paid off, if the Coin will admit of it, before the closing of the Mint.—

5th. Whatever shall remain of gold—or silver Coin, Bullion, Clippings or Grains, must be returned on warrant to the Treasurer, who will take such measures for its security as he may think expedient.

6th. The Officers of the different Departments will take measures to secure all the Works in every part of the Mint, together with the Tools, Implements and Machinery belonging to their respective departments so that they may not be injured or even visited by any person whatever during their absence without leave. —The Chief Coiner will also see that all the Presses are secured and the Mechanism put away in a separate place.—

7th. The Chief Coiner, with the Engraver will particularly attend to the positive Destruction of all the Spoiled Dies, so that no possible use may be made of them for Coinage in case they should be stolen, not so much as for a Pattern.—

8th. All the good Dies must be boxed up and sent to the Bank of the United States, an official List being first taken of them and left with the Director's Clerk.—

9th. If practicable with safety, the Chief Coiner or his Clerk will now and then visit the Mint, to see that all remains as left.

10th. Mr. Sharpe [9] will draw up a short Article in writing for such Workmen as choose to sign, purporting that they engage to return to their different employments, when the Mint shall again be opened, in consideration whereof they shall respectively receive half of their original pay while the Mint is shut up extraordinary, in four weeks after their return, let the Mint be shut up longer or shorter. —All who refuse to sign will be of course discharged.—

11th. The Horses will be put out to pasture under the care of Mr. Eckfeldt.—

12th. All the Books and Files of Papers must be carefully locked up in a box or chest, and carried to the Bank of the United States, being first sealed with the Seal of the Mint.

13th. The different Keys of the Mint had best be also lodged in the Bank in a box carefully secured and sealed.—

14th. The Doorkeeper, in case he will stay, will be carefull to suffer no visitors of any description to enter the Mint during the absence of the Officers, without very urgent necessity—He will also carefully patrole the Works every Half hour during the night.—

15th. The above directions are not to interfere with the respective Officers absolutely discharging every workman they can do without in case of the Mint again opening.

16th. If the Door Keeper should be obliged to leave the Mint, the old Watchman must be engaged to attend to the Mint as formerly, for which he shall receive the same sum as he received in 1798.

Elias Boudinot Director.

Ten days later, Boudinot appended the following order:

The Officers of the Mint having signed the Certificate mentioned in the beginning of the above order, let the Mint be shut up, the Men discharged for the

---

[9] Ludwick (or Lodewick) Sharp(e), clerk to the chief coiner.

present, till called for again.—It is presumed that the above directions have been strictly complied with—Septr. 24, 1803.—

Elias Boudinot DM.

Ill-equipped, crowded, its operations hindered by inept laws and annual plagues, the Mint was indeed an object for sympathy. Worst of all, its coins were largely exported because Congress refused to correctly value them. The silver dollar had been overvalued in relation to the Piece of Eight, and was now becoming less valuable than a dollar's worth of gold. In 1803, France adopted a ratio of 15½ to 1, and after that time U.S. gold coins served mainly as a commodity for export.

United States silver dollars were likewise exported since they could be exchanged in the West Indies for the heavier Spanish and Mexican pieces of 8. The latter were then shipped to the Mint for recoinage into U.S. dollars, and the operation repeated *ad infinitum*. As a result of these abuses Mint Director Boudinot suspended the coinage of silver dollars and gold eagles in 1804. The practice was confirmed in the following year by an order from President Jefferson to Secretary of State Madison.[10] Jefferson likewise requested Boudinot's successor, Robert Patterson, to confine the coinage to smaller denominations. On March 29, 1807 Jefferson wrote to the Director:

I should approve of your employing the Mint on small silver coins, rather than on Dollars, & gold coins, as far as the consent of those who employ it [i.e., the depositors] can be obtained.[11] It would be much more valuable to the public to be supplied with an abundance of dimes & half dimes which would stay among us, than with dollars & eagles which leave us immediately. Indeed I wish the law authorized the making of two cent & three cent pieces of silver, and golden dollars, which would all be large enough to handle, & would be a great convenience to our own citizens.

But if Spanish dollars poured into the Mint from the West Indies, they also left the country in large numbers, en route to ports beyond the Cape of Good Hope. These coins were in particular demand in China where, because of a prejudice against anything new, they enjoyed a premium of four per cent over the U.S. dollar. In fact, the celestial merchants paid a higher premium on the worn Carolus (Charles IV) dollars, which issue had ceased in 1808, than on the subsequent, less abraded Ferdinand dollars. From 1792 to 1811, pieces of 8 in American circulation commanded a premium over U.S. dollars ranging generally from one fourth to one per cent. For bullion dealers it was the West Indies game played in reverse. Only at rare intervals, when the American premium on Spanish dollars reached four per cent, did these coins remain long in our circulation. The Bank of the United States suggested a palliative to Director Patterson, who on December 14, 1805 wrote to President Jefferson:

Sir: A Committee from the Directors of the Bank of the U. States have represented to me, as Director of the Mint, that in order to prevent, as much as possible, the exportation of Spanish Dollars, so injurious to the general interest of the country, it is their wish, as well as perhaps that of most of the other Banks in the U. States, to send this species of money, of which there are now considerable quantities in their vaults, to the Mint, for the purpose of having it coined into half dollars and smaller coins of the U. States, provided the Mint can give them assurance of having a return of their deposits in a reasonable time.

---

[10] Neither Boudinot nor Jefferson, but Congress alone, had the actual authority to suspend any coinage.

[11] It is doubtful whether Patterson ever gave the depositor a choice.

In a letter to Jefferson dated April 2, 1807 Patterson explained why the output of low denominational silver was so small.

> With respect, Sir to *small coins*, the practice of the Mint has been, and still continues to be in strict conformity with your wishes and instructions. No Eagles nor Dollars have been struck during the last two years. Quarter Dollars, Dismes, & half Dismes are struck whenever desired by the depositors, or not particularly objected to. But in truth, nearly the whole of our Silver Bullion (chiefly Spanish dollars) come through the Banks, and it is very seldom that they will consent to take any coin less than half dollars.
>
> Small Spanish Silver coins are extremely plenty, I believe in most of the commercial towns, and as their nominal and circulating value is considerably above their real intrinsic value,[12] they will neither be sent to the Mint, used in Manufactures, nor carried out of the country, but indeed are daily increasing by importation. Small Coins of the U. States will therefore be less necessary for the sake of change, while foreign small silver continues to be a circulating medium. We lately struck at the Mint nearly a quarter of a million of Silver dismes: it is however with the utmost difficulty, that we can prevail upon any of the Banks to accept of them, and in fact nearly half the number still remain in our vaults.

During the first two decades of the Mint, large quantities of Spanish doubloons flowed into the country through Natchez and New Orleans, but after that time the proliferation of low value bank notes gradually extinguished the circulation of gold coins in America.

It is unfortunate that early Mint reports do not indicate precisely when one metal had disappeared from circulation and its coinage was continued solely for the profit of bullion dealers. By 1826, however, according to the report of Director Samuel Moore, a premium of four to six per cent was being paid on gold bullion for export. At the same time, the Mint received large deposits of silver, principally from the Bank of the U.S. and other banks, but also from Mexico, South America and the West Indies.

The half dollar had become the "coin of the realm," and in 1826 no other silver was issued. In 1827, only 4,000 quarters were struck, and in 1829 and 1830 none at all. Between 1812 and 1819, dimes were issued for only one year, and the coinage of half dimes was suspended from 1806 to 1828.

Thus, despite the advantage that silver enjoyed at the Mint, the total number of quarters, dimes and half dimes issued during its first three decades was less than one coin for every living person.[13] Although the demand for gold coins remained unabated, deposits increased to some extent in 1824 when South Carolina began to furnish large quantities of bullion, and again in 1830 when Georgia, which had never previously supplied any gold, made deposits in excess of $200,000. In that year the Mint almost tripled its previous output.

---

[12] That is, because they were very worn.
[13] Neil Carothers, *Fractional Money*, John Wiley & Sons, 1930.

CHAPTER 10

Congress vs. the Mint

"THE RESIDENCE OF THE PRESIDENT being in High Street, now called Market, only two or three squares from the Mint, he was in the habit of visiting it daily, as we are informed, and manifested a deep interest in its operations." So wrote J. R. Snowden in 1861 [1] quoting a tradition which had doubtless been handed down by the venerable Adam Eckfeldt. Indeed, when Congress had all but forsaken the Mint, Washington took particular pains to forecast its success.

On November 19, 1794, a month after the first delivery of silver coins, he announced:

"The Mint of the United States has entered upon the coinage of the precious metals, and considerable sums of defective coins and bullion have been lodged with the director by individuals. There is a pleasing prospect that the institution will, at no remote day, realize the expectation which was originally formed of its utility."

Nevertheless, an inquiry was soon made in Congress regarding progress at the Mint. On December 9, Rep. Elias Boudinot testified that he had gone to the Bank of the United States to obtain cents, and was told that none were available, the Bank itself being unable to procure them from the Mint. Boudinot then went to the Mint where he was informed that cents were not coined at a greater rate because there was no place to vend them! He said that the annual expense of the Mint was $24,000 and that each cent it coined cost the public several cents, though he did not know exactly how many. In New Jersey, far more cents had been coined in a few months than had been coined altogether

---

[1] James Ross Snowden, *Washington and National Medals*, 1861.

at the U.S. Mint, and at one fortieth the expense.[2] Several other members of the House complained about the shortage of copper coins and marveled at the Mint's explanation. Finally, a committee of three members, headed by Boudinot, was appointed to examine and report on the Mint and suggest means to increase its efficiency.

The debate was considered at some length, the following day, by James Callender, Congressional recorder for the *Pennsylvania Gazette*. Callender, a Scottish writer, had fled to America to escape prosecution for sedition after publishing an unflattering account of British political history.[3] He at once aligned with Jefferson, becoming an implacable foe of Hamiltonian or Federalist principles. Although Jefferson had laid the foundations of our coinage, and been in over-all charge of the Mint until resigning his cabinet post in December 1793, it was Hamilton who was popularly identified with the institution. The Mint thus became a symbol of "Federalist excesses" and was attacked by the same parties who espoused the Jeffersonian cause.

Callender compared the Philadelphia Mint with the "nominal Mint" at Edinburgh, Scotland, which maintained employees at an annual cost of £1000 but issued no coinage. He then added:

> It is not wonderful that such abuses are to be found in an old, worn out, and rotten system like that of Britain, which is just about to tumble into pieces. But the remarks in Congress yesterday, concerning the American mint, may lead this country to pluck the *mote* from her own eye, before she touches the *beam* of her neighbor's. . . . It has been said, that a greater part of the money hitherto expended on the mint, was on charges incident to the *beginning* of a work, and that this charge would hereafter be lessened. This pretence has not even the *vestige of plausibility*. In 1794, twelve thousand two hundred and eighty-five dollars were consumed, not in buying implements for coining, nor in building furnaces, but for a director, an assayer, a chief coiner, an engraver, a treasurer, three clerks and the workmen. If all these officers are necessary at present when only seven thousand three hundred and fifty dollars of cents are struck off, then twice the number will be wanted, when twice the quantity of cents are coined, and so on.

Callender said that while the country could have a thousand tons of cents struck at Birmingham at practically no additional cost, the people were forced to use "dirty paste board."[4]

With these choice words still ringing in their ears, Boudinot's committee began its investigation of the Mint. Boudinot plied the officers with confidential questions and received strangely contrasting accounts from Voigt and Cox. Whereas Voigt strongly defended the Mint, Cox gave a pessimistic and exaggerated report of the Mint's shortcomings, apparently with the intention of promoting his former partner John Harper. He recommended Harper as "a practical man who operated in the Jersey Coppers," and who would provide "such Information with respect to the proceedings of coinage as will appear almost incredibable [sic] when contrasted with the present proceedings."[5]

---

[2] Although the price of copper had risen since passage of the original Mint Act, Boudinot's calculations were ridiculous and must have included, on the Mint's side, the entire cost of the establishment.

[3] *The Political Progress of Britain*, Edinburgh, 1792.

[4] Callender was probably referring to the paper money of the states—primarily New York, Pennsylvania, New Jersey, Maryland and Rhode Island. These were still circulating, and were redeemed at late as 1800-10.

[5] Harper had worked with Cox in the New Jersey coinage, though not as a co-contractor. See Frank H. Stewart, *History of the First United States Mint*, 1924; also Walter Breen, "The United States Patterns of 1792," *The Coin Collector's Journal*, March-April 1954; and R. W. Julian, "The Harper Cents," *The Numismatic Scrapbook Magazine*, Sept. 1964.

Harper, at Boudinot's invitation, came to the Mint and suggested a number of ways to improve the coining department. His visit (or rather visitation) in the wake of James Davy seems to have been ill-received by Voigt and Eckfeldt who probably feared for their jobs. Harper, as we earlier noted, complained that the presses (apparently those sent over by Droz) were too complicated, and he constructed a simpler model which was subsequently copied by Eckfeldt. Harper's ultimate ambition was to secure a contract with the Mint for coining its coppers. For this purpose he had built a planchet cutter and coining press, and engraved dies from which, in the presence of the investigating committee, he struck several pattern cents. Raymond Williamson has pointed out the probability of these being the "Jefferson Head" cents, a view elaborated upon by Breen and now generally accepted.

Although Harper failed to obtain his contract, he was offered the modest position of assistant coiner which he respectfully declined.

At the same time that Congress was probing the Mint for ways to increase its efficiency, a blunt solution was offered by the outgoing Secretary of the Treasury Alexander Hamilton. On January 31, 1795, his last day in office, Hamilton wrote to President Washington:[6]

Sir: Previous to the leaving my present office, there are a few points which I think it my duty to bring under the consideration of the President.

The first regards the present state and arrangement of the Mint.

It is certain that this establishment is capable of producing very important benefits to the community. At this moment, when an unusually large and sudden exportation of silver has produced a very inconvenient scarcity of that species of money, the full activity of the Mint would be of primary utility. Large quantities of silver lie in the banks and other places in ingots, which, if turned into coin, would be of the greatest advantage to trade, and to all pecuniary operations, public and private.

Hitherto the Mint has comparatively done nothing. This is a matter both of surprise and complaint with all that part of the community whose dissatisfactions are the less known because they are not lightly promulgated. The institution itself, by not fulfilling the public expectation, grows into discredit, and those who have had the principal agency in its establishment are wounded by a growing disrepute, which is attributable truly to an insufficient execution. The President probably knows better than I do, what have been the causes of the deficiency. They may afford a justification; but, uninformed as I am, I cannot help thinking that with due exertion the business of the Mint might have been far more matured, and its present powers of action far greater than they are. And I am led to fear that as long as it continues under its present management the public expectation will be disappointed. The director, though a most respectable and excellent man, can hardly be expected on several accounts to give that close and undivided attention to it, which in its first stages, is indispensable.

There is another point in relation to the same subject, on which I should have been silent as long as I could have been supposed to have any personal motive to influence my opinion. But now that this is at an end, I yield without hesitation to my convictions of the public interest, in presenting, with the greatest deference those convictions to the consideration of the President. They amount to this, that the mint establishment will be most advantageously for the service of the United States placed under the superintendent of the department of the Treasury.

It is obvious that that establishment forms a most material link in the money

---

[6] *The Works of Alexander Hamilton*, Vol. 5, edited by John C. Hamilton, Charles S. Francis & Co., 1851.

system of the country. This system, as it regards public operations, is the management of the department of the Treasury. It follows, that in the theory of the case, there is an intimate relation between this department and that establishment. The law constituting the mint, also establishes some relations between them.

The fifth section refers to the judgement of the Secretary of the Treasury [regarding] the competency of the sureties to be given by the officers of the mint.

The fourteenth section, providing for the exchange of the bullion for money, with the deduction of one-half per cent., towards defraying the expenses of the mint, makes it the duty of the Secretary of the Treasury to furnish the mint from time to time, whenever the state of the Treasury will admit of it, with such sums as may be necessary for effecting those exchanges. To engage the Secretary to dispossess the Treasury with confidence of large sums for such exchanges, it is necessary that he should be very certain of their regular and punctual return. The assurance of this would be not a little strengthened by that intimate knowledge of [the] situation which would result from the duty of Superintendency. The efficient operation of this provision is of no small consequence to the economy of the establishment. Hitherto its situation has been such as to preclude absolutely the effect of it.

Moreover, the Secretary of the Treasury, called daily and habitually, to observe the progress of money transactions, awake to everything which can affect them well or ill, because the credit of his department depends upon it, must be more likely than any other officer, to feel a due sensibility to the efficient and proper course of the mint, and consequently to exert himself to give it such a course.

The Post Office, on the other hand, if the idea which has repeatedly appeared in Congress be adhered to, that of rendering it an instrument of the improvement of the public roads instead of a means of revenue, may without inconvenience be placed under the department of State, while the mint establishment is transferred to the Treasury. . . .

Despite this exhortation Washington took no steps to alter the arrangement of the Mint.[7] We can assume that the President was influenced by Boudinot report, which the House committee laid before Congress on February 9, 179. Boudinot described operations at the Mint and the difficulties it had faced. H summary was sympathetic, entirely exculpating Rittenhouse and the other officers. In fact, Boudinot went so far as to state (which was ridiculous) that the coins lately executed were superior to any made in Europe.[8]

Nevertheless, the Mint still labored under several disadvantages which might be removed by additional legislation. Boudinot recommended that 1) provision be made for a melter and refiner; 2) the Mint charge depositors of substandard bullion 2¢ per ounce on silver and 4¢ per ounce on gold; 3) it receive su standard bullion in gross quantities of no less than two hundred ounces of silv or twenty ounces of gold; 4) it increase fineness of silver coins to .900; 5) due the rising price of copper, the President be authorized, at his discretion, reduce the weight of the cent by two pennyweights; 6) the Mint vend its cer to one bank or principal collector in each state, in proportion to the populati of the state; and 7) preference in working deposits be given to those standard or better fineness.

On February 26, Boudinot introduced a bill containing these provisio which passed in the House the following day. For some reason, the four

---

[7] The Treasury Department was not given direct control over the Mint until the Act of March 1835.

[8] Boudinot's hyperbole was so well known in Congress that any exaggerated statement, from wh ever source, was called a "Boudinot."

provision was expunged in the Senate, and the bill, thus amended, was enacted on March 3.

Despite Boudinot's favorable report, criticism of the Mint continued and on June 30, 1795 Rittenhouse, physically worn and disheartened, resigned. He died a year later.

Perhaps no one fanned the embers of the controversy with such fervor as James Callender. In a rather partisan publication called the *Annual American Register for 1796,* Callender renewed his chastisement of the Mint. Referring to Hamilton's 1790 report, he said:

> One chief objection to an American mint, though not stated by Mr. Hamilton, seems to be that there is a constant drain of money *out of* the continent, as well as into it. Thus American gold or silver coin would be constantly exported, almost as soon as struck, while the perpetual influx of Spanish silver might augment that confusion in our current money, which is at present extremely troublesome.

Callender's next object of attack was the management of the Mint. Although he took particular pains to vindicate Rittenhouse, he demanded to know why the Mint had claimed to be unable to vend its cents.

> Whenever it was known in Philadelphia that a parcel of cents had arrived from the mint at the bank, every storekeeper who heard of it hasted to seek them. It was a matter of favour to get cents in change for silver. The persons, therefore, at the mint who told such an absurd story, acted improperly.

But Callender reserved his most pointed squibs for the Mint's clerks. The three who were now employed, he said, did nothing, and yet the Mint was asking for a fourth.

> It is affirmed by people who frequent the mint, that they have been at a loss to find a clerk there, and that some of the receivers of these salaries of five hundred dollars do not once enter it, unless perhaps to sign a receipt for their wages. They are to be found regularly doing business at other places.

At the time Callender wrote, the Director and assayer shared one clerk, and the chief coiner and the treasurer each had their own. Callender said that the fourth clerk was wanted for the purpose of counting the copper coin. "The depth of his calculations," he jibed, "will not put him in danger of a head ache." But the matter would not end even with a fourth clerk, for "The committee farther menace us with the necessity for a *Refiner and Melter.* This battalion of pensioners afford one, among many good reasons, why the public in sea port towns, have been paying a shilling per dozen for onions half rotten, and half a crown for a couple of chickens, that a hungry cat would pick to the bones, without risk of a surfeit."

The enemies of the Mint were gaining in force and number. Some had been moved by the clamor of private patronage, while others wished to contract with the Bank of the United States.

As of October 27, 1795 the Mint's second Director, William De Saussure, had also resigned. In a letter to Washington, De Saussure repudiated the persistent attacks against the Mint, and on November 1 the President replied with his characteristic sympathy:

> I cannot, at this moment of your departure, but express my regret, that it was not in accordance with your views to remain in the Directorship of the Mint: Permit me to add thereto, that your conduct therein gave entire satisfaction.

Elias Boudinot, who had already been selected for the appointment, succeeded De Saussure on the following day.

On December 8, Washington presented to Congress a report of the outgoing Director who urged a reduction in the weight of the copper coins. De Saussure also observed that there were no federal laws to punish counterfeiting, that private mints were boldly operating, and that an attempt had been made to steal dies and implements from the Mint. Lastly, he recommended that the Government purchase the Cromley lot, in order to prevent intrusion into the interior lots of the Mint. None of these suggestions were immediately acted upon.[9] Boudinot had already recommended the weight of 168 grains for the cent. After some discussion between the Director and the Secretary of State, and further promptings from De Saussure, Washington finally authorized the reduction on December 27.[10]

It is ironic that Boudinot, who provoked the first investigation of the Mint, now found his own administration under fire. The attack began in earnest on January 19, 1796 when a bill for annual appropriations was brought before the House. Representative Williams moved to expunge the clause containing items for the Mint. Mr. Sedgwick opposed Williams on principle. He said that an appropriations bill should conform exactly to the state of public engagements, and where establishments had been formed and salaries provided, they should determine the appropriations. But it was not right, by withholding appropriations, to seek to destroy establishments formed by the whole Legislature.

Williams agreed to confine his resolution to one clause—that for purchasing the Mint's copper. He maintained that every cent cost ten cents to make, and that it was profitable to melt down the cents and sell the copper back to the Mint.

This was a mere embellishment of Boudinot's own exaggerated remark. Williams' amendment was nevertheless agreed to by a large majority, whereupon Mr. Nicholas of Virginia moved to strike out other clauses—for payments to mechanics, stationery, etc. Mr. Smith inquired whether the Mint was to be altogether suspended. John Page objected to dispersing the workmen who could not be easily collected again. He said that the copper coins, even if expensive, were of great benefit to the country, particularly to the poorer classes. The Mint, Page believed, was more important than most gentlemen realized.

Mr. Hartley was of a different opinion. He had once gone to the Mint on business for a country bank, and seen its operations performed. He said: "The institution is a bad one, and badly conducted. It has been most scandalously carried on, and with very little advantage to the public. If the institution is not to be better carried on than it has been, it ought to be thrown aside."

On the third day the debate was still raging. Representative Giles wished to postpone any appropriation to the Mint until another investigation could be made. This motion, however, failed, and the amendment for striking out the appropriation to purchase copper was finally defeated 44 to 38.

But the matter did not end there. On November 29, Boudinot was called upon to explain the high expenses of the Mint. He attributed these to the

---

[9] It was not until 1806 that Congress declared counterfeiting illegal in the United States.

[10] But, as Carothers notes, the President did not issue a proclamation until January 26, 1796, the date that is generally, though erroneously, assigned to this Act.

manner in which they were required to assay, melt and refine the bullion. Boudinot asked for the appointment of a permanent melter and refiner,[11] and the establishment of a $10,000 bullion fund. The bullion was to be purchased at market price and kept in the vaults until there was a sufficient quantity to coin. The Director said he had seen "with regret, an opinion generally prevailing, that the establishment is unnecessarily expensive, and less productive than was rationally expected by its advocates and friends."

By the Act of April 2, 1792 the Secretary of the Treasury had been directed to furnish the Mint, whenever practicable, with a bullion fund. This was not done, and Hamilton intimated that the Treasury Department could not safely comply with the provision so long as the Mint remained under another authority. The result was that many depositors brought bullion to the Mint and, being unable to secure an immediate exchange for coin, took it away again. Boudinot appealed to Congress to enforce the law, but received no other satisfaction than silencing, for a time, the more voluble of the Mint's critics.

✿   ✿   ✿

A meeting in July 1799, between Matthew Boulton and Robert Leslie, an American watchmaker, inventor and mechanic, seems to have stimulated renewed interest in Boulton's plan. Leslie had already distinguished himself by inventing the rod pendulum for taking measurements, and drastically reducing the number of parts in a watch. He was considered by Jefferson to be one of the greatest living mechanics, and when Leslie moved to London in 1793, he was given every assistance by Thomas Pinckney, the American minister in England.[12] Leslie is listed as "Clock & Watch Maker, No. 230 Oxford Street, London." On July 18, 1799 he wrote to Boulton:[13]

> Since my return to town I have seen Mr. King [14] and informed him of the conversation I had with you concerning the Mint, and your offer of Supplying the United States with your Aparatus for Coining, with which he seems much pleased, so much So, that if it is agreeable to you, I will do myself the pleasure of making you another visit, in order to make necessary arrangements to carry the plan into Effect, which I have no doubt will be to our advantage.

Another letter on this subject, dated November 6, 1799, can be found among Director Boudinot's fair copies. Boudinot wrote to Boulton:

> I am preparing to lay before Congress, an entire new plan of a Mint as I am dissatisfied with our present Establishment. To enable me to do this with Precision, will you be so good as to let me know what you will charge for a compleat Apparatus of a Mint on your own best approved plan, with a steam Engine equal to the force of 8 Horses constantly at work, the whole shipped on board a Vessel bound for this Port, so that Congress may have a view of the entire Expence by adding the freight & Insurance. There is an Opposition in Congress with the Minority to the Mint at any Rate, therefore it will be necessary for me to have an accurate Estimate of all the Expences attending it, that the Extent of the Advance may be known, as if Congress should come into the Measure, an express appropriation may be made for it, as no Money can be issued from our treasury without it.

---

[11] Although the Act of March 3, 1795 had provided for this office, a commission was not yet delegated.

[12] See Jefferson's letter to Pinckney, April 24, 1793, Library of Congress collection.

[13] *Matthew Boulton Papers,* Assay Office of Birmingham, England.

[14] Rufus King, the American minister in England.

Nothing seems to have come of Boudinot's inquiry, and on March 14, 1800 a Senate committee recommended abolishing the Mint. The chairman, James Hillhouse, had been a partner of James Jarvis in the Connecticut Company for Coining Coppers. His report declared that:

> To furnish coin sufficient for a circulating medium throughout the United States, would be impracticable, unless the powers of the Mint should be greatly increased, and the practice of melting down the coin, and the exportation to foreign countries, prevented, which can be done by debasing the coin, a measure which the Committee cannot recommend.
>
> The providing a fixed and permanent standard, by which the value of property contracts for money, and foreign coins, shall be regulated, is an object of great importance. This may be effectually done without the aid of a permanent mint establishment; for it is not an indispensable requisite, that the whole circulating medium should be of the coins of the United States. . . .
>
> An authority might be, by law, vested in the Bank, for ascertaining the intrinsic value of coins of a new impression, by assaying them at the expense of the United States: for these purposes the present Mint Establishment cannot be necessary. . . .
>
> The furnishing a supply of cents and half cents, sufficient for circulation, would, in the opinion of the Committee, be a desirable object, but they are well satisfied, that the Mint, upon its present establishment, will not furnish such supply, the efforts of almost seven years having done very little towards it. Perhaps a more economical and the most effectual mode would be by contract. . . .
>
> As the removal of the Mint, must be attended with expense, and probably a derangement of many of the officers, if a change of the system is to take place, the present is beyond a doubt the most convenient time for effecting it.

On April 24, while this report was still under consideration, Congress passed a law obliging depositors to pay the expense of refining substandard bullion.

On May 5, however, the Senate resolved to abolish the Mint and contract for coinage with the Bank of the United States. The bill was received in the House the following day and debated on the 10th.

Representative Gallatin was unwilling to invest the Bank, a private corporation, with the authority of coinage. He said he would rather see the coinage discontinued and the implements of the Mint sold. Gallatin moved an amendment to continue the Mint at Philadelphia until the expiration of its present term, March 5, 1801. The motion was carried, and after a show of resistance the Senate finally acceded on May 13.

During 1801, bullion deposits dwindled to practically nothing, and the Mint became a haven for the idle. Curiously, no one outside the Mint seems to have understood the cause of its unproductiveness which was thus attributed to indolence and inefficiency. Even President Jefferson appears confused as we find him conferring with Robert Leslie (now returned to America) on the virtues of a double cylinder coining press.

Leslie suggested that several pairs of dies be fixed to each roller in order to stamp the planchets in groups. This method, he said, would be more expeditious, and abridge the expense of the operation. Encouraged by Leslie's enthusiasm, Jefferson wrote to Boudinot on May 23, 1801 asking him to allow the construction and trial of an experimental model. "You know," the President cautioned, "the disposition of the legislature is [to] discontinue the establishment of the Mint on account of its expence, and there is a possibility not to say more that the design will be resumed."

Leslie delivered the letter to Boudinot at the Director's house, and explained how the "double cylinder" press worked and would expedite coining. To his surprise, Boudinot remarked that this was of no advantage since the men were already unemployed more than three-quarters of the time. Leslie said that, if this were the case, the machine might enable the Mint to dispense with some of its workmen. Boudinot, apparently with some emotion, rejected the proposal. He replied that each man was in charge of a certain operation and had to be retained and paid by the year in order to be ready when wanted. Nevertheless, Leslie might present his plan to Voigt and the other officers, and an appointment was accordingly arranged for eleven o'clock the following morning.

What occurred at this most interesting meeting is described in a letter from Leslie to Jefferson, dated June 2, 1801.

Leslie was taken to a large upstairs room where he found Boudinot surrounded by a great assemblage of workmen. There were so many people, he said "that at first I fancied myself before a committee of the whole house, but on Mr. B's asking for several by name, who were not present, I found I was only before a part of the body." After Boudinot had read Jefferson's letter aloud, he asked Leslie to explain the machine. When the latter finished, Voigt remarked that he had seen the same kind of press in Germany. This was followed by a general discussion of the practicability of the double cylinder. Several objections were answered by Leslie when suddenly the whole party, with one voice, denounced the machine. Voigt said that the gold and silver planchets underwent thirty-two operations before they were ready to receive an impression, and if the first operation took one day, the second took another, and so on, for thirty-two days. Thus, an improvement in striking would save only a few hours work in one day out of thirty-two, and not be worthy of notice.

Voigt's thirty-two operations must have included many subdivisions, and perhaps the labors of the various clerks. When Leslie tried to learn the nature of these operations, he was entertained, at length, with pointed anecdotes about attempts that had been made to deceive and defraud the Mint by charlatans and pseudo-inventors.

On June 16, Boudinot wrote to Jefferson that the double cylinder would prove as expensive as the present mode of striking the coins. Boudinot enclosed a letter of Voigt which further maintained that Leslie's machine would not permit the use of master dies and would bend the planchets and produce oval coins.[15]

On June 30 (as though on Leslie's behalf) the Mint was ordered to suspend every superfluous workman. Sensing the temper of Congress, Rufus King, the American minister to England, wrote to Boulton on September 14, 1801:[16]

Sir: The American mint was first established, and so far as respects the machinery upon no very good plan at Philadelphia: Doubtless the President will prefer that the coinage be minted at the City of Washington, the seat of Government, and where the other principal offices are now established—It has occurred to me to revive the Project of procuring for this purpose, the improved mint, which no other place can furnish so advantageously as Soho. In order therefore that I may in recommending this measure, be able to speak with accuracy respecting the

---

[15] Despite this rebuff, Leslie continued to devote his thoughts to the Mint. In a letter to Jefferson, dated August 3, 1801, he described a method he had developed of casting silver in a metal mold and suggested that the Mint prepare its planchets in this manner.

[16] *Rufus King Papers,* New York Historical Society collection.

Expense, I take the Liberty of enquiring what was the Price of the Mint first to Repair, or in other words what a comple[te] one would cost us.

I likewise should be obliged to you to state the probable annual expense of keeping the machinery in repair, and whether from your idea of the skill of our workmen, they would be able to repair it.

With great respect, etc.

King's plan does not seem to have made much headway, and with the new year the Mint again found itself caught in a political crossfire. This time the attack came from Republican forces in the House. The Mint was pictured as a "Federalist creation," monarchical, unproductive, expensive and personifying centralized power. On January 29, 1802 Representative Giles proposed a bill for abolishment, and on February 8 debate commenced. Giles said he had opposed the Mint from the beginning and that the Government should not maintain an establishment the expense of which surpassed the profit. He showed the deficiencies of the Mint and proposed that Congress contract with the Bank of the United States. Mr. Smith maintained that it cost half a dollar to coin each cent, but later in the debate retracted the statement as a "lapsus linguae." He nevertheless protested the cost of the copper coinage and favored a contract with Birmingham (i.e. Boulton). Mr. Bayard replied ironically that we could likewise send to Westminster for our legislation and save the expense of four to five hundred thousand dollars a year. A national coinage was, besides, emblematic of our sovereignty. Bayard said that if, on inquiry, it should be found proper to abolish the Mint, he would join, but that he was not ready "without reflection or distinction to go any length with those who seemed actuated only by an indiscriminate rage for pulling down and destroying establishments."

John Randolph called attention to the enormous percentage of Spanish coin in circulation. He said that sovereignty gave the *right* to establish a Mint, but that it was no more affected by using foreign coin than by using foreign cordage or cannon.

Giles insisted that it was unnecessary to wait for any further information from the Mint. "There is a difference," he said, "between this and other countries. Other nations need to coin their own money; it is not with them the general, but the partial good; it is aggrandizement of individuals, the trappings of royalty. Here it is true you established a mint; you have raised armies and fleets, etc. to create an executive influence; but what do the people say now? They send men here now to govern, who shall not govern for themselves but for the people."

This, of course, was mere party line. If any public establishment in America were actually *shorn* of royal trappings and individual aggrandizements, it was the Mint.

Mr. Rutledge suggested that inquiry be made with the Bank of the United States to learn whether and on what terms it would coin copper before abolishing the Mint.

Only Griswold and Bayard observed (what was a patent fact) that the Mint's expenses accrued from coining the precious metals, and that the copper coinage actually paid its own way.

Rutledge moved to refer the resolution for abolishing the Mint to a select committee, and the motion was carried 54 to 33. Only two years earlier, the

House had killed a Senate bill for abolishment, but now it was likewise menacing the Mint. On March 4, when the end seemed near, Robert Scot wrote to Secretary of the Treasury Gallatin, soliciting a government contract for coining copper.[17]

"I need not omit informing you," he added, "that in the first establishment of the mint, I relinquished a profession, at least equally productive and beneficial as that of the engraver's place in the mint, which I have filled, and I believe without reproach, ever since; by the loss of which, I shall be left without resource, being so long out of the practice of my former profession, that I feel an incapacity to prosecute it with any more effect."

Gallatin may have seriously considered Scot's proposal, for on March 22, Boudinot wrote to the Secretary:[18]

Sir: I am honoured with your letter of the 10th inst. and hasten to give you the best answer that I can, with regard to the real and personal estate of the Mint establishment, &c., &c. This consists of—

Two lots on Seventh Street between Market and Arch Streets, a dwelling house on the north lot, and a shell of a house on the south lot, which last lot widens on the rear to about 60 feet, on which the stable stands. These lots pay a ground rent of 27-50/100 dollars per annum.

A lot on Sugar Alley, at the rear of the above, 20 feet front on the Alley, and about 100 feet deep.

A frame building improved for a large furnace, in the commons at the north end of Sixth Street, of little value, the ground being merely loaned to us.

As to personal estate, this consists wholly of—

The copper planchetts on hand, amounting to about 22 tons.

Three horses, good for little but for the use of the Mint. The machinery of the Mint, of no value but for the use of the Mint.

Five striking presses with machinery.

Three cutting presses.

One milling machine.

Five pairs of rollers, great and small.

One drawing machine.

Three pair of smith's bellows.

A set of blacksmith's tools.

A large number of hubs and dies on hand, of different denominations.

Carpenter's tools.

Seven stoves.

One turning lathe.

Six sets assay scales, and sundry adjusting scales.

Furniture in the clerk's rooms.

Various implements used in the several departments.

About 2000 bushels of charcoals.

Engraver's tools. Potts, bottles, &c., &c. An old horse cart and geers.

About 2000 fire brick; a considerable quantity of old iron.

It is impossible to ascertain the value of these articles, as most of them are of but little consequence, except for the use of the Mint or to persons who may intend to put them to the like uses, and if sold at public sale, probably will not bring half their real value. The machinery of the Mint, may last a year longer with small repair, but after that, will cost about 300 dollars to put them in good repair. The horses may also last another year, but must then at farthest be replaced by others.

If it should be thought best to continue the Mint, the establishment should be rendered permanent, and the machinery should be moved by steam instead of horses, which would in some measure reduce the annual expenses of labor, as

---

[17] *American State Papers,* Finance, Vol. 1.
[18] Ibid.

almost the whole of it could be carried on with the same original force. Our lots are much too small, by which we are greatly cramped as to room. They are now very valuable being in the heart of the city; their price would purchase a very advantageous lot in a less public place, and buildings might be now planned, so as to reduce the expenses of a Mint. But I am perfectly satisfied, that no modification of the Mint could be contrived to lessen them below 17 or 18,000 dollars per annum, though if a larger quantity of bullion could by any means be provided, a greater quantity of coin could be annually made with the same expense, although I am, individually of the opinion, that its present issue of about 500,000 dollars annually, in addition to the current coin of the Union, is sufficient for the present welfare of the United States.

It is the absolute necessity of strict and regular cheques, throughout the whole establishment, that makes the expense of the Mint so great, and this cannot be dispensed with, under any modification that can be proposed. I verily believe, that under no given circumstance, can the necessary coin of the United States be produced with safety to the Government at a much less expense than it is at present, and I believe, that, in the consideration of the subject, it would not be safe, to estimate the expense, at any rate, much under 20,000 dollars.

In the above estimate of expenses, it should be remembered, that the copper cents may produce a profit of 500 dollars per annum, that ought to be credited against the expenditures of the Mint in future, which reduces the amount considerably.

I have the honor to be very respectfully, Sir, Your obedient humble servant,

ELIAS BOUDINOT, Director.

Two gentlemen, in Philadelphia, of respectable Character, have requested me to submit the following propositions on the subject of the Mint.

They will engage to coin on the following terms, and will give ample security for the performance of the contract.

Copper for the difference in weight.
Small silver for three percent.
Dollars for two and a half,
Gold for one and a half,

} on the values

Provided, the United States will give them such part of the present machinery, belonging to the mint, as they may want, with the use of the building.

On April 2, Giles again presented his bill to abolish the Mint. It was read twice and deferred. We can imagine the demoralizing effect such proceedings must have had upon the Mint's employees, most of whom worked from 6 a.m. to 7 p.m., six days a week, while receiving the barest remuneration. Dr. Sheldon has pointed out that the majority of blundered cent dies assign to the periods of agitation against the Mint (i.e. 1794–96 and 1800–03) when the employees expected at any time to be discharged.[19]

On April 17, Director Boudinot wrote to President Thomas Jefferson:

The Director of the Mint being informed by the public News Papers that a Bill has been brought into Congress for abolishing of the Mint, cannot consistent with his duty, omit respectfully to represent the case of some of the officers, clerks and workmen of the Mint, to the President.

The Salaries and Wages allowed in the Mint, have not been increased since the first Establishment of the Institution notwithstanding the great rise in the prices of every necessary of life, for several years past. They have submitted to a bare subsistence without complaint from the Idea that their employment was permanent, while they behaved well, and that Peace and reduced prices of food would give them an opportunity of making up former deficiences. Add to this that

---

[19] Dr. William H. Sheldon (with the collaboration of Dorothy Paschal and Walter Breen), *Penny Whimsy,* Harper & Bros., 1958. (One can also cite similar examples among the other denominations.)

their constant habits in the Mint have made it difficult for them, at once, to return to their former occupations with advantage. If the Mint should be abolished, it will be sometime before they can get again into full employment and of course must suffer essentially, even as to their necessary support. The Director therefore submits their case to the Consideration of Government, and does not doubt, but some small provision will be made for them in case of their intire [sic] dismission from public service.

In this representation it is not meant to include the Director, Assayer or Treasurer, as neither of these do depend on their Salaries for support.

On April 22, the debate was resumed with its customary warmth. Mr. Smith opened the proceedings by suggesting that Congress contract for its coinage with the Bank of the United States.

Giles remarked that "if we turn to the report of the Director, we shall find that he himself supposed the gold and silver coinage unnecessary." This was sheer fabrication.[20]

Giles now peddled a softer line which ostensibly assumed the Federalist position. He had earlier attacked the Mint as monarchical only to hear it praised as an emblem of sovereignty. Actually, there was little difference between the Federalist view of sovereignty and the Republican view of monarchy. Giles said that sovereignty consisted of the power to coin or not to coin, and he didn't think it worth $30,000 annually simply to prove that such a power existed. As for the copper coins, these were of little consequence where he lived since the people would not accept them.

On April 26, the bill to abolish the Mint was passed in the House and sent to the Senate where, surprisingly, it failed to obtain a third reading. To complete the reversal, the Senate, on March 3, passed a bill to prolong the continuation of the Mint at Philadelphia.[21]

On December 17, the abolishment bill was again introduced in the House, this time by Mr. Randolph. Randolph attempted to force a debate on the 21st, but failed when Mr. Griswold advised waiting for the new annual Mint report. On the following day, however, Randolph partially succeeded after remarking that he had not seen a gold coin for two years. Mr. Lowndes professed to have seen many, and said the shortage was in any case due to the large quantities held by banks which preferred gold because it expedited their monthly counting operations. Lowndes maintained that there was $2,000,000 in gold in the Bank of the United States.[22] The subject was finally postponed.

On December 20, Voigt wrote to President Jefferson,[23] suggesting possible improvements in the Mint. He said that with its destruction imminent, he had "reflected with a good deal of attention on the most economical and advantageous plan of conducting the business," and conceived how "in the construction of the machinery great improvements might be made not only to facilitate the

---

[20] In his annual Mint report of February 18, 1802 Boudinot had written that "the greatest part of the gold bullion was received in ingots and lumps imported from foreign ports, which, had it not been for the mint, would have been exported as remittances to Europe, but has now become an addition to the current coin of the United States." Moreover, the Director had estimated, in his special report to Gallatin, that the coinage of a half million dollars annually was necessary for the nation.

[21] The Act of July 16, 1790 provided for all offices to be attached to the seat of the Government, which was now Washington.

[22] If so, it must have included foreign coins or uncoined bullion, for the Philadelphia Mint's entire gold output through December 31, 1802 was only $1,860,170, and not all of that sum had gone to the Bank of the U.S.

[23] *The Papers of Thomas Jefferson,* Library of Congress collection.

work and save labour; but also to give a more beautiful impression on the coin."
Voigt's recommendations would have come with better grace if he had
not ridiculed Jefferson's own efforts to increase the Mint's efficiency. In any
case, the President seems not to have replied, and there is no evidence that
Voigt ever broached the subject again.

With the new year, a gleam of hope touched the Mint. On January 10, 1803,
Representative Gregg suggested that if the Mint's lots could be sold to
advantage they might try to purchase a more propitious site. The "Committee
of Revisal and Unfinished Business" was directed to investigate the subject, and
chairman John Davenport wrote to Boudinot the same day, inquiring also on
the expediency of purchasing a steam engine. The Director replied on the 18th,
enclosing a copy of the Mint's inventory.

> With our present experience, I should think that a new and compleat Mint,
> exclusive of a Steam Engine (with the expence of which I am unacquainted)
> might be built for fifteen thousand Dollars, not including the Site, which I should
> not consider as costing anything, as if well chosen, its rise in value, in a few years,
> might more than double its first cost. However, about half the value of the present
> real Estate, would be fully equal to the purchase.
>
> This having literally answered your request, shall I take the liberty to suggest,
> what is really the effect of longer experience, and a closer application to the sub-
> ject, than before. We have hitherto been supplied with the precious metals, beyond
> our highest expectations, but a continuance of an equal supply in future, cannot be
> looked for with any degree of certainty, unless Congress in their wisdom can
> point out some new source of supply. We never yet have coined a single Dollar
> of the precious metals for Congress.[24] On this view of the subject I conceive the
> present Establishment may answer for some years to come, as well as it has for
> several years past, with the small expence of a few hundred dollars, and par-
> ticularly for the purposes of getting rid of a trifling incumbrance in our local
> situation. The supply of bullion is not such, as to render a Steam Ingine [sic] so
> necessary, as to justify the expence, unless a new mint should be thought eligible,
> in which case I would advise its adoption without hesitation.

On January 21, the House, in a more munificent mood, directed Davenport's
committee "to inquire into the expediency of continuing the Mint at Philadelphia, and whether any alterations or improvements might be made."

On the 25th, Davenport read Boudinot's report and submitted it to the
committee. No further recommendations were made, and on March 1, the
House concurred in the Senate's bill to retain the Mint at Philadelphia.

The bill was enacted on March 3. Its lease was renewed after five years,
and further extensions were made until May 19, 1828 when the Mint was
authorized to continue "in force and operation, until otherwise provided by
law."

❖   ❖   ❖

The Act of February 9, 1793 had legalized, for a limited time, the circulation of several foreign gold and silver coins, and fixed the rates at which
they were to pass. Because of the continuing shortage of U.S. coins, the
Act was renewed on February 1, 1798 and again on April 30, 1802 and April
10, 1806. It was then allowed to expire, and no further attempts were made
to revive it until April 1815, when a group of Maryland bank presidents
petitioned Congress to reinstate the several foreign coins. It appears that the
banks had received large quantities of these coins and were now unable to issue

---

[24] That is, only from private deposits.

them. Secretary of the Treasury Dallas recommended the petition to Congress, which legalized the coins by the Act of April 29, 1816. The provision was renewed in 1819, 1823, 1827 and 1834.

     ❋   ❋   ❋

On March 27, 1806 Senator Tracy introduced a bill for the coinage of double dimes and billon two-cent pieces. The obverse of the double dime was to bear the inscription "XX cents" instead of a Liberty head. In the original printed bill, the weight of the two-cent piece was left blank, and the words "silver and copper" were subsequently crossed out. The bill, as amended on April 12, fixed the weight of this coin at $30\frac{7}{10}$ grains, consisting of $6\frac{4}{10}$ grains silver and $24\frac{3}{10}$ grains copper. The obverse was to bear a large 2 with the word "cents" below, the reverse an eagle as on the silver coins. Over the protests of Director Patterson, the bill passed the Senate on April 16. It was reintroduced on December 19, and again assailed by Patterson.[25] The Director's principal target was the two-cent piece which he said would be difficult (and thus expensive) to produce and easily counterfeited. Moreover, the difficulty in extracting its component metals would render the coin useless to silversmiths and unacceptable to the public. The bill passed the Senate on February 13, 1807, but again died in the House.

Between 1816 and 1829, three individual solutions to the coin shortage were proposed. Congressman Erastus Root thought that reform should begin with the copper coinage. On January 19, 1816 he told members of the House that "the want of a national circulating medium had been a topic of much complaint," and that what served for small change would "scarcely be accepted by the servants at the taverns." In a letter to Secretary Dallas on January 24,[26] Root inquired whether it wouldn't be advisable to reduce the weight of the cent to ninety-six grains, and make copper coins a legal tender up to the value of a dollar. If such a plan were adopted, Root also recommended the coinage of a two- and four-cent piece and the interdiction of privately manufactured coppers. All of these proposals were rejected by Director Patterson and Secretary Dallas.

Three years later, Representative Lowndes of South Carolina presented a lengthy report [27] in which he proposed to reduce the fine weight of the dollar in gold from 24.75 to 23.79 grains, and in silver from 371.25 to 356.4 grains. In the first instance the coinage was free; in the second, the depositor would pay a seignorage of 14.85 grains, or the difference between the old and new weights. The seignorage would not represent a loss to the depositor unless he meant to vend the coins as bullion, for their face value would remain the same. Lowndes also wished to reduce the legal tender of the quarter, dime and half dime to less than five dollars. The plan, though ignored, was well conceived in every way. The bi-metallic ratio of 15.6:1 would have stopped the exportation of gold, and the seignorage on silver created a genuine fiduciary coinage as later adopted by Congress.

In 1820, Secretary of the Treasury Crawford suggested a ratio of $15\frac{3}{4}$ to 1, and the substitution of billon coins for the clumsy, overweight coppers.[28] He

---

[25] Walter Breen, "The Secret History of the Gobrecht Coinages 1836-1840," *The Coin Collector's Journal*, Sept.-Dec., 1954.
[26] *American State Papers*, Finance, Vol. 3.
[27] Ibid.
[28] Ibid.

said that the difficulty in working a silver-copper alloy would, in itself, be security against a flood of counterfeits. Crawford then answered the other objections advanced by Patterson:

> Although the expence of such a coinage should be twice as much as that of an equal number of silver coin, still it might be advantageous. Small change, both of silver and copper, may be abundant in Philadelphia, the seat of the mint; but it is not generally so elsewhere. If it were, tickets of 6¼, 10, 12½, 25 and 50 cents, issued by mayors and corporation officers, and dollar bills torn in two pieces, for the purposes of change, would not be employed for that purpose. The fractional parts of a dollar are so indispensable in the transactions of individuals, that any thing which assumes that character will be employed. If the tickets, which, at this moment, form so great a portion of the change of this City, and of various other places, are employed for that purpose, it is inconceivable that the community should refuse to permit a compound coin of silver and copper to circulate, containing the intrinsic value which it represents, merely because for manufactures it will not be worth more than brass or copper, and that the expense of refining will be equal to the value of the silver. Change, that is, the fractional parts of a dollar, is so indispensable to the community, that its inapplicability to manufactures, and its exemption from liability to exportation, instead of forming objections, are recommendations in its favor.

Crawford's report was likewise rejected, and during the entire history of the first Mint, Congress watched supinely as bank notes, miscellaneous scrip, and lightweight foreign silver coins did service as a national currency.

CHAPTER 11

The Closing Years

ON DECEMBER 10, 1828 DIRECTOR SAMUEL MOORE wrote to John Sergeant, chairman of the House committee on the Mint:

The inadequacy of the present accommodations of the Mint has become so obvious and the unsightly aspect which the buildings present is so little suitable to its character as a National Institution, that I must ask leave to consult you on the expediency of bringing the subject before Congress. Many members of both Houses have, on visiting us, expressed their surprise and solicitude on the subject, and I persuade myself that a general wish would be evinced to place the Mint on a less discreditable establishment. Unless therefore, the present short session should seem to you an unpropitious period, will you please to take the measures relative therefor, which may seem best.

Something more than a simple appropriation being requisite, you will judge whether a special Bill through the formality of a Committee will not be indispensable. Authority to purchase a suitable lot in a new position, or to enlarge the present one by the purchase of adjacent ground, as either might be found most judicious, would be necessary, as also to sell the buildings and lots now occupied, if the Mint should be erected on a new site.

The sum required to accomplish the object, in such manner as to afford all proper facilities for the accommodation of the Mint, would probably be not less than one hundred thousand dollars. Space and apartments adapted to the introduction of that system of machinery in which the coinage is effected by steam power ought to be considered as a part as to a Mint establishment. The structure should be very substantial, devised and executed with studious care, and present an exterior neat and not inelegant.

I touch only cursorily on this topic now, but will go more into detail if deemed necessary, when the direction the subject will take is ascertained. The general facts are familiar and obvious to you. There are points less obvious which can be given in ample illustration of the privations and impediments by which the Mint is now embarrassed.

Your attention to the welfare of the Mint last session has marked an epoch in its history. I hope you may have the pleasure of promoting its prosperity still farther through the liberality of the present Congress in relation to this Institution.

On December 15, the House appointed a committee to enquire "into the expediency of making further provision for the support and extension of the Mint establishment." The committee solicited a report from Director Moore who complied on the 23rd. (This report is referred to in Chapter 7.) After describing the present site, Moore suggested the possibility of purchasing the adjacent ground and rebuilding the institution.

> To construct this Establishment on the present site of the Mint would require that the ground extending to the fourteen foot alley on the South and to the private court on the North and embracing the lot F on the East should be purchased. These with the ground already occupied by the Mint would form an area 90 feet in front and 150 feet deep, leaving a vacant space of ten feet on the East. It is believed that these additional lots might be obtained at from twelve to fifteen thousand dollars. Not much advantage could be derived from any of the buildings now occupied by the Mint—except No. 3, which might be retained, and made to form a part of the arrangement delineated.
>
> The expence of constructing the requisite buildings may be estimated at from 50 to 60 thousand dollars. Much would depend on the stile of the front edifice. It should be in good taste. The extent of the appropriation would afford some criterion by which to judge of the expectation entertained in this regard. The other buildings should possess all the advantages of exterior which well adjusted proportions, symmetry and aptitude could exhibit. This is a cheap and enduring stile of beauty in an edifice.
>
> The question of the stile of the principal edifice is a public concern of some little moment, and will claim consideration. My special object is an official establishment which may accomplish the design of this Institution with promptitude commensurate with the expectations of the Government and the wants of the public.
>
> To Secure this capacity for enlarged operations the new combination of machinery devised and executed by Mr. Boulton and adapted in some of the Mints of Europe ought to be had in view and a suitable position appropriate for its erection and employment at an early period. This topic has been the subject of some preliminary enquiries addressed to Mr. Boulton in 1827. From his reply it appears that so much of his system of machinery as it might be desirable to introduce would cost about £7,000 at Liverpool.
>
> It is understood that machinery of this description constructed by Mr. Boulton for a Mint in South America is now in New York for sale. If this should be found adaptable to our purpose it would be judicious to embrace the opportunity of securing it: the expence it is presumed would be as low as the price charged by Mr. Boulton at Liverpool.
>
> If the Committee perceive in the consideration presented sufficient reasons for an extension of the Mint establishment I beg leave to ask that the measure may not be deferred if practicable to accomplish it during this session. In every Department repairs have been procrastinated where it was possible in the belief that something more than repairs would eventually be deemed proper. The roof of our front building is in a decayed state, and ought to be renewed if it is to be used much longer: the state of other of the buildings has been before mentioned, and it is proper to add that the boiler of our steam Engine has been in use since 1816 and it is not proper to rely on it much longer—it is wished that when renewed, it should form a part of the improved establishment with a proportional enlargement. Up to the present time the power of the Mint has been generally adequate to the coinage demanded without vexatious delay. The time can not be far distant, and it is probably very near, where the demand will exceed its capacity. On the whole I trust the Committee will be of opinion that it will be wise to authorize an

extension of this establishment, and expedient to do so now. A considerable time must elapse before anything can be accomplished effectually. Every step will require to be taken with studious care that there may be nothing deficient or superfluous.

The committee will I hope excuse the expression of some sensitiveness on account of the repulsive aspect which the group of buildings appropriated to the Mint presents. A transient allusion to this alone is intended. Were I however to pursue this consideration with some earnestness, I should be sustained by the tenor of the remarks made by all the members of Congress who have visited us—a feeling of concern having been uniformly expressed by them that an exterior so unsightly should characterize an institution so eminently national.

Moore subsequently drafted two different forms of a bill for erecting a new Mint. He submitted these to Sergeant on December 31, adding: "It is desirable that the liberty of selecting a new site may be given without presenting the idea of removal and that course to be attained in both forms but the first appears to be most likely to prevent the members from entertaining loose views in this respect."

On March 2, 1829 Congress granted appropriations for enlarging the Mint, and on April 30, a new site was purchased by the Government from Ann Poyntell and a Mr. and Mrs. R. A. Caldcleugh. During the same month the Mint was offered a set of Boulton's machinery from two men in New York representing the Anglo Mexican Mining Co. Director Moore finally decided that the machinery would be unsuitable for the proposed new Mint.

On May 31, 1830 Congress authorized the President to cause the entire Mint property to be sold, when and on such terms as he deemed best for the public interest.

At this point, our chronology becomes confusing. In a letter to Matthew Robinson Boulton on August 19, 1830 [1] Moore indicated a desire to enlarge the Mint on the old site. He enclosed a diagram of the Mint property, which embodied the proposed alterations. The three principal buildings were to be replaced by a single unit.

In the end, however, Moore must have found the old site inadequate, for beginning on July 2, 1832 Poulson's *American Daily Advertiser* ran the following advertisement:

> United States Mint Property under authority from the President of the United States, will be sold at Public Sale on Thursday, the 19th of July, 1832, at 8 o'clock in the evening at the Merchants Coffee House:
> The site of the old Mint, together with the improvements thereon, and a quantity of valuable machinery. The premises embrace a lot of ground situate on the east side of Delaware Seventh Street between Market and Arch Streets in the City of Philadelphia, containing in front or breadth on said Seventh Street 36 feet, 10 inches, and in length or depth 99 feet, together with a contiguous lot of ground in the rear of the above containing in front 17 feet on a 14 feet passage way called Sugar Alley and in length or depth 56 feet 10 inches, and also another lot of ground fronting said alley 20 feet 6 inches and extending in depth 88 feet dividing from the last described by a 4 foot passageway.
> The improvements are a large double house on Seventh Street 36 feet 10 inches in front, 3 stories high, conveniently divided, affording accommodations to the various offices and vaults and a part of the operating machinery and also a range of shops extending about 17 x 80 feet across the rear of the premises.
> The machinery comprises a steam engine of 10 horse power, together with a

---

[1] *Matthew Boulton papers.* Assay Office of Birmingham, England.

complete system of rolling apparatus for hot or cold rolling, together with a drawing table connected with the steam power, all now in daily use, with a variety of other implements, furnaces, etc.

Subject the first two described lots to an annual ground rent charge of 21 dollars and the last described lot to an annual ground rent charge of 6 dollars and 50 cents.

The premises and machinery will be offered either separately or together, as may be considered most advantageous to the United States and to those persons inclined to purchase.

Terms, etc. at sale.

S. Moore, Director.
C. J. Wolbert, Auctioneer.

N.B. A draft of the above may be examined at the Merchants Coffee House and at the premises by applying to Mr. Eckfeldt, Chief Coiner of the Mint. Persons desirous to purchase may obtain all necessary information relative to the machinery, &c.

Because of delays in completing the new building, the old Mint was withdrawn from sale. In January 1833, its machinery was removed to the new site, where it was used until 1835. In that year the threadbare engines were hauled back to their original home, and on October 8, the first Mint finally passed under the hammer. It realized a trifling $10,100.

PART III

THE SECOND PHILADELPHIA MINT

The Second Philadelphia Mint. Lithograph published by J. T. Bowen in 1840.

CHAPTER 12

Mechanization Comes to the Mint

IN ITS LONG AND VARIEGATED HISTORY, the second Mint offers many contrasts to its predecessor. The forces that caused this transformation were both internal and external. Mechanization was, of course, fundamental. It increased the output of the Mint tremendously, and dignified its labors. It also resulted in a certain psychological ease and idiosyncrasies of conduct which, as Horace Greeley used to say, "make mighty interesting reading."

The discovery of vast gold deposits in California, the Western territories and some Southern states, of silver in the Appalachians; the working of new metals and new alloys; and above all, the lobbying by the gold, silver and nickel interests, largely assign to the era of the second Mint. The same may be said of the establishment of branch mints and the re-organization of the Mint under the Treasury Department, finally with its headquarters in Washington, D.C.

The lot on which the second Mint was built extended from the northwest corner of Chestnut and Juniper Streets to Penn Square. It had a front of 150 feet, and was 204 feet deep. The cornerstone was laid on July 4, 1829, on the Juniper Street side, about forty feet from Chestnut.[1]

The Mint was finished and occupied in January 1833. It was designed by architect William Strickland after the celebrated Grecian Temple on the river Ilysus, near Athens. The building was made of white marble, with Ionic por-

---

[1] This cornerstone was discovered in May 1903, when the building was razed. It weighed three hundred pounds, and revealed an old-fashioned candy jar with a petrified cork. The jar held three coins, two newspapers, and a scroll giving a skeleton history of the old Mint and the establishment of the new one.

ticos in the front and rear. Its interior court was enclosed by terraces reaching from the principal and second stories.

For two years, the new Mint plodded along with the machinery of its fore-runner. Director Moore, who for several years had contemplated the purchase of an entire system of machinery from Boulton, finally decided to send a special agent to the principal European mints and refineries, to learn the best features of each. Moore hired an assistant assayer for this purpose, and obtained an appropriation to send him abroad. At the recommendation of his brother-in-law, Robert Maskell Patterson, Moore selected Franklin Peale, who embarked in May 1833. Peale remained in Europe for about two years and, upon his return, introduced many valuable improvements in the Mint technology.

OPERATIONS[2]

Engraving

In 1836, the production of dies at the Mint was revolutionized by the pur-chase of a reducing pantograph—the French *Tour à Portrait de Contamin*, or Portrait lathe. Instead of cutting the device into a steel die blank, the engraver now sculptured a clay or wax model about six inches in diameter. From this a plaster casting was made which, in its turn, served as a model for a metal casting. For some years castings were made of fine iron, but these apparently proved too hard for convenient hand finishing. After various experiments at Sellers' foundry, brass was selected as the most suitable material.[3]

The portrait lathe operated on the principle of a three-dimensional panto-graph. A long, rigid bar, or lever, ran along the front of the lathe and hinged at the farthest left-hand side, to a fulcrum. At a short distance from the fulcrum a very sharp graver, or cutting tool, was fastened to the lever. The graver faced a soft tool-steel cylinder (the hub blank) which was fixed on a large, solid wheel. Toward the right end of the lever, a pointed steel stub was mounted directly opposite the casting.

By means of a spring at the upper end, the lever was drawn in, causing the graver and the tracing point to touch the center of their respective models. The models were now rotated in an equal counter-clockwise motion, with the two points gradually working their way to the edge. In this duet, the tracing point was the leader, and its motions were precisely reproduced on the hub in a smaller ratio, the proportion being established by the distance between the two tools. After every complete revolution, a screw mechanism lowered the right end of the lever slightly, placing the two tools closer to the edge of their respec-tive models. The entire operation was repeated several times until the design was sufficiently blocked out. Even then, however, it was comparatively rough and required a good deal of hand finishing before the master hub could be used to sink a master die. Lettering, except for the mintmark, was added to the

---

[2] The principal sources consulted for this section are: 1) Waldo Abbott, "Making Money," *Harper's Monthly Magazine*, Nov.-Dec. 1861; 2) Annual reports of the Director of the Mint: 1875, 18
[3] George Escol Sellers, "Early Engineering Reminiscences; The United States Mint (Part II)," *American Machinist*, May 18, 1893.

Contamin reducing lathe, cutting a hub. The following sketches of Mint operations are re-produced from "Harpers Monthly Magazine," Nov.-Dec., 1861, and "Harpers Weekly," June 19, 1880.

latter, after which working hubs and dies were made in a multiplying press. late as 1860, a large, manually operated screw press was used for this purp but it was eventually superseded by an hydraulic press.[4]

The date and mintmark were punched only into the working die as th would otherwise restrict the use of the hub. In 1840, compound punches w the first two numerals of the date were used in the dies of large cents and h dollars, and three-figure punches for those of the smaller coins. Breen sugge that three-figure punches of larger size may have proven too difficult to pur by hand. By the 1860's, however, they were probably standard procedure most denominations, as indicated by the 1865-S over inverted 186 ten-dol gold piece. That a four-figure date punch was used on at least one denomin tion prior to 1860 is proven by the 1858 over inverted 1858 half dime.

On November 30, 1866, the Mint's engraver James B. Longacre wrote Mint Director William Millward concerning an improved reducing lathe vented by C. J. Hill of London:[5]

"Dear Sir . . . My attention was called to the "reducing machine" about f years ago, from specimens sent to the Mint by the inventor C. J. Hill of Lond purporting to be produced by the operations of his machine which were so m superior to any other machine reductions I had seen, as to create some doubt to the accuracy of the representations of the process by which they were p duced; and I was induced to open a correspondence with an artist friend resid in London on whose judgment I could rely, to make further inquiries; his re satisfied me of the value of the invention, but Mr. Hill would not then agree construct and furnish the machine, preferring to keep it in his own hands a take orders for the work produced by it; he has since however as I have learn parted with his interest in the invention to the Messrs. Wyon, who it seems n propose to furnish the machine.

The work produced by this machine judging from the specimens before me so far superior to that of our present machine (which was constructed many ye ago in Paris) or any other in existence of which I have knowledge—that I c sider it extremely desirable the Mint should possess it—if it can be obtained fair terms and guaranteed to produce work equal to the specimens now submitt It is scarcely possible to overrate the value of such a machine in its relation to work required for the coinage, provided the Mint can have the entire and absol control of its operations without restriction by the patentee.

A Hill machine was purchased by the Mint in September 1867, and us from the following year.

Trial impressions dating as late as 1877, indicate that lettering was s punched by hand into the master die, rather than sculptured in the origi model.[6] Using letter uniformity as another criterion, we can assume that th was standard procedure as late as 1892. Again, certain blundered numerals (on one variety of the 1894 Indian cent), and slight differences in positioni indicate that dates were punched into each working die throughout the peri of the second Mint.

---

[4] The Mint Director's Report for 1893 mentions the installation of an hydraulic press to repl the large screw press hitherto used to strike medals (and apparently proof coins). It is thus p sible that a screw press was used for hubbing until, or even after, this date.

[5] *Papers of James B. Longacre*, Library Company of Philadelphia collection.

[6] This was due not to any deficiency in the Hill machine, but apparently to the ease with wh the engraver could punch letters into the die.

Large copper flan used to test punches. Obverse shows impression from incomplete hub made in 1876. This arrangement does not appear on any known pattern. Reverse shows punches for various denominations together with 1877 date.

ASSAYING

Gold

Although the basic method of assaying gold was not altered after Peale's trip, three important modifications were introduced. The first was to melt down the deposit, creating a uniform mixture before taking an assay sample. This was a more accurate and expeditious method than taking a sample from each separate, and probably heterogenous, mass of bullion. The second innovation was to "quart" the sample before cupelling it. The third was the adoption of the metric system, with fractional divisions to one ten-thousandth part.

* * *

Following the discovery of gold in the Southern and Western United States, several assay offices were established in addition to the branch mints. A graphic description of the New York Assay Office is given by Waldo Abbott in the November 1861 edition of *Harper's Monthly Magazine.*

The bullion is brought in by every conceivable class of persons. The greater part comes through banks and brokers, brought by sturdy porters or jaunty clerks; but much is brought by miners from California or Pike's Peak, and by emigrants from every land. A bearded Californian, fresh from the steamer, will not infrequently walk into the room, throw off his upper garments, and take from his waist a belt filled with golden scales which he has worn during the whole voyage. The precious metals come in every possible shape. There are bright bars stamped with the British crown—the value of five thousand dollars, compressed into brick; there are Napoleons and sovereigns, with the imperial and royal effigies as bright as when they left the mint; doubloons, ducats, and joes, and all the miscellaneous coins of Europe. There is gold dust washed clean in mountain streams, and nuggets, rough but rich, worn into uncouth shapes by the waters of ages. There is plate and jewelry of every kind and form—rings, bracelets, broaches, and chains; vases, dishes, forks, and spoons of gold, silver, and not infrequently, as subsequent assay shows, of counterfeit metal; these having performed their duty of use or adornment, and now worn out or unfashionable, are sold for their value as metal. . . .

The bullion having been weighed, the depositor takes a receipt for it. This is beautifully engraved, with a vignette of the American Eagle, printed in crimson, and signed by the Treasurer of the mint.

Another improvement in the gold assay was introduced in 1867, when the glass mattrass used to boil the nitric acid was replaced by platinum thimbles with fine slits at the bottom. These obviated the necessity of decanting the old solutions since the thimbles drained themselves into a large platinum evaporating dish.

Silver

In reply to a query of Congress, Director Samuel Moore on January 22, 1831 [7] reported that silver had hitherto been assayed by cupellation. He added:

> No silver assays have been made here in the humid way. The subject having however, attracted the attention of foreign assayers and chemists, and the probability being great that they may be led to select this method, under some modifications, in preference to cupellation, a series of experiments will be considered worthy of attention with us, though the practice . . . of referring frequently to a proof piece, renders us less sensible to the necessity of a change in this regard. A facile process in the humid way would, however, be decidedly preferable.

The humid process was introduced at the Mint in 1835 by Franklin Peale who had studied the method at P. N. Johnson's refinery in England.

The ore was first melted in a black lead and clay crucible which had been lubricated with fine charcoal. A small portion of the fluid metal was then poured quickly into water, and the resulting granulation assayed. [8]

A quantity of the silver-copper granulation (weighed for exact determination) was dissolved in a glass bottle containing nitric acid. To this the assayer added a solution of salt, the latter being of the exact weight necessary to convert 1000/1115 parts of pure silver into silver chloride, at the same time leaving the copper unaffected. The bottle was then shaken violently to make the white curdy chloride settle at the bottom, leaving the liquid above clear, although slightly colored by the remaining metal. Thus, unless the silver was far below coin standard, a very small fraction would remain unprecipitated in the solution. More saline solution, of one tenth normal strength, was now added in minute and measured decimal doses by means of a small hand pipette. This raised a white cloud on the surface of the solution, and from the density of the cloud, the assayer judged how much salt was required to complete precipitation. Additional decimal doses were then added until the rest of the silver was converted.

To ascertain whether or not the strength of the salt solution had been altered by atmospheric changes or other influences, the assayer measured out the quantity required to precipitate 1000 parts of silver, which he tested against 1004 parts of absolutely pure silver. If the solution were unaltered, four additional decimal measures would be necessary to precipitate the whole of the silver. If a disparity arose, the other assays were corrected accordingly.

---

[7] Register of Debates in Congress, H.R.

[8] Silver and copper inevitably separate as the mixture is poured into, and solidifies in, the mold. The silver is drawn toward the area of greatest heat, the copper away from it. Thus, the metal in the lower part of both the mold and the pot, and in the interior of the ingot, will be of higher quality than the rest. For this reason, the metal was exposed to cold water, producing homogenous granulation from which an accurate assay could be made.

Cupellation and parting of silver.

The one defect in the humid process was that it did not permit a comple
extraction of mercury, which reacted the same way as the silver did to t'
solvents and precipitants. This was finally overcome by adding to the nitr
acid ten grams of acetate of soda in crystals, plus a little free acetic ac
which held the mercury in solution.

Refining

Improvements in the refining of gold made cupellation unnecessary. The go
bullion, combined with three times its weight in silver, was brought to fusie
in one of the furnaces, then ladled out with a long-handled dipping cup, ar
flung with a jerk into a tub of cold water. The reason for granulating the met
in this particular operation was to present as much of its surface as possible
the acid. After the water had been drained off, the flakes were placed into larg
porcelain vessels, containing nitric acid.

The vessels were arranged in rectangular lead-lined troughs, which we
placed in a water bath kept boiling by steam jets issuing from copper coi
This arrangement was known as the "corroding house," or "parting house
Each vessel in the corroding house had a stonewood lid, and was enclosed
woodwork with sliding doors, allowing the copious nitrous fumes to escaj
through the chimney; but occasionally these still became sufficiently heavy
cause serious annoyance. Abbott described the nitrous fumes as presenting
brilliant appearance so that many who watched them from the street belo
supposed that vast quantities of gold were passing into the air.

The nitric acid was gently boiled for about six hours, reducing most of th
silver to a dark green solution of silver nitrate. This was carefully decante
through a gold siphon and transferred into large, round precipitating va
where we shall find it again after a little while. In the meantime, the near
pure gold, appearing to be anything but what it actually was, remained at th
bottom of the vessel in the form of a dark brown granular sediment. Perhaj
a twentieth of one per cent of the silver nitrate still remained, and to remov
this, the gold was showered with warm water in a large tub which had,
the bottom, a strainer composed of alternating layers of muslin and filterir
paper. This "finishing" operation, which generally took from eight to ten hour
was later shortened by treating the gold a second and a third time wit
nitric acid.

Clean and pure, but still in granular form, the gold was taken to an hydraul
press. There, about a peck of it was placed in a "stave," or mold, with sli
at the bottom, and squeezed under some eighty tons pressure which forced ov
the remaining water and compressed the gold into a long solid cake, or chees
as it was called. Although the top and bottom of the cheese were still rath
dull, its sides, polished by the friction of the stave, were lustrous. To expel ever
bit of moisture, the bars were then baked in a steam oven, broken up, melte
and cast in iron molds lubricated with pitch and rosin. After cooling suf
ciently, the bars, now weighing about seventeen pounds each, were washe
with dilute sulphuric acid to remove any film of iron oxide and restore the
full brilliance.

During all this time, the silver nitrate, which we left as a dark green flui

Refining: granulating the deposit.

Refining: the corroding house.

Refining: precipitating and parting the silver.

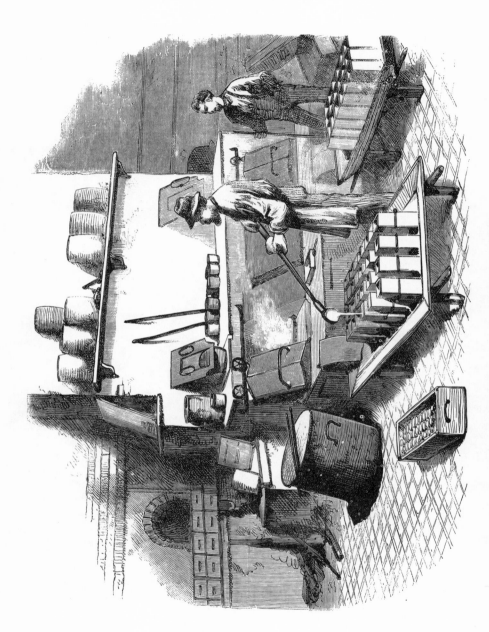

Alloying the metal and casting ingots.

in the precipitating vats, was poured into an immense tank and subjected to a strong solution of sodium chloride (common salt), brought in by pipes leading from reservoir tanks in the attic. The mixture was thoroughly stirred, transforming the greenish solution into a curdy white substance composed of silver chloride and nitrate of soda. Continued stirring reduced it to a smooth pulpy condition. It was then drawn off by stop-cocks into large filtering boxes where it was drained several times through cotton cloth. The purified, or "sweetened," silver chloride, as it was now called, was scooped out of the filter tank with a copper scoop shovel, and transferred to a lead-lined reducing vat where it was washed with hot water and treated with a quantity of pure granulated zinc. In this "reduction process," the materials were mixed by manually operated, oar-like paddles, producing zinc chloride and metallic silver. With reduction complete, a small amount of sulphuric acid was added to remove the remaining zinc. The pure silver was then scooped out, again filtered, and washed in hot water. Like the gold, it bore in this state little resemblance to a precious metal, appearing more like a dull, grey heap of ashes. Finally it was conveyed to the drying cellar where it was compressed by an hydraulic press into long, hard cakes. These were heated to redness in a drying oven, and melted and cast into bars.

In 1875, various improvements in the refining of gold were introduced at the Philadelphia Mint. To begin with, the heavy nitrous fumes from the corroding house were conveyed to a coke-burning furnace in the attic where they were destroyed.

The silver chloride solution, which had been previously stirred by hand, was now moved by an arrangement of mechanical stirrers, driven by steam, and reversible in motion. A mechanical mixing apparatus was built to quicken the parting of the silver and the production of zinc chloride in the reduction process.

Instead of "finishing" the gold with nitric acid, which refined it to about .995 fineness, sulphuric acid was introduced, producing bars of .998 or .999 fineness. Five furnaces or stoves were built, each supporting a small iron pot, with the whole arrangement encased in a lead-lined box to receive and carry off the sulphureous fumes.

The hydraulic press was powered by a small steam engine, and a large settling vat was placed in the courtyard, plus another smaller one in the basement, to intercept traces of the precious metals carried along by the washing operations.

Alloying

After refining, the cakes of metal were sprinkled with powdered charcoal to prevent oxidization, and melted in crucibles in the furnaces of the melting room. Each furnace was given one crucible, or melt, at a time, and was capable of handling four in a day. When properly alloyed, the melt was ladled out with a triangularly-shaped cup, held by a pair of tongs, and poured slowly into narrow rectangular molds. These molds were bound together in pairs, the unit actually consisting of three pieces—two long U-shaped strips, and a center piece forming a partition between the two. The construction was held together by a band with a fixed screw.

As soon as a mold had been filled, it was passed to a second man who dismantled it and, with heavy gloves, threw the two red-hot ingots into a tank of water. Afterwards the ingots were dipped into a very weak solution of sulphuric acid. The gate end of the ingot was cut off in a "topping machine," and the little fringe which accrued from the parting line of the mold was filed off by hand. The ingots were then stamped with their melt number and sent to the chief coiner.

Coining

The rolling machines, which had been powered by steam since 1816, were improved in two important ways. First, the engine was furnished with a throttle valve to control its speed during the irregularities inherent in the rolling operation. Secondly, the expensive gearing was dispensed with, and the distance between the rollers was regulated by a dial arrangement with a crank handle. The Mint had four rolling machines that were kept in a fixed, graduated series, allowing the ingot to pass successively through each.

The draw bench was improved by an arrangement of weights that, fixed to a nearby wall, automatically drew the carriage back to its starting position, ingeniously reducing the speed as it approached the iron stand.

Situated in the rear of the rolling mills were six planchet cutters, driven by steam and operating on the principle of an eccentric wheel, as described earlier.

In 1850, due to the enormous increase in gold deposits, the Mint hired forty women to supplement their adjusting staff. This was done at the suggestion of Franklin Peale who adjudged the labor as "being entirely suited to their capacity." In 1860, the female adjusters received $1.10 a day for ten hours work, a sum considered generous by current standards. Abbott describes them as appearing "happy and contented and chatting and laughing merrily" as they worked "with apparent recklessness, scarcely glancing at planchet or scales, but seemingly guided by their touch." Yet the work could not have been wholly pleasant, for the scales were so sensitive that no draft could be allowed to enter the room which was thus poorly ventilated and, on warm days, very uncomfortable.

Sometime in the 1860's, the practice was introduced of adjusting only the gold coins and silver dollars. The overweight planchets were filed lightly on the edge and, after striking, hardly ever showed the adjustment.

The other slightly heavy or light pieces were coined separately, then mixed together, allowing each delivery to present a balanced weight.

Gold coins, except for the dollar, were counted by hand, and weighed in the aggregate before being placed into bags. Gold dollars, silver and minor coins were counted in a "counting board," a wooden tray partitioned by copper strips. The board could be worked with such facility that twenty-five dollars in five-cent pieces were counted in less than a minute, then emptied through the front of the tray into a drawer.

Shortly before leaving the Mint, in December 1854, Franklin Peale ordered a beautiful and delicate automatic scale from France which seems never to have been employed. Since the scale was adapted only to half eagles, Peale may have intended to redesign it for a more general use. The scale was arranged so that the planchets, on being placed at one end, were carried through

Top: rolling the ingots. **Bottom**: drawing the ingots to the exact width of the planchet.

Cutting planchets out of the strips.

Adjusting the planchets—a feminine vocation.

a hopper and then deposited, one by one, onto a balance. If the coin were too light, it failed to move either of the two counter-weights and was automatically tipped into a bin containing other underweight pieces. If the weight were correct, the coin moved the first counterweight, causing the chute to shift slightly. The coin was thus tipped into a second bin. If too heavy, it moved both counterweights, and the chute moved still further, dropping the piece into a third bin.

A. L. Snowden, during his appointment as chief coiner (1866-76), introduced the "Seyss Automatic Weighing Machine," which, by a superior application of the same principle, weighed planchets of every denomination. The planchets were fed into their respective tubes and forwarded piece by piece to be weighed and assorted. At the end of the machine there was an electrical apparatus which sounded an alarm if more than one planchet at a time found its way onto the balance.

In 1836, the old milling machine was replaced by a beautiful steam-powered model. The new milling machine, however, was used only to "upset," or raise, a rim around the coin. Edge lettering was discontinued, and the reeding was applied by means of a close collar during striking. The milling machine stood about three feet high, and had three long brass piling tubes leading to grooves of different sizes. The operator dropped about thirty planchets down their respective tube, at the bottom of which the lowest planchet was caught by a revolving feeder and forced edgewise between a large revolving disc and a fixed segment. The space between the disc and the segment was slightly less than the diameter of the planchet, whose edge was squeezed inward and upward, receiving a mill, or rim, all around. At the end of four revolutions, the planchet was released, falling into a receptacle below. The drive shaft of the machine, concealed in a hollow column, rotated the milling wheel by means of a cam. So dextrous was the mechanism that 120 double eagles or 560 half dimes could be milled in a single minute.

Before stamping, the planchets were annealed and cleaned, then dried in a large drum, which was steam-heated, and filled with a quantity of very pure basswood sawdust. Afterward, the sawdust was removed and the planchets were kept revolving for an hour to burnish their surfaces by the constant friction. Finally, they were steam-heated over a warming pan and brought to the presses.

On September 26, 1835 Director Robert Patterson wrote to the Secretary of the Treasury:

> We have just completed under the superintendence of Mr. Peale, a model of a coining press, formed from plans which he saw in successful operation in France and in Germany, and possessing many very manifest advantages over the Screw press now employed at the Mint. Among these one of the most important is that [it] admits the immediate and easy application of steam power. At present our larger presses require the operation of three men each, while I am sure that one man could attend two of the new presses. The work too may be done much more rapidly,—a desideratum of which we now feel the necessity.

The first working model of the press was built during the following year by Merrick, Agnew & Tyler, under the direction of Rufus Tyler who afterward served as chief coiner of the New Orleans Mint.

The press worked by a toggle, or knee, joint, the principle still employed

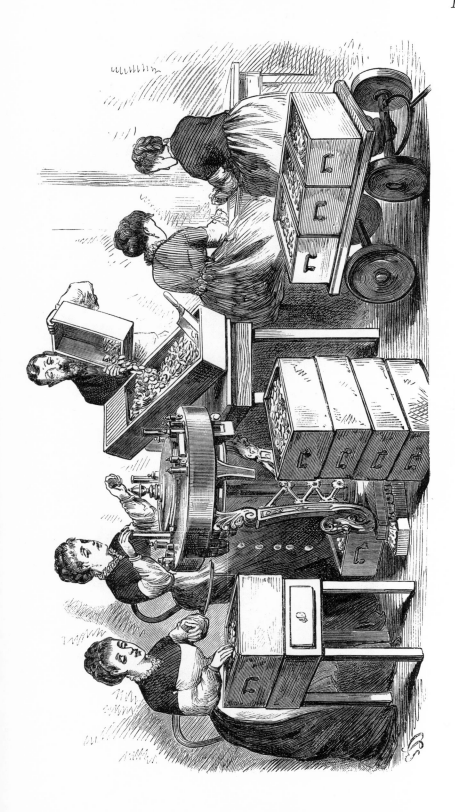

Milling the planchets.

Steam-powered coining press.

in coining presses. The joint is alternately pushed forward and pulled back by a rotary motion in the rear of the press. When the joint is retracted, a linkage of movements causes the lower die to rise through the collar, receiving a planchet that has been automatically fed by the layer-on (a mechanism simulating the action of human fingers). The die then sinks back into the collar, and the upper die is brought down with great force. The faces of the planchet are stamped and, almost simultaneously, its edge is forced against the corrugated collar, resulting in the familiar reeded edge. Then the toggle joint is pushed forward, the dies separate, and the coin is ejected.

In addition to its automation, the new press had the advantage of applying a force equal to that of the screw with only a fraction of the power required by the latter, with its vibrating motion and inherent loss through friction. The one disadvantage of the steam press was that its fast-action blow brought up the relief of the coin less perfectly than the "squeeze" of a screw.

In 1858, the coining press was redesigned by David Gilbert, and its arch made solid to prevent extraneous vibration. This model was used at the Mint until 1874, when it was replaced by another, constructed along lines suggested by the then chief coiner, A. L. Snowden. The new machine is said to have utilized a "solid stroke," which registered a progressive force. This resulted in coins of better relief, and greatly increased the life of the dies.

CHAPTER 13

New Designs

IT WOULD HAVE BEEN OUT OF CHARACTER for that able and energetic Director Samuel Moore to overlook any possibility of improving the coinage. Under his aegis, William Kneass had overhauled the quarter dollar in 1831, and other changes were soon to follow. In 1834, Kneass redesigned the gold coinage and introduced a new Liberty head on the half dollar. The latter emerged gradually, over several dies, and shows many slight variations on the 1834-36 coins. Kneass also reduced the stars, letters and numerals on the half dollar as he had earlier done on the quarter. During the following year he made comparable changes in the obverse of the large cent.

In May 1835, Director Moore announced his resignation, to become effective July 1. Accordingly, on May 26, a commission was given to his brother-in-law, Dr. Robert Maskell Patterson.

On June 16, Moore wrote to Secretary of the Treasury Woodbury, asking permission to hire Christian Gobrecht as second engraver.[1] He said that this would be necessary to meet the demands of the new branch mints authorized by Congress.

> Mr. Kneass, our present Engraver . . . is an acceptable, popular and very useful Officer; perhaps one of the most rapid in execution in the U. States. I do not know whether another could be found, whose celerity in his profession could have sufficed to furnish all the dies we have necessarily employed within the past five years. The intensely studious care with which Mr. Gobrecht executes is

---

[1] Walter Breen, "The Secret History of the Gobrecht Coinages, 1836-40," *The Coin Collector's Journal*, Sept.-Dec., 1954. Most of the following pertinent correspondences were originally printed in this source. Certain differences will be noted in the present printing, which was copied directly from papers in the National Archives.

not more remarkable than the quickness of Mr. Kneass in multiplying copies—united they would make a force in this department of the Mint sufficient, it is believed, for the whole establishment including the Branches.

While Woodbury was still pondering this request, Kneass suffered a stroke that left him partially incapacitated. The new Director, Robert Patterson, immediately requested and received permission to employ Gobrecht, who began working at the Mint the following month. Patterson had already hired the Philadelphia artists Thomas Sully and Titian Peale to prepare new designs for the coinage, and Gobrecht arrived just in time to take his place among the historic trio.

Patterson maintained that, in an emblem, it was necessary to avoid the individuality of a portrait. A man of great self-confidence and dogmatism, he suggested for the obverse a design similar to that on the reverse of the English copper coinage. Liberty thus emerged as a refurbished Britannia, her trident replaced by a staff and pileus.[2] Shortly before his stroke, Kneass made a sketch based on Patterson's conception. This was remodelled by both Peale and Sully, and on October 15 Gobrecht's copper-plate impression was submitted to Secretary Woodbury.

On January 8, Patterson sent impressions from a study die to Woodbury and President Jackson, both of whom approved the design. Woodbury regretted, however, that the Liberty pole had not been placed somewhat higher so that its foot was visible. In his reply of January 14, Patterson observed that this could not be done except in a standing figure, in which the size would be reduced by one third. He said that the objections to this were "almost insuperable," and that the design would be "wholly unfit for the smaller coins."[3] Then, to prove his superior judgment, Patterson listed his own objections to the approved design.

It is true that in our first attempt the pole is not thrown sufficiently back from the figure, and this is in part due to a fault in the left arm and shoulder, the latter of which, as you have probably observed, is too low, and too far from the neck, and the former of which is too prominent, requiring to be subdued and thrown back by being made flatter. A similar fault exists in the face, which we find to be very much improved by flattening the cheeks. The right arm is too muscular, and the articulation at the elbow is not properly marked. The right hand was at one time beautiful, but was injured by yielding to an injudicious criticism. The index finger of the left hand is too much in the position of pointing. There is too much confusion of drapery about the left breast, and near the right hand. The knees are too *lumpy,* the articulations not being shown with sufficient distinctness.

On April 9, Patterson submitted an improved die of the obverse together with a pen sketch of the reverse. Anent, he wrote:

The die for the reverse is not yet commenced, but I send you the drawings which we propose to follow,—the pen sketch being that which we prefer. The drawing is true to nature, for it is taken from the eagle itself,—a bird, recently killed, having been prepared, and placed in the attitude which we had selected. . . . The absurdity of the shield sticking to the breast of a bird is avoided,—the shield, with its thirteen stripes, being placed with the figure of Liberty, on the face

---

[2] Former Director Moore was strongly against the use of the pileus on our coinage. In a letter to Woodbury, dated July 9, 1834, Moore quoted Jefferson, who had deprecated the symbol, saying "we are not emancipated slaves."

[3] In the twentieth century, the mint found the standing Liberty designs of Saint-Gaudens, Weinman and MacNeil, fully practicable.

Drawings behind the Liberty seated coinage: dated sketch by William Kneass, painting by Titian Peale, and sketch by Thomas Sully. Library Company of Philadelphia and American Philosophical Society Library.

Rejected designs for the reverse of the coinage by Titian Peale. The eagle within the square border was copied by Gobrecht on a pattern half dollar of 1838 (see the following plate). *American Philosophical Society Library.*

of the coin. The arrows and branches are also removed from the eagle's claws, as contrary to nature and good taste. A constellation of stars, equal to the number of states, is distributed, irregularly, over the sky, supposed to be seen beyond the eagle, instead of having 13 equal stars stiffly arranged in line around the margin.

In a letter of April 11, Woodbury replied:

. . . No objection to the proposed emblems is worth noticing, except that the attitude of the eagle for flight on its prey is considered best in the one where India ink is used, and for distant flight that with the pen, tho' in the 1st, perhaps the mouth should be closed.

On April 14, Patterson wrote again:

I am glad to find that our dies and designs for the new coinage meet your approbation. Your suggestion that the mouth of the flying eagle should be closed had also been made by me to the artist, and the change was tried; but the effect was thereby injured on two accounts,—first by taking away from the spirited appearance of the bird, and secondly by smoothing down the feathers on the neck, which are never ruffled except when the mouth is open. There has been great difficulty in getting a good design for the eagle. I am confident that not less than thirty sketches have been rejected; indeed we feared, at one time, that the flying eagle would have to be abandoned entirely.

In November 1836, the Mint began to issue new half dollars from dies designed by Gobrecht. The Liberty head was finely drawn and very beautiful. However, no change was made in the heraldic eagle despite the omission of the motto. Patterson, on the 8th, enclosed ten specimens of the coinage with the following letter to Secretary Woodbury:

Sir, I have the pleasure to send you herewith, and to beg you to exhibit to the President, the first specimens of our coinage of Silver by Steam, executed this afternoon. The milling, [i.e. reeding] as well as the striking, has been done by the new machinery, and the steam-power; and the saving of labor, and the acceleration of our work, will be very great. Heretofore we have used two screw presses for coining half dollars,—one of them only occasionally. The smaller of these presses required three men to work it, the larger four.[4] The steam press, with a single hand to feed the planchets, will do more work than these two presses with seven hands. You will observe too, that the work is better done. The old coin was struck in what we term an *open collar;* this is struck in a *close collar,* which makes the edge of the pieces thicker, and gives a mathematical equality to their diameters.

I think, also, you will not fail to see a considerable improvement in the impressions themselves. We do not, indeed, consider this as a new coin, such as the dollar will be; yet both the face and the reverse have been altered in many particulars, as you will see by a comparison with the old half dollar. These alterations, including a change in the diameter of the piece, are such as we introduced in the quarter-dollar, and have met the approbation of the government.

I shall, in a short time, send you some impressions of the new dollar. We are busily engaged in making a press suitable for coining it. Very respectfully, etc.

Patterns for the dollar were made the following month, and quickly retired because of criticism of the conspicuous Gobrecht signature in the field. A second obverse die was then cut in which the name was placed in tiny letters on the rock.

In 1837, the seated Liberty design was introduced on the dime and half

---

[4] Compare this with Boudinot's 1795 report, which stated that six men could work three presses, if all were in the same room.

Top: 1836 pattern dollar by Gobrecht; 1840 dollar (adopted design), Robert Ball Hughes after Gobrecht, reverse by Gobrecht. **Center:** 1836 half dollar (adopted design) by Gobrecht. **Bottom:** 1838 pattern half dollar by Kneass and 1839 by Gobrecht.

dime. In place of an eagle, the denomination was spelled out in the center of the reverse, and enclosed by a wreath.[5] In 1838, Gobrecht redesigned the Liberty head on the gold coinage, and made a pattern for a new half dollar. In the same year, the constellation was removed from the reverse of the pattern dollar, and stars were placed along the obverse border of the half dime, dime and quarter. Kneass designed a pattern half dollar (the so-called "sunburst head"), and in the following year, introduced the ephemeral "silly" and "booby" head varieties of the cent.[6] In 1839, Gobrecht designed another pattern half dollar, but soon afterward, Patterson apparently decided to standardize the silver coinage with the Liberty seated figure. In 1840, the Director commissioned the eminent Anglo-American sculptor Robert Ball Hughes to perfect the device,[7] and the artist complied by lowering the relief, refining the proportions and dynamics of the figure, and adding a graceful fold of drapery from the right elbow.[8] Surprisingly, the flying eagle was replaced on the dollar by the old heraldic bird which Patterson had scornfully repudiated, and the designs thus adopted remained on the silver coinage for over a half century.

---

[5] This was in conformity with section 13 of the Mint Act of Jan. 18, 1837.

[6] Kneass died in office Aug. 27, 1840.

[7] Georgia S. Chamberlain *American Medals and Medallists,* privately printed, 1963.

[8] For some reason, the Hughes design was never used on the half dollar.

CHAPTER 14

A Workshop for Their Gain

IN 1834, THE STATE DEPARTMENT instructed Director Moore to send gift sets, containing one of each coin in use, to the King of Siam and the Sultan of Muscat. Although the eagle and silver dollar had not been struck since 1804, they were never demonetized by Congress, and were technically still in use. Moore, literal to a fault, decided that both pieces should be represented. Accordingly, he authorized the preparation of antedated dies from which a number of impressions were taken. The Director's motive was undoubtedly innocent, but his act was a flagrant violation of two laws; first, because the coins did not bear the year of their date, and secondly, because the weight of the eagle did not conform with the Act of June 28, 1834, passed prior to its striking. *Moreover, Moore did not know that the 19,570 silver dollars issued in 1804 were struck from leftover 1803 dies, and that no genuine 1804 dollar ever existed!* [1]

The Director had broken two laws and played a hoax, but all, at least, for an official purpose, and without the prompting of pecuniary gain.

In 1835, two duplicate sets of specimen coins were ordered by the State Department. Whether additional impressions were made at that time, or by Mint employees a few years later, eight 1804 dollars struck from these antedated dies are now known. In 1842, two of the dollars were prominently displayed in the Mint, and a year later, to augment the coin cabinet, Curator William DuBois traded one to a prominent Philadelphia collector without troubling to inform him when it was made. DuBois had joined the Mint in

---

[1] For the most complete account of these celebrated fantasy coins see *The Fantastic 1804 Dollar*, Eric P. Newman and Kenneth E. Bressett, Whitman Publishing Co., 1962.

1833, and was employed in Moore's office when the 1804 dies were engraved. Possibly he only wished to preserve a tradition, but the result was a second hoax, this time without official sanction, and swindling a citizen out of some valuable coins.

There was yet one more link to be forged in this chain of dishonor, and it was wrought with consummate skill by the chief coiner Franklin Peale. In one of the most absurd biographical sketches ever palmed off as history, Evans[2] says of Peale: "Mr. Peale's administration as Chief Coiner may be said to mark an era in the mechanics of minting. Being specially fitted, by natural genius as well as education, for the position which he adorned, his mildness, integrity, gentlemanly bearing and high moral and mental culture constituted him a model officer. His connection with the service lasted until 1854."

In order to more fully savour this encomium, it is necessary to examine each of the statements individually. That Peale's administration marked "an era" in the mechanization of the Mint is, of course, literally true. The portrait lathe, steam coining press, and humid assay were all improvements that he introduced after his trip to Europe—a trip financed by the Mint for this purpose, and one which might have been undertaken by several of its mechanics.

On April 15, 1852 Peale, with his characteristic humility, wrote to Mint Director Eckert: "I boldly claim to have done for the Mint and my country, much that will entitle me gratitude." The letter then describes how, during his special mission to Europe, Peale "saw the indispensable importance of securing balances for weighing," and how he "gave to this important subject his best powers of reflection and experiment." The resultant balances, he tells us, "were made from his own drawings, and under his personal inspection," and "after trial in daily use for many years, have been found entirely satisfactory to a degree hitherto unattained in any country."

For the record, Peale's famous assay scales were built by Burton Saxton[3] in London, excepting only three that were brought in an unfinished condition to the Mint. The melter and refiner, Richard McCulloh, later testified that Peale's only contribution to these was his insistence that "the knife edges should be fastened to the beam without any means of adjusting them which caused much difficulty and rendered it necessary to adjust them by fitting them to the ends of the beam and filing those ends, a troublesome and uncertain operation."

The balance in the melter and refiner's room was likewise built by Saxton as was, almost entirely, the gold balance in the Weigh Room. In fact, the only balance Peale actually constructed was the one for silver in the Weigh Room; and for this, a beam was shipped from Washington.

Peale also built an improved drawbench, which cost the Mint between $1,500 and $2,000. The machine dispensed with the horizontal pulley, drawing the ingot-strip through the plates by means of a piston rod. The only disadvantage was that as soon as the strip passed through the plates, the piston

---

[2] George G. Evans, *Illustrated History of the United States Mint and Coinage*, 1885. Peale was appointed assistant assayer in 1833, melter and refiner in 1836, and chief coiner in 1839, assuming this last office upon the retirement of Adam Eckfeldt.

[3] Saxton, an ingenious inventor and mechanic, was later engaged as an instrument maker for the U.S. Coast Survey. He also constructed the balances which Congress sent to foreign governments. Saxton improved upon the accuracy of the famous French assay scales by substituting palladium for steel, and allowing the beam to rest on agate and the scales and dishes to hang from rubies.

was driven with tremendous force against the end of its cylinder, causing a violent concussion and endangering everyone in the vicinity. The bench was used only briefly (earning the epithet of "Peale's machine gun"), then deposited in the loft as useless.

Peale also introduced a large lathe for turning rolls, which cost the Government at least $2,000. Although he once admitted that the lathe had never worked and probably never would, he later blamed its failure on the Mint's adoption of cast-iron rollers.

To expedite the operations of melting and refining, Peale purchased, from his relative George Sellers, an expensive set of molds for casting large ingots with an accompanying apparatus for pouring. Unfortunately, these were not adapted to the rolling machinery and thus proved useless.

Joseph Canby, one of the workmen, later testified that he and the machinist William Snyder, had spent between $1,800 and $2,000 to construct a single scale for Peale. Although Peale, in turn, blamed the men for their extravagance, he neglected to add that he had afterward tried to gild the beam and other parts with gold!

Perhaps the most spectacular of Peale's inventions was the "noisy sofa." When sat upon, its cushions emitted a great trumpet blast, ostensibly as an alarm. It had taken four of the Mint's workmen two weeks to build the piece, which was thereafter used to terrify children and annoy female visitors. The sofa cost nearly $200, and originally adorned Peale's own office. Later, it was appropriated by his old friend, Director Patterson.

For fifteen years Peale's "experiments" were financed by the systematic filching of petty sums which were used to augment the general Mint fund. The Act of January 18, 1837 specifically stated that no depositor should be charged in excess of "the actual expense to the Mint of the materials and labor employed." The fourteenth section, however, declared "that when gold and silver are combined, if either of these metals be in such small proportion that it cannot be separated advantageously, no allowance shall be made to the depositor for the value of such metal." Patterson, twisting the word "proportion" to mean "amount," declared that silver should not be parted when its aggregate value was less than five dollars. He thus invoked a seignorage by which the poor depositor (for obviously the practice had no effect on the rich mine owner) was cheated of up to five dollars in silver every time he stopped off at the Mint with less than about seventy ounces of gold. Patterson's rationale for this swindle was that the parting took proportionately too long on small deposits and delayed the coinage. Strange as it seems, this explanation was accepted as satisfactory by two Secretaries of the Treasury, Woodbury and Meredith, who in 1837 and 1849 consented to the practice.[4]

Inspired by Patterson's dictum, the refiners of the New Orlean's Mint often failed to even part the silver, with the result that the ostensibly fine gold used for coining was debased. In 1849, an anonymous letter in a Philadelphia newspaper openly insinuated that the Mint was debasing its coins, and that loans on U.S. gold were refused by the Bank of England.[5] In a published letter, dated November 24, 1849 to a member of Congress, Patterson vehemently denied the

[4] See the following correspondences: Patterson to Woodbury, Jan. 28, 1837; Woodbury to Patterson, Feb. 1, 1837; Patterson to Meredith, May 22, 1849; Meredith to Patterson, May 29, 1849.
[5] *Bankers Magazine*, January 1850, p. 572.

charge even though he had admitted earlier to the President [6] that the New Orleans Mint gold coins for 1847 had been assayed, after several trials, at only 898.2. The matter was revived in a communication from the Hon. Abbot Lawrence, while minister in England; then contradicted by the new Director of the Mint, George Eckert, in a letter dated April 2, 1852 to the Secretary of the Treasury; [7] next imputed by Senator Gwin on December 29, 1852 and investigated by the Senate and Secretary of the Treasury Corwin; and finally confessed to, on January 17, 1853 by a red-faced Eckert who nevertheless defended the Mint's right to filch silver from its depositors! [8] *Bankers Magazine* was of a different opinion. In its February issue it declared that "to deny to the depositors the silver they carry to the Mint . . . and then to use that silver for coining three-cent pieces, is but to defraud them of the premium which their silver is worth." Secretary of the Treasury Corwin agreed, and soon put an end to this time-dishonored custom.

On January 16, 1850 Peale wrote to Patterson suggesting the replacement of certain boilers and, incidentally, a renovation of the surrounding area of the Mint. After careful calculation, Peale announced that the work could be completed for $20,800. Patterson at once recommended the measure to the Secretary of the Treasury, on whose approval the amount was appropriated by Congress, May 15, 1850. When Peale spent an additional $12,000, Patterson appropriated—without appropriation—the profits arising from the high seignorage on the new silver three-cent pieces.

When, in 1853, the Senate asked Director Eckert by what appropriation he was using the seignorage on these coins to defray Mint expenses,[9] he replied that it had been done by the formula "other available funds," which he himself had inserted into an appropriation bill laid before the ways and means committee; and "if there was any irregularity or illegality in the use of them [the profits] the committee seems not to have discovered it or made it known;" and furthermore, that "if the Mint should be deprived of the authority to use the balances of gain accruing from its operations in separating [i.e. parting the silver], or of the three-cent coinage, our appropriations would have to be enlarged precisely in proportion to the means thus taken from it."

In other words, if Congress, entrusting the Director of the Mint with public money, had been deceived by the formula, "other available funds," which he inserted into a minor appropriations bill for the purpose of arrogating more than $70,000, it had no right to complain. And furthermore, if the Director were deprived of the "authority" to continue his hanky-panky, he would be forced to resort to the lawful process of requesting appropriations!

Congress tacitly expressed its opinion of Eckert's philosophy on March 3, 1853 when it inserted the following provision into an appropriations bill:

> It shall be the duty of the Superintendent of the Mint, to cause to be paid annually into the Treasury of the United States the profits of the Mint, and to present a quarterly account of the expenditures of the Mint to the Secretary of the Treasury.

Having disposed of the first part of the Peale myth, we shall now take up

[6] Letter of April 15, 1848.
[7] *National Intelligencer*, April 7, 1852.
[8] Senate Document No. 21, 32nd Congress, 2nd Session.
[9] Ibid.

that "mildness, integrity, gentlemanly bearing and high moral and mental culture [which] constituted him a model officer."

In a letter to President Fillmore, on August 1, 1851 Professor Richard Mc-Culloh, the erstwhile melter and refiner of the Mint, preferred several charges of misconduct against Franklin Peale and McCulloh's successor, Professor James Booth. McCulloh accused Peale of "lavish and unnecessary expenditure of public money without adequate appropriation or useful effect," of "unofficer-like and demoralizing proceedings," of "malicious intermeddling with the duties of other officers of the Mint and false representations of their conduct," and of "appropriation to his own benefit or gain to which he was not legally entitled." He concluded that Peale was flagrantly unfit to hold office.

The first of these charges has already been discussed and we may now proceed to the second, namely the "unofficerlike and demoralizing proceedings." McCulloh charged, among other things, that Peale had utilized the services of Mint workmen for his own purposes.

In the subsequent investigation, Phineas Rowan, a workman at the Mint, testified that he had spent two days in plastering Peale's own house, and a half day shaking out his carpet.

Robert Wallace stated that he and John Rickard had once spent two days in "cutting the panels out of framing under the stairs of Peale's house and putting in gauze wire," that he fixed a window sash at Peale's house and did other jobs there from time to time. He said he had repaired music stands, a number of chairs and several other articles for Peale. The stands appear to have been used for the Musical Fund Society of which Peale was a member, and Patterson a co-founder.

One of the most voluble deponents was William Snyder, an erstwhile machinist of the Mint, who resigned because of the "intolerance and malversations" of Peale. Snyder testified that on the occasion of the Musical Fund Society fair (which was held for the sole purpose of collecting money for that society), Peale, who at the time was busy making kites in the Mint workshop, stopped Snyder from building a government scale in order to have him make some juggler's apparatus. Then Peale came to the fair dressed as a Turk, and performed circus tricks with the Mint equipment while Patterson sat in the front row cheering him on! Snyder said that whenever Peale's archery club held its outings, the Mint's workmen were assigned to fixing tents and making bows and arrows and other equipment.

Snyder also maintained that Peale had caused a turning lathe to be built in the Mint that was chiefly used to make things for the private use of Peale and other privileged persons; that workmen were required to repair tin utensils, shower bath fixtures and sundry articles at Peale's residence; that the modern trellis in front of Peale's house had been made at the Mint; that cast-iron tables for Peale's home were fitted up at the Mint; that Peale's old furniture was repaired and his old silver cleaned at the Mint; that old silver plate brought to the Mint by depositors to be coined was frequently appropriated by Peale for the price of old metal; and that one of the workmen was suffered to drive Peale's daughter around in a carriage!

Joseph Canby testified that he had been employed to convert a tamborine into a parlor drum with keys for Peale's wife. On one occasion Canby had spent three days polishing a brass mirror in the house of Rembrandt Peale, the

renowned artist and brother of Franklin. Another time, Canby and Jonatha
Tompkins had spent two weeks making an alarm bell and fixtures for Peale
residence.

In a separate testimonial, nine of the Mint's workmen complained that Pea
employed them during the regular hours of the Mint for his own purpose an
without compensation, though they had heard he occasionally gave gifts fe
such favors to others.

McCulloh had also charged Peale with "appropriation or benefit to his ow
gain to which he was not legally entitled." As a matter of fact, Peale was usin
the Mint's machinery and workmen, during the regular hours of their emplo
ment, to conduct a full-time, highly lucrative medal business. Castings suitab
for reduction were supplied by outside artists, but Peale supervised the prepara
tion of dies and planchets and personally received remuneration for the wor
This was done despite the fact that Patterson's inquiry to President Va
Buren, of whether the Mint might strike private medals *on a non-profit basi*
was ignored by the Congressional committee to whom it was referred, and a
act of August 23, 1842 forbade any public official to receive additional unautho
ized compensation.

The only flaw in Peale's medal business was that he had to depend for he
bullion on the melter and refiner. So long as his friend Dr. Jonas McClintoc
held this position there was no problem. But in 1846, McClintock resigned an
was succeeded by Professor Richard McCulloh.

McCulloh was one of the most ingenious men ever employed by the Min
and in 1849 he greatly increased the output of the refinery by introducing th
use of steam to heat the stone and porcelain vessels. His improvements, hov
ever, were at first ignored, then suppressed. Today they have been complete
forgotten. McCulloh fought a losing battle, first from within the Mint, the
outside of it. It is perhaps well that his story is told.

In the beginning, McCulloh never questioned Peale about the propriety
his medal business, but furnished him with whatever gold and silver he ordere
Gradually, however, McCulloh grew suspicious and, to exculpate himsel
offered to obtain the bullion for Peale's medals from the War Departmen
When Patterson declined this proposal, McCulloh and Peale reached an agre
ment whereby the medal would remain in the latter's custody until he had r
turned the bullion. Peale, however, soon found the new arrangement "incor
venient."

The situation reached a head on August 17, 1849 when Peale, receiving a
order to furnish a gold medal for General Scott, applied to McCulloh wh
answered: "Under the present circumstances, I must decline to furnish yc
with gold and silver, for the manufacture of medals."

Peale did not ask a second time, but obtained his bullion from the treasure
of the Mint.

In a letter to Patterson, on August 23, McCulloh explained why he had fe
obliged to refuse Peale. He reminded the Director of prevailing laws, addir
that "within the Mint, the workmen, with few exceptions, believe it wrong an
unauthorized by law, that they should be required to labor for the pecunia
benefit of an officer."

On the following day, Patterson replied:

Dear Sir:—I have read with care your communication of the 23rd inst.; but I will now confine my answer to the circumstances which gave rise to it. I have therefore, only to say, that as you are responsible for the bullion placed in your keeping, you have a perfect right to decline an interchange of any part of it, even for other bullion of equal value, and even if required for the purposes of the Government, if such be your will in the case. Yours with sincere friendship, etc.

What a revealing letter this is! Patterson admits he has no wish to discuss Peale's medal business, and then tacitly accuses McCulloh of obstructing the Government through the due process of law!

McCulloh again wrote to Patterson on the 25th, clarifying things, and calling attention to the fact that Peale had made an extra medal for his own benefit. This letter apparently went unanswered, and there is no further correspondence on the subject for over a year.

In the meantime, McCulloh continued to refuse Peale bullion for his medal business, and the latter retaliated by enraging McCulloh's "accomplished and meritorious assistant" Professor J. B. Reynolds. According to McCulloh, Peale declined to accept deliveries of bullion from Reynolds, insisting that they should never be made by anyone of inferior rank. Peale then dissuaded Patterson from introducing the office of assistant melter and refiner for which Reynolds was provisionally employed. This proved to be the last straw, and both Reynolds and McCulloh resigned.

McCulloh now launched his own campaign against Patterson and Peale, as can be seen from the following article of November 14, 1850 in the *New York Evening Express*:

> It does not appear by the published laws of the United States that Congress has ever given authority to persons employed in the Mint thus to convert it into a *workshop for their gain*, nor even that medals may be made in the Mint for the Government, as a source of pecuniary benefit to its salaried officers . . . The whole business is corrupt, and the officers engaged in it deserve the severest censure. And if the President has overlooked such official misconduct, then Congress should see to it, and deal with those who have thus abused the responsible stations they occupy as they justly merit.

The article was forwarded by President Fillmore to Secretary of the Treasury Corwin on the 18th. Corwin, in turn, sent it to Patterson for an explanation. The Director's reply was most remarkable. He admitted that the manufacture of medals, national or private, was without justification of law, and formed no part of the Mint's business. He excused it, however, on the (imagined) ground that there had been no one outside the Mint competent to execute the work. Moreover, Peale had assured him that "the use of the machinery is all the advantage accruing to him, and does not in any way interfere with the usual Mint operations." Curiously, this explanation, which actually explained nothing, was accepted by Secretary Corwin, and the issue allowed to drop.

It must be conceded that the assurance was not wholly false. Coining operations had *not* been interfered with because they were daily attended to by Adam Eckfeldt who, despite his retirement, continued to faithfully perform the work. Eckfeldt served as gratuitous chief coiner until only a few days before his death in 1852. Peale then wrote a frantic letter to Director Eckert about the necessity of hiring an assistant.

❉   ❉   ❉

McCulloh was succeeded as melter and refiner by Professor James C. Booth, the most renowned chemist of his day, and publisher of an *Encyclopedia of Chemistry,* to which the former was a contributor.

After leaving the Mint, McCulloh invented a method of parting gold by the use of zinc instead of silver. Booth then announced an invention of his own, which he threatened to run in competition with the zinc process unless McCulloh agreed to a merger. Being at a decided disadvantage, McCulloh finally gave in. Booth tried out both methods early in 1851, and on February 6, wrote to Director Patterson:

Dear Sir: Having completed my experiments on the processes for refining, so far as to form an opinion of their relative merits, I herewith submit that opinion to you.

By the process at present pursued at the mint a sufficient amount of gold may be refined, in all probability, to meet the deposits—say as much as eight or nine millions per month; but there are objections to the process which it would be very desirable to obviate, if practicable. The process is attended with the evolution of a very large amount of noxious and disagreeable vapor, the avoidance of which I believe to be impracticable, except to a limited extent; and this vapor is not only inconvenient and injurious to the workmen, but is likewise highly objectionable to those residents of the city who are in the vicinity of the mint. The process is one of the most expensive, requiring more manual force to melt the mixed gold and silver, and to carry it through the refining process; more fuel to melt three times as much metal as there is gold in the mixture; and a large amount of the most costly of all common acids, together with a large consumption of zinc to recover the silver employed in refining. Add to these the large amount of silver upwards of $200,000 removed from circulation, and retained only for the purpose of refining gold. In most other points, the present process is an excellent one.

Mr. McCulloh's process consists, in the substitution of zinc for silver in the present operation, whereby a low temperature is required for melting the gold and zinc, diminishing greatly time, fuel, and labor. In the next part of the process cold and dilute sulphuric acid is used to remove the zinc, and obtain the gold and its silver in a pulverulent state, so that the nitric acid will then remove the silver readily from the gold. So far, the process is everything that could be desired, requiring but one precaution, that is, the due regulation of the heat when melting gold and zinc together, for too high a temperature is apt to volatilize the gold with the zinc. This can, however, be entirely guarded against. The only difficulty hitherto experienced, in carrying out this process, lay in the brittle character of the gold; and the difficulty of obtaining it in a malleable state, in any of the experiments hitherto made, except the last. I have not been able to obtain it in tough condition upon a *test,* whether with or without lead or copper, nor in black lead crucible; but it can be toughened in a sand crucible, or on a hearth of a reverberatory, whether a bone ash test or not, by the use of ordinary means.

Now, as a reverberatory can be constructed, on which several hundred thousand dollars of gold can be daily toughened, I think that the process of Mr. McCulloh is, in all respects considered, the best that could be adopted at the U.S. Mint. It is next attended with far less expense than the present method, and with no noxious fumes, and a larger amount of gold may be operated upon in the same space, and in the same time.

The process of myself and Mr. C. Morfit consists of dissolving gold by means salt, nitre, and oil of vitriol, or by muriatic acid and nitre, in stoneware or glass vessels by steam heat, or a sand bath, or in well-secured wooden vessels by steam blown into the liquid. Immediately after solution is effected, copperas is added to the solution to precipitate the gold. The gold and chloride of silver being filtered and washed, the chloride of silver is extracted from the gold by a solution of salt or an alkaline hyposulphite; or the chloride is reduced by zinc, washed, and the reduced silver extracted by nitric acid. This process recommends itself by the low cost of materials, in which respect it excels all others, by a complete extraction of silver from the gold, if necessary; by the convenience of using different kinds of vessels, according to the opportunities of procuring them; and by the use of less acid than any other process. Since, however, its use would not be a gain in the time required for refining, over the present process, and its introduction would require a total change of apparatus and arrangements in order to carry it out most successfully, attended with loss of time in making such change, I do not recommend its adoption in the Philadelphia mint. But as wooden vessels can be used with this process, and as it requires a very small amount of acid, it might be advantageously adopted in California, or where the use of much acid, or of stone or glass vessels, is objectionable on the score of expense. In such places under the above circumstances, it is the best of the three processes.

In conclusion, therefore, I would respectfully recommend the adoption of Mr. McCulloh's process at the U.S. Mint, since it can be introduced without interfering with the operations of the Mint, and presents the advantages above specified.

Unfortunately, Patterson was much too ill-disposed toward McCulloh to consider the merits of his invention. McCulloh pressed for news, and Booth hemmed and hawed, finally admitting that his own process had failed. This was all McCulloh had to hear. Realizing he had been duped, he forced Booth to relinquish his partnership in the zinc process.

Not long afterwards, Booth tried out the zinc process at the Philadelphia Mint and declared it a failure. McCulloh, incredulous, arranged for a trial at the New Orleans Mint, where the process was proven highly successful. He then appealed to the Secretary of the Treasury to have it retried at the Philadelphia Mint, this time in his own presence. The request, though granted, was ignored by Booth as unnecessary. The vindictive Patterson wrote to McCulloh that "the interest, integrity, and energy of Mr. Booth should be regarded as giving the fullest assurance that the work would be perfectly done, if confined to him alone."

Booth now enjoyed his revenge. He tried the process without McCulloh's supervision, and reported that a large quantity of gold had been volatilized and escaped up the chimney. McCulloh protested to President Fillmore, arraigning Booth and Peale, as well as the management of the Mint generally. McCulloh was now convinced that the trial of his process had been sabotaged by Booth. He said that volatilization would never occur if an alloy of gold and zinc were properly made, at a temperature below redness, by dissolving gold bars in the melted zinc. The letter was forwarded to the Secretary of the Treasury, and on December 26, acting Secretary Hodge, instructed Director Eckert to give McCulloh's process a fair trial. McCulloh was to direct the operation and pay for any additional expenses incurred by the process. Any savings would be applied toward the cost of erecting the necessary furnaces. The process had been patented by McCulloh, and the Mint could adopt no part of it without his consent.

McCulloh spent the whole of January, and up to February 5, 1852 at the Mint, constructing the special furnaces which he required. While tearing down the furnace Booth had built for the earlier trial, McCulloh discovered more than seventeen ounces of gold which were said to have been volatilized! A year later, McCulloh described the trial to Secretary Corwin.

5,000 ounces of zinc had been melted, for the purpose of quarting 1952.72 ounces of gold. The gold bars were heated to incipient redness to prevent their chilling the zinc, then dissolved. The zinc-quarted gold was melted in a granulating furnace from which it flowed down, through a valve, in eight streams into a large copper kettle of water placed in the cellar below. But McCulloh made one mistake. Instead of fastening the pipe which led to the copper kettle, he simply gave orders that it should not be moved. As a result, some mysterious person raised the pipe, permitting a draft to sweep upward and clog the valve with solidified metal. McCulloh then reconstructed his apparatus in such a way as to prevent a repetition of the incident. The second quartation met with success, and the grains of metal were pronounced more uniform, finer, and thus more easily acted upon by the acid than those poured by hand. Moreover, none of the alloy could be spilled in the furnace or on the floor, since it was carried directly from the retort into the reservoir of water.

McCulloh gathered the grains in a scoop, and as he was called out of the room, he placed them on top of one of the melting furnaces. When he returned, the grains were gone and, in fact, they were never seen again. Undaunted, McCulloh began for a third time and soon produced another batch of granules. He refined these in dilute sulphuric acid which removed the zinc and left the gold and silver in a pulverulent state. The silver was now separated by immersion in nitric acid, using first a weak solution, then a strong one which rendered the gold fine and perfectly tough. Finally, the gold was parted with dilute sulphuric acid and alloyed in a black-lead crucible. Contrary to Booth's assertion, the gold proved to be both softer and tougher than that produced by the usual method. On striking one bar against another, remarkably soft, large dents were made; and when clipping off the corners of several bars there was not the slightest evidence of crystalline fracture. The zinc process involved fewer operations and less fuel, produced a smaller "sweep," and required no additional silver for quartation.

Everyone who witnessed McCulloh's trial pronounced it a complete success, including Woods Baker of the U.S. Coast Survey, who had been selected by acting Secretary Hodge to assist in the operation. Eckert himself was so pleased with McCulloh's furnace that he proceeded, surreptitiously, to apply it to the work of the Mint despite their prior agreement. McCulloh forbade the Director to employ the furnace, and Eckert retaliated by stopping McCulloh's experiments. The Director wrote to Corwin that the gold refined by the zinc process might prove unfit for coinage and interrupt the business of the Mint.

On August 3, 1852 McCulloh submitted a lengthy record of the trial (and his tribulations!), together with all the testimonials, to Secretary Corwin.[10] Eckert offered his own comments on the 17th, to wit, that McCulloh's process (which had been tried again by Booth in McCulloh's absence) failed to part the silver more thoroughly than did the usual method of quartation. On October 12, the Director wrote to Corwin that "a series of trials has been made by us with a view to the more complete extraction of silver from gold and to test the advisability of such extraction on grounds of economy.[11] The results have been very satisfactory, and have shown that we may with great ad

---

[10] *Report made to the Hon. Thomas Corwin, Secretary of the Treasury by Professor R. S. Mc Culloh of his Operations at the Mint of the United States, in Refining California Gold by hi Zinc Method,* Gideon & Co. printers, Washington, 1852.

[11] This no doubt utilized the apparatus Peale claimed to have invented in 1852 for "filterin and recovering minute particles of metal, usually lost during the washing, cleaning and whitenin of the coin."

vantage to the depositors and without disadvantage to ourselves, refine the silvery gold as high as 990 thousandths."

Eckert then proceeded to bill McCulloh for the wastage resulting from the zinc process, to which on November 26, McCulloh replied from Princeton:

Sir: I have delayed to reply to your communication of the 4th of Sept. last, until I should have put an end to all pecuniary questions relative to the trial of my zinc method of refining gold, by paying to you the balance exhibited in your statement of account. That having been done, you have now my answer.

You could not have made of me any demand to which I would not have acceded, unless the same had been so very extortionate that duty would have compelled its resistance; for I have been resolved from the first to permit no question of accountability on my part to be a matter of debate between the mint and myself.

In final settlement of account, I therefore saw first to admit your aforesaid statement, though it was fraught with error and injustice.

That bullion should have been received from the depositors and charged to the melter and refiner, Prof. Booth, at one assayed valuation, and then have been delivered and charged to me at a different and higher valuation, based upon special assays, made by order and for the purpose, was a proceeding which needs no comment.

But as you have sought to justify it, by the pretext, that said special assays were more accurate, I may remark that I cannot see in their comparative results, exhibited in pages 26 and 51 of my printed report to the Secretary of the Treasury, any data for such an opinion. They, however, furnish proof that the process of assaying, as conducted in the mint, is attended with much uncertainty.

You were mistaken in asserting that your proposed allowance for gold wastage 4/10 thousandths, is slightly above the credit claimed by me. By reference to Section 44, page 17, of my aforesaid report, you will find that the latter amounts to 53/100ths per thousands, when freed from the masking effect of the deductions usually made from assays for depositors.

There are some minor and unimportant points of difference between us, which I shall pass over without remark.

And in conclusion, I would observe that you seem strangely slow to learn, that experiments tried in the melting and refining department of the Mint, under charge of Prof. Booth, concerning the relative merits of my zinc method of refining and that now employed, have proved to have been grossly inaccurate and unworthy of credit. Nor can I admit, therefore, that the result of any late experiment, performed in said department and without my concurrence, could be a proper basis for that conventional determination of the ordinary gold wastage, stipulated with the Treasury Department to be made between you and myself,—notwithstanding that I have acceded to the corresponding pecuniary demand made by you. Very respectfully etc.

But the matter did not end there. In a letter to McCulloh dated January 28, 1853 Eckert snidely remarked that he was investigating the latter's charges against Peale and Booth "solely for the satisfaction of his own mind." That the Secretary of the Treasury had ordered the investigation a year and a half earlier was of no account!

Eckert showed Peale the charges preferred against him by McCulloh, but withheld the corroboratory statements made by the other workmen. Peale's reply of April 15, 1852 is an amusing bit of sophistry. By accusing Peale of "lavish and unnecessary expenditure without useful effect," McCulloh (Peale said) was in effect charging the Director and the comptrolling departments in Washington with "gross neglect of duty." Again, by assailing Peale's manufacture of medals, McCulloh was attacking "the late venerable and much loved

Adam Eckfeldt" who had been appointed by Washington and whose precedent Peale was merely following. After felicitating himself on the "special mission" to Europe by which he "brought the Mint machinery to perfection," Peale wrote:

"My labors in perfecting these instruments have been freely bestowed without charge or compensation, or other benefits to myself personally than the confidence and satisfaction which result from their use."

Alas, poor Peale! One would think he had toiled for years in the Mint without pay, when he actually received a chief coiner's salary for doing almost nothing!

Again, Peale wrote: "The trifling advantage which the chief coiner derives from the manufacture of medals, is not at the expense of the United States, as charged. The only advantage he derives from his position is in the use of the old coining machine, now dispensed with for Mint operations."

Ignoring the impropriety of the word "trifling," one still finds in this statement much worth examining.

Peale's claim, that he derived no other advantage in manufacturing his medals than "the old coining machine, now dispensed with for Mint operations," was a manifest lie. In the first place, it would imply that he procured his planchets ready made from outside the Mint, whereas nine workmen testified to Eckert that "such of us have worked in melting, casting, filing or rolling ingots into strips for his medals," and that "he was not in the habit of paying for the work we done for him." In the second place, Peale virtually monopolized the portrait lathe which belonged to the engraver's department; and lastly, his "old coining machine" was still very much in use by the engraver to sink dies.

When Peale collected old medal dies for the purpose of restriking and peddling specimens, this too was a public service. Thus, he wrote:

> Although the law devolves no duty upon the chief coiner in reference to the collection and custody of dies and medals, yet at an early period after entering on my office, I formed the plan of collecting in the Mint, for permanent preservation, as extensive a series as was possible of our national, state and private medal dies. A few of the former, which were in the Mint, I catalogued and arranged at once. . . . Without such pains they would probably, in a few years, have been lost or destroyed; now they are likely to be permanently preserved, and copies of medals from them may be, if necessary, at any time reproduced. As the law assigns no duties on the subject, it is desirable that it shall be made the interest of the chief coiner to assume them himself, by allowing him the privilege of striking copies when required. Not for myself do I make this remark, for I shall preserve these dies, while they remain under my influence, as sacred deposits, of too great value to be neglected or lost without regard to any ulterior interest.

In investigating the charge of connivance against McCulloh, Eckert moved with unusual alacrity. He questioned Booth and Peale, both of whom maintained that the zinc process had failed and should not be given another trial. Peale even produced an affidavit from ex-Director Patterson stating that the former had "always expressed a favorable opinion of the process," and that Patterson did "not recollect to have ever heard [from Peale] a single suggestion adverse to the plan." On receiving three such unprejudiced testimonies Eckert concluded that he need not allow McCulloh the opportunity to furnish contradictory evidence, and assured Corwin the process was too risky to be retried.

With the assistance of Peale and Booth, Eckert was enabled to complete his investigation of McCulloh's charges in less than two years. To Secretary Corwin, the Director wrote that he had been influenced in his opinions "more from general impressions than by any written memoranda." For this reason he had "purposely avoided a dry recital of evidence or documents, or any argumentations commentary thereupon" which he supposed "would be tedious, and superfluous to the department." In lieu of this, the Director submitted his own opinion: that Peale was "eminently fit" for his position, "by his mechanical talents and general acquirements, by his valuable experience acquired both in the institutions of Europe and in office here, and by his close attention and scrutiny into all the details of coinage." Eckert concluded that the perfection of the machinery was largely due to Peale's talents and labor, and constituted "an enduring test of his official conduct." In fact, the bulk of Eckert's report is nothing more than a recitation of Peale's own letter to the Director [12] with all its sophistries and falsehoods.

The only other testimony which Eckert referred to was a verbal one given by the foreman of the machinists. This was to the effect that Peale had not utilized the services of the workmen since the heavy influx of California bullion. To whatever extent the statement may have been true, it certainly did not pertain to Peale's medal business, which continued as usual.

On receiving a copy of Eckert's letter, McCulloh wrote to Corwin, requesting that the Secretary himself review all the testimonies in the case. Corwin agreed, and Eckert, piqued at the interference, took the occasion to further recommend Peale's virtues. This correspondence took place on January 29, 1853, and within a few months both Eckert and Corwin were succeeded by new officers. In July, the dauntless McCulloh, still seeking justice, published a lengthy tract called *The Proceedings of the late Director of the Mint in relation to the official Misconduct of Franklin Peale Esq., Chief Coiner and Other Abuses in the Mint,* in which he published and reviewed much of the correspondence and other evidence relating to the case.

Although the pamphlet did not immediately accomplish all McCulloh would have wished, it had an effect of sorts, for on August 30, 1853, Director James Ross Snowden [13] wrote to the new Secretary of the Treasury James Guthrie:

I have your favors of the 27th, 28th and 29th inst. in reference to making medals at the Mint for Representative Adams & Co. for exhibition at the World's Fair at New York, and for the Massachusetts Mechanic Association. It is proper that I should call your attention to the fact that the making of medals in the the Mint has heretofore occasioned unpleasant remarks. It has been objected to, because the material and machinery of the government has been used for private purposes and made a source of profit to some of the persons employed in the Coining Department. I have myself very great doubts whether it is legal or proper to make medals except such as may be ordered by the government. If they are made for other purposes I am of opinion that no charge should be made except for the intrinsic value of the metals used. Heretofore considerable profits have been made by the persons who have executed the medals. It seems doubtful also whether the government ought to interfere with private enterprise by manufacturing free of charge or otherwise any work of a private character. I may further remark

---

[12] Peale to Eckert, April 15, 1852.
[13] At the time Snowden took office, Peale was attempting to fuel the wood-burning annealing furnaces with anthracite coal. The experiment cost the Mint several thousand dollars and destroyed the furnaces. Snowden, amazed at this reckless waste, forbade Peale any further exercise of his ingenuity.

that in order to meet the public demands for gold and silver coin I am running the coining department twenty hours a day, and it would be inconvenient at this time to make these medals. If however it is your wish after considering the objections I have presented, that they should be made I will make every possible effort to comply with your request.

Guthrie must have agreed, for on August 24, 1854 he issued a series of Mint regulations, which included the following:

No profit can accrue to any officer of the Mint by reason of the legitimate operations thereof, and no private or extra official work can be done therein, with or without compensation or reward by an officer, clerk, or workman. In case of the violation of this rule, the Director, if the offender be a workman, will forthwith dismiss him, or if an officer or clerk, report the fact to the Secretary of the Treasury.

In a letter to Snowden on September 5, Guthrie clarified the purpose of this provision:

The regulation, which is designed to preclude private business of all kinds and private calls on the officers and men, as well as some others, may appear to be unusually stringent. Still I cannot think they can operate oppressively: such regulations have, at various times, been applied to the Executive department of the Government here and even where they are not adopted as an inexorable rule, exertions have been made to induce a compliance with their spirit. Recent occurrences at the Mint appeared to point out the propriety of rules as strict, as have theretofore been adopted in other public establishments, not merely to insure greater safety but to reinstate the Institution in the public confidence . . .

Guthrie's reforms seem to have been ill-received in certain quarters of the Mint. What exactly occurred we must leave to the reader's imagination, for the pertinent correspondence is now missing. It is clear, however, that Snowden wrote to Guthrie preferring charges against Peale, and that Guthrie in turn wrote to the President who, having no one else to write to, dismissed Peale at once. Still clinging to his ledgers, Peale left the Mint on December 2, never again to return. The shock generated by this "discharge" seems to have muddled the minds of certain Mint contemporaries, who gave out the story that Peale was replaced because of the doctrine of "rotation in office." This concoction (which probably originated with Peale's old friend, the Curator, Nestor and fabulist of the Mint, William DuBois[14]), passed current despite the fact that the same political party was in office when Peale was dismissed as when he had been appointed!

Peale subsequently petitioned Congress for $30,000 as remuneration for having freely given his inventions and improvements to the Government. The memorial, though colored throughout with the usual Peale hyperbole, was attested to by former Director Eckert, melter and refiner Booth, foreman of the refinery John J. Morell, and foreman of the coining room George Eckfeldt.

In the Senate, the committee on claims reduced the amount to $10,000 because the inventions and improvements had been undertaken at the expense of the Mint. Mr. Wade of the committee introduced the memorial on May

---

[14] Some of the stories related by DuBois are indeed fantastic. In a paper read before the American Philosophical Society in June 1861, he stated that in 1814 "the melters at the Mint carelessly emptied some gold into a pot of copper from which cents were coined [and] it gave trouble at the counter of the Mint for many years afterwards in consequence of numerous inquiries and offers to sell." DuBois had apparently forgotten that in 1814 the Mint purchased its copper planchets ready-made from England.

23, 1856, along with a bill for Peale's relief. The bill was debated and passed on July 25, after Peale's claims excited the wonder and approbation of Senator Richard Brodhead. Brodhead had apparently been influenced by his nephew Henry Linderman, who was then chief clerk of the Mint.

In the House, the bill was shuttled around until July 22, 1860 when it was deemed unworthy of further consideration. It had already been passed three times by the Senate. On May 28, 1870 the bill was again introduced in the Senate, but failed to pass. Then, on February 8, 1873 Mr. Foster of the House committee on claims, reported the same bill for the relief of Anna E. Peale, the only child of (the now deceased) Franklin Peale. The bill passed both houses without debate, and was enacted on March 3, 1873.

The date of the bill's final appearance is significant. In less than a week, the President was to sign comprehensive legislation which Henry Linderman had co-authored, and which would inevitably place the latter at the head of all the mints. Although Linderman already exerted a powerful influence in Congress, the victory of the Mint bill greatly enhanced his position and prestige. In March, he was appointed Director of the Mint Bureau in Washington, and on April 30, with his expressed approval, Caroline Peale presented to the Mint a marble bust of her late husband Franklin, "to be set upon a pedestal, in some position, where it may be open to the inspection of visitors and preserve his memory to future generations." The writer has been unable to learn the location of this bust at the present time.

❋ ❋ ❋

The "retirement" of Franklin Peale closed a chapter in the history of scandals which distinguish the second Philadelphia Mint. But that was all that it did. Director Snowden, for example, was so intrigued by Peale's collection of coin and medal dies that he soon hatched a scheme of his own. Snowden wished to complete the collection of Washington medals in the Mint cabinet, and to augment the modest appropriation set aside for this purpose, he ordered the restriking of rare coins and patterns which had trade value. Ironically, the coin in greatest demand was the 1804 dollar, of which no genuine specimen had ever been struck. Snowden located the antedated obverse die and ordered a new reverse to be engraved. The project was duly completed, but before the Director could act, a curious thing happened.

There was at this time in the Mint a young man named Theodore Eckfeldt, son of the foreman of the engraving room, George Eckfeldt, and nephew of the principal assayer Jacob Eckfeldt. Theodore had first been hired as a youth, and served in the coining department under Franklin Peale. According to McCulloh's testimony, Peale confided that he had discharged the young man for stealing. Nevertheless, about a month after the incident Peale, together with the boy's grandfather Adam Eckfeldt, wrote an affidavit testifying to Theodore's honesty and worth, so that he could procure other work. A few years later, an additional workman was needed for the Mint, and among the applicants was Theodore Eckfeldt, now a married man and still armed with the affidavit of his grandfather and chief coiner Peale. On the strength of this reference, Theodore was rehired and became once more a regular employee. In fact, he was reassigned to Franklin Peale, who placed him on night watch, a post of trust and extra compensation.

Sometime during 1858, Theodore's fancy turned toward the 1804 dollar dies. Either on his own, or in connivance with other Mint employees, he stole the dies and struck off several pieces, peddling them around town for $75 each.

The new 1804 dollars seem not to have fooled many people, for Theodore, with his limited facilities, was unable to letter the edges. One piece was struck over a cut-down 1857 Swiss shooting thaler, and this bizarre creation still adorns the Mint collection, now at the Smithsonian Institution.

Embarrassed by a number of pointed inquiries, Director Snowden took great pains to recover the dollars, and afterwards denied the incident had happened.

Young Eckfeldt was apparently forgiven for his boyish pranks, for in 1861 he was observed peddling rolls of patterns to dealers between Boston and Philadelphia. By 1866, public criticism of the Mint had grown so persistent that Director Pollock issued a circular letter in which he promised to destroy all the old dies at the end of each calendar year. Pollock, however, retired before the year was over, taking his good intentions with him. His successor, William Millward, remained at the Mint until April 1867. Millward's appointment was never confirmed by Congress, which finally selected Henry Linderman in his place.

An avid coin collector, Linderman brought out of hiding the several plain-edge 1804 dollars that Eckfeldt had struck in 1858, and which William DuBois testified were destroyed. The edges were now lettered, and the coins, accompanied by certificates of their genuineness (written by DuBois and other Mint officials), were again let loose upon the guileless collectors.

In 1868, after carefully restriking a number of impressions from each of the old dies, Linderman magnanimously allowed the lot to be destroyed. It must be noted that Linderman, unlike Snowden and Pollock who indulged their fancies for the sake of the Mint collection, caused the striking of numerous artificial coins solely for his own benefit. In 1888, when his collection was put up for auction, several of these pieces were confiscated by Treasury agents as being in violation of the 1873 coinage law which he had helped draft! The most famous coin in the Linderman collection was a Type II 1804 dollar for the completion of which the Director himself was responsible. Years after his passing, Linderman's wife deponed that the coin was one of the few genuine dollars struck in 1804, and that her husband, being unable to afford to purchase it outright, had paid in several installments.

It is difficult to determine just when the "workshop" closed its doors for good. In *Counterfeit, Mis-struck and Unofficial U.S. Coins* (Arco; New York 1963), the writer has chronicled the history of some of its more famous productions, including the clandestine issue of 1884 and 1885 trade dollars. In the latter year, Director James Kimball began an extensive inquiry into Mint irregularities, which culminated in his thunderous declamation of 1887. No superintendent since then has had the temerity to return to the "wild woolly days," although a few individualistic experiments (such as the 1913 Liberty Head nickels) have occurred from time to time.

CHAPTER 15

The Gold Interests Take Charge

IN HIS REPORT OF MAY 4, 1830 Secretary of the Treasury Ingham offered suggestions for a coinage reform. He maintained:

1) That for a decade or more, the mean ratio of 15.8 : 1 had prevailed in England and France and could thus be relied upon as accurate; but as gold was less important than silver, which could not be replaced by a paper currency, it should be slightly undervalued; that the ratio, and the weights of the unit in fine and standard metal, should be expressed in definite numbers (i.e., without an endless fraction) to facilitate calculation, and that 15.625 : 1 was in all respects the best ratio.

2) That a large volume of paper currency prevented a stable ratio, and necessitated periodic adjustments in the legal value of the metals.

3) That if, under the circumstances, these adjustments were undesirable, only one metal should be maintained, of which silver was preferable for its use in small transactions.

The Senate finance committee disputed Ingham's conclusions. On December 15, committee chairman Nathan Sanford presented a report which favored complete bi-metallism at a ratio of 15.9 : 1.[1] He believed that:

Our system of money, established in the year 1792, fully adopts the principle that it is expedient to coin and use both metals as money; and such has always been the opinion of the people of the United States . . .

Each of the two metals is peculiarly convenient for purposes to which the other is not well adapted. Silver is divisible into pieces of small weight and small value, and is convenient for payments of moderate amount, but is very inconvenient

---

[1] Senate Doc. 3; 21st Congress, 2nd Session.

when large sums are paid or transported. Gold, containing the greatest value in the smallest compass and weight, cannot be well used in pieces sufficiently small for very small payments, but is eminently suited for large payments and long transportation. These different advantages cannot be enjoyed without the use of both metals: neither metal can conveniently be used as a measure of value, in the form of bullion; and when only one of the metals is coined, the great convenience of using the other in the form of coins is denied. . .

Those considerable and durable variations, which after a due adjustment of the coins, are sufficient to expel either species of coins from currency, are of slow progress. When they take place, the remedy is, to act again upon the principle which led to preceding adjustments, and to conform the coins to the actual relative value of the two metals.

Sanford's arguments were the same as Hamilton had used four decades before. The idea that occasional adjustments in the legal ratio of the two metals could maintain an equilibrium between them was, of course, hazardous. At best it would breed a circulation of coins of all different weights, with the heavier pieces (unless they were immediately recalled) being sold at a premium or melted down. Moreover, Congress had shown no inclination to make such adjustments, but permitted the nation to limp along indefinitely on a defective ratio. Sanford said that any ratio lower than 15.9 : 1 would be "altogether insufficient to ensure the circulation of gold coins in this country."

The Senate report was, in turn, refuted by that of a select House committee. On February 23, 1831 the chairman, Campbell P. White, said:

The committee . . . feel compelled, reluctantly, to withhold their assent to the opinions preferred in support of the double standard. They cannot admit, that by rejecting one of the metals, any of the injurious consequences predicted would ensue. . . There are inherent and incurable defects in the system, which regulate the standard of value in both gold and silver; its instability as a measure of contracts, and mutability as the practical currency of a particular nation, are serious imperfections; whilst the impossibility of maintaining both metals in concurrent simultaneous, or promiscuous circulation appear to be clearly ascertained. . . The standard being fixed in one metal is the nearest approach to invariableness and precludes the necessity of further legislative interference. . .

Nevertheless, White did not actively oppose bi-metallism, and after reviewing the theories of several renowned economists, he remarked that "such discordancy of opinion amongst writers distinguished for profound and philosophical views, and practical knowledge of the subject under consideration, perplexing and embarrassing."

He thus concluded that it did not really matter what standard was adopted or whether the proportion of money consisted of gold, silver or both. If, however, bi-metallism were selected, White preferred Ingham's ratio of 15.625 : 1 with both specie coined at a fineness of .900.

On May 25, 1832 White wrote to Mint Director Samuel Moore:

It is highly important that gold should not be so estimated as to displace silver from our currency, when the state of foreign exchange may be such as to induce the export of specie.

White again recommended the ratio of 15.625 : 1.

On June 30, White's committee presented another report to the House strongly urging an exclusive silver standard.[3]

---

[2] H. R. Report 95; 21st Congress, 2nd Session.
[3] H. R. Report 496; 22nd Congress, 1st Session.

Silver is the ancient currency of the United States, the metal in which the money unit is exhibited, the money generally used in foreign commerce, and that description of the precious metals, in the distribution of which we exercise an extensive agency. The committee, upon due consideration of all attendant circumstances, are of the opinion that the standard of value ought to be legally and exclusively, as it is practically, regulated in silver.

[Bi-metallism was impracticable because,] if their [gold and silver] relative values were adjusted with the utmost precision, unavoidable vibrations would speedily disturb the accuracy of the adjustment; and experience teaches that the difference of a minute fraction of one per cent will cause either metal to be withdrawn from circulation; a provident government must guard against these alterations, as the public convenience and satisfaction require the steady use of the customary coin.

If bi-metallism were still preferred, the committee thought it should be adopted on a subsidiary basis. Accordingly, White presented a revolutionary bill to end the rivalry between gold and silver.[4] The eagle and silver dollar were to be coined free at a ratio of 15.625 : 1, but all other denominations would be fiduciary, with a limited legal tender. Section 3 provided for the issue of five-, three- and two-dollar gold pieces, at 22½ fine grains per dollar, and a fractional silver coinage at 360 fine grains per dollar. The fiduciary gold was intrinsically worth about five per cent less than its face value, the silver three per cent. The former was a legal tender up to $10, the latter to $5. The devaluation of both metals was, of course, no more necessary than tying both ends of a boat to the pier. Ideally, the bill should have reduced the dollar in the same proportion as the fractional silver, and left the coinage of gold free.

The fifth section directed "that the die used in fabricating the subsidiary currency shall exhibit on the face, as heretofore, the value, and on the reverse, the weight, in grains, of each coin." This was a curious provision considering that no U.S. coin had ever shown the denomination on its obverse side.

The bill was read twice and committed.

On February 19, 1834 White reported a similar but more comprehensive version of the bill. The fine weights of the gold eagle and the silver dollar were fixed, respectively, at 237 6/10 grains, and 371¼ grains, with an alloy of ten per cent. The ratio was thus fixed at 15.625 : 1.

Then a remarkable thing happened. On June 21, when the bill was presented for final disposition, White, without warning even his committee, introduced a substitute for ordinary bi-metallism at a ratio of 16 : 1. This action amazed several members, but was heartily approved by Messrs. Clowney of South Carolina and Jones of Georgia, both representatives of important gold producing areas. In fact, Jones boasted that he had talked "freely and candidly" to White who thereafter agreed to present the substitute bill. Jones offered several specious arguments in favor of the change. He said, for example, that while the ratio originally proposed was 15.625 : 1, the relative devaluations of the subsidiary gold and silver coins would bring it up to about 16 : 1. This was pure nonsense. The subsidiary coins could not have been purchased from the Mint except at face value, and so the question of their relative intrinsic values never arose. After a long and vigorous debate the bill was passed by the House 145 to 36.

Contemporary pro-Jackson newspapers celebrated the House victory as a

---

[4] H. R. bill 603. The bill also gave a legal tender of ten cents to the copper coins.

triumph over the Bank of the United States.[5] In truth, the bill was of little
concern to the Bank, whose notes enjoyed public confidence and could easily
circulate alongside an inflated gold currency. Nevertheless, the "armageddon"
story made good reading, and masked the real objection to the bill—namely
that it overvalued gold and would eventually drive out silver, not bank paper
In a typical piece of party propaganda the Jackson-fed *Washington Globe*
reported:

> The Bank forces opposed a furious opposition and fought, like the ancient *villien*
> till the stars disappeared in the evening. The great battle was fought on Saturday
> and occupied the whole day. Be it remembered that this Saturday was the 21s
> day of June, just at the summer solstice; when days are longest and hottest. It wa
> evidently the tactics of the Bank leaders, if men can be called leaders who ar
> themselves both led and driven by the mammon they serve—it was evidently thei
> tactics, first, to stave off the bill till the next session; next to befog it in a wilder
> ness of mystification; and finally to sink the relative value of gold and silver to
> ratio below 16 to 1; which would have defeated the great end of getting gol
> into circulation as a national currency. Upon these three tacks the ultra-bankite
> made fight, and developed in such force, about mid-day, as to show that *time wa*
> their great *resource*, and that their plan was to protract the struggle into the en
> suing week. The friends of gold then determined upon a permanent sitting ti
> the bill was passed. They renounced all idea of adjourning at the end of the day
> and evinced an invincible determination to sit out the question. This brough
> things to an issue, and towards sunset, the triumphant vote was taken, and resulte
> in an overwhelming majority for the just and truly American ratio of 16 to 1.

Senate opposition to the gold bill was curiously half-hearted, despite the fac
that everyone admitted the inaccuracy of the 16 : 1 ratio. After a short debat
the bill was passed by a vote of 35 to 7, becoming the Act of June 28, 1834.
In an exultant mood, the *Globe* declared:

> Those who talk of a NATIONAL CURRENCY, we point them to the *gol*
> *region* in Virginia, the Carolinas, Georgia, and the contiguous portions of east Te
> nessee and Alabama. *There* is material for a NATIONAL CURRENCY!
> Contrary to their will the Bank party, even in the Senate, have been oblige
> to vote for the measures of the administration, deemed essential to carry on
> policy. By public opinion they have been forced to vote for the GOLD BILL
> which is a treasure of deadly hostility to the interests of the Bank, will supe
> sede its notes, and is the harbinger of a *real* SOUND CURRENCY. The peop
> are now enabled to see the policy of the administration, and to see that it wou
> give them GOLD instead of PAPER. The great bank attorney, Mr. Clay, w
> bold enough to vote against this bill; but he could carry only six of the Ba
> Senators with him. The mass of them, although they voted for the bill with t
> utmost reluctance, dared not tell the people, "We will deny you gold, and for
> *you to depend for a general currency on the notes of the mammoth bank.*" Th
> they were forced to minister to the triumph of the administration.
> The great bills have passed. The triumphant measure is adopted. Gold—tl
> cherished currency of all nations—a currency banished from the United Stat
> for a whole generation by the power of bank legislation—this precious curren
> once more appears in our land, and, in defiance of bank power, will diffuse a
> spread itself throughout the country, and become the familiar inmate of eve
> industrious man's pocket. Such is one of the first fruits of the great measure
> removing the oppressions of a lawless and gigantic moneyed power. What no

---

[5] Despite its obviously beneficial effects, the Bank of the United States was an unpopular
stitution. It was attacked by the gold advocates, who resented the predominance of bank pa
as a currency, and by private bank interests whose oftentime precarious growth was checked
the national bank's moderating policies. President Jackson, influenced by his infamous "kitch
cabinet," vetoed the Bank's recharter and its term thus expired in 1836.

has become of all those predictions that the currency would be ruined—that there would be nothing but broken bank notes to be seen in the land! The new law is to take effect on the 31st inst., but already gold is in circulation! Already the rare and precious metal is jingling in the pockets, and glittering in the hands of the people. Already many travellers have supplied themselves with it, and will be able to traverse the country without the danger of receiving, or the humiliation of offering to pass, the counterfeit imitations of a wretched paper currency.

On July 12, *Niles' Weekly Register* took the *Globe* to task for what it called "the golden humbug."

One of the leading "humbugs" of the day is what is called the "gold bill," concerning which the *official* "Globe"—the "organ" of the powers that be, has many silly or worse than silly paragraphs.

The stuff about the majority of the Senate doing a thing "contrary to their will," &c., is hardly worth a remark. The *"bank party," "interests of the bank," "bank attorney," "bank senators," "mammoth bank,"* and *triumph of the administration,* are mere *setting poles* to make a HURRAH. The stockholders of the bank have a present deeper interest than any other class of persons in the United States, in the preservation of a "SOUND CURRENCY," in which the debts due to them may be paid, and their capital refunded—if the *"glory"* of the "Globe" is consummated in the prostration of that establishment.

Now if the whole interest which "the government" has in the bank is paid off in "glory," and the "hurrah boys," (as Mr. Van Buren calls them,) are content with that, the private stockholders of the bank of the United States will require a "sound currency" in the large sum of $37,546,217 to refund their capital and satisfy the surplus profits earned! And, as it is determined that the bank shall be closed, all this money will be needed by them in the space of three years from the 3d of March next, being the utmost limit to which the power of the Bank will extend, even in the settlements of its own concerns! Where is such a *glorious glory of Gold* to come from? The "gold region of Virginia," and other States? Bah! It will require a Midas, with an ass's ears, to make a *long* bray about this! Every one does not see his way clear to pay off honest debts to the bank at the rate of three or four cents in the dollar, though having many *illustrious* examples of such operations before him—and every body does not furnish "twine, blanks, and paper," to the Post Office, or receive 8,376 dollars for publishing a single advertisement, for less than three months, or at the rate of more than 100 dollars a day! The diggers get gold for the sweat of their brows, and other men have to give them the *quid pro quo;* but these chief brawlers about gold, obtain it by genuflections and brawlings, having well oiled knee joints and brazen faces. Call over the names of these men—and call to mind their former proceedings as to money matters, and we may well smile at some of their shoutings about a "sound currency." But they are now thrifty through fawning, and have "waxed fat" on the "spoils of victory." They must, however, sometimes think—and if so, must know the folly of this "humbug." But custom has also made it natural for them to mislead the people; and, as the *Esquimaux,* from habit, would prefer a piece of whale's blubber, though half putrid, to a fresh killed canvass back duck, so these, from habit, prefer high pressure statements, or arrant falsehood, to the soberness of reason and plainness of truth.

If this be not so—why such hurrahings about the "gold bill?" Has one of Mr. *Ritchie's* "mare's nests" been discovered? Was it only just now thought of to advance the *legal* value of our gold? Did any one oppose the principle of the bill? We have not heard of one. But while all agreed that the *legal* value of gold ought to be raised, as measured by silver, some opposed the bill as it passed under the apprehension that the rate of gold was placed too high; and we shall be much pleased to find, a short time hence, that they and ourselves were mistaken. We think it possible that within the space of three years, a bill of the Bank of the U. States, if to be paid in dollars, may be more valuable than a new made eagle. We would have avoided the danger of this by more closely regulating the comparative value of the metals which compose our coins—that is all that should have been done, and so much ought to have been done long ago.

The bank has a very small, if any, interest in this matter, whether its charter shall be renewed or not. Its notes are better than the new gold coins will be and so will remain as long as they are permitted to circulate among the people, because of the greater cheapness and safety of their transportations; but if the gold bill has any sensible effect on the currency of the country at an early day, it is the *state* banks that will feel it, in reduced circulations, *and the hurrah will be on the other side!* If a man has ten 1000 dollar notes of the Bank of the United States, and goes into the office at New Orleans, he may get a draft on Portland, if he pleases, for ¼ or ½ per cent if not at par—and the further cost of remittance will be 25 cents for postage; but if he has $10,000 in gold at New Orleans, it will cost him at least 2 per cent to pay a debt with it at Portland. And besides, in the first mode of remittance there is no risk—but the second is attended with much hazard and delay. In an interruption of exchanges, the office at New Orleans cannot give a draft on Portland, though gold be laid on the counter for it, unless at a rate of premium that will pay for the cost and insurance of the transportation of the gold, to satisfy the debt made at Portland, with *interest,* on account of a less rapid remittance than the mail is expected to furnish. Every business man understands this, and it is not worth while to say more about it. Persons will no more deal in gold than in paper, without a view to profit. If exchanges are to be made in gold, the costs of transportation and insurance must be added to the premium or interest that shall be charged.

The reference made to the "gold region" as a "national treasure," is stupidly ridiculous. The countries that produce the most gold are among the poorest in the world. *Ignorance* and *poverty* and *misery* abide in them, and the laborers are degraded *working machines.* There is no exception to the rule. As a branch of the national industry, and in places where there is a surplus of labor, the digging for gold may be well enough—but it is seldom more profitable than digging for potatoes. A quantity of potatoes worth $100, is just as valuable as $100 in gold, with this difference, that it is the owner of the potatoes, and not of the gold, who *commands* the market—for persons do not eat gold. And what is this flourish of trumpets about the "gold region"—*this* "national treasure"? Why the makers of buttons, horn combs, and wooden clocks, in Connecticut, might gather to themselves as much gold annually as is produced in all our mines and washings; for their wares are worth more money in the market. England produces neither gold nor silver—and yet lent money to Mexico, Peru, Brazil, &c. Holland had no mines, but yet was the banker of nations!—It is a *productive industry* that gathers and retains gold and silver. Without that, no matter what may be the legal enactments about gold, the metal cannot be retained amongst us. It will seek those countries wherein labor is best rewarded. The "national treasure" is the successful industry of the people, the wheat grower, cotton planter, and cod fisher.—Strike out even the fisherman from the productive classes, and the gold that we obtain from our mines will not remunerate the value lost—though the gold were found in a heap and ready coined for use.

So much for the *hurrah!* We have long desired a new regulation of the legal comparative value of gold, but think that the rate established is about two per cent too high. If such is not the case, we shall be as well satisfied with the passage of the gold bill as Col. Benton or Mr. Polk can be—but without making any noise about it.

Another article in the *Globe* intimated that the Mint was too dependent on the Bank of the United States, and might try to delay the new gold emission until after the fall elections. The editor suggested that a close watch be kept over the Mint's officers to prevent such an occurrence. By August 1, however, the new coins were already bagged and awaiting distribution. The original plan of adding the entire date to the design was abandoned, and on August

2, the Treasury Department issued a proclamation to assist the public in discriminating between the new and old issues:

> As the date could not, by law, be altered, but the cap and motto be legally omitted, and would serve plainly to distinguish the new impression, that course has been adopted at the Mint till the commencement of the next year, when the motto will probably be restored, and the date of the new year, instead of the omission of the motto, will be sufficient to indicate the change in the coin.

Ironically, the new coins were attacked by Whig journals as premature and hastily contrived. Numerous editorials painted stories of the counterfeits already in circulation, and predicted that quarters would be gilded and passed off as half eagles.

* * *

It was not long before the Dixiecrats in Congress, emboldened by success, began a new promotion to establish southern branch mints. On Feb. 20, 1835 Senator Waggaman of Louisiana introduced a bill for this purpose, which he "urged from consideration of the great importation of gold and silver into New Orleans and the great risk and expense incurred by sending on all the bullion from the south to be coined at Philadelphia." Senator Calhoun of South Carolina supported the bill, adding that the expense of establishing branch mints would be less than that of transporting bullion and coin to and from Philadelphia. Mr. Benton favored additional mints as a means of providing more "hard money" and dispensing with the "rag system."

A warm debate followed. Calhoun tried to steamroll the bill through the Senate, but failed when Henry Clay insisted on receiving an account of the proposed expenditures "not a syllable" of which had been rendered. Further opposition was led by Senator Hill who maintained that the salaries of the officers were placed at nearly a third higher than would be expected elsewhere in the union. The proposed New Orleans Mint was his special target. Hill said that New Orleans had a sickly season lasting from three to six months, when operations would have to be suspended. The upkeep of such a mint would be far greater than the expense of transportation to and from Philadelphia. Hill preferred Louisville, Kentucky which would prove less costly, and was centrally located for the western country. He said that a large part of the gold coined at New Orleans would not be from bullion or native gold, but from foreign specie which was already legal tender. Thus, he reasoned, the argument that branch mints would create a more plentiful supply of coins was largely fallacious. There were, besides, enough gold coins already in circulation.

Senator Frelinghuysen of New Jersey also spoke against the bill. He said that the branch mints would require an outlay of half a million dollars, and create an additional annual expenditure. Frelinghuysen pointed out that the amount of bullion received from North Carolina was $800,000 and that the cost of establishing a mint was $30,000. He said that Calhoun's estimate of five per cent for the cost of transportation from New Orleans to Philadelphia was exaggerated, the Director of the Mint having calculated the figure at less than two-and-a-half per cent. Moreover, the Director had suggested only one branch mint, and the Treasury Department had not indicated that others were required.

Clay remarked that gold imports from the Atlantic coast had totaled $5,000,-

000 for the previous year. Even if the entire sum had been received at New Orleans, the cost, he said, of transporting it to Philadelphia would have only been about $375. Clay wished to have the bill recommitted in order to reduce the number of proposed mints.

Senator Waggaman objected, saying that this would prevent its passage during the present session. He accused Clay of being "very disingenuous" in his argument. Waggaman maintained that a certain percentage of the value was always demanded by carriers because of the risk involved in transporting gold or silver. If the sum transported from New Orleans to Philadelphia were $5,000,000, a charge of 2½ per cent would not be $375, but $125,000. He said that New Orleans exported more American articles than any other city in the United States. It would doubtless receive a large part of its payment in specie and its exports were expected to grow.

Clay insisted that the transportation charge was figured by the pound. He said it had been quoted by the Director of the Mint at 1¼ cents per pound, including insurance. Moreover, if the real facts of the case were known, it would be found that the expense was borne by the banks. Clay also disputed the assumption that export payment would be made largely in specie.

When the debate closed, it had not yet been determined whether the annual cost of transportation to the Mint was $375 or $125,000. The bill was finally put to a vote, and passed 24 to 19. It was whisked through the House without debate and enacted on March 3, 1835.

The Act provided that "Branches of the mint of the United States shall be established as follows: one branch at the city of New Orleans for the coinage of gold and silver; one branch at the town of Charlotte in Mecklinburg county, in the state of North Carolina, for the coinage of gold only; and one branch at or near Dahlonega, in Lumpkin county, in the state of Georgia, also for the coinage of gold only."

The Act of June 28, 1834 had established a bi-metallic ratio of 16.002 : 1. It reduced the gold unit to 23.2 grains fine, with an alloy of 13/129 parts. This resulted in a figure as clumsy as that which had nearly driven Albion Cox to distraction four decades before. Mint Director Samuel Moore inveighed against the alloy and pressed for new legislation which would also create a bullion fund, and provide statutory recognition for the 168-grain copper cent authorized by President Washington in 1795.

Out of these recommendations grew the first of our two comprehensive revisionary Mint laws. Numerous proposals were offered to improve the coinage, and some of considerable merit were rejected. Among these was a bill providing for subsidiary dimes and half dimes, and light-weight copper coins with a legal tender up to ten cents.

A revisionary bill was finally passed on January 18, 1837. The new law provided a uniform fineness of .900 for the gold and silver coins. The gold unit was increased from 23.2 to 23.22 fine grains, while its standard weight remained 25.8 grains. The standard weight of the silver dollar was reduced from 416 to 412½ grains. The new legal ratio between the two metals was thus 15.998 : 1.

Another important provision gave the Mint a $1,000,000 bullion fund to purchase and coin bullion in advance of deposits. The charge on immediate exchanges was abolished, and the 168-grain cent was finally acknowledged by Congress.

Among the provisions rejected by Congress while considering the revisionary Mint bill was one for coining gold dollars. On March 14, and again on March 23, 1836 Director Robert Patterson (who opposed the innovation) submitted patterns for a dollar to Secretary Woodbury. Provision for a gold dollar was included in a draft of the Mint bill, but finally rejected after Patterson's appearance before a Congressional committee on December 12, 1836.[6]

Nevertheless, on December 21, the *Philadelphia Public Ledger* urged the issue of not only a gold dollar but also a double eagle.

> On Monday last, we stated that the silver dollar, the coinage of which has been suspended since 1805, was soon to be issued from the mint. We exceedingly regret this, because the silver dollar is a very cumbrous coin, will interpose an obstacle to the circulation of small gold coins, and increase the prejudice already existing in favor of paper, from its lightness. Nobody will encumber himself with silver dollars, when he can obtain any substitute. Twenty are an encumbrance in a pocket, and induce the possessor to regard silver, for money, almost as he would iron wedges or brick bats. A man might travel for five years, and carry gold enough in his pocket to pay his expenses for the whole period; while the same amount of silver would require a yoke of oxen to draw it.
>
> With this well founded objection against silver, it will never supersede paper, while with a gold coinage, paper would soon be driven from circulation, excepting for large sums.
>
> A silver dollar is not so convenient as two halves, and weighs precisely as much. Neither is a half dollar so convenient as two quarters, while it weighs precisely as much. It is therefore judicious to make silver coin as small [as] possible, and to coin no silver in any piece which the value can be conveniently given in gold. The dollar is the smallest gold coin that would be convenient, and as it would be eminently so, neither silver nor paper should be allowed to take its place. Therefore as gold in dollars is better than silver in dollars, no silver dollars should be coined; and as silver in quarters can perform the office of silver in halves, and another office besides, we should be well pleased to see no other coins than quarters, dimes and half dimes. For two years to come, we should wish to see the whole gold coinage confined to dollars. If we are to have larger coins, let them be in gold. In addition to the eagle, which has the size of the half dollar, we would recommend the double eagle, which of the size of our silver dollar, would contain the value of twenty.
>
> We are surprised that those who perform such anxiety to procure a gold coinage, should commend a coinage which will impede the circulation of gold, and sustain existing prejudices in favor of paper.

It was another eight years before the gold dollar was again proposed. On January 22, 1844 Director Patterson wrote to Secretary of the Treasury, John C. Spencer:

> Sir, I have been called upon to present my views to the Committee of Ways and Means as to the propriety of introducing the coinage of gold dollar pieces, and I have done so, in a letter sent to the Chairman[7] by yesterday's mail.
>
> As one of the elements on which they are to form their judgment, I have caused some pieces to be struck, from dies prepared for a similar occasion in 1836.[8] It is right that the head of the Treasury Department should also be furnished with one of these specimens, and I therefore send you the enclosed piece. Its weight is 25.8 grains; its volume but little more than ⅔ds of that of the half dime, the smallest of our coins.
>
> The opinion to which my reflections and inquiries have led me is adverse to the

---

[6] Walter Breen, *The Secret History of the Gobrecht Coinages.*

[7] James McKay, a Representative of North Carolina, one of the largest gold-producing areas in the country.

[8] These are evidently the specimens with obverse and reverse aligned instead of inverted.

proposed innovation in our coinage. If it should be ordered, however, the piece sent to you is not offered as a model to be followed. The obverse should bear the head of Liberty, like our other gold coins. In the reverse, however, I think that the figure of the eagle should be omitted as in the dime and half dime.

The Secretary replied on the 27th, soliciting Patterson's further views. In a letter dated January 31, Patterson stated that the only justification for a gold dollar was that it was only one sixteenth the size of a silver one. But it would, in fact, be "too diminutive" and if counterfeited, less easily detected by weight. The Director added that small gold coins were unpopular, and that the only ones in use anywhere—the Spanish and Colombian "dollars" (i.e., half escudos)—had not been coined for twenty years. Moreover, the issue, if adopted by Congress, would mean increased labor and expense for the Mint.

Patterson seems to have had his way, for on March 23, McKay's committee reported adversely on the coining of gold dollars. Two years later, when the committee was again directed to inquire into the subject, it reported as before. Toward the end of 1848, however, the discovery of gold in California changed the economic scene almost overnight, infusing new life into the gold interests.

On January 25, 1849 McKay introduced a bill for the coinage of gold dollars. After a second reading, the bill was referred to the House ways and means committee, of which McKay was conveniently still chairman. The bill excited a lively discussion in the press, even regarding the shape of the coin.

The *Washington Union* praised the bill as a further step in driving out the ragged paper currency. On the 27th, it quoted a letter to the editor which suggested the issue of an annular dollar:

> Dear Sir: I beg to lay before you a mode for coining the gold dollar, to which I would most respectfully ask the favorable attention of the public.
> I need not say much on the subject, and the importance of this coin. The structure of what I propose is as follows:
> In circumference the same as a five-cent piece of silver, with a square hole in the center, (a design of which I have). Leave out the eagle and Liberty cap, and insert on one side thirteen stars, "one dollar, 1849," or whatever year it may be coined in; and on the other side a "wreath," and the words "United States of America." The outer edge milled much the thickest, and scientifically decreasing to the inner edge, according to a scale which the knowledge of the director of the mint and his associates could exactly fix.
> The object of the square hole is to make the coin thicker and broader, and to enable every person to ascertain the difference at any time, either night or day, between the gold dollar and a five-cent piece. I have understood that one of the most plausible objections to the gold dollar has been this apprehension of seeming identity, and consequent liability to imposition. The square hole in the centre will at once enable any person to detect an attempt at fraud in the payment or exchange of coins to which I have alluded. Very respectfully etc.—P.W.

McKay seized upon the idea (if, indeed, he hadn't authored the article), and then, in a sanguine mood, determined to push for the coinage of double eagles. Patterson responded coolly. In a letter of January 30, he wrote to the Congressman:

> Dear Sir: I have to acknowledge the receipt of your letters of the 27 and 28 insts. and you will see from the enclosed form of a bill that I have complied with your request.
> There can be no other objection to the Double eagle except that it is not needed. It will be a handsome coin, between the half dollar and dollar in size.

I send you six specimens of the gold dollar, three of standard gold and three of gilt silver. The form proposed in this article to which you called my attention is very objectionable. So also is the plan devised in England in which a silver coin has a gold plug in the center.

A more favorable opinion was expressed the same day by the *Washington Weekly Globe.*

Mr. McKay has introduced a bill into the House of Representatives to authorize the coinage of one dollar gold pieces at the mint, which will pass, we hope, *nemine contradicente.*

We go for gold, for gold coin, for the gold dollar, and for golden opinions, could we be but fortunate enough to win them. That the gold dollar should find objectors among those who are interested in maintaining a sound, tangible, metallic, unfluctuating and non-depreciating currency, surprises us much; but there are, it seems, some who, blest with microscopic powers of vision, perceive, or think they perceive, obstacles and inconveniences—the gold dollar would be too small, might be lost, or might be paid away in the dark, or by the blind for a five-cent piece. Well, this might all happen, we admit, but it would not happen often; and we venture to assert that, allowing for all sorts of accidents and mischances, there would not be lost in ten years as large a sum with the gold dollar as there is lost with the paper dollar annually. But if provision is to be made against every possibility of losing money, we know but one way of coming at it effectually—that is, never to have any.

A writer in the Union, in order to obviate objections to the gold dollar, proposes to coin it with a hole in the centre. We do not see the necessity of this. In some parts of South America gold dollars are very abundant, and are found to be very convenient; but they have no hole in them. They are thin, and present nearly double the surface, probably, that a five cent piece does. Why not coin them so here, if it is desirable that they should be broader than a half dime? But we care nothing about the size, or the shape, or the effigy, or the milling. Give us the gold dollar, and be it thick or thin, broad or narrow, with or without the hole, we will give it a hearty welcome.

McKay now conferred with fellow Democrat Charles Atherton, of the Senate finance committee, about promoting the expanded bill. McKay could expect the opposition of Whigs in the House, and an amendment providing for double eagles would make passage even more difficult. But, if Atherton introduced the new bill in the Senate, McKay could offer the amendment with better grace.

Atherton presented his bill on February 1, and McKay followed on the 20th. The House debate began the same day. McKay admitted that objections had been made to the size of both coins. The dollar, it was contended, was too small and would be easily counterfeited, and paid out in the dark for a half dime. Again, the double eagle would be subject to undue abrasion.

McKay might have easily disposed of these objections. Quarter eagles, for example, were not paid out in the dark for dimes, and if double eagles were more susceptible to abrasion than lower denominations, they would also circulate less. In any case, the double eagle would be smaller than the silver dollar. Curiously, McKay did not advance any counter-arguments, but assumed a defensive position. He said that the Mint was obliged to pay out whatever denomination depositors requested, and if no one wanted dollars or double eagles, none would be coined.

Taking advantage of McKay's irresolution, Whig Representative Joseph Ingersoll assailed the bill. He said that Director Patterson "warmly objected" to the new denominations, and that the dollar had met with little favor when suggested some years previously. Only Spain issued such a "toy coin," and her disturbed economic condition could well be the result. "A little piece of precious metal, scarcely perceptible to the eye or touch, may be a plaything for the idle, or counter for the card table—perhaps a little addition to a lady's purse in her morning's shopping, or a medium of fraud upon the post office laws, by lurking concealed under the seal of a letter. Beyond these fanciful purposes it has none."

Moreover, new denominations would require the construction of additional dies and machinery, and might disrupt the "happy organization" of the Mint. Worse still would be the possible consequences of such a precedent.

"It seems," Ingersoll continued, "great coins are to be issued as well as small ones. If eagles' wings are to be clipped down to a standard so small that they will fail to perform their office from their insignificance, they are, as the bill proposes, to be doubled into a ponderous and unparalleled size. Bad as the increase of metal is, it is not half so bad as its wasteful diminution. We have dollars of silver. It is idle to have dollars of gold. Is it intended to carry the experiment still further, and duplicate all the denominations of coin? Make gold half dollars, gold quarter dollars, gold dimes, and gold half dimes, and you have enough; but may it not lead to making silver quarter eagles, silver half eagles, and silver eagles? Ponderous coinage once existed among a simple and warlike people. If it is to be introduced again, iron or tobacco will suit as well as gold."

Mr. Hudson, a Whig representative from Massachusetts, agreed with Ingersoll. He repeated the objections McKay himself had raised, but failed to answer. Hudson said that Patterson had furnished the House committee with a genuine gold dollar and a counterfeit piece, and that the majority of members were unable to distinguish one from the other.[9]

During all this time, McKay was strangely silent. But Democrats Jones and Nicoll came to the rescue. Jones inquired whether the gentleman from Massachusetts could distinguish in the dark between a hundred dollar bill and a shinplaster of one dollar. Nicoll added that all of the talk about counterfeits was greatly exaggerated. More important, he said, was the fact that the country now called for these coins. The gold dollar was particularly essential to communities where small notes were disappearing. Whig Representative John Rockwell tried to table the bill, but his motion was overwhelmingly defeated. The amendment calling for the double eagle was then agreed to, and the bill was passed in the House by a large majority. After token resistance the Senate concurred, and the bill was enacted on March 3, 1849.

Interestingly, the opposition of Congress to the new gold coins was rather mild compared to what followed in the Mint itself.

To begin our story properly, we must go back to July 1844, when the death of Christian Gobrecht left the Mint temporarily without an engraver. Among the aspirants for the office were Charles Welsh, a Philadelphia banknote engraver, and Allen Leonard, a modestly talented engraver who had modeled the John Quincy Adams Presidential medal for the Mint.

A third contender was James Barton Longacre, the well-known Philadelphia portrait engraver, and publisher of *The National Portrait Gallery of Dis-*

---

[9] Patterson's "counterfeit" was nothing more than a gold-gilt silver coin made at the Mint.

tinguished Americans. Longacre ignored Patterson's good offices, securing the appointment through Senator Calhoun.[10] If Patterson resented the slight, however, he was more annoyed by Leonard's importunities. In the following letters to Secretary of the Treasury Walker, we see the Director's attitude toward Longacre change from grudging toleration to genuine enthusiasm. The first, dated August 20, 1845, reads in part:[11]

> The present incumbent, Mr. Longacre, is a gentleman of excellent character, highly regarded in this community, and has acquired some celebrity as an engraver of copper; but he is not a Die-Sinker. Indeed I do not know that he has ever made an attempt in this art. For the mere routine work of the Mint, however, it is not required. So long as one can rest contented with our present coins, the making of dies used for the Mints will be a mere mechanical operation, and the office of Engraver little more than a sinecure. I confess, however, that I am not myself contented with our coins as works of art; and if I knew a man of real taste, talent, and skill, who could make for us a new set of original dies, I would not hesitate to recommend him for the appointment at the Mint. But I do not know any such person in the United States, and I doubt if there be one.

Patterson added that Leonard's medal of President Adams had not given "satisfactory evidence of his ability to make the dies required for the Mint," and that the artist was cutting another die in low relief to better exhibit his work. On December 19, after rejecting Leonard's new die, Patterson wrote to Walker:[12]

> This is not all we want. We require an artist of taste, judgment and inventive talent; a man who can devise as well as execute. Now the mechanical skill of the die-sinker is even a subordinate qualification, with which we could almost entirely dispense. If the artist, after making his design, be able to model in wax, so as to make a medallion of three or four inches in diameter, in low relief,—all the rest can be done by ordinary workmen. A cast of the medallion is made in iron, and from this, by the aid of a portrait lathe, a die is cut, which is a perfect fac-simile of the original, reduced to the size required. Some of the medals executed at the Mint,—one of Franklin, and the Indian Medals of President Tyler,— were struck from dies made in this way. The original dies of our dime and half-dime were also cut by the portrait lathe, set in motion by the steam-engine.
> The present incumbent in the office of Engraver of the Mint,—a Mr. Longacre, —has shown, as I think, more taste and judgment in making devices for an improved coinage here than have been exhibited by any of his predecessors. He has shown too that he is quite competent to make the required models from his drawings, and he is now engaged in this work. I think that it will be successful, and he will be able, if not interrupted in his labors, to accomplish the improvement in our coins which is so desirable. I hope, therefore, that his tenure of office will not be interrupted until I am able to lay before you, and through you before the President, the evidence of his skill and taste.

When we bear in mind that Patterson was chiefly concerned with discrediting Leonard, the above letter becomes more intelligible. We can understand, for example, why the Director could "almost entirely dispense" with die-sinking, when it was actually required to complete every single working die. Again, there is no evidence that Patterson ever sent samples of Longacre's "skill and taste" to Walker, or that the Director's enthusiasm for the engraver outlasted Leonard's persistence.

Longacre had never been very popular with the other officers who were

---

[10] Longacre's appointment dates Sept. 16, 1844.
[11] Georgia S. Chamberlain, *American Medals and Medalists.*
[12] Ibid.

a clannish group comprised of Patterson's own friends and relatives. Being a man of humility and dignity, he contented himself with a solitary existence, and despite his incompetence as a die-sinker managed for some years to avoid any serious encounters, even with the irascible Peale. But with the adoption of new denominations in 1849, the engraver's office at once became the cynosure of the Mint, as well as an unwitting obstacle to Peale's medal business. The bone of contention seems to have been the Contamin lathe, which rightfully belonged to the engraver's department, but which Peale monopolized to make his medal dies. Peale thus began an insidious campaign to undermine Longacre's position, with the aim of having models for new coinage dies made by contract outside the Mint. For the rest of our story, we have culled largely from Longacre's correspondences with Director Patterson, Secretary of the Treasury Meredith, and the erstwhile melter and refiner Richard McCulloh.[13] In relating the background to Secretary Meredith, Longacre, on February 18, 1850 wrote:

> About a year ago, when the act of Congress adding two new denominations to the gold coinage was a subject of discussion, I was informed by a gentleman in the Mint, that he feared measures would be taken in relation thereto prejudicial to my position, intimating that a purpose existed on the part of another officer to have the engraving of the *dies* executed elsewhere and by some other hand than mine. Knowing the law designating my duties, I immediately waited on the director and apprized him that I was ready to commence the work. He assented to my suggestion, and requested me to commence making a model in wax for the *head*, which I accordingly executed, and subsequently engraved the dies for the gold dollar. The engraving was unusually minute and required very close and incessant labor for several weeks. I made the *original dies* and *hubs* for making the working dies twice over, to secure their perfect adaptation to the coining machinery. I had a wish to execute this work single handed, that I might thus silently reply to those who had questioned my ability for the work.
>
> The result, I believe, was satisfactory, but I then found I had tasked myself too severely for my health; and knowing that my labor would necessarily be increased with that which was to follow, I took occasion to say to the director, in the month of May last, that my department was not strong enough for such an emergency; as it rested with him legally and properly to order such assistance as I might require. I was surprised to find that he objected to making any addition to the force of my department by the employment of any person to assist me, saying that for that matter he saw no objection to having the engraving done out of the Mint—that it might be done by contract, as it was in France—that if it could not be done in this city, it might be done in any other part of the country or even in Europe.[14] This remark closed my lips against any further application for aid; the law required that I, as the proper officer, should engrave all the dies for the Mint, and left it to the discretion of the director as to what assistance should be given me. I could not direct or control any work done out of the Mint, or by contract; I was not so empowered. I proceeded as well as I was able with the work necessary to produce the dies for the double eagle. I made a design and model of the *reverse*. The plan of operation selected for me was to have an *electrotype mould* made from my model, in copper, to serve as a pattern for a cast in iron. The operations of the galvanic battery for this purpose were conducted in the apartments of the chief coiner. The galvanic process failed; my model was

---

[13] Drafts of most of the following Longacre letters are found in the Library Company of Philadelphia collection. The whole of the correspondence is preserved in R. S. McCulloh's pamphlet *The Proceedings of the late Director of the Mint in relation to the official Misconduct of Franklin Peale Esq., Chief Coiner and Other Abuses in the Mint*, July 1853.

[14] Patterson had evidently gone so far as to contact the French engraver Louis Bouvet who, in the same year, furnished patterns for a half eagle. No correspondence relating to this interesting issue remains in the archives.

destroyed in the operation.[15] I had, however, taken the precaution to make a cast in plaster from my model, previous to subjecting it to the action of a galvanic battery. From this cast, as the only alternative, I procurred a metallic one which, however, was not perfect; but I thought I should be able to correct the imperfections in the engraving of the die with more economy of time than in making a new model; this was a laborious task, but seasonably completed, entirely by my own hand. The die had then to be hardened in the coining department; it unluckily split in the process.

I had then to go to work with depressed spirits to overcome this unexpected misfortune to my work. When I had got through this, the original die was still to be finished for the head, and all the *hubs* to be made. For all this no assistance was yet provided for me, nor was it until late in October that I received authority to procure it. I had then to look for one qualified for the work, and at liberty to undertake it. Through the good offices of my friend, Mr. Wright, of New York, I was, in November last, enabled to obtain the services of a young man[16] whom he had instructed, and who has rendered me valuable aid. But the days had now become short and dark, and the light of my only room in the Mint was frequently rendered more obscure by the smoke of the steam engines and the melting and refining furnaces.

By December 24, 1849 Longacre had finally completed a pair of double eagle dies. Peale at once rejected these as unsuitable, and wrote complainingly to Patterson:

> Sir—It is with extreme regret, and after the most ernest endeavors to overcome the difficulty, that I am compelled to inform you that the impression upon the new die for the double eagle cannot be brought up by the usual coining process. The depth of the head of the obverse is such, that the steel will not sustain the degree of pressure necessary for a perfect impression.
>
> To this is to be added the minor disadvantage of the projection of the head beyond the border of the coin, preventing its being "piled" (as it is technically expressed) and exposing it to abrasion.

The only presently located 1849 double eagle, which is in the Smithsonian collection, altogether belies Peale's charge. The coin has excellent relief and, according to Breen, stacks perfectly.

But Peale had "spoken," and that was the end of the matter. Longacre was ordered to reduce the relief in his model and make a new obverse die. Meanwhile, on the strength of Peale's testimony, Patterson had decided to hire a new engraver. On Christmas Day, the Director wrote to Secretary Meredith, complaining of Longacre's "want of skill in die-making." Meredith inquired whether a replacement could be found, and Patterson immediately suggested the brilliant New York City engraver and die sinker C. C. Wright.

Longacre, ignorant of these events, continued to work on his new double eagle dies, which he completed on January 12, 1850. Despite a growing complaint over the delay, Peale refused to try the dies until the evening of the 26th. He then notified Longacre that the relief still wouldn't come up because of the relative position of the head to the eagle,[17] and that the former must be changed. Longacre, incredulous, appealed to Director Patterson. In a long letter dated the 30th, he described the various delays caused by the coining department, as well as the details of the latest trial.

---

[15] Under the circumstances, Peale's adoption of a process not normally used at the Mint, together with its catastrophic failure, seems more than coincidental.

[16] Peter F. Cross.

[17] If the depth of impression is too great at opposite points of obverse and reverse dies, the corresponding relief will not be fully brought up.

... The result of the trial ... was not satisfactory to me as an artist, as it respects the character of my work; and the further alteration which was required, involving carefulness and delicacy in the operation, to guide me intelligently whilst occupied therewith, it was important that I should have by me, for the time, one of the pieces then struck; but on asking the chief coiner for one of them for this purpose, he declined complying with my request, on the ground of some alleged or apprehended difficulty in making up his accounts; and on my offering to deposit the value in his hands from my own pocket, solely with a view to expedite the public business, he refused absolutely and on any terms to allow me the use of one of them—and on my inquiry as to what he expected me to do under such circumstances, proposed the alternative, which I was constrained to accept—of an impression to be taken in silver.

I am justified, therefore in assuming that this test is considered a fair one, by the party assuming or claiming the privilege of deciding. I have accordingly compared this impression in silver with those of the current gold coins in previous use at the Mint, and the deficiency in the character of the coin from want of fullness, is not much, if anything, to the disparagement of my work as it now stands. Could I have seen a coin of the same size fully brought up by the same machinery, I should have experienced no difficulty in adapting my work to the capacity of the striking machinery at the first; but I have no knowledge of any coin here of corresponding type being perfectly brought up by the process now in use.

I would say that it is more desirable to me to make the dies for the coin in question as perfect in execution and adaptation as may be attainable by all the skill that can be brought to bear upon them; and I shall prefer to follow your direction to this end rather than any other, only let me not be held accountable for the consumption of time occasioned by casualties, omissions, or untimely revisions occurring in departments other than my own, nor bear the charge of imperfections that have a legitimate habitation elsewhere.

The "direction" in which Patterson planned to lead Longacre was different than the artist anticipated. As Longacre described it in a later correspondence (Sept. 2, 1851) with Richard McCulloh:

To that letter a written reply was not given; the director noticed verbally some of the points on a visit to my office-room; but the complaint of official obstructions in my intercourse with the chief coiner, was not adverted to. A few days after however, I received another visit from the director, when he informed me that he had painful intelligence to communicate to me; which was, that I was to be removed from office; that the communication from the executive authority of the Government was imperative, and urgently advised me to send in my resignation. It was the unexpected character of this interview, which impelled me to seek one with the Secretary of the Treasury, from a conviction that a purpose so unfriendly on the part of that officer, could only have been formed, in the absence of correct information, as to my position, and the proper discharge of my official duties; and which information it then became a duty to myself to convey, in such a manner as would admit of no prejudicial intervention.

The result was such as to justify, to the fullest extent, the apprehension I had entertained ... I became satisfied that my position as an officer of the Government, as well as the discharge of my duties, had been mostly unfairly represented and that by communications emanating from the Mint, without my knowledge. One fact will suffice to show the grounds of my conclusion. On exhibiting an impression from the dies I had just finished, he inquired with evident surprise, what had become of the *dies* from which it was taken, implying that he had been informed they were broken, when at the time I knew them to be in perfect order as I told him.

Longacre was thus temporarily reprieved—an interference for which Patterson never forgave him. On March 12, the Director wrote to Secretary Meredith

Sir, The first coinage of the Double Eagles has been executed today, and I send two of them, for the President and yourself.

They have been struck with all the force that could be raised,—even to such a degree as to injure the dies,—and yet the impression is not perfect. The face is still too much in relief.

Still courting revenge, Patterson wrote again to Meredith on April 1, suggesting the adoption of Peale's plan.

Sir, When I informed Mr. Longacre,—the Engraver of the Mint, of the determination of the President respecting him, he went, as you know, immediately to Washington, and obtained leave to finish his dies. This extension of time having lapsed, I feel anxious to know whether any decided steps are intended in this important matter. If the office is to be vacated, I would propose that the vacancy not be filled, until we can have time to test an experiment, the object of which is to show that the office of Engraver of the Mint has become unnecessary, and even cumbersome, and might profitably be abolished by law.

In the end, the conspiracy failed. Longacre stayed on, and, in fact, outlasted by a good many years the two men who had unjustly sought his removal.

* * *

As a result of the gold rush, California swiftly grew into a thriving seaport area. But the expansion was not altogether a blessing. Paper currency had never circulated on the Pacific coast, and the supply of coins was quickly absorbed by the Customs House which refused to accept gold dust or nuggets in payment of duties. To resuscitate trade, various private firms began to issue their own gold coins and on September 19, 1850 California Senator Gwin introduced two bills, one providing for assay offices at Stockton and Sacramento City, the other for the manufacture of large-denomination gold coins in the Mint, its branches and assay offices. The coins were to be .980 fine, and cast in an hexagonal shape in values from $100 to $10,000.

Patterson opposed both bills. He was particularly averse to the ingot-coins, insisting that their manufacture was impracticable and thus useless. As an alternative, he proposed the issue of ordinary ingots, of any value, chiefly designed for international exchanges. By the end of 1850, Gwin had failed to secure passage for either of his bills, and was forced to settle for a single assay office at San Francisco. Finally, in July 1852, after California had suffered two money panics, Congress took decisive action, establishing the San Francisco Mint.

* * *

On January 13, 1851, Representative Duer accused Director Patterson of deliberately making the gold dollar too small and thick in order to provoke criticism. Patterson retired in July, and in the following year new patterns for an annular gold dollar and half dollar were struck at the Mint. The subject, however, was not resumed in Congress, and in February 1853, *Bankers Magazine*, quoting from the *Philadelphia Public Ledger*, reported:

This [the annular dollar] is a more convenient coin in size than the present dollar, but as the public are now familiar with the size and shape of the present dollar, it is probably well enough to continue them, and authorize gold half-dollar pieces of the ring shape proposed, by which the inconvenience now experienced from want of change would be greatly relieved. The half dollar of ring shape would be as large as the present gold dollar, and yet would be readily distinguished by touch from the whole dollar.[18]

Nevertheless, on April 19, 1853 Secretary of the Treasury Guthrie wrote to Mint Director Pettit:

So many complaints have been made about the size of the gold dollar—its liability to be lost or paid thro' mistake for small silver coins that it would seem to be expedient to adopt some other form.

It is understood that a specimen of a gold dollar proposed to be issued with a hole in the centre was some time since submitted to the Department, but if such was the case, it has been lost or mislaid.

Be pleased to take the matter under consideration and to submit a design for a Ring Dollar.

Pettit replied on the following day:

. . . To my regret I find that no specimen remains of the annular gold dollar but I enclose a piece in silver which exactly represents the size, thickness, & general appearance of what was struck in gold.

The preparation of an annular coin involves several mechanical difficulties, and it would probably prove a very tedious piece to strike. Nevertheless, these difficulties are not insurmountable, if that form should be thought desirable.

I may state, also, that it would be possible to enlarge somewhat the diameter of the gold dollar, and yet preserve its present shape. The enclosed gold piece may serve as a specimen to show the extent to which the size may be increased if deemed proper.

In a letter to Guthrie dated May 10, Pettit said that the production of annular gold dollars was necessarily slow, and that the coins would not permit standard devices. He suggested, instead, "an oval shaped, or an angular shaped coin" which would present much less mechanical difficulty, hold standard devices, and be more beautiful.

Pettit died suddenly on May 31, and was succeeded four days later by James Ross Snowden. Guthrie, with a peculiar stubbornness, wrote to Snowden on June 7:

The Department is very solicitous that the gold dollar should be put into circulation in a more convenient form than that now in use, and it is hoped that there are artists in the country sufficiently skillful to devise some emblems of liberty which may be impressed on the annular coin in a manner so as to comply substantially with the law.

During 1854, the Mint began to issue three-dollar gold pieces, provision for which had been inserted by the gold interests in a subsidiary coinage bill passed February 21, 1853. With Patterson retired and Peale more or less subdued, Longacre's only difficulty seems to have been in selecting designs for the anomalous issue.[19] An undated draft among the Longacre papers reads:

I have rarely, if ever felt more perplexity in determining on the nature of a device appropriate to the issue, than in respect to the intended coin of the value of three dollars—Its approximation in size & weight of necessity, to the coin already in use and extensively so—of the value of two and one half dollars, known as the "quarter eagle," makes it important that it should bear a distinctive character, in the device and inscription, which should be peculiarly striking, and obvious in order

---

[18] Among the Longacre material (at the Library Company of Philadelphia) is a drawing of 1852 annular gold piece inscribed with the curious notation: "intended as coinage for the blind."
[19] The Secretary of the Treasury was authorized to select original devices for the coin.

prevent, or guard against the danger in circulation of passing or receiving one piece for the other.

It does not fall into the regular series or multiples of the other denominations which constitute the national currency; and it is therefore anomalous, excepting only the three cent coin.

Longacre met the challenge with conspicuous success. On the obverse of the coin he placed his "Indian princess," a beautifully modeled classical head in feathered tiara; on the reverse, a composite wreath of corn, wheat, cotton and tobacco enclosing the denomination.

As a further solution, the three-dollar piece was made proportionately wider and thinner than the other gold coins. Following the same principle, Snowden asked Longacre to prepare modified dies for the gold dollar. This idea had been suggested in Congress two years before, and recommended to Guthrie by former Director Pettit. But Guthrie's heart was set on a coin with a hole in the middle. In a letter of May 24, 1854 he suggested to Snowden that the planchets and the holes could be cut out in the same stroke. Snowden's displeasure is evident from his reply of the 26th:

> . . . I may here remark that by my direction, the Engraver of the Mint is now engaged upon a pair of dies for a gold dollar of *enlarged diameter,* which a dollar's worth of gold will readily bear, and which will make the coin much more convenient for handling. My attention was called to this proposed change from the fact that we were enabled to make the diameter of the three dollar gold coin much greater than the difference in the value of the quarter eagle would at first view seem to be practicable, and yet the thickness of the three dollar coin is quite sufficient. The proposed new one dollar piece will have the same devices as the lately issued three dollar coin, which I am happy to find are universally admired. As soon as specimens of this dollar are ready they will be submitted to the examination of the department.
>
> The mechanical difficulties in the manufacture of annular coins, are not trivial. They do not lie so much in the cutting out of the planchets, as your letter supposes, as in the stamping and throwing off.
>
> We are fully aware, that the hole would be of use in another respect than the one already named; that is for tying in bunches of a given number as the Chinese do. It would also be a good mode for distinction by the touch. Against these two considerations, let us place the fact, that by cutting out the centre, the piece is very much weakened, or in plain terms, "its back is broken," and further, there is no nation on earth, barbarous or civilized, which has thought it worth while to make this sort of coin, except the Chinese.

The "expanded" dollar was placed into circulation during the same year. Longacre had modeled a new obverse, similar though not identical to that of the three-dollar piece. But the design was too faintly relieved, and in 1856 the artist replaced it with a reduction from the larger coin.

There is an interesting correspondence among the Longacre papers concerning the engraver's ideas on coin designs, and in particular those of the three-dollar piece. The letter is dated August 21, 1858, and was written to Director Snowden, apparently in reply to a recent criticism.

> Dear Sir, In asking your attention to this communication I hope to present a sufficient apology in the matter of which it treats:
>
> I have not been accustomed to consider myself responsible for the *designs* and *devices* of the coinage, unless those designs originated with myself: This has not been from any desire to avoid responsibility where it justly belonged; but from the obvious propriety of the case.

Gold coinage and patterns. **Top row:** 1836 pattern dollar by Gobrecht, 1849 experimental dollar (engraved) by Longacre, 1852 experimental dollar by Longacre; **2nd row:** adopted designs for the dollar, all by Longacre; **3rd row:** 1852 experimental half dollar (obverse struck from reverse die for half dime) and three-dollar piece (adopted design) by Longacre; **bottom row:** double eagle (adopted design) by Longacre.

The *execution* of a die &c. belongs to the engraver in every case; but the design does not, unless made by, or originating with him. An Engraver, strictly speaking, is very frequently placed in a position, where he cannot exercise a discretionary power in respect to the design from which he is required to work, without appearing to conflict with the very authority under which he is employed: This fact induces a habit of acquiescence; which unfortunately for him, is sometimes construed to his disadvantage. As for instance, when a design from another hand is placed before him; the defects of which may be apparent to his own judgment, he yet perceives no alternative (without a collision of opinion which it is not his interest or desire to provoke) but to use skill in making the best of it; because nothing short of a radical change of the whole affair would suffice to remove the defects he perceives to be inherent.

I am led to these remarks, not from the fact that some injustice has been done to my position, by the want of a correct understanding and proper discrimination on the part of those who assume the right of public criticism (This being a casualty to which those who are called to serve the public in places of higher importance are equally subjected;) but from expressions coming from authority to which I am more sensitive, I fear that I am liable to suffer on a point, where the work fairly subject to animadversion, has never been within my legitimate control, simply because the *design* and *execution,* have been improperly blended, when they ought to be regarded as entirely distinct.

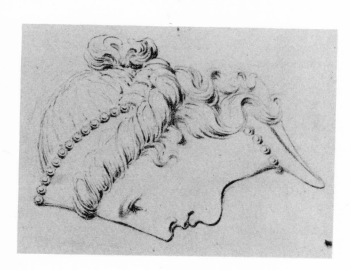

Designs for Liberty head by James B. Longacre. The coronet and plumed headdress types were adopted successively on the gold dollar, the feather headdress on the cent. *Library Company of Philadelphia.*

While thus stating the limitation to which the proper duty and consequent re sponsibility of the engraver is restricted: I would not have it inferred in my own case, that I should decline the responsibility of *design,* if it were timely and au thoritatively presented for my acceptance: it would rather enhance the value and interest of my place in the public service.

These remarks are rather more personal and extended than I desired to make: but I conceive them necessary to disembarrass the position, which the subject I pro pose might otherwise be thought to involve.

My thoughts were early turned to the subject of appropriate design in our coinage: but I found it surrounded with greater difficulties than I had apprehended from the conflicting views of those who claimed to be heard if not to dictate. The extent and variety of their views discouraged me from pursuing the course I should in all probability otherwise have taken.

The first opportunity I had, of giving any practical expression of my own on the subject, occurred under your favor, in respect to the Three Dollar coin. The more consideration I have given to this expression, I am but the better satisfied of its ultimate adaptation: I allude more especially to the design on the *obverse.*

The strongest antagonism I had previously met, was from the *cognoscenti* who were the advocates of the Greek and Roman models: and I know and feel the powerful subjection which is ever held by this idea over the Artist mind; but on deeper analysis, I am persuaded, too much has been conceded to this influence. The original type which the roll of ages has made venerable, had its origin in those remote periods, when the history of nations is mixed with fable or mytholog cal romance. The question I would ask then, is this: Why should we in seeking type for the illustration or symbol of a nation that need not hold itself lower than the Roman virtue or the Science of Greece; prefer the barbaric period of a remo and distant people, from which to draw an emblem of nationality: to th aboriginal period of our own land: especially when the latter presents us with characteristic distinction not less interesting, and more peculiar than that whic still casts its chain over the civilized portion of the older continent? Why n be American from the spring-head within our own domain?

A precedent has, in fact, already been prepared for us, by the most emine artists abroad; Canova in Sculpture, as seen in the design for the monument Nelson; and Gerard in painting, as in the emblematic frontispiece for the wo of Humbolt and Bonpland: to say nothing of minor authorities so numerous now to place the question of appropriateness beyond cavil.

From the copper shores of Lake Superior to the silver mountains of Poto from the Ojibwa to the Araucanian, the feathered tiara is a characteristic of t primitiveness of our hemisphere, as the turban is of the Asiatic.

Nor is there anything in its decorative character, repulsive to the association *Liberty,* with the intelligent American: to us it is more appropriate than t *Phrygian cap;* the emblem rather of the emancipated slave, than of the independe freeman, of those who are able to say, "we are never in bondage to any man.' regard then this emblem of America, as a proper and well defined portion of o national inheritance: and having now the opportunity of consecrating it as memorial of Liberty, our liberty, American Liberty: why not use it? One mo graceful can scarcely be devised: we have only to determine that it *shall* be a propriate and all the world outside of us, cannot wrest it from us.

The objection made to this emblem on account of its correspondence with, supposed deviation, from, European armorial bearings; is not sufficiently inte gent to deserve much consideration. The objectors have probably seen the cr of the Princes of Wales, consisting of three *ostrich feathers*: This armorial cr in this connection, has no higher origin than the battle of Crecy, where it v assumed by Edward the Black-Prince by right of conquest from the slain Ki of Bohemia the unfortunate ally at the time, of the King of France: but t probability is, that the natives of this continent had worn their own feather he attire for ages before; with a right at least equal to that of any of the feudal tentates of the dark ages of Europe; without the motto of "Ich dien" attach to it.

* * *

In 1854, San Francisco bankers presented a memorial, asking to be furnished with large denomination gold coins. Senator Gwin appealed to Secretary of the Treasury Guthrie who recommended to Congress the coinage of gold pieces of $100, $50 and $25, called the union, half union and quarter union. A bill providing for the coinage of the union and half union was passed by the Senate on June 16, but died in the House and was never raised again.

Notwithstanding this one failure, the gold interests, in two decades, had conquered virtually every horizon. They achieved a favorable ratio for their metal, added new denominations, accommodated the producers with branch mints, and then watched gold coinage emerge from literal obscurity to become the predominant specie. During all this time, little effort was made at the Mint to improve the face of the gold coins. Gobrecht's designs still remained on the $2½, $5 and $10 pieces, and seem vastly inferior to Longacre's work.

On October 20, 1857 Anthony Paquet was appointed assistant engraver of the Mint. Paquet possessed a very modest talent, and his dies, with but one brief exception,[20] were never adopted on the coinage. A peculiar ugliness in portraiture, stiffness in anatomy, and tall, thin lettering distinguish the work of this artist. Paquet designed a pattern double eagle in 1859, and the following year Longacre contributed a beautiful pattern half eagle showing Liberty with a starry cap. It is unfortunate that the latter was never adopted.

* * *

The attempts to establish international bi-metallism belong properly to a a period taken up in a later chapter. Yet, their beginnings overlap our present chronology and are thus included here.

As early as 1854, Dr. J. H. Gibbon of the Charlotte mint had reported on the advantage of a uniform system of decimal weights and measures in the coinage of commercial nations. The idea was developed in the September 1859 issue of *Hunt's Merchants Magazine and Commercial Review,* and during the next two decades frequently considered by Congress.

At the invitation of the French government, an international monetary conference met at Paris on June 17, 1867. The representatives of eighteen countries voted almost unanimously in favor of a single gold standard based on the French metric system, with the five-franc piece as unit. Gold coins conforming to this standard were to be a legal tender among the nations agreeing to the action of the conference. It was further proposed to coin gold pieces equal to 25 francs. At the final session of the conference, the members resolved to submit these decisions to their governments for diplomatic approval.

On January 6, 1868 Senator Sherman introduced a bill to reduce the weight of the half eagle to 124 9/20 grains (the weight of 25 French francs), and that of the other gold denominations proportionately. The value of the gold coins was to be stated both in dollars and in francs. The bill also required a revaluation of the silver coins to conform with the French standard, new emblems and inscriptions, and the discontinuation of the silver dollar, half dime, and three-cent piece.

On March 18, Director Linderman wrote to Secretary of the Treasury McCulloch that "inasmuch as the Emperor of France caused a specimen of International coin to be struck, it would seem proper for us to return the compliment,

---

[20] The reverse of one variety of the 1861 double eagle.

Gold coinage and patterns. **Top:** 1836 half eagle (adopted design) by Kneass, 1838 and 184[ ]eagles (adopted designs) by Gobrecht; **center:** 1859 pattern for a double eagle by Paque[ ]**bottom:** 1860 pattern for a large diameter half eagle by Longacre, 1868 pattern for inte[ ]national five-dollar piece by Paquet.

and make a Five Dollar Gold piece, according to the new weight & diamet[ ]proposed."

The original models for the coin showed an American eagle on the obver[ ]and an emblem representing Concord on the reverse. The eagle had bee[ ]copied from a recently deceased bird, apparently the famous Mint masc[ ]"Peter" who was mortally injured after perching upon a large flywheel. The[ ]models were subsequently abandoned in favor of the more traditional Liber[ ]head and wreath. Appropriately, the pattern was designed by the Mint's Frenc[ ]German engraver, Anthony Paquet.

Strenuous opposition to the international coinage bill was led by the Tole[ ]Board of Trade which predicted that a change of standards would cause gre[ ]confusion. Moreover, Great Britain showed no inclination to relinquish h[ ]own time-honored monetary system. The bill thus died a natural death,[21] a[ ]Congress turned to the less ambitious task of creating a metric minor coina[ ]But that is another story.

---

[21] Nevertheless, Linderman ordered a pattern for an international ten-dollar piece in 1874.

CHAPTER 16

Subsidiary Silver Coinage

ON NOVEMBER 8, 1834 *Niles Weekly Register* reported that half dollars were being sold at a one per cent premium for export. The writer concluded: "Thus we see the beginning of what was predicted, that the alteration in the 'gold bill' would drive a large portion of silver out of the country."

Oddly enough, the silver shortage did not materialize. If silver were exported, it also flowed into the country (despite the adverse ratio) from Mexico, where silver mining had resumed on a large scale a few years before.[1] American trade was thus furnished for the first time in history with a well-regulated supply of coins. This supply was interrupted by a bank panic in 1837, but thereafter it increased steadily, and by 1843 was greater than could be absorbed. On February 21 of that year, New York merchant Philip Hone observed: [2]

> There is an absolute plethora of specie in this country; no more certain indication of the prostration of commerce and disordered state of trade. The banks in New York have two dollars in gold and silver for every dollar in circulation, lying like an ingot in the vaults, producing nothing and unable to get into circulation.

The year 1849 was the last in which true bi-metallism flourished in the United States. Thereafter, as a result of the gold rush, silver coins sharply appreciated and were exported. At the beginning of the year, however, there was still a plentiful supply of silver change, including millions of small Spanish pieces. The levy and fip[3] circulated in the East for twelve and six cents respec-

---

[1] Neil Carothers, *Fractional Money.*
[2] *The Diary of Philip Hone,* edited by Allan Nevins; Dodd, Mead and Company, 1927.
[3] i.e. the one and half bit pieces. Levy was a corruption of eleven pence, fip of five-and-a-half pence—the early values of these two coins in Pennsylvania reckoning.

tively[4] and, if generally a nuisance, were more easily divisible than the dime and half dime without resorting to cents. When sold as bullion, however, the Spanish coins were heavily discounted. At the Mint, two-bit pieces were received at 23 cents, levys at 10 cents, and fips at 5 cents. Even then, many of the pieces were so badly worn that the Mint lost money on their recoinage. In January 1849, a House committee suggested the issue of a debased three-cent piece which, exchanged on par for the Spanish fractions, would offset the pecuniary advantage of the depositor.

Committee chairman Samuel Vinton asked the advice of Director Patterson who replied on the 18th:

> A *three cent piece* would certainly be a convenience and would be particularly so, if, as has been proposed, the postage of letters should be reduced to this sum. Specimens . . . which have been struck from dies hastily made, will show the appearance of this coin. The first contains 50 and the second 60 per cent of silver.[5] At these two proportions the pieces will retain their appearance tolerably well . . . It is very questionable, however, whether the convenience of such a coinage would justify an interruption in the unity of our standards, and the circulation of a low alloy.

The *Washington Globe* was of a different opinion. In a Christmas day (1849) editorial it declared:

> It would be an improvement in our currency, if there were a two-and-a-half or a three-cent piece of silver, or of a mixture of silver and copper. There is everywhere in Spanish America a silver coin called a *cuartillo*, which is the fourth part of a *real* (12½ cents), the cuartillo being of course 3⅛ cents. This is the smallest coin; and instead of a smaller, eggs are used in some places, and in others grains of cacao. A three-cent piece would be found to be very useful and convenient, as it would not then be necessary to use the copper cents to the extent they are now used, which though answering every purpose for which they were intended, are still heavy and inconvenient, and copper being very soft and very oxidizable, is not particularly well adapted for either tasting, smelling, or handling.

On May 14, Mr. Dickinson of the Senate finance committee introduced a bill for the coinage of a silver three-cent piece.[6] The coin would weigh 12⅜ grains, in proportion to the other silver denominations, but be only .750 fine. It was to be sold for small Spanish and other foreign silver coins, and have a legal tender limit of twenty cents.

The House proposed an alternate bill which discounted the nominal value of Spanish fractional coins by twenty per cent, and required a twenty-cent piece to facilitate their withdrawal. Neither bill passed.

In January 1851, a House committee introduced a bill to reduce the postage rate from five to three cents and provide for Dickinson's three-cent piece. In a debate on the 13th, Representative Duer said he favored having both a postage rate and a coin of two-and-a-half cents. The three-cent piece would increase the inconvenience of the five- and ten-cent coins and further perpetuate the Spanish fractions. Representative Matteson offered an amendment embody-

---

[4] Until many years later, cents did not circulate in the South and West, and the bit passed in these areas at a par with the dime.

[5] The first weighed 22 grains, and was worth 2.96 cents; the second weighed 18½ grains, and was worth 2.99 cents. Patterson evidently did not know that the Senate intended to have a high seignorage on the coins.

[6] The bill also provided for the coinage of a billon cent. This will be described in the following chapter.

ing Duer's proposals, which was rejected. The bill passed on March 3, 1851.

Physically, the three-cent piece was the same as Dickinson proposed, but its legal tender was increased to thirty cents, and its original purpose, which was to buy up the Spanish fractional coins, forgotten. In its ultimate form, however, the bill was even more revolutionary than its predecessor. Carothers rightly observes:

> After resisting for sixty years every attempt to introduce any form of fiduciary silver coinage Congress adopted a subsidiary silver coin as an adjunct to the postal service, without realizing that the first step had been taken in the relegation of silver to the status of a subordinate monetary material.

Early in 1851, while the bill for a three-cent piece was still before Congress, the Peale-Patterson-Longacre controversy entered a new phase. Longacre completed sketches of the proposed coin and, with Patterson's grudging consent, prepared dies and struck several trial pieces, one of which he enclosed in a letter of March 2 to Secretary Corwin.[7] It is evident from the letter (and its consequences) that Corwin understood the delicacy of Longacre's position.

> Dear Sir: I send you the enclosed privately, that I may have the opportunity of making my own explanation.
> It is the first impression taken from the dies I have been preparing for the Three cent piece ordered by Congress—and which dies still being in process of adjustment for the coining machinery—it is necessarily to some degree imperfect—but as you will no doubt receive the same advice officially, I have thought it might be acceptable to you to receive my own explanation of the design which the enclosed is sufficient to illustrate—
> That portion of the act referred to which prescribes my duties in relation to the coin is in these words: "The said coin shall bear such devices as shall be conspicuously different from those of the other silver coins and from the gold dollar, but having the inscription United States of America, and its denomination and date.
> On so small a coin it is impossible that the device can be at once conspicuous and striking unless it is simple—complexity would defeat the object—
> For the *obverse* I have therefore chosen a *star* (one of the heraldic elements of the National crest) bearing on its centre the shield of the Union, surrounded by the legal inscription and date: For the *reverse* I have devised an ornamental letter C embracing in its centre the Roman numeral III, the whole encircled by the thirteen stars—I think I have obtained the object of the law—but it would be very gratifying to me to have your candid opinion, provided your health should be such as to allow of your making a response to my communication in a private way—with very high respect & deep solicitude for your health—I remain, etc.
> P. S. I should observe that the low relief of the coin is not to my taste if it could be avoided, but it is made necessary by the *thinness* of the piece, and the necessity of adapting the depth of the engraving to the powers of the press in striking it—

After posting this letter, Longacre showed trial impressions to Patterson and the other officers, receiving a generally favorable reaction. But the malevolent Peale finally persuaded Patterson to reject the design and order Longacre to substitute devices which Christian Gobrecht had used in making pattern gold dollars in 1836. When this plan failed to obtain Longacre's approval, Peale himself made up the dies, using Gobrecht's old punches. Patterson, ignoring the fact that the engraver was legally authorized to prepare all coining dies, submitted Peale's pattern, together with Longacre's, to Secretary Corwin on March

---

[7] Papers of James B. Longacre, Library Company of Philadelphia collection.

25. The following day, acting Secretary Hodge pointedly replied that the three-cent design from the "new dies" had been approved, and not that from the "old dies."

* * *

By 1851, silver was flowing out of the country at an enormous rate, and Ambassador Abbot Lawrence advised Congress to adopt a fiduciary coinage as England had done in 1816. The coins were to retain their present fineness but have their weight sufficiently reduced to discourage melting. Although Congress was about to authorize a debased three-cent piece, most of its members considered a fiduciary coinage dishonest, believing it would bring a flood of counterfeits and then depreciate. They even feared it would lead to a single standard and reduce the number of coins in circulation.

On February 1, chairman of the Senate finance committee R. M. T. Hunter suggested the possibility of coining dollars, halves, and quarters of mixed gold and silver in equal values. Later in the month the committee, in avowed desperation, reported a fiduciary coinage bill. The half dollar was to be reduced about 7¾ per cent, and the small silver coins, which were less apt to be exported, 7 1/5 per cent. The coins were to have a legal tender limit of five dollars.

The *New York Journal of Commerce* approved of the bill, saying:

> The scarcity of silver change is daily becoming more and more annoying to our businessmen; the banks are robbed in every possible way of their halves and quarters, and persons are now engaged in collecting dimes and half dimes from all sources, for the sake of the premium. Various remedies have been proposed by our shrewdest financiers to obviate this difficulty, among the most prominent of which is the creation of a currency of small coins, which shall have a *current* value above their intrinsic worth, and thus be retained in the country.

Secretary of the Treasury Corwin also supported the bill but recommended a uniform fiduciary standard of 384 grains to the dollar. This amendment was adopted, and the bill re-introduced in March 1852. In an apology to Congress the Senate committee explained that it did not adhere to the fiduciary principle and was suggesting it only as a temporary expedient. When the value of silver again stabilized, free coinage would be resumed at the corrected ratio.

After passing unanimously in the Senate, the bill was delayed in the House where, as Carothers notes, the ways and means committee "was more exercised over an attempt to move the Mint to New York."

In his report of January 15, 1853 Corwin urged the House to resume consideration of the bill:

> The inconvenience arising from the scarcity of silver coinage still continues, and to such an extent as calls loudly for some legislative action to remedy the evil.
>
> I see no remedy for this great existing evil but the adoption of the principle embraced in the bill which passed the Senate during the last session, making new issue of silver coinage of such reduced weight as will allow it to circulate with the gold coinage of established weight and fineness.
>
> The principal objection which has been urged against the proposed new silver currency is, that it could not, without a violation of contracts, be made a legal tender for the payment of debts, and that gold would, therefore, hereafter be the only legal tender. It is true that heretofore the laws of the United States have recognized the coin of either metal as a legal tender; and if it was at the option of the creditor to select which he would receive, there would be a very serious objection to changing either the weight or standard fineness of any portion of the

coin. But this is not the fact, as it rests with the debtor to say with which description of coin he will pay his debts; and the natural and inevitable consequences of the premium which silver now bears have been to establish, practically, gold as the only legal tender.

Opinion on the whole seems to have grudgingly endorsed Corwin's view. In a *New York Tribune* editorial of February 7, Horace Greeley wrote:

We give way to this debasement as inevitable but we protest against any further, and we insist that Congress guard now against the possibility of further progress on this downward path. Let it now be solemnly enacted that gold is the national standard of value, and that our present gold coinage shall never more be debased or interfered with. Let every promise to pay imply so much gold as would fulfill that promise according to our present legally established standard. Then if silver becomes more or less plentiful, let the silver coinage be altered to conform to the fact, but let the standard of gold be unvarying evermore—silver being used as change or counters, and never being a legal tender for debts, except for sums below five dollars. If a dollar means anything in particular, it is high time for decisive settlement as to precisely what it *does* mean.

In the House, opposition was led by Andrew Johnson. After admitting his ignorance of the bill, Johnson ridiculed it in a witless manner. He claimed that Congress had no right to alter the ratio of its coinage, and even if it had, it should not exercise it. Johnson said that the object of the Constitution had been to create a uniform currency, and the law of 1834 had defeated this object by placing into circulation coins intrinsically different from those already current. He believed that the country had no need of any further currency legislation. At one point Johnson declared:

I look upon this bill as the merest quackery—the veriest charlatanism—so far as the currency of the country is concerned. The idea of Congress fixing the value of currency is an absurdity, notwithstanding the *language* of the Constitution—not the meaning of it . . . If we can, by law, make one hundred and seven dollars out of one hundred dollars, we can, by the same process, make it worth one hundred and fifty dollars. Why, sir, of all the problems that have come up for solution, from the time of the alchemists down to the present time, none can compare with that solved by this modern American Congress. They alone have discovered that they can make money—that they can make one hundred and seven dollars out of one hundred dollars. If they can increase it to that extent they can go on and increase it to infinity; and thus, by the operation of the Mint, can the Government supply its own revenues. The great difficulty of mankind is solved; the idea that so much money is wanted all over the world is at length at an end.

The bit about the Government making "one hundred and seven dollars out of one hundred dollars" was particularly absurd. What Johnson failed to realize was that the gold depositor, under current laws, made one hundred and four dollars from every hundred he brought to the Mint.

After three consecutive days of debate, the bill passed the House by a three-fifths majority and was signed into law February 21, 1853.

For all its fretting and fuming, Congress had barely reduced the silver coinage below its intrinsic value. The silver dollar, which it left unchanged to preserve a bi-metallic currency, continued to be exported and was never seen in domestic circulation. Without realizing it, the country had entered onto the gold standard.

On the following day, Director Eckert wrote to Longacre regarding a change of devices in the silver coins.

Dear Sir, In view of the late act of Congress, reducing the weight of the half dollar &c, it becomes necessary, in my judgment, to make such a change in the devices or inscriptions as will distinguish the coins of the old from the new issue, and I have to request of you to make such suggestions as appear to you pertinent to that object.

It may perhaps be thought necessary, by the Department to introduce finally, for such coins, entirely new devices; but at present I do not so much ask you to consider that point (though I should be pleased at any time to receive such designs for an alteration as you may have to offer), but rather to point out such minor and easily executed changes in the present dies as will suffice to discriminate the new coins, satisfactorily, from the old.

One suggestion which has been made impresses me favorably; it is to make a change in the reverse of the half & quarter dollar assimilating them to the dime & half dime; that is introducing a wreath, with the name of the coin enclosed. It would be well, if this change were made, also to introduce a new design of the wreath in the dime & half dime. Such alterations, in connection with *arrows* at the dates, as you have formerly proposed, might suffice. It is probable that we have already punches that would suffice for such borders, or that we could procure such already made, so that the delay in making the alterations need not be very great.

It is probable that you will need some assistance in preparing the new dies. If such should be the case I will be ready to accede to any request you may make on that subject. Very truly yours.

Longacre replied on the 28th:

Dear Sir: In compliance with your request of the 22. inst. that I would make such suggestions as were pertinent to the object contemplated by the late Act of Congress, reducing the weight of the silver coin &c. I have given such attention to the subject as the time would allow; and proceed briefly to state the result of my conclusion.

The time allowed by the law, is too short to warrant any elaborate revision or alteration of the present devices, as there is no permanent force in the Mint, attached to, or within the control of, my office, applicable to the work that is, or would be required beyond the labour of my own hands; and the uncertainty that rests upon the availability of transient or temporary aid, is too great to incur the risk of delay that might ensue; besides; to legalize so material a change, as has been suggested in the reverse of the present dies for the half and quarter dollar, would require, as I understand, at least a conference with the head of the department to authorize the substitution:[8] which would necessarily involve a farther consumption of the time to which the operations must be limited.

I would therefore respectfully suggest the following changes, to be made on the obverse and reverse, respectively, of the silver coins now in use.

On the obverse of the coins I propose to mark the place of the date, somewhat in the manner represented on the next page, [i.e., with facing arrow heads] designated by the letter D.

On the reverse, I propose for the half and quarter dollar to cover the space between the Eagle and the inscription with rays radiating from the centre of the piece—or what in heraldic language is termed a "glory," and for the dime and half-dime, to join the wreath or garland at the top, in the manner represented by the drawing on the next page marked B. The arrangement of the reverse of the half and quarter dollar will be understood by the drawing marked A.

I should take pleasure in submitting other designs for the changes that have been suggested; but that more time will be required to make them, especially in the formation of a wreath, for which there ought to be an original design and model, if it is determined to introduce such a change on the reverse of the coin: and that more time will be required for its adaptation and arrangement; for all

---

[8] It would actually have required an act of Congress, as the devices were fixed by law.

which there does not appear to be room in the present emergency. Very respectfully Yours &c.

* * *

By the Act of March 3, 1853 the three-cent piece was changed to conform with the fiduciary standard. The new coin weighed 11.52 grains and was .900 fine. Longacre added two extra outlines to the star, and the piece was issued with this design from 1854 to 1858, after which one of the outlines was deleted.

Section 7 of the same act authorized the selection of new devices for the fiduciary coins by contract with a private artist.

> . . . The Secretary of the Treasury is hereby authorized to regulate the size and devices of the new silver coins; . . . and that, to procure such devices, as also the models, moulds, and matrices or original dies for the coins, discs or ingots authorized by said act, the Director of the Mint is empowered, with the approval of the Secretary of the Treasury, to engage temporarily for that purpose the services of one or more artists, distinguished in their respective departments, who shall be paid for such services from the contingent appropriation for the Mint . . .

It would be interesting to learn the origin of this particular section. Eckert does not seem to have been responsible and, in fact, he just ignored the provision. In a letter of March 31 to Secretary of the Treasury Guthrie, the Director enclosed specimen quarters with Longacre's alterations. He wrote: "The clamor of the community for an issue of the new coin is very great, and until the devices are settled (which by law devolves upon you) we cannot enter upon the coinage." Guthrie sent his approval five days later, and the "arrows" design was used on the subsidiary coinage through 1855.

On June 3, 1853, James Ross Snowden became the ninth Director of the Mint. Although the issue of subsidiary coinage had already begun, Snowden resolved to initiate new designs in conformity with the law. We can imagine Longacre's chagrin when the Director, in a circular letter dated July 26, announced:

> The director of the mint, under the sanction of the 7th section of the act of March 3, 1853, authorizing new devices for the silver coinage of the United States, and with the approval of the Secretary of the Treasury, invites the cooperation of artists, engravers and other persons of taste to aid him in effecting that object, and requests such as may be disposed to forward to him, before the first day of October next, such designs as they may deem appropriate to that coinage.
>
> The law having imposed no restrictions in relation to the devices, the director abstains from advancing any suggestions on the subject, it being his wish that the designer should be entirely untrammelled in the exercise of his judgment and skill.
>
> An impartial examination will be made of the designs which may be furnished in accordance with this request; and for those three which shall appear best fitted to the object in view, a competent and liberal remuneration will be made.

On December 29, Snowden wrote to Guthrie that the designs submitted in response to his letter were unsatisfactory. He enclosed the three best offerings, drawings of a Mr. Nohl of San Francisco and Mr. Chapin of New Jersey, and a medallion of Mr. [William?] Barber of Philadelphia.

* * *

The Act of February 21, 1853 specified how the Mint was to purchase its bullion for the subsidiary coins, and distribute those coins.

Section 3 stated that "in order to procure bullion for the requisite coinage of the subdivisions of the dollar authorized by this act, the treasurer of the

Mint shall, with the approval of the Director, purchase such bullion with the bullion fund of the Mint."

Section 4 added that the subsidiary coins "shall be paid out at the Mint, in exchange for gold coins at par, in sums not less than one hundred dollars."

Section 5 reiterated these terms: "No deposits for coinage into the half dollar, quarter dollar, dime, and half dime, shall hereafter be received, other than those made by the treasurer of the Mint, as herein authorized, and upon account of the United States."

The intention was crystal clear. By ordering the Mint to pay out subsidiary coins only at face value, in exchange for gold, Congress made certain that no more would be issued than were required for circulation. Director Eckert, however, anxious to procure a supply of bullion for the coinage, conceived a plan by which to obey the law nominally and still defeat its intention. On February 26, he wrote to Guthrie:

> In anticipation of the time when, by law, we shall be allowed to issue the new silver coin lately authorized, it seems to be incumbent on us to take some measures to procure a supply of bullion for the coinage. How this shall be most readily and economically effected may be a matter of some doubt. After considerable reflection on the subject it has seemed to me that the most expedient method will be for the Mint, with the approbation of the Department, to establish and publish a fixed price for certain classes of silver, to be paid to all comers who may offer the same. In the first instance the payment should be in gold, but it would be an additional inducement, to banks particularly, if we should undertake to replace that gold with the new coin, to those who furnished us silver, and in the order of priority . . .

Not having heard from Guthrie, Eckert wrote to the Secretary again on March 12, calling attention to the fact that the Act was to have gone into effect on the first of the month. Eckert now threw off all pretense of obeying the law, and proposed to Guthrie that the Mint exchange subsidiary coins for gold or silver at the option of the seller.

Still receiving no answer, Eckert proceeded on his own to initiate the illegal practice. On March 31, the Treasurer of the Mint, E. C. Dale, issued the following circular letter:

> By virtue of the 3d section of the Act of Congress, approved Feb. 21, 1853, the Treasurer of the Mint, with the Approval of the Director, gives notice that he is prepared to purchase silver coin and Bullion delivered at the Mint, on the following terms, viz.:
>
> For dollars of Mexico, Peru, Bolivia, Chili (restamped), and Spain, for Francs for silver coins of the United States other than three-cents, the price paid will be $1.21 an ounce gross.
>
> For Thalers of Sweden and the Northern States of Germany, $1.01 an ounce.
>
> For Silver bars, $1.21 for each ounce, at standard fineness (9-10ths) as determined on assay at the Mint.
>
> The payment will be made in gold coins, or in silver coins of new emission, at the option of the seller. Parties furnishing silver to the Mint, according to the terms of this notice, will receive a preference, in exchange for the new coin, according to the order of priority of their sales to the Mint.
>
> It is expected that an emission of new coinage will be made by the middle of April.
>
> The prices herein fixed will be continued until further notice.
>
> E. C. Dale, Treasurer
>
> Approved
> G. N. Eckert, *Director*

The Mint price of $1.21 per ounce was sufficiently high to attract a flood of silver whenever the market value dropped even slightly, and it virtually annulled the seignorage on the subsidiary coins.

On April 2, acting Director Robert Patterson,[9] wrote to the National Bank of Kentucky, calling attention in underlines to the fact that the Mint was paying out subsidiary coins for silver bullion.

Five days later, Guthrie wrote to Patterson approving the arrangement, and paving the way for an incredible fiasco.

More than one historian has blamed Director Snowden for launching the fiasco, even though he was not appointed until two months later. The letters quoted above indict his predecessor, George Eckert. By 1872, however, Eckert had been forgotten, and Representative William Kelley laid the whole responsibility on Secretary Guthrie. Ultimately, Kelley's judgment must prevail. As head of the Treasury Department, Guthrie was obliged to at least read the coinage law and know its provisions.

Eckert's resignation from the Mint was followed by the appointment of Thomas M. Pettit [10] on April 4, 1853. Just two days later, Pettit issued a circular letter of his own, which read:

> The law regulating the new coinage of silver, leaves it optional with the Director of the Mint to pay in whatever denomination of coins he prefers. It has been deemed that the quarter dollars are the most useful of all silver coin, and the whole force of the Mint is now and has been engaged since the 1st instant, upon them only. It is useless, therefore, for parties to order returns in various coins.
>
> For silver sold to the Mint in accordance with the "circular," a check on the paying-teller, with value thereon, is given; this can be *drawn in gold or silver, at the option* of the seller. If, however, the silver be mixed, in other words, if it is composed of various kinds, a memorandum receipt is given, and when an assay is made and the net value determined at $1.21 per ounce, this receipt is released on the paying-teller . . .

A few weeks later, Pettit died suddenly, and chief clerk Robert Patterson was again placed in temporary charge. Patterson served as acting Director until a few days after Snowden's appointment.

In late May, Secretary Guthrie furnished the Mint with sufficient bullion to coin $200,000 worth of the new silver coins, "with a view to the accommodation of the business community of New York." John A. Dix, the assistant Treasurer of the U.S., sent a circular letter to New York banks, informing them they could obtain the coins, in amounts of two thousand dollars, in exchange for gold. Dix appears to have been the first and only official to comply with the new law.

When the demand for subsidiary coins began to exceed the Mint's production, Snowden worked out a plan somewhat resembling that originally proposed by Eckert. In a circular letter of July 27, the new Director announced:

> The director of the mint gives notice that from and after the 15th day of August next, payments for silver purchased for the mint at Philadelphia, and at the branch

---

[9] Robert Patterson III, chief clerk of the Mint, and son of former Director Robert M. Patterson.

[10] Upon Eckert's resignation, chief clerk Robert Patterson managed to have sixteen letters plus three petitions (from the American Philosophical Society, the Medical School of the University of Pennsylvania, and the Bankers and Bullion Dealers of Philadelphia) recommending his appointment as Director. President Pierce, however, chose Judge Pettit. After Pettit's premature death, J. R. Snowden was appointed, and on June 6, 1853 Patterson resigned as chief clerk, being replaced by Henry Linderman.

mint, New Orleans, will be made three fourths in silver coins of new emission, and one fourth in gold. In accordance with existing arrangements, the whole price will be advanced in the first instance in gold, and as the new coin is ready for issue it will be paid out, in the proportions specified, in exchange for the gold returned by the parties selling silver, and in the order of their priority of sales . . .

Snowden's insistence on paying for one fourth of all bullion purchases in gold was the largest concession the Mint ever made to the law of 1853. On the other hand, the Director continued to advertise for silver at prices frequently above the open market. More silver was coined in 1853 and 1854 than for the dozen preceding years—and the new coins remained in circulation. In fact, there was no place for them to go, since they could neither be redeemed at the Mint, nor paid to the Government in taxes. By 1855, they clogged the channels of trade, and the Mint itself acquired a large surplus.

In a rather confused appraisal of the situation, a Washington correspondent of the *New York Courier* reported: [11]

> The Treasury is now burthened with the custody of over five millions of dollars in small change, from half-dollars to three-cent pieces. Two or three years ago, there was a universal complaint of the scarcity of small coins, either American or foreign. Mr. Hunter's coinage bill was passed, slightly reducing the actual value of our silver coin, and providing for more rapid manufacture. The expected results have followed. The wants of circulation have been fully supplied; but another less desirable consequence has ensued, to wit: this small change has become a drug. People will not take it, and the law makes it legal tender in sums of not over five dollars. Though the inconvenience of an inadequate supply of small change was a serious one, prudent financiers expressed doubts of the soundness of the remedy adopted at the time it was proposed. Orders have been issued to suspend the coinage of quarters and halves, and the operations of the Mint are much reduced.

By now, sheer necessity should have driven the Treasury Department to comply with the law. Instead, in July 1855 Secretary Guthrie ordered Snowden to pay out only silver for silver and gold for gold. The action, which was supposed to force the coins on depositors, resulted in a stalemate. Creditors and even banks refused to accept subsidiary coins in sums above the five-dollar legal tender limit. Finally, on April 25, 1857, acting Secretary of the Treasury Clayton ordered Snowden to stop his purchases and to instruct the New Orleans Mint to do likewise. He said that the influx of silver was threatening to produce a large surplus in the Treasury.

Snowden, in desperation, asked for legislation to raise the legal tender limit of the subsidiary coins to fifty or even one hundred dollars. On January 5, 1858, Senator Slidell introduced a bill to increase the limit to twenty-five dollars. He said that the bill was recommended by the treasurer of the Mint, and that its provision was not objectionable since there was no seignorage on the coins. This statement obviously referred to Mint practice, which gave much of the seignorage to the depositor. Slidell said that the purpose of the bill was to drive out small bank notes, and "that by proper concerted action on the part of the Treasury and the different mints, a very large amount of silver could be put into circulation without any cost to the Government."

The bill was referred to the Senate finance committee which reported unfavorably on February 2.

When the subsidiary coins had become a national nuisance, Snowden de-

---

[11] Quoted in the Sept. 1855 issue of *Bankers Magazine*.

cided to give them a new look. In 1859, Longacre and Paquet each submitted patterns for a new half dollar, and on October 25, the Director recommended Longacre's design to Secretary of the Treasury Howell Cobb:

> Sir: For the purpose of improving the silver coinage I have caused several new dies to be prepared, from which were struck, the few specimens I placed in your hands during my recent visit to the capitol.
>
> I now am prepared to recommend the adoption of the one which I personally expressed a preference for during my interview with you. It may be described as follows:
>
> 'On the *obverse,* an ideal head of Liberty, crowned with oak, and cotton, *legend, United States of America,* and the word *Liberty* on the ribbon, and the date of the piece beneath. The *reverse,* a wreath composed of cotton, tobacco leaves, sugar cane, Indian Corn, and wheat, with oak leaves, the productions of the different sections of our country. Within the wreath the inscription *Half Dollar.* I may state that the *reverse* of the coin is secondary to the obverse and should be so regulated as to admit of a fair and full *striking up* of the device on the main disc. The wreath greatly facilitates the full expression of the head. The present silver coins are difficult to bring up, not only because of the full figure of liberty, but because the eagle occupies the field immediately opposite to it. Again, the eagle properly and particularly belongs to the gold coinage.—they are even named for it, the "eagle, double eagle, half eagle, quarter eagle." They are the legal titles and it is not proposed to alter the gold coinage. But to place the same devices on the silver seems to be a solecism although sanctioned by long usage.
>
> The silver coin has become a subsidiary coinage . . . a mere matter of change, not being legal tender beyond a limited amount; this consideration renders it less important to cover it with all the national emblems. Gold is the effective currency, and on that the eagle is stamped.
>
> For a number of years past the eagle has been omitted on the dime and half dime, and a plain wreath substituted. The adoption of the devices now recommended will enable us to introduce a uniformity into the silver coin, as the same head and wreath on the specimen half dollar is well adapted to the quarter dollar, and the dime and half dime.
>
> I must beg your early attention to this communication in view of the fact that we must immediately commence the preparation of the working dies for the next year for the Mint and its branches.

Neither Snowden, who favored abolishing the eagle from the silver coinage, nor Cobb, who rejected the proposal because the eagle had for "so long a period appeared as a device," realized that the matter lay entirely with Congress. With Cobb's approval, however, the composite wreath was adopted on the dime and half dime, replacing Gobrecht's laurel design.

* * *

The Civil War wrought drastic changes in the economy. To help defray expenses, Congress, in July 1861, authorized the issue of paper currency. Though not expressly payable in coin, the notes were so redeemed, and people cashed them in such quantity as to defeat their purpose. In December 1861, banks suspended specie payments and the Treasury quickly followed suit. The following year, Congress introduced legal tender notes, giving statutory recognition to their gold value. The issue proved unpopular and sharply depreciated. Subsidiary coins, which were valued in relation to the notes, likewise depreciated, becoming worth more as bullion than as fractions of paper currency. Many were melted down, but the majority were exported to Canada and South America. In the panic to obtain small change, even cents were hoarded, and private firms and individuals pressed into circulation every conceivable sub-

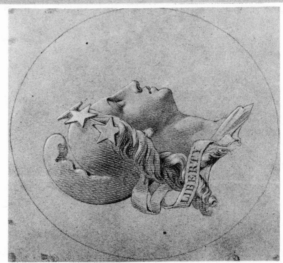

Sketches by James B. Longacre for obverse of standard silver (reduced weight) coinage. *Library Company of Philadelphia.*

Subsidiary coinage designs: **Left:** three cents, 1850 pattern by Franklin Peale after Christian Gobrecht; 1852, adopted design by Longacre. **Center:** 1859 patterns for half dollar by Longacre and Paquet. **Right:** 1863 experimental aluminum postage currency dime by Longacre. **Bottom:** 1869 patterns for standard silver (reduced weight) coinage.

Circular in Relation to Deposits of Silver Bullion

For Coinage, Purchase or Manufacture into Fine Bar

At the Mint of the United States.

The Regulations of the Mint of the United States at Philadelphia in relation to Receivi
Silver Bullion for Coinage in Dollars, to be made into Fine Bars, or to be purchased
and paid for in Half Dollars or smaller Silver Coin.

THE following are the usual forms in which Silver Bullion is received :—

Foreign Coin, U. States Coin issued before 1853, and U. S. whole Dollars and defaced coins issued since.

Plate, Bars, Kings, &c., containing but a small portion of base metals.

Native Lumps and Grains, comparatively free from earth and stone, and the copper not exceeding seventy-five per c

"It shall be lawful to refuse any deposit of less value than $100 (One Hundred Dollars in coin), or bul unsuitable for the operations of the Mint."

To produce a value of $100 (One Hundred Dollars), from pure Silver to that which contains 75 per cent Copper, will require from 75 to 300 ounces Troy Weight.

Ordinary Silver Bullion, such as Coin, Plate, Bars, Kings, &c., about the fineness of U. S. Coin, will require 82 to 90 ounces.

A receipt is given for each deposit, and it is kept entirely separate until after it is melted, assayed, and the e value ascertained.

The value is calculated on the weight after melting.

Deposits of Silver are paid in Silver. If a Silver deposit contains the value of over one Dollar in Gold, cle parting charges, the value will be estimated and paid in Gold Coins.

The charges for refining and separating Gold from Silver, are only the actual cost varying from one third or cent to six cents per ounce.

The charge for coinage in dollars is half of one per cent.

The charge for making fine Silver Bars is one-half cent per ounce on the Fine Silver.

There is a charge of half of one per cent. United States Internal Revenue Tax, on all bullion received at the excepting bullion that has been taxed and has the U. S. Stamp on it.

Silver Bullion is purchased by the Mint at 122½ per ounce, standard fineness ⁹⁄₁₀ths pure Silver, and paid Silver Coin of less denomination than the Dollar.

The weight of one hundred U. S. whole Dollars of the present issue is 85.9375 ounces.

The weight of $100 (one hundred) in U. S. Half Dollars or smaller Silver Coin is 80 ounces.

The following U. S. Coins will produce at the Mint, at the present rate of purchase, about as follows :—

Dollars coined before 1837, . . 104.5 cents each. Half Dollars coined before 1837, . 52.2 cents
"   "   since   "   . . 105.0   "   "   "   "   since   " to 1853. 52.5

Quarter Dollars are proportionally less productive of premium, while Dimes and Half Dimes coined before 1853 lost rather more by wear, on an average, than the premium would make up.

Fine Silver will produce 136½ cents per ounce.

American Plate usual manufacture 120 to 122 cents per ounce.

Genuine British Plate, 125.8.

Deposits are usually paid on the third day after they are received.

The Mint recognises no depositor except the person that presents the Bullion at the Mint.

Persons at a distance can employ the Express Companies or their business connections to deposit for them one connected with the Mint is allowed to make such deposits.

Parties sending by Express, should always send their instructions with the package, and have their name and of business or residence plainly written on the outside of it.

MINT OF THE UNITED STATES,   }
    Philadelphia,   186 .   {

H. R. LINDERMAN,
DIRECTO

Mint circular of 1867-68 showing illegal method of purchasing bullion for the subsidiar coinage. *Library Company of Philadelphia.*

stitute for coin. Postage stamps, fractional parts of bank notes, private bills of credit, underweight foreign coins (which also were quickly hoarded) and, finally, an enormous variety of copper tokens came into use.

Congress rejected the suggestion of Mint Director Pollock to reduce the weight of the subsidiary coins by twenty-five per cent. Instead, in July 1862, it legalized the use of postage stamps as currency. The plan was adopted on the advice of Secretary of the Treasury Chase, without the approval of the Postmaster General. No provision had been made to increase the manufacture of stamps, and the insatiable demand quickly exhausted the post office stock.[12] Congress then authorized the issue of small fractional notes, and for more than a decade these circulated in the absence of coins. In the meantime, Mint Directors Pollock and Linderman continued to buy silver bullion with subsidiary coin for the benefit of the bullion dealers. Except on the West Coast, where paper money had been resolutely refused, almost every silver coin struck at the Mint was immediately exported or melted down.

Although Chase had tacitly rejected the idea of lessening the weight of the subsidiary coins, the Mint's assayers Eckfeldt and DuBois conducted experiments of their own with reduced-weight silver coins for the purpose of replacing the fractional U.S. notes.[13] They proposed the issue of dimes and quarters at a fine weight of from 200 to 220 grains per dollar, to be alloyed with aluminum, which would add bulk to and strengthen the planchet. The coins were to be inscribed "Exchanged for U.S. notes/Postage Currency (the denomination) Act July 1862." Pollock recommended the idea to Chase in a letter of May 15, 1863, attempting to convince the Secretary that the original postage currency act did not specify the material from which the notes were to be made.

Chase apparently demurred, and during the whole of the war he conceived no greater reform in the coinage than the addition of a religious motto.

When, in April 1869, Pollock was reappointed Director of the Mint specie payments had not yet resumed. He again urged the adoption of reduced-weight silver coins "for change" in lieu of the fractional paper currency. In his annual report of October 24, 1870, the Director suggested the issue of subsidiary coins weighing as little as 140 grains to the half dollar. He said that the proposition had been endorsed by leading financiers and commercial newspapers. A number of patterns were struck in 1869 and again the following year. Longacre passed away January 1, 1869, and the dies were prepared from his designs by William Barber. They are among the most beautiful essays in our numismatic series.

---

[12] Carothers, (pgs. 170-177), gives an interesting account of the controversy between Secretary Chase and Postmaster Blair over the responsibility of issuing and redeeming the postage stamp currency.

[13] Dr. J. Hewitt Judd, *United States Pattern, Experimental and Trial Pieces,* 3rd edition, Whitman Publishing Co., 1965.

CHAPTER 17

Experiments in Copper

ALTHOUGH THE COPPER CENTS HAD GROWN IN CREASINGLY UNPOPULAR due to their size and tendency to blacken and become foul, the Mint resisted any change in the coin until the mid-nineteenth century.

Nevertheless, in March 1836 Peale and Gobrecht conducted unofficial experiments with a billon two-cent piece of ninety percent copper and ten percent silver.[1] Provision for the coin was included in a draft of the 1837 revisionary Mint bill, but finally dropped after Peale showed that billon could be easily simulated by silver plating and pickling copper.

In October 1837, Dr. Lewis Feuchtwanger urged Congress to substitute small coins of German silver[2] for the old coppers, offering to furnish the Mint with any amount of the compound.[3] Senator Benton forwarded the proposal to Mint Director Patterson who rejected it, among other reasons, because German silver was already manufactured in at least five almost indistinguishable proportions, and was difficult both to produce and assay.

"Nickel," he wrote, "which is a characteristic constituent of German silver is chiefly obtained from a mineral called copper nickel, and from the refuse of smalt-works. It is never found, and cannot be practically obtained, wholly free from cobalt; and it likewise contains arsenic and iron; and as these metals are in variable proportions, the compound into which they enter cannot be uniform

---

[1] Walter Breen, *The Secret History of the Gobrecht Coinages—1836-40.*
[2] William L. Schultz, "Why the Feuchtwanger Composition Metal Coins Received Their Knock out Blow," *The Numismatist,* Nov. 1938.
[3] Feuchtwanger struck pattern one- and three-cent pieces which he distributed to promote his plan.

But there is another difficulty in the manufacture. When the ingredients are introduced into the crucible, and fused together, a portion of the zinc is volatilized, and must be replaced by a fresh quantity, and thus, also it is rendered impossible to obtain a compound of uniform proportions."

Patterson's opinions were evidently supported by Professor James Booth, who was then teaching at the Franklin Institute. Patterson quoted Booth as saying: "An arduous and expensive assay is necessary to determine the proportions of the ingredients in argentan [German silver], and requiring for one analysis, at least two weeks. The copper may readily be estimated; the arsenic, if there be some present, with much more difficulty; the amount of iron is not ascertained without much trouble; it is exceedingly difficult to separate the zinc and nickel with accuracy."

Patterson replied to Benton on January 4, 1838, and for a dozen years thereafter no further change was considered. By 1850, however, the rising price of copper made cents unprofitable to coin, and a bill was introduced on May 14 to authorize a billon substitute.

During the following month the *Philadelphia North American and United States Gazette* reported:

> We have examined specimens of coins lately struck at the Mint, to illustrate the bill presented in the United States Senate, by Mr. Dickinson, for the coinage of *one-cent* and *three-cent* pieces.
>
> The cent piece is designed as a substitute for the present copper coin, and contains the proportion of silver—one tenth—expressed in its legend. The effect of this infusion of precious metal, small as it is, beside lightening the color perceptibly, is to reduce greatly the bulk of the coin of that denomination, and to make it much more convenient and portable. Its weight is 25 grains, while that of the present cent is 168. It is annulated, that is, it has a *large round hole* in the center, which is a novel feature, and has been introduced for the sake of the following advantages: it extends the diameter of the piece to a proper measurement, being the same as that of the dime, which is as small as could be desired for such a coin; it affords a distinctive mark, by which the piece may be recognized and safely paid out even by touch; it affords a facility to retailers to put the pieces up in parcels, say of a hundred or thousand, by *stringing* them, or putting them on an upright stake or file; and lastly, the complexity of manufacture will throw some impediments in the way of counterfeiting, if that is to be apprehended. Should the bill pass, dies for this piece will, we learn, be got up with more care, and more show of art, than in this specimen, which is only a temporary illustration for the use of Congress.

Patterns for an annular cent were struck in 1850 and 1851. The inclusion of silver was believed necessary to make the coin acceptable to the public. "Without this precious metal," Director Snowden later remarked,[4] "the piece was so light and worthless as to be incapable of circulation." But the advantage of intrinsic value was offset by the cost of recovering the silver, as well as by the difficulties which the perforation caused in striking and ejecting the coin.

On February 20, 1851 Dickinson informed the Senate that the House had omitted the billon cent from their bill for a three-cent piece. "The time has come," he said, "when cheap postage, retail dealers, newspaper rates, &c., require something more portable than the present cent piece." Dickinson made an amendment to include the cent, but withdrew it two days later on the

---

[4] Letter of Director James Ross Snowden to Secretary of the Treasury James Guthrie, May 26, 1854.

advice of Senator Rusk, who thought it would delay and perhaps prevent passage of the bill.

Nevertheless, something had to be done. Snowden consulted Professor Booth, now melter and refiner at the Mint. Refuting Patterson's argument (to which he himself had contributed), Booth advised the adoption of German silver, and launched a project for the local manufacture of nickel. Early in 1854, he prepared experimental pieces in three nickel alloys, including two proportions of German silver. Booth described his results to Director Snowden in a report dated March 25:

Cents: 1838, adopted design by Kneass; 1844, adopted design by Gobrecht; 1850, '51 experimental annular billon cents; 1853 experimental German silver cent struck with regular obverse die for quarter eagle.

While it is desirable to possess a coin which shall represent the unit of the Dollar, the size and weight of the copper cent, hitherto used for this purpose renders it objectionable as the representative of so small a value, so that it is disliked as a coin in the northern & middle states, & has no currency in the Southern

Since no single metal, possessing qualities requisite for coinage, can be found of an intermediate value between silver & copper, so that a cent-coin of less size & weight than the copper-cent could be made; a proper substitute for such metal may be found among alloys.

Of all the alloys known, which can fulfill the conditions above stated of qualification for coinage & of proper value, an alloy of copper, nickel & zinc, known in commerce as German silver, Albata, Argentan & Packfong, appears the most suitable. The advantages of using this alloy are that its constituent metals can be obtained in reliable sufficient quantity & of reliable quality as ordinary commercial articles, that the alloy is readily made, that it will take a good impression in coinage, that it presents a good appearance & possesses properties differing from gold & silver, & that it will wear well, even better than copper . . .

Booth added that counterfeiters would have no new advantage, since the appearance, feel, and ring of a German silver coin, were so different from those of a silver one. Nor did the problem of assay arise, since assays were not conducted on the cents. Booth suggested a twenty per cent seignorage to keep the coins from being bought up when market fluctuations made this profitable.

On March 18, and again the following month, Snowden sent pattern impressions in German silver to Guthrie. On the latter occasion, he suggested the issue of a 100-grain copper cent. He said it was the Government's stamp, not the intrinsic value, which cause minor coins to circulate. Considering that Snowden understood the fiduciary principle, his proposal was conservative. The 100-grain cent weighed more than two modern cents, and had a larger diameter than the quarter.

On May 24, Guthrie proposed the coinage of annular German silver cents and 2½ cent pieces. But if the latter were adopted, the cents were to be coined in bronze. Snowden vetoed the idea, replying on the 26th that it was his desire to diminish, not increase the diameter of the cent.

Despite Booth's assurance, German silver was rejected because of its resemblance to silver. Booth then unloaded his nickel interests, and the Mint began experimenting with other alloys. In addition to the 100-grain copper cent, patterns were struck in French bronze (95% copper, 4% tin and 1% zinc) and oroid. The latter was an innovation of Booth, who added more tin to the alloy to prevent tarnish, and give the coins a nearly golden color.[5]

In his annual report for 1854, Snowden advised the adoption of the bronze cent and the discontinuation of the half cent which he said was useless: "People will not take the trouble to make a cent with two pieces of money." The new cent would be paid out for the old coppers, and have a limited legal tender.

However, when Booth resumed his experiments with nickel, Snowden vacillated. In drafting a bill, he left the content, shape and devices of the new cent to be determined thereafter by himself, with the approval of the Secretary of the Treasury. The President would then legalize the issue by proclamation.

The cent was to have a legal tender limit of ten cents, and be sold by the Mint for U.S. or Spanish fractional silver coins at their face value. Although the Spanish coins were well worn and usually passed at a twenty per cent discount, the seignorage on the cent would compensate for the Government's loss, and encourage deposits. The half cent was to be abolished.

The bill was introduced in the Senate on March 25, 1856. On April 16, Mr. Hunter on behalf of the Senate finance committee amended it to provide for a 96-grain cent, of at least 95 per cent copper, with an admixture of other metals. Congress had retrieved its authority. The bill passed, and was referred the following day to the House ways and means committee.

Meanwhile, Booth completed his experiments, and on July 11, Snowden wrote to Secretary of the Treasury Guthrie:

> Sir: In a former communication respecting an alteration of the cent coinage I took occasion to say I had requested the melter and refiner to prosecute further experiments with a view to the ascertainment of the most suitable alloy for that coinage. These experiments were not completed, chiefly because the Mint was in a dismantled condition when the bill relating to the coinage of cents was prepared, in the fifth section of which it was proposed to allow the proportion of metals in

---

[5] J. Hewitt Judd, *United States Pattern, Experimental and Trial Pieces.*

the new coin to be determined hereafter, in the manner therein stated. Subsequently, the department and the Finance Committee of the Senate deemed it proper that the proportion of metals should be authoritatively fixed by law, whereupon the section was amended as the bill subsequently passed the Senate, in which it enacted that the proportion of other metals than copper shall not exceed five per cent.

Recent experiments have induced us to prefer an alloy in which the proportion of other metal than copper shall be greater than is above stated, namely an admixture in which in every hundred parts of weight of metal there shall be eighty-eight of copper and twelve of nickel. This alloy seems to possess all the desirable characteristics for a cent piece. I have accordingly caused some specimens to be struck, fifty pieces of which I send you by Mr. Colmesnil, an agent of the department.

To prevent expense and delay we have used the half cent dies. The specimens will show that the mixture receives a good impression from the dies and exhibits its color and general appearance.

It will be seen that, in its external character, it differs entirely from gold, silver and copper, preserving the pure red tone of the latter, with the light color of nickel. The color is peculiar and it is believed will be more acceptable than any graywhite or brassy mixtures, or that in which the copper more largely prevails; for it seems to be desired by the public that not only a smaller cent than the one now in circulation should be struck, but that we should get rid of the copper, on account of its liability to blacken and become foul.

The infusion of twelve per cent of nickel which is a metal of considerable value —elevates the character of the material, and besides the advantages of color and general appearance will enable us to make a cent of less weight and at the same time preserve some just proportion between the intrinsic and the nominal value of the coin. The present legal cent weighs one hundred and sixty-eight grains; the specimens I send you weigh about seventy-two grains, and I propose that as a proper weight. It gives a sufficient seignorage and is represented by a convenient decimal, namely, fifteen hundredths of an ounce, which will afford a proper facility in the calculations of the mint, they being kept, as you are aware, in troy ounce and decimals of the ounce.

The value of the metal in rolled sheets is fifty-four cents per pound; the piece to weigh seventy-two grains (fifteen-hundredths of an ounce), the seignorage without estimating the cost of cutting and striking, would be eight per cent. This is considerably less than the seignorage on the pieces as proposed by the bill as it passed the Senate, but it is large enough to effect the recoinage contemplated and the withdrawel of the small Spanish coins and old cents, as is provided in the other parts of the proposed law.

I cannot speak with certainty, in the absence of actual trials, of the effect of wear and keeping on the color of the metal; but it will certainly tarnish less from keeping than the alloy which is proposed in the bill which passed the Senate and far less than pure copper; and in the pocket it will probably maintain nearly the color which it now presents, becoming rather of a darker reddish hue. It cannot be easily imitated by the cheaper brass or bronze, as these have a decided yellow instead of red tone, and I know of no other alloy which can be readily substituted for it.

To carry into effect the views herein presented it will be necessary to amend the Senate bill now pending in the House in the fifth section by striking out "ninety six grains, or two-tenths of an ounce," and insert "seventy-two grains, or fifteen hundredths of an ounce;" strike out "four grains," and insert "three grains" as that will be a sufficient remedy for the diminished piece; and strike out "five percentum in weight of metals" and insert "one-eighth in weight of other metals."

The section would then read as follows:

"Sec. 5. And be it further enacted, That the standard weight of the cent coined at the Mint shall be seventy-two grains, or fifteen hundredths of one ounce, troy with no greater deviation than three grains in each piece; that said cent shall be composed of copper, with an admixture not exceeding one eighth in weight of other metals, which may render it more suitable for the purpose of coinage and such shape and device as may be fixed by the Director of the Mint, with the approbation of the Secretary of the Treasury."

I submit the matter to your consideration and for such action upon it as you may deem expedient. I have the honor to be, etc.

A week later, Booth himself wrote a long letter to Guthrie, explaining the merits of the new alloy and urging the Secretary to "directly or mediately [sic] procure in the House (or its committee) a modification of the existing or proposed law."

On December 17, Snowden wrote to Missouri Representative John Phelps of the House ways and means committee, reminding him of the bill. The Director said that he was "'pressed on all hands, and from every quarter, for the new cent—in fact, the public are very anxious for its issue."

Phelps reported the bill on the 24th. It had been amended to provide for Booth's copper-nickel cent, and to reduce by twenty per cent the Mint price on Spanish coins. Debate centered around the subject of legal tender. Representative Jones of Tennessee strongly opposed the measure.

JONES: "Does the gentleman propose to make the new cent coin a tender in the payment of debt?'

PHELPS: "We do."

JONES: "Where is the authority on the part of the Government, or a State, to make a copper coin a legal tender? If the gentleman will permit me, I will move to strike that portion of the bill out. The Constitution says that the States shall make nothing but gold and silver coin legal tender in payment of debts.

PHELPS: "I have this reply to make to the gentleman from Tennessee. The Congress of the United States has power 'to coin money and to regulate the value thereof.' That is one of the specific grants. It has the power to regulate what shall and shall not be money, and what shall and shall not be its value. The provision of the Constitution to which the gentleman refers is a limitation on the power of a state. It provides that 'no state shall make anything but gold and silver coin a tender in payment of debts.' We do not propose in this amendment that these cent pieces shall be a legal tender above the value of ten cents. . ."

The bill was finally postponed for two weeks. When it emerged on January 14, 1857, the legal tender provision was omitted. On the floor, Representative Whitney moved to strike out section eight which in no way related to the rest of the bill and authorized the Mint to strike medals "for the several states, incorporated companies and societies." It was the second time Congress had been asked to condone this unauthorized practice by ex post facto legislation. Whitney said that the medalist business was still very young in America and the Mint's competition discouraged it and was "calculated to destroy the improvement which is now going foreward." The amendment was adopted the following day, when the bill passed and was returned to the Senate for concurrence. On February 4, Senator Hunter reported a further amendment to permit redemption of the Spanish coins at face value for a period of two years. The amendment was agreed to, and the House concurred on the 18th. The bill was enacted February 21, 1857.

Snowden estimated that there were some $3,000,000 in Spanish coins outstanding, in addition to the cents. He purchased a new pair of rollers and three cutting presses, and for the first time in over a half century, the Mint prepared its own cent planchets. On May 25, the date of the small cent's debut, Snowden wrote to Secretary Guthrie:

> The demand for them is enormous . . . We had on hand this morning $30,000 worth, that is 3,000,000 pieces. Nearly all of this amount will be paid out today. The coinage will go forward, however, at the rate of 100,000 or more pieces per day and the demand will be met as well as we can.

A colorful description of this enormous, and perhaps unprecedented run on the Mint, was given in the *Philadelphia Bulletin:* [6]

> Every man and boy in the crowd had his package of coin with him. Some had their rouleaux of Spanish Coin done up in bits of newspaper or wrapped in handkerchiefs, while others had carpet bags, baskets and other carrying contrivances, filled with coppers—"very cheap and filling," like boardinghouse fare.
> The officiating priests in the temple of mammon had anticipated this grand rush, and every possible preparation was made in anticipation of it. Conspicuous among these arrangements was the erection of a neat wooden building in the yard of the mint for the special accommodation of the great crowd of money-changers. This temporary structure was furnished with two open windows, which faced the South. Over one of these windows was inscribed the words "cents for cents," and over the other "cents for silver." Inside the little office were scales and other apparatus for weighing and testing coin, a goodly pile of bags containing the newly struck compound of nickel and copper, and a detachment of weighers, clerks, &c.
> The bags containing the "nicks" were neat little canvas arrangements, each of which held five hundred of the diminutive little strangers, and each of which bore upon its outside the pleasant inscription "5." Just as the State House bell had finished striking nine o'clock the doors of the mint were thrown open, and in rushed the eager crowd—paper parcels, well-filled handkerchiefs, carpet bags, baskets and all. But those who thought that there was to be a grand scramble, and that the boldest pusher would be first served, reckoned without their host. The invading throng was arranged into lines which led to the respective windows; those who bore silver had the post of honor assigned them and went to the right, while those who bore nothing but vulgar copper were constrained to take the left.
> These lines soon grew to an unconscionable length, and to economize space they wound around and around like the convolutions of a snake of a whimsical turn of mind. The clerks and the weighers exerted themselves to the utmost to meet the demands of all comers, and to deal out the little canvas bags to all who were entitled to receive them; but the crowd grew apace, and we estimated that at one time there could not have been less than one thousand persons in the zigzag lines, weighed down with small change, and waiting patiently for their turn.
> Those who were served rushed into the street with their money bags, and many of them were immediately surrounded by an outside crowd, who were willing to buy out in small lots at an advance of from thirty to a hundred per cent., and some of the outside purchasers even huckstered out the coin again in smaller lots at a still heavier advance. The great majority of those who came out "made tracks" with their bags of money, and not an omnibus went eastward past the mint for several hours that did not, like the California steamers, carry "specie in the hands of the passengers." Those who made their way homeward a-foot attracted the attention of passers-by by their display of specie bags, and we doubt much whether, in the history of the mint, there was ever so great a rush inside the building, or so animated a scene outside of it. It was, in effect, the funeral of the old coppers and of the ancient Spanish coins, and the giving of a practical working existence to the new cents.

---

[6] Reprinted in *Bankers Magazine,* August 1857; also, Eric P. Newman, "An Excited Mob Besieges the Philadelphia Mint Money Changers," *The Numismatic Scrapbook Magazine,* October, 1962.

In the course of a few weeks, the new coin will be plentiful enough at par, the Spanish coins will go out of the hands of the brokers [7] just as they have already disappeared from ordinary circulation, and as regards the old cents there will be "nary red" to be seen, except such as will be found in the cabinets of coin collectors.

By the end of September, demand for the small cents had far outstripped production, and Snowden instructed the treasurer to receive the Spanish silver pieces by tale, in exchange for U.S. gold and silver coins. The Spanish coins were still flowing into the Mint a year and a half later and, at Snowden's request, Congress on March 3, 1859, extended the redemption clause for another two years. By 1860, the number of cents in circulation was more than could be absorbed. Congress repealed the redemption clause on July 25, but Snowden on his own authority perpetuated it for more than a year. In its October 1861 issue, *Bankers Magazine* announced that the practice had finally been discontinued. The magazine quoted the *Philadelphia Press* as saying:

> This regulation will doubtless be regarded by many of our citizens as a judicious one, in as much as the large issue of the new nickel cents has rendered them almost as much of a nuisance as the old Spanish currency. Many persons who have obtained for the latter, at its nominal value, a much larger number of cents than they could legitimately use, have used them to pay bills of one, two or three dollars, and as this custom has been extended, it has caused considerable inconvenience.

Artistically, the new cent was less than inspiring. Longacre had copied the flying eagle from Gobrecht's pattern dollar, and the composite wreath from his own one- and three-dollar gold pieces. Snowden suggested that Longacre replace the eagle with the head of Columbus. On July 17, 1857 the engraver replied that the idea was "entitled to consideration," but "how can it be relieved of any of the objections that have theretofore prevailed against the introduction of the head of Washington upon the coinage of the United States?" In the following year, Longacre substituted an Indian head (or rather a Caucasian head in Indian headdress), and introduced a plain laurel wreath on the reverse.

* * *

After it passed from Booth's hands, the project for manufacturing nickel broke down and was abandoned, leaving the Mint dependent on foreign sources. In 1863, Joseph Wharton, a local metallurgist, became interested in nickel and was evidently encouraged by Mint Director Pollock to undertake its extraction. But even before Wharton had begun, Pollock changed his mind, and proposed the adoption of a bronze cent.

In his annual report of October 1, 1863 Pollock wrote:

> A great benefit to the country was effected by the act of 1857, reducing the size of the cent. It is to be regretted the idea still prevailed that it was necessary to put into the coin, if not an equivalent, at least a large proportion of real value. To this end, and for other reasons, an alloying metal was sought, which should command a comparatively high price in the market, without being properly a precious metal . . . The change was well intended, but the experience of other countries, and indeed of our own, has taught us that it was unnecessary liberality, and that all the nickel we have used has been so much money wasted . . . Whilst people expect a full value in their gold and silver coins, they merely want the

---

[7] Carothers notes that brokers were purchasing the Spanish coins at a discount on the open market, exchanging them for the new cents at face value at the Mint, then using the new cents to purchase more of the Spanish pieces.

inferior money for convenience in making exact payments and not at all for the value of the copper, tin or nickel which may be present. If the law makes it a cent of legal tender, to a proper and sufficient extent, then it is a cent to every one using it, even if its intrinsic should be only one-tenth of its nominal and legal value. If any further proof of this fact should be demanded, we have only to refer to our own recent experience, when illegal cent tokens of the size of the legal cent were made and freely passed, although they contained no nickel, weighed on the average about 51 grains, and were worth not more than one-fifth of a cent . . .[8]

Nickel derives its name from a certain unpleasant allusion,[9] indicating its character, and which, in a metallurgic sense, it honestly deserves. It is very obstinate in the melting pot, requiring the fiercest fire, even when in alloy with copper. It commonly makes a hard mixture, very destructive to dies, and all the contiguous parts of the coining machinery. . . .

On the whole, it may now be advised, and even urged, that the law of coinage be modified so as to provide that the cent, retaining its present size and devices, shall be composed of 95 per cent. copper; remainder, tin and zinc in suitable proportions . . .

Again, on December 8, Pollock wrote to Secretary of the Treasury Chase:

Sir: In my last annual report I recommended the disuse of nickel in the cent coinage, and the substitution of the alloy lately introduced in France and England called bronze. It is composed of copper, tin, and zinc, and makes a beautiful and ductile alloy. This change in the material of the cent is not only desirable in itself but has become a necessity from the advance price of nickel (for a supply of which we are at present entirely dependent upon the foreign market, paying for it in gold or its equivalent), and the great uncertainty of procuring an adequate supply for the future from any source at a price within the legal limit.

Besides this, nickel is itself objectionable as an alloying metal. It is harsh, brittle most difficult to melt, requiring the fiercest fires even when in alloy with copper and is very destructive of dies, machinery, &c., thus increasing the cost of production, which will soon exceed the value of the product if the price of copper, labor coal, &c., continues to advance, as it is almost certain to do. In that event, the coinage of the cent must cease.

It is not proposed to change the size or devices of the cent, only the weight. The weight of the new coin would be forty-eight grains or one tenth ounce troy. This will secure a coin in every respect superior to the slumpy nickel.

I also propose for your consideration the coinage of a *two cent* piece, same material and double the weight of the cent, and with such devices and motto as may be approved by you.

This piece would be a great public convenience, and its coinage, in my opinion should be authorized. The devices are beautiful and appropriate, and the motto on each such, as all who fear God and love their country, will approve. I prefer the "shield and arrows" to the "head of Washington," on the obverse of the coin They are submitted for your consideration.

If you approve of the proposed change in material and denomination, the inclosed bill, prepared with care, can be submitted to Congress for their action.

Permit me respectfully to suggest that immediate action is necessary, for nickel is retained it will be impossible to meet the enormous demand for cent and the increasing cost of production may compel a cessation of that coinage. The demand for cents is now far beyond our ability to supply it. The substitution bronze for the nickel alloy was examined by the commissioners of the last annual assay in February, and was by them cordially approved. The commission consisted of Professors Joseph Henry, Washington, District of Columbia; John Torrey, New York; Alexander, Baltimore; Rogers and Rand, Philadelphia; Judge Putnam, Boston

---

[8] These tokens were placed into circulation during the Civil War to relieve the shortage of cent Pollock was evidently impressed by the fact that the tokens circulated freely while the Mint copper-nickel cents passed at a premium or were hoarded.

[9] i.e., Nick, the devil.

Hon. H. McCulloch, Washington, District of Columbia, and the three *ex officio* members from Philadelphia. The opinions of such gentlemen, though not officially expressed, are deserving of consideration. Yours, etc.

On March 5, Chase submitted Pollock's letter and bill to Senator Fessenden, chairman of the finance committee. However, no action was taken, and on March 16, Pollock again wrote to Chase:

Sir: The continuance of the cent coinage is now not only a question of *price*, but supply. Our present stock of nickel will be exhausted in a few days, and an adequate supply cannot be obtained from any source. Our foreign correspondents inform us that nickel cannot be furnished at present prices, nor can any considerable amount be had for some months.

We are thus shut up to the home supply, from the works of Mr. Wharton; but if we could receive all made at his establishment the amount would be wholly insufficient, would be from five hundred to eight hundred pounds per week, not more than one half the amount required under ordinary circumstances. Something must be done by Congress, and that at once, to meet the constant and overwhelming demand; our daily orders range from two to five thousand dollars; our daily production about one thousand dollars. We cannot increase it, for we cannot procure the material. The wants of the public could be fully met by substituting bronze for the nickel alloy. But private interests have induced opposition to this proposition.[10] Can these private interests be reconciled, and at the same time the public interests and convenience be promoted? I think they can, by reducing the weight of the nickel cent from seventy-two to forty-eight grains, and continuing the coinage of the nickel alloy at this reduced rate, making a more convenient and desirable coin, and at the same time authorizing the coinage of a two cent bronze piece. This will meet the wants of the people and Government, and be satisfactory to Mr. Wharton and his friends. Although every consideration of public interest and convenience requires the abandonment of nickel, yet the plan now proposed, if adopted, will greatly aid the Mint in meeting a demand that is unceasing and increasing. I inclose an amendment or new section to the supplement forwarded some weeks ago, embracing the present proposition. If bronze is substituted, or the submitted plan be adopted, a clear revenue of at least two hundred or two hundred and fifty thousand dollars will, under the present demand for cents, annually accrue to the Government. I hope the subject will receive the early and favorable action of Congress. Yours etc.

Chase referred the letter to Fessenden, adding: "I concur with the Director in thinking that the public interests and convenience require the abandonment of nickel and the substitution of bronze for one and two cent pieces, as provided by the bill already submitted."

The bill was introduced by Senator Clark on March 22. Pollock's letters were read by the Clerk and apparently influenced the proceedings, for the bill on being thrice read was passed without debate.

A few weeks later, Wharton published a pamphlet in which he suggested the adoption of a unified minor coinage of one-, two-, three-, five- and ten-cent pieces, composed of 25 per cent nickel and 75 per cent copper.[11]

The plan was rebutted on April 20, when a select House committee unanimously endorsed Pollock's bill. Then Thaddeus Stevens, the powerful and influential representative from Pennsylvania, from the very district where Wharton operated his mine, rose and announced his opposition to the bill. He

---

[10] Wharton had several influential friends in Congress who, for many years, espoused the cause of nickel.

[11] Joseph Wharton, *Project for Reorganizing the Small Coinage of the United States of America,* April 15, 1864.

said that the former legislation had "induced several gentlemen to embark on the difficult project of working nickel mines," and that one man (Wharton) had spent $200,000 in opening a nickel mine and preparing the machinery which was now able to supply all the nickel wanted in the country. But except in coins or for alloying German silver the metal had little use. "Shall we destroy all this property," he thundered with patriotic fervor, "because by coining with another metal more money may be saved to the Government?" Such, he said, was bad policy. Besides Congress had already approved the nickel cent which would not rust like the "brass" one now proposed.

Mr. Kasson, chairman of the House committee, said that the new metal did not at all resemble brass. Neither could he admit the thesis that the Government, in purchasing an article from a producer, was bound by him in perpetual mortgage. Such a principle, he said, was without precedent in the House or any other legislative body. The bill was thereupon put to a vote and passed, becoming the Coinage Act of April 22, 1864.[12]

---

[12] For the first time, the minor coins were given legal tender status, the cent up to ten cents, the two-cent piece up to twenty cents.

Cents: 1855 experimental cent for proposed reduced-weight copper coinage; 1856 (adopted design) and 1858 patterns for copper-nickel cent; regular issue Indian cent with 1859 and 1860 reverses. All of the foregoing by Longacre. **Two cents:** 1836 billon experimental pattern by Gobrecht; 1863 experimental pattern and 1864 adopted design by Longacre.

CHAPTER 18

Nickel Makes a Comeback

THE WIDESPREAD HOARDING OF COPPER-NICKEL CENTS apparently baffled contemporary observers as much as it did later economic theorists. On December 11, 1863 the *Philadelphia Ledger* remarked:

The coinage of cents [for Nov.] exceeds four and a quarter millions of pieces, and for the last year and a half or two years, the monthly average has been as much. In the face of this fact and the notorious scarcity of cents in circulation, the question may well be asked, "Where are all the cents?" Being depreciated below their nominal value they are not exported, and considering what a nuisance their abundance was before the suspension of specie payments, and their immense coinage since, it is a general wonder where they can all be hid.

Hoarding, along with a dwindling nickel supply, finally led to the adoption of a bronze cent and two-cent piece. These new coins circulated widely and without interference, gradually replacing the copper tokens which had inspired their adoption. Meanwhile, experiments continued at the Mint.

On December 21, 1863 Pollock sent to Secretary Chase a hastily made pattern for a bronze three-cent piece. The coin was as large as the old cent, and the Director did not recommend its adoption. He said that experiments would be made with an aluminum three-cent piece and half dime.[1] In the following year, however, Chase authorized the issue of a three-cent postage currency, setting the stage for new nickel agitation. Arguing that coins were more desirable than paper for small change, Wharton's friends gained the support of Representative Kasson, the House coinage committee chairman who had previously opposed the continuation of nickel. On March 3, 1865 (when the wide circulation

---
[1] J. Hewitt Judd, *United States Pattern, Experimental and Trial Pieces.*

243

of the bronze cent and two-cent piece had made a three-cent coin superfluous) Kasson introduced a bill for a copper-nickel three-cent piece. The coin was to weigh 30 grains and consist of 75 per cent copper and 25 per cent nickel. On the same day, the bill was whisked through both houses without debate and signed into law.

With Kasson's conversion, and no immediate hope for restoring specie payments, Pollock tempered his opposition to nickel coinage. In his report of June 30, 1865 the Director stated:

> From this nickel alloy, a coin of the denomination of five cents, and which would be a popular substitute for the five cent note, could easily be made. This suggestion, however, is respectfully submitted in view of the probable withdrawel of the smaller denomination of the fractional paper currency, and as preparative and aid to its accomplishment. This to continue only until the resumption of specie payments, or for a fixed and limited period. In a country abounding in the precious metals, and with silver generally in excess, in time of peace, of all demand for coinage or other purposes, tokens or coins of inferior alloy should not be permitted to take the place permanently of silver in the coinage of pieces above the denomination of three cents.

Pollock subsequently prepared a bill to authorize a five-cent piece of no more than 60 grains, consisting of 75 per cent copper and 25 per cent nickel. Compared to the three-cent piece, the new coin was disproportionately heavy. The House coinage committee further increased the weight to 5 grams (77.1 grains), ostensibly to express it in metric units. Of course this could have been done with a weight of 4 grams (61.72 grains), but with less satisfaction to Joseph Wharton. The bill passed without debate on May 16, 1866.

In selecting new devices, Longacre may have been influenced by the following comments in a June 1865 issue of the *New York Journal of Commerce*:

> But why can we not have the head of Washington on our Coinage now? The cent is the coin in most common use, and on that it ought to be placed. We respectfully urge it on the attention of the Director of the Mint. Let us have a few patterns with the head of Washington submitted to the Treasury Department, and do a good thing by thus adopting the memory of Washington as a special object of veneration.

Longacre refused to discard his Indian head cent, but in making patterns for a five-cent piece he modeled two different Washington heads as well as a head of Lincoln. On May 28, 1866, Director Pollock wrote to Secretary of the Treasury Hugh McCulloch:[2]

> Sir, I have the honor to forward for your selection and approval specimens of the five cent piece, the coinage of which has been recently authorized.
> No. 1: Obverse,—the "Union Shield resting on tied arrows," peace, &c. Motto "In God we trust," and date. Reverse,—13 stars set in rays, U.S. of America, and figure &c. "5 cents."
> A neat and unique design, and differs from the devices on all of our other coinage. This specimen is in my opinion before all the others in artistic beauty, significance, and diversity. I would respectfully recommend its adoption.
> No. 2: Obverse—"Head of Washington," Motto, "In God we trust," and date. Reverse—same as No. 1; a neat and elegant design.
> No. 3: Obverse—"Head of Washington," U.S. of America and date. Reverse Wreath and figure &c. "5 cents."

---

[2] Lee Hewitt, "Adoption of Five-Cent (Nickel)," *The Numismatic Scrapbook Magazine*, 1961.

No. 4: Obverse—"Head of Washington," Motto, "In God we trust," and date. Reverse. Wreath and figure "5."

The above are respectfully submitted for your consideration. Be pleased to notify me of your decision as early as convenient, so that the dies may be prepared for the coinage of the specimen selected.[3]

Pollock must have delivered the letter in person, for three days later the assayer William DuBois wrote to Longacre:[4]

The Director has returned from Washington having taken with him a choice of devices for the five cent token, but strongly recommending the starry circle; which was adopted. . . . It is truly pleasing to see a man pass the life of three score and ten and yet be able to produce the same artistic works as in earlier days.

In truth, the design was not very pleasing. Longacre had adapted the shield of his two-cent piece, but its heraldic beauty was lost by omitting the scroll, reducing the arrows, and surmounting the shield with a cross.

Some years later, Joseph Wharton justly remarked:[5]

The diameter of this coin being too small for its weight, it has an awkward and humpy appearance, and is entirely devoid of resonance. The design of its face strongly suggests the old fashioned pictures of a tombstone surmounted by a cross and overhung by weeping willows, which suggestion is corroborated by the religious motto. It is a curiously ugly device.

A more pungent criticism of the "shield nickel" appeared in the August 1866 issue of the *American Journal of Numismatics*. The editor was critical of the fast and loose distribution of patterns at the Mint, and after seeing a number of the twenty-eight varieties of the new coin, exclaimed:

Though collectors have long ceased to regard the true issues of the "Government copper-head factory," better known, perhaps, as the United States Mint, as of any value, they may be interested in the information that the ugliest of all known coins, the new five cent piece, is out, as oysters are served in some places "in every style."

Though specimens are refused to Societies and individuals, they are readily procured in Philadelphia through the agents of the young gentleman at the head of that department.

At present the price of a set of four, struck in "putty" and various metals, with copper gold dollar included, is $35, though the expected purchaser is informed in every case, that as the owner is very anxious to sell (somebody?) he will take $30. Collectors are advised to wait a little, when it is expected that *the owner's* anxiety will increase to such an extent that he will be glad to take any amount, however small, above their legal value.

* * *

When, in 1867, Longacre removed the rays from among the stars, many persons thought that one or the other of the two varieties was counterfeit. Rumors grew so persistent that the Mint considered abandoning the shield and starry circle altogether, and a number of new models were prepared. However, no further changes in the five-cent piece were adopted until 1883.

In a letter to Secretary McCulloch, on June 12, 1867 Longacre enclosed a five-cent pattern for an aluminum coinage which he recommended as a means to retire the fractional paper currency.

---

[3] Probably because of violent southern resentment, Pollock ignored Longacre's Lincoln head design.

[4] *Papers of J. B. Longacre*, Library Company of Philadelphia.

[5] Joseph Wharton, *Memorandum Concerning Small Money and Nickel Alloy Coinage*, 1877.

Dear Sir, I know not how far it may coincide with the present or future polic of the Government—but it has appeared to me as a desideratum, that the portio of the circulating medium—designated as fractional currency should possess a intrinsic value in the material of which it is composed, which it has not now.

If this view should be entertained now, or hereafter: it is important to find c suggest a material that would meet the exigency. The use of Aluminum for th purposes of coinage, was suggested by its peculiar qualities as I became acquainte with them: especially when I ascertained that it was employed successfully i Paris for the purpose of striking medals.

The most formidable objection I have encountered to the use of this metal fe such purpose is, that being comparatively, a *new metal,* and as yet known chief to men of science—it is difficult to assume a fixed value—which must depend upo the expense of its reduction from the ores.

This objection is however more specious than real; its manufacture is alread the subject of competition in France and England, and the cost in large ordei has varied as little during the past five years, as any other metal; the preciou metals not excepted.

The characteristics which claim a favourable consideration for this material fe such purpose, among others are these.

1. The facility and certainty with which it can be distinguished from all othe metals in use or known, arising from its remarkable place among the *specif gravities* of metals; its extreme lightness, presenting a greater safeguard again adulteration or spurious imitation, than even the opposite quality of gold, whic may be regarded as occupying nearly the other end of the scale of metallic gravitie

2. It is less liable to discoloration from mere atmospheric exposure than ar other metal used as a circulating medium except gold.

3. It is malleable and fusible at a modest heat.

4. Its relative value—which would give for the value of five cents, intrinsicall a piece of the size of the Half Eagle; one of the most desirable sizes of coin fe extensive circulation, for which there would be no danger of mistaking it, eve in the dark, to say nothing of color.

5. These considerations have induced me to prepare for the purpose from die designated and engraved by myself—the accompanying specimens, correspondin in size with the coin above mentioned, in order to exhibit fully and fairly unde the usual process of coining, the fitness of the metal for the requisite operation

It is not my object to press these suggestions in the way of matters of mor immediate importance; they are presented rather as a contribution to the publ service, should any change of policy or necessity occur to indicate their relativ importance to the future coinage. With the highest respect etc.

Longacre submitted his letter to the new Director Henry Linderman wh forwarded it, together with his own adverse comments, on the 14th. Linderma said that the supply and price of aluminum were uncertain, and that for th minor coins it was unnecessary to use a metal of high intrinsic value.

It seems that the Director was already committed to the nickel interest After admitting in his first annual report that the copper-nickel three- an five-cent planchets had worn out the Mint's machinery and broken an enormou number of dies, Linderman framed a bill to create copper-nickel cents an dimes. All of these coins were to have uniformly proportioned weights, and a alloy of not less than 25 per cent nor more than 33 per cent nickel. Linderman willingness to increase the proportion of nickel by eight per cent, after he ha already complained of the alloy's intractability and advised a modest value fc the minor coins, throws some doubt on his official motives.

The Director enlisted the support of Pennsylvania Representative Willia D. Kelley who, conveniently, was chairman of the House Committee on coinag

Standard copper-nickel alloy: 1865 three-cent piece, regular issue; 1866 experimental patterns for five-cents with Washington and Lincoln head; 1866 "shield" five-cent piece and modified 1867 reverse, adopted issues; 1867 experimental aluminum pattern for five-cent piece. All of the foregoing by Longacre.

weights and measures. Kelley thought that the weight of the cent should be fixed at one gram. In furnishing Congress with experimental planchets, the chief coiner, A. L. Snowden, found it necessary to enlarge the cent to one-and-a-half grams. Kelley distributed the planchets to members of his committee, and on February 23, 1868 wrote to Linderman:

> Some members think the one & a half gram planchet too small for a coin of such common use as the one cent, & others object to the size & weight of the ten cent planchet as excessive. It was, however, suggested that by making the one & a half gram planchet thinner in the center with a thicker edge or by making its whole surface as thin as the one gram planchette the difficulty would probably be overcome.

In a letter to Linderman dated March 16, Snowden said that a one-and-a-half gram cent was the smallest that could be coined properly. Moreover, the copper-nickel dime would be so large that "no steel would be found with tenacity enough to withstand the blow." To facilitate the striking of five-cent coins, Snowden wished to increase their diameter from twenty to twenty-two millimetres.

Provision for the dime was omitted when Kelley introduced the bill on March

25. It was read twice, referred back to the committee and ordered printed. On February 25, 1869, it was again introduced by Kelley.

Debate centered around the provision for purchasing nickel. The bill left it to the Director of the Mint to make his purchases "in like manner as other materials for the use of the Mint are purchased." The provision was ambiguous to say the least, and would have given the Mint an absolute discretion in the matter. Missouri Representative Pile moved an amendment to make the materials for the nickel coinage "so far as practicable, of domestic origin." He added that there was a large deposit in his state. Mr. Hooper, sensing Pile's motive, suggested that the amendment be modified by inserting the phrase "at equal price." Pile said he did not think that his amendment would put the Government to the disadvantage inferred by Hooper, and that he disliked confining it absolutely to the same price because he understood that native ore was preferred even if it cost a little more. This way, he said, the Government would "stimulate the development of that branch of industry, and in the end would benefit the country." Pile finally agreed to alter his amendment to read that "in the purchase of said materials preference shall be given to domestic production if at a cost not exceeding twenty per cent more than the foreign materials." The bill, as amended, passed the House but died in the Senate.

In the next session it was re-introduced by Mr. Kelley. There was a heated debate on March 15, when Kelley offered an amendment which would again leave the purchases of nickel to the discretion of the Director. Representative Butler of Massachusetts insisted that all purchases be made by public advertisement, with the contract given to the lowest bidder. Kelley said he could not consent to such an amendment unless Butler changed his wording to the "lowest and best bidder." He said that the quality of nickel varied considerably. In answer to a question by Representative Maynard, Kelley asserted that the "best nickel" came "from a mine in Pennsylvania." Butler thought that the phrase might be worded "by the lowest bidder for pure metal." Butler was strongly backed by Mr. McCormick of Missouri. McCormick said that he probably represented the largest nickel interest in the United States, and he wanted his people to have a chance to bid. Butler offered his amendment the following day, amidst another flurry of debate. The bill was finally recommitted.

When it emerged on March 30, it included Butler's amendment. The bill passed the House but failed again in the Senate.

With Pollock's reappointment as Mint Director in May 1869, the nickel interests bided their time. Everything hinged on Linderman who, according to some, would soon return. But just how soon, and in what new role, no one then could guess.

CHAPTER 19

The Mint Act of 1873

IN HIS ANNUAL REPORT FOR 1869, Secretary of the Treasury Boutwell called attention to the growth of the Government's mining and coining interests. He said that these now required a Bureau, located in Washington, and headed by a special officer under his direction. He also recommended abolishing the coining charge to discourage the exportation of bullion to foreign mints.

Several weeks later, Boutwell asked John Jay Knox, the deputy-comptroller of the currency, to prepare a bill which included these provisions, as well as every important statute in effect relative to the Mint and coinage. The bill was to be a grand revision, like the Mint Act of 1837, which had grown obsolete through the passage of alterations. It was to dispense with any outmoded provisions, and revise to best purpose those retained. Having prepared his bill, Knox solicited opinions from various Treasury Department and Mint officials, past and present, including former chief clerk Robert Patterson, Franklin Peale, James Ross Snowden and Henry Linderman. Linderman, in fact, was chosen by Boutwell to assist Knox in the final casting of the bill.

Of paramount importance was the reorganization of the Mint as a Bureau which would also direct the collection of statistics. Anent, Boutwell remarked:

Although the mints and assay offices are nominally in the charge of the Treasury Department, there is not, by authority of law, any person in the Department who, by virtue of his office, is supposed to be informed upon the subject, and none on whom the Secretary of the Treasury can officially rely for information as to the management of this important branch of the Government business.

At this time, the branch mints and assay offices were headed by superin
tendents, each subordinate to the Director at Philadelphia. Knox said that thi
was unjustified since the output of the Philadelphia Mint was only about one
sixth that of its sister mint at San Francisco. Besides, the supervision of th
Director, in this respect, was really nominal. In 1856, the melter and refiner o
the San Francisco Mint incurred losses amounting to nearly a quarter of
million dollars, none of which was recovered. Subsequently, an investigatin
committee and then a special agent sent by the Secretary of the Treasury foun
great irregularities in that particular department. In 1866, large discrepancie
between the books of the chief coiner and the treasurer of the San Francisc
Mint led Knox to personally investigate the institution.

In 1869, according to Knox, examinations of the branch mints at San Frar
cisco and Denver, and the New York Assay Office "disclosed other irregularitie
resulting in large losses to the Government, which might easily have bee
prevented by periodical examinations conducted by competent persons."
seems that the New York Assay Office had practically gone into business fc
itself. When the local supply of coin was plentiful, the officers allowed favore
bullion dealers to borrow gold bars on deposit, though these were legally r
quired to be in the Treasury. And when coins were scarce, they issued una
thorized certificates, or Government obligations, amounting to many millior
of dollars for loans of bullion. Sometimes the obligations shown by the not
even exceeded the value of the deposits! Knox said that it was only with gre
difficulty he had been able to find a copy of the Treasury Department regul
tions for the transaction of business. Clearly, more stringent control was nece
sary.

In 1869, Linderman relinquished the management of the Philadelphia Mir
which would soon become a subordinate post. For the next three years,
held a roving commission, gathering experience and priming himself for l
appointment as first Director of the Mint Bureau. In 1870 he was asked to i
vestigate the San Francisco and Carson City Mints, and the following ye
was sent by the Government to examine the coinage systems of various E
ropean nations. In 1872, he helped erect a refinery at the San Francisco Min

In the meantime, James Pollock had been reappointed Director of the Mi
Pollock probably did not learn what was brewing until Boutwell sent him
draft of the revisionary bill for his comments. On January 28, 1870 he replied

> The main feature of the bill lies in the first section, the creation of a new offic
> the director of the minting system of the United States, to have his office in
> Treasury Department at Washington. Now, apart from all personal consideratio
> whoever may be the Director of the mints, &c., his office should not be in Wa
> ington, but in one of the principal mints of the United States. The Director,
> be efficient and fitted for his duties, should know the daily operations of a m
> from actual personal inspection, should see and know the details of its worki
> be personally familiar with all the requirements of its respective departments. T
> he could not do if his office is to be at Washington, however roving his comn
> sion may be. He must depend for all his information in relation to mints and as
> offices upon the superintendents of these establishments, and any opinion he n
> form must come to him from those officers who are in daily contact with
> actual operations of the mint. Therefore the proposed Director can do no m
> than transmit to the Secretary of the Treasury what the Secretary of the Treas
> now receives direct, and without the intervention of such officer. There is no

---

[1] *Annual Report of the Director of the Mint, 1896.*

and no advantage, then, in the proposed directorship. It would be the creation of a new office not required by any consideration of public interest, and consequently the useless expenditure of government funds.

Again, casual visits to the mints and assay offices cannot possibly enable the Director to gather as certain information, or form as reliable opinions upon practical questions or operations, as those resulting from the daily observations of an officer in the mint of such operations, and carried on for a long time. If the superintendents are men of ability and integrity (and none other should be appointed), he (the Director) could not alter the information given him by them, nor ought he to risk giving different opinions on practical questions, because he is necessarily, by absence and want of familiarity with their working, not qualified to hazard conjectural opinions at variance with those based wholly on practice. Either, therefore, the proposed Director will transmit the information and opinions he receives from his superintendents, *unaltered* or *modified*. If unaltered, then he is a useless intermediate between the superintendents and the Secretary of the Treasury; *if altered,* he will create confusion and trouble arising from his interference in matters of which he has practically no knowledge.

Elsewhere in his letter Pollock said that the difficulties, which existed or had existed in the mints and assay offices, originated "not in the system itself, but in a disregard of its provisions, and the rules and regulations for the government of the Mint and branches, as prescribed by the Director with the approval of the Secretary of the Treasury." Pollock also commented on other parts of the bill, concluding that the whole was hasty, defective and unnecessary.

Knox sent a copy of the bill to former Director J. R. Snowden, who replied on March 10, 1870. Snowden also rejected the idea that a Director could manage the Mints more efficiently from a distant city.

Linderman himself commented on the bill in a letter dated January 25, 1870. He said that since 1861 (when Pollock was first appointed) new and inexperienced men assumed the duties of Director with every change of Presidential administration, and that they required supervision by an officer in Washington. Linderman's argument ignored the fact that the proposed Director in Washington was himself to serve for only five years.

The bill also introduced other new provisions:

1) The office of treasurer was abolished, and its duties were transferred to the superintendent.

2) The coining charge of one-half per cent was abolished in order to encourage depositors.

3) The silver dollar, which had long ceased to circulate in the country, was discontinued.

In his original draft, Knox had substituted a fiduciary dollar weighing 384 grains, but on Linderman's advice the denomination was dropped. Louis Garnett, manager of the San Francisco Assaying and Refining Works proposed the issue of a commercial dollar,[2] to be coined for the sole purpose of competing with the Mexican peso in Chinese trade. The Chinese were so averse to anything new, they even rejected the more modern pesos because of slight modifications in the design. They likewise discredited standard U.S. dollars, forcing American bankers and merchants to import the earlier pesos at a premium of seven-and-a-half per cent above their bullion value.

The commercial dollar was to weigh 420 grains (three-quarters of a grain fine more than the peso) and bear on the reverse its weight and fineness in-

---

[2] Porter Garnett, "History of the Trade Dollar," *American Economic Review,* March 1917.

stead of an eagle. The idea was endorsed by Knox and Linderman who believed that the superior value and workmanship of the coin would appeal to the Chinese mentality. To further distinguish it from the standard dollar, Linderman named the new denomination a "silver union." Knox recommended the coin in his report to Boutwell, but made no provision for it in his revisionary Mint bill.

4) The minor coins were to be replaced by a uniform copper-nickel series such as Linderman had already proposed. Pollock, in his letter to Boutwell vigorously attacked the measure:[3]

> These sections embody the provisions of the copper-nickel bill, providing for a new one, three, and five-cent coin, presented to and not passed by the last Congress. There exists no necessity, no consideration of public interest or convenience for a change in the present bronze, and copper-nickel coinage, and the substitution of that proposed in these sections. In appearance, in size, weight, and artistic device, the present is fully equal to the proposed base coinage; and as regards the bronze in comparison with the nickel cent suggested, it is superior in every pretension, economy, convenience, easy recognition, &c. The copper-nickel cent would be a small, inconvenient coin, so small as to be almost useless; and the cost of the production, after a careful calculation by some of the most experienced officers of the Mint, would be equal to its nominal value in *gold.*
>
> It costs as much (material excepted) to make a copper-nickel cent as a gold double-eagle.
>
> If every consideration of economy and a desire to prevent useless waste of the public money condemns the authorizing of the coinage of a nickel-copper one-cent piece, why introduce a *three* and *five*-cent piece of the same metals and proportions, when the existing coins of the same denominations are equal, if not superior, to the proposed.
>
> Then, again, the proposition to abolish the *silver* five-cent piece, in aid of the nickel coin, is one that would be by common consent condemned, particularly in a country like ours, abounding in silver ores, and near the day of the resumption of specie payments.

Snowden rejected the nickel coinage for a different reason. He believed that the low intrinsic value of the three- and five-cent pieces would eventually bring a flood of counterfeits struck in the same composition. With respect to the latter coin he was, in fact, quite correct. Snowden nevertheless lamented the late copper-nickel cent, which he himself had introduced.

Franklin Peale disliked the copper-nickel alloy in general, and Robert Patterson could think of no greater advantage than the (imagined) difficulty would present to counterfeiters. Linderman alone, whose nickel bill Knox was virtually restating, endorsed the measure. Linderman said:

> The substitution of a copper-nickel one cent piece for the bronze coin of the same denomination will be objected to on the ground that the latter is more easily manufactured than the former; while admitting the fact that the alloy composed copper, tin, and zinc, usually termed "bronze," is more malleable than the copper nickel alloy, experiments made at the Mint prove that the manufacture of the copper-nickel cent, such as you propose, is entirely practicable; moreover, it may be stated that the more difficult the alloy is to manipulate, the less liability there is to have counterfeiting of the coins therefrom successfully carried on. In this respect the argument is decidedly in favor of the copper-nickel piece. It is proper to add that experience shows copper-nickel coins to be no more liable to counterfeiting than the existing silver coins.

---

[3] *The Annual Report of the Director of the Mint, 1896.*

What Linderman neglected to add was that the silver coins were widely counterfeited. Moreover, nickel had been a favorite of counterfeiters since the late 1830's, when large quantities of half dollars were struck in German silver.

On the strength of Linderman's endorsement, the measure was allowed to stand. But the most amazing testimony concerning the copper-nickel coinage was offered by Knox himself. Under his list of reasons why the Director should be removed to Washington, he wrote:

> The expense of the manufacture of this [minor] coinage has been paid from the gain arising from the conversion of copper, bronze and copper-nickel into coin having a nominal value much exceeding its intrinsic value. The amount paid into the treasury during the past twelve years from this source has been $4,225,000, so that the minor coinage has been manufactured at a cost of more than one-half of its nominal value. If the manufacture of this coinage had been under the supervision of an officer not influenced by the clamor for patronage, and independent of all local pressure, its cost would not probably have been more than one third of its nominal value.

The ironies in this statement are almost inexhaustible. To begin with, the officer most influenced "by the clamor for patronage" was none other than Linderman. Secondly, it was, with slight exceptions, Linderman's own copper-nickel coin bill Knox was proposing. Thirdly, Linderman co-authored the final draft of Knox's bill which was accompanied by the statement condemning Linderman. And fourthly, it was to be Linderman's job, as Director of the Mint Bureau in Washington, to stop the abuses of former Director Linderman of Philadelphia.

Knox said that the new bill effected an "entire change in the manner of issuing silver subsidiary coinage." This change, however, was in practice, not in law. Knox had discovered that for sixteen years the Mint was illegally purchasing its silver bullion above market price, with subsidiary silver instead of gold coin. He wrote:

> The effect of the mint practice has been to put in circulation silver coins without regard to the amount required for purposes of "change," creating a discount upon silver coin and bringing loss upon holders of any considerable amount. . . . The coins thus issued have accumulated, and are now at a large discount in Canada and California, and will again become burdensome at home when brought into circulation. The correct method of issuing silver coin is, as was originally contemplated: to purchase with gold such an amount of silver bullion at market rates as is needed for coinage into fractional parts of a dollar; to issue the silver coins only in exchange for gold at par, and to require the manufacture of such coinage to cease whenever there is evidence of a redundancy. In the proposed bill the language is clear and explicit on this point.

It was inevitable that at least two of the reviewers (Patterson and Peale) would comment on the engraver's office. Peale said that the artistic quality of the coins had "hitherto been lamentably, if not disgracefully deficient." He refused even to admit that there was such a person as a Mint engraver, acknowledging only a die-sinker who, he said, did nothing but punch in current dates.

Patterson added:

> The duties of the engraver are defined in a manner somewhat different from those of the old law. In the progress of art the whole system of preparing *working* dies for coins has been changed, and has become mechanical instead of demand-

ing the graver's tool. When *new devices* are required the necessity of a new or original die arises, and a high style of art is required,. The engraver who may be at the Mint is not, necessarily, the person best qualified for such a work. In France, the government, when a new coin is to be issued, selects the most appropriate device and die from a *concours*, or competitive trial, in which the best artists are requested to participate. Perhaps it is to this cause we may attribute the perfection reached in the coinage of that country. Without insisting that this is the best plan, it is surely judicious to change the present law, which gives to the one person, who may happen to be engraver at the Mint, a monopoly on preparing new devices and dies where new coins or changes of old become expedient.

Patterson's idea was incorporated into the bill, permitting the Treasury Department to engage outside artists in the preparation of original dies.

The bill, as finally drafted by Knox and Linderman, was the most exhaustive in the history of our coinage. It embodied the ideas of more than thirty persons distinguished in economics, and its seventy-one provisions required a year and a half to prepare. The only fact it overlooked was that neither gold nor silver coins were in circulation, nor would be until the gold value of the greenbacks rose and specie payments were resumed.

The bill was introduced by Senator Sherman on April 28, 1870, and again with some amendments, on December 19. It was debated on January 9, 1871, and might have passed without opposition but for the fact that the Senate finance committee had reinserted a coining charge which was repugnant to the western silver interests. After some debate, the charge was retained and the bill passed the Senate on January 10.

The following day, the bill was sent to the House committee on coinage, weights and measures, where it was amended and reported back by Representative Kelley on February 25. It was then redirected to the committee, and finally brought back by Kelley on January 9, 1872.

Representative Potter of New York asked Kelley whether the bill changed the value or weight and fineness of any coins or provided for any new coin. Kelley replied in the negative, despite the fact that the bill was to replace the bronze cent with a copper-nickel coin.

Potter was far from satisfied. In cross-examining Kelley, he referred to the bill as "this Pennsylvania contrivance" which, with its nickel coinage, would give "a monopoly to the gentleman in Pennsylvania." The discussion was resumed with greater warmth the following day. Mr. McCormick, representing the Missouri nickel interests, introduced an amendment to provide for open bidding on the nickel and copper purchased by the Mint. Kelley remarked that the regulations for procuring gold and silver would be sufficient "to secure something like integrity in the purchase of nickel." Since the coinage of gold was free and unlimited, Kelley's statement was meaningless. McCormick acidly replied that the primary object of the bill was apparently to "affect the manner in which nickel should be purchased," and that there were "in the United States more places producing nickel than the state of Pennsylvania."

The bill was finally recommitted. On April 9, it emerged with sundry amendments, and was reported by Mr. Hooper who made a long explanatory speech. One of the new amendments provided for open bidding on nickel. Another, requested by the bullion dealers, legalized for two years the sale of subsidiary coins for silver bullion, even though this practice had been patently exposed and condemned by Knox.

Patterns by William Barber. 1870 standard silver (reduced weight) dollar; 1872 dollar, "Amazonian" design; 1872 eagle.

During the previous Congress, the coinage committee had interviewed a New York bullion dealer who admitted making $75,000 to $100,000 a year by exporting subsidiary coins to South America. Moreover, his colleague was netting a good deal more. The committee was so impressed that they acceded to the dealer's demands for non-interference by the Government. Hooper said:

> Prior to the suspension of specie payments, in 1861, silver coins appear to have been issued in excess of the requirements of the public, and were at times sold at a small discount from their nominal value, probably for the reason that they could be obtained at the Mint at less than their nominal value. The principle or system of issuing silver coin at their nominal value, in exchange for gold only, is undoubtedly the correct one, as it gives the Government the benefit of the seignorage, and restrains their issue to the wants of the public for these subsidiary coins. A proviso, however, has been added to this section, authorizing the present practice to continue in force for two years from the 1st of July next, to meet the special requirements for the subsidiary silver coins in commercial transactions with some of the South American States. This provision, however, applies only to the Mint at Philadelphia and the assay office at New York.[4]

A third amendment provided for Knox's fiduciary silver dollar.

The bill was severely criticized by New York Representatives Brooks and Potter. Brooks said:

> I move to strike out section 1 of the bill. I frankly avow that my object in doing so is to end this bill. It seems to me that this is the most farcical spectacle that Congress can present at this time when Uncle Sam is covered all over with rags [i.e., paper currency], from head to foot, and there is not a portion of his garments fit to wear in public, for all is so ragged; when no member of this House has seen a silver dollar or a golden eagle, except as a curiosity in a museum, for some four or five or six or seven years, and when there is no probability of seeing another golden eagle for some six or seven years to come. . . .

Potter agreed, adding that Congress should have introduced instead a bill to restore specie payments. He said that so long as the paper dollar was worth less than a real one, fiduciary coins would pass at a depreciated rate. Moreover, he could not resist the conviction that the bill had been designed to make room for a particular person (i.e., Linderman).

Kelley riposted that those who opposed the bill were dupes of the banks that wanted to delay specie payments, and of the bullion dealers who were making enormous profits under the old laws. He said that the dealers opposed the bill because it substituted a fiduciary silver dollar, but he ignored the new provision which would force the Government to share its seignorage with these dealers. Potter, in turn, needled Kelley about his patronage of Wharton, and the debate closed without anything more being accomplished.

On May 27, Hooper introduced a substitute bill which he said had been submitted to the House members who had "taken a special interest in the bill." He announced that it met with "universal approbation" in the form he now offered it.

Mr. Brooks believed that his constituent, Mr. Potter, did not concur with the substitute, and asked Hooper to postpone his motion until Potter took his seat. Hooper not only refused, but insisted on having the bill voted upon

---

[4] During the previous year, San Francisco Mint officials on their own authority had refused to pay out the subsidiary coins for anything but gold.

without its even being read. The most important change was in the weight of the subsidiary coins. The half dollar was increased from 192 grains to 12½ grams (192.9 grains), and the smaller coins proportionately, the entire purpose of which was to establish a metric system, the "small step" toward international coinage.[5] The bill passed by an overwhelming vote of 110 to 13, and was printed in the Senate on May 29.

In November, Linderman issued a special report, in which he advised the substitution of a commercial dollar for the fiduciary coin. He said:

> The facts . . . indicate the gradual but eventual certain adoption of the gold standard, and consequent demonetization of silver by all commercial countries. Not only is the tendency to adopt gold as the sole standard and measure of value, but to use paper money redeemable in gold as the bulk of the circulating medium.
>
> The true policy of this country under these circumstances is to seek a market in China for its silver bullion; and to do this it must be put in form to meet a favorable reception in that empire.
>
> The United States silver dollar of 412½ grains has never been well received in China, nor amounted to much as a coin of commerce, for the reason that its bullion value is less than that of the old Spanish dollar, and its successor, the Mexican dollar. . . .
>
> From the great advantages in rates and time, the vast business of Europe with China and Japan, which was formerly done by direct remittances, is now transacted to a large extent by cross exchange through San Francisco, and will undoubtedly increase as her advantages for arbitrating such exchanges shall become better known. . . .
>
> After consulting with some of the leading businessmen of San Francisco, as well as with some of the most prominent and intelligent Chinese merchants as to its probable success, I do not hesitate to recommend, in lieu of our old dollar, a new coin or disk, which shall be slightly more valuable than the Mexican dollar, to be made only upon request of the owner of the bullion, and to be paid for by him.
>
> It is not proposed to make the new coin or disk a legal tender in payment of debt, but simply a stamped ingot with its weight and fineness indicated. Its manufacture can therefore in no wise give rise to any complication with our monetary system, and neither in theory or principle differ in any respect, it being of *uniform* weight and fineness.
>
> If this new coin should be accepted at all as a medium in our trade with China, it will doubtless very soon supersede the Mexican dollar, and there is no reason why it should not in a short time command a premium of 6 or 8 per cent. . . . It will not be a coin of circulation, or legal-tender in payment of debts, but simply an agent in our commerce with foreign countries.

The Senate adopted Linderman's proposals, and the bill, amended in this and other respects, was debated in December, and again in January 1873. Not only the trade dollar (as it was now called), but the gold dollar, three-dollar piece, and silver coins were to show their weight and fineness instead of the conventional eagle design. Sherman said that the silver coins were being revalued to the French standard "and in order to show this wherever our silver coin shall float—and we are providing that it shall float all over the world— we propose to stamp upon it instead of our eagle, which foreigners may not understand, and which they may not distinguish from a buzzard, or some other bird, the intrinsic fineness and weight of the coin."

Sherman's insistence on having the weight and fineness stamped on subsidiary coins which were mere tokens, and on the trade dollar where Chinese

---

[5] Although this weight was finally adopted, common usage has nevertheless prevailed, and our coinage continues to be reckoned in grains.

merchants would never understand them, is amusing and incomprehensible. The amendment for expunging the eagle device was defeated.

The bill, further amended to strike out the copper-nickel cent, was passed in the Senate on January 17, and sent back to the House which refused to accede to the amendments. The matter was finally arbitrated by a conference committee of both houses which produced a compromise bill. Confused and weary, Congress passed the bill without further debate. It is known today as the Mint Act of February 12, 1873.

The most significant provisions of the new law were:

1) The reorganization of the Mint as a Bureau, with its Director in Washington.

2) The discontinuation of the two-cent piece, silver three cents, half dime, and silver dollar.

3) The adoption of a trade dollar, weighing 420 grains. Contrary to its expressed purpose, the trade dollar was included with the silver subsidiary coins and made a legal tender up to five dollars.

CHAPTER 20

The Silver Crusade

THE ORIGIN OF THE FREE SILVER MOVEMENT dates from a period when the new Mint bill was still before Congress. In 1871, following the conclusion of the Franco-Prussian War, Germany adopted an exclusive gold standard. She exported two thirds of her $350,000,000 silver stock, converted the rest into a new subsidiary coinage, and withdrew the old silver coins from circulation. As a result, silver quickly depreciated, first in the neighboring countries, then, gradually, throughout the world. France, anticipating a flood of silver deposits at her mints, suspended silver coinage, and the other nations of the Latin Monetary Union followed suit. These circumstances, coinciding with the discovery of rich silver mines in the western United States, ushered in an era of "cheap silver."

By 1874, the bi-metallic ratio had widened to 16.7 : 1, and the mining interests thought it profitable to have their silver coined at the San Francisco Mint.[1] Imagine their surprise to learn that the free coinage of silver dollars had been discontinued the previous year! An agitation followed, during which several pious Congressmen feigned ignorance of the repeal, maintaining it had been worked into the Mint bill surreptitiously.

On August 5, 1876, for example, "Silver Dick" Bland, the Representative from Missouri, told the House:

"The act of February 12, 1873 was a fraud, because its title gave no clue to the real intent of the act. The record shows that the act was stealthily passed, without reconsideration and without debate."

---

[1] The reader will recall that for two years the San Francisco Mint had refused to sell subsidiary coins except at face value for gold.

The gravity of Bland's lie becomes apparent when we realize that the bill was printed altogether eleven times and debated for nearly three years. As for the silver dollar, it had long ceased to circulate within the country, and its discontinuation by law merely acknowledged economic fact. The status of the coin can be appreciated from the remarks of Senators Conkling, Sherman, and Bogy on March 30, 1876:

CONKLING: "Will the Senator allow me to ask him or some other Senator a question? Is it true that there is now by law no American dollar?"

SHERMAN (chairman of the finance committee): "I will answer the Senator from New York, that since 1853 the use of the silver whole dollar has been discontinued, and none has been issued. That has been so since 1853."

CONKLING: "Is it really true that there is now by law no American dollar and no power to issue it?"

SHERMAN: "There has been no silver dollar issued since 1853, and my impression is that the law of 1853 did not confer the power, but the law of 1873 cut off the power, in my judgment, if it existed."

BOGY: "The power to issue existed from 1853 to 1873, but since 1873 I think there has been no power."

At no time during debate did the Act of 1873 offer a standard dollar, nor any Congressman protest the omission. When Kelley introduced the bill he said it had been considered as carefully as any measure in his experience, and that the committee "proceeded with great deliberation, to go over the bill, not only section by section, but line by line and word by word."

Representative Hooper had specifically explained to the House why the dollar was being dropped, saying:

> This dollar, by reason of its intrinsic value being greater than its nominal value, long ceased to be a coin of circulation, and is melted by manufacturers of silverware. It does not circulate in commercial transactions with any country and the convenience of these manufacturers, in this respect, can better be met by supplying small stamped bars of the same standard, avoiding the useless expense of coining the dollar for the same purpose.

To which Kelley added:

> It is impossible to retain the double standard. The values of gold and silver continually fluctuate . . . Hence all experience has shown that you must have one standard coin which shall be a full legal tender, and then you may promote your domestic convenience by having a subsidiary coinage of silver which shall circulate in parts of your country as legal tender for a limited amount.

On another occasion, Representative Kelley maintained that those opposing the bill were dupes of the bullion dealers who were making exorbitant profits trafficking in the old standard dollars.

After passage of the Act, its legislative history and provisions—including the repeal of the silver dollar—were discussed in the commercial and banking press. Instead of reacting critically, Congress, in June 1874, passed a general revision of the Act which not only omitted the silver dollar, but deprived the earlier dollars of their legal tender.

As the price of silver continued to decline, the agitation for free coinage at a 16 : 1 ratio increased inversely. By 1878, the movement was in full swing, and Representative Kelley, with his India rubber conscience and amenability to partisan interests, emerged as a champion of "free silver." On March 9, 1878 he declared:

> In connection with the charge that I advocated the bill which demonetized the standard silver dollar, I say that, though the chairman of the Committee on Coinage, I was ignorant of the fact that it would demonetize the silver dollar or of its dropping the silver dollar from our system of coins as were those distinguished Senators, Messrs. Blaine and Vorhees, who were then members of the House.

Even more incredible is Kelley's statement on May 10, 1879:

> All I can say is that the Committee on Coinage, Weights and Measures, who reported the original bill, were faithful and able, and scanned its provisions closely; that as their organ I reported it; that it contained provision for both the standard silver dollar and the trade dollar. Never having heard until a long time after its enactment into law of the substitution in the Senate of the section which dropped the standard dollar, I profess to know nothing of its history but I am prepared to say that in all the legislation of this country there is no mystery equal to the demonetization of the standard silver dollar of the United States.

A still greater mystery was the source of Kelley's recollections . . .

The "friends of silver" contended that demonetization was responsible for the depreciation of silver and general depression. In support of their view, they cited Hamilton's remark that to demonetize either metal would cause a coin shortage, sinking of prices, and great distress. This argument overlooked some embarrassing facts. First, there was no federal paper currency when Hamilton spoke, and the few private banks issued only a small volume of notes. Secondly, Hamilton's demonetization meant literally that one or the other metal would not be used for coinage. The demonetization of silver wrought by the Mint Acts of 1853 and 1873 was only a *limitation* in its monetary use. Correctly administered, these laws would have provided a subsidiary coinage in exact proportion to the nation's requirements. Moreover, no demonetization, real or imaginary, could have affected the currency in 1873, since there had been no gold nor silver coins in circulation for a dozen years.

Such homely truths were best ignored, and the Act became widely known as the "Crime of 1873." The friends of silver referred to "the deep-laid plot" that had been engineered by a foreign conspiracy in order to increase our national debt, which would thus have to be paid in gold.[2] They even went so far as to accuse the English economist Ernest Seyd of having foisted the conspiracy. This charge was predicated on a remark made by Representative Hooper during the course of a House debate on April 19, 1872, that Seyd had read the first draft of the bill and furnished him with many valuable suggestions which were incorporated into it. On May 9, 1892, Frederick A. Lukenbach, a citizen of Denver and member of the Produce exchange, is said to have deponed before the Clerk of the Supreme Court that Seyd confidentially admitted to having received £100,000 from a European syndicate to bring about the desired legislation.[3] The only flaw in this testimony is the fact that Seyd was an avid bi-metallist who had urged Hooper to support the coinage of both a standard silver dollar and half dollar![4]

---

[2] *Silver in the Fifty-First Congress*, National Executive Silver Committee, 1890, Washington, D.C.
[3] *Silver and Gold Money*, John C. Henderson, 1893.
[4] Senate Misc. Doc. No. 29; 53rd Congress, 1st Session.

By 1873, a dollar bill had again become worth more than the intrinsic value of two subsidiary half dollars, making it possible for the Treasury Department to purchase silver bullion with greenbacks, coin the bullion, and redeem the outstanding fractional notes.

There were two reasons for not doing so. First, if the gold value of the greenbacks should again decline, the subsidiary coins would be exported. Secondly, it was illegal to issue subsidiary coins in exchange for paper currency. Linderman, however, in true Mint tradition, ordered the Government offices to issue the coins as change, which amounted to the same thing.

The action was not only illegal but ill-advised, for just two months later the value of the greenbacks declined, resulting in the disappearance of the new coins. Despite the fiasco, Senator Sherman, in December 1874, introduced a bill to redeem the fractional notes with subsidiary coins. Since the value of the coins and the notes were just on par, the decision was hazardous. After a bitter debate, the bill was enacted on January 14, 1875, becoming the Specie Resumption Act.

* * *

For some years following the gold rush, inflation had stayed the need of small coins in California. No dimes were struck at the San Francisco Mint until 1859, and no half dimes until 1863. Thereafter, the coinage of half dimes increased steadily, and during 1872 and 1873 the output at San Francisco almost equalled that of its entire nine preceding years. The figure would have even been higher but for the fact that the coin was abolished by the Act of February 12, 1873. Since minor coins were not struck at the San Francisco Mint, the loss of the half dime caused some difficulty in making change. Many items were priced at a dime, or "short bit," and persons paying for one of these with a quarter had often to accept a dime or Spanish bit as change. To alleviate this problem, Nevada Senator J. P. Jones, in February 1874, introduced a bill for the coinage of a twenty-cent piece. The bill was supported by Director Linderman, and enacted on March 3, 1875.

On August 7, 1874 Superintendent Pollock sent to Director Linderman the first patterns for a twenty-cent piece. The obverse design had been modeled by Joseph Alexis Bailly, a French-born Philadelphia sculptor, who furnished the Mint with a casting from which to make the hub. The reverse was evidently the work of William Barber. Pollock said that the coin too closely resembled the quarter, and he directed Barber to prepare additional patterns.

On March 31, 1875 Pollock submitted impressions from new dies, and promised Linderman that two or three additional varieties would be ready by the following week. On April 5, he wrote to the Director:

> Sir, I herewith enclose specimens of the twenty cent piece for your examination. Two in silver and two in copper are, as to design &c. in conformity with our present coinage. To distinguish these more readily from the Quarter dollar we have made the edge plain, not reeded. The other specimens, two each of silver and copper, are peculiar in design, very beautiful, but not conforming to our other coinage. They cannot, therefore, I presume, be adopted. . . .

One of the latter coins referred to by Pollock was undoubtedly Barber's "sailor head" design, with a shield device for the reverse.

On April 12, Pollock sent Linderman additional patterns showing the denomination as "⅕ of a dollar" and "20 cents." He said that he preferred any

Twenty-cent pieces. 1874 pattern, Bailly/Barber; 1875 patterns and adopted design by Barber.

of the previous designs to these. Linderman replied that the pattern with a shield device was very beautiful and would have been adopted but for the law. Instead, he selected the devices most resembling those on the other silver coins.

In a letter of the 15th, Pollock said:

> We propose to enlarge the legend "Liberty" by enlarging the shield a little, and whilst enlarging the scroll in which the letters are placed, to *raise* the letters instead of sinking them, as on the specimen sent [i.e. returned] to me. This raising of the letters will improve the appearance of the obverse, and make the word Liberty much more legible.

Despite its plain edge, the twenty-cent piece was constantly confused with the quarter. A bill for its repeal was introduced in July 1876, and finally passed May 2, 1878.

*   *   *

The passage of the Specie Resumption Act was followed by a sudden fall in the gold value of the greenbacks, making the new law inoperative. The Mint continued in the meantime to purchase bullion, coin it, and store the specie in the Treasury vaults. Gradually the value of the greenbacks rose to a point where subsidiary coins could be safely emitted. On April 17, 1876, Congress directed the Secretary of the Treasury to issue the coins in exchange for fractional paper currency, and by the Act of July 22, 1876, permitted their sale for greenbacks as well.

For a time it seemed too good to be true. In its June issue, *Galaxy* said that the appearance of silver coins had created such a sensation, people were again hoarding the pieces, and it was "almost as hard to get a dollar changed now as in 1861." Then, after taking a long look at the old, nondescript Liberty, the magazine added:

> Why is it that we have the ugliest money of all civilized nations? For such undoubtedly our silver coinage is. The design is poor, commonplace, tasteless, char-

Pattern half dollars of 1877. **Top and center rows** by George Morgan; **bottom** by William Barber

acterless, and the execution is like thereunto. They have rather the appearance of tokens or mean medals. One reason for this is that the design is so inartistic and so insignificant. That young woman sitting on nothing in particular, wearing nothing to speak of, looking over her shoulder at nothing imaginable, and bearing in her left hand something that looks like a broomstick with a woolen nightcap on it —what is she doing here?

As a result of such complaints, the engraving department, which already employed four artists (chief engraver William Barber, assistant engravers Charles Barber, Anthony Paquet, and William H. Key), was further enriched by the addition of George T. Morgan. Morgan had formerly worked for the British Royal Mint, and was hired in October 1876 as "special engraver" under a loose interpretation of the 8th section of the 1873 coinage law. He at once set to work making "improved" designs in competition with William Barber.

A letter of August 6, 1877 from Pollock to acting Director Robert Preston enclosed no less than thirty-two different pattern impressions in copper for silver coins. These are attributed as follows: By Barber (six) $1, (ten) 50¢ (two) 10¢; By Morgan (twelve) 50¢; By Paquet (two) 50¢. Several of these have apparently not survived.

Pattern half dollars of 1877 (continued). **Top and center** by William Barber; **bottom** by Anthony Paquet.

So far as the public was concerned the novelty of the silver coinage soon wore off. By the latter part of 1877, the continued depreciation of silver had begun to bring back the hundreds of millions of subsidiary pieces from Latin America, Canada and the West Indies, where they were now comparatively less valuable. This influx clogged the channels of trade, creating conditions similar to those prior to the Civil War. The situation was described in the November 1878 issue of *Bankers Magazine:*

> Under existing laws, or, at any rate, under the executive administration of existing laws, the people are subjected to constant annoyance and loss from our subsidiary silver. Probably the new coinage of that description under the Resumption Act of January 14, 1875, would not of itself have been sufficient to cause the glut and depreciation which we are witnessing. But the quantity in existence of the subsidiary silver of former coinage has proved to be far greater than anybody supposed. Those old coins have come out from their hiding places in such numbers, that the old and new together are more than can be floated at par with our actual currency which is the greenback, inasmuch as there is no government redemption of those coins, and inasmuch as the Government will only receive them for taxes less than five dollars, or when the tax exceeds the sum, then for only any fractional part of a dollar. The result is that many banks decline to receive them on deposit, or in large payments, and all business establishments which

receive a good deal of money in small sums, find themselves overloaded with these coins and unable to get rid of them without considerable loss. This is a practical, every-day grievance, to put an end to which is among the first duties of Congress.

The following month, Secretary Sherman suspended subsidiary coinage, and on June 9, 1879 an act was finally passed for its unlimited redemption.

Meanwhile, the silver interests and the mono-metallists were locked in battle and no one could foretell the result. In 1877, Director Linderman projected plans for a quintuple eagle, and ordered the striking of patterns. The aura of mystery surrounding these coins [5] has given rise to many fanciful theories, obscuring the purpose for which they were obviously intended.

Mintage figures indicate that the double eagle was by far the most popular gold coin, and that a still larger denomination would have been a great success. Moreover, Linderman, as a gold standard advocate, was undoubtedly interested in extending the monetary use of the metal.

On April 25, 1877 he wrote to Superintendent Pollock:

> Sir: In striking an experimental Fifty-Dollar piece, you will please instruct the Coiner to test the practicability of the Coinage of that size in the ordinary manner & by the use of the Large Press recently put up.
> When I was last at the Mint I told the Engraver to have the relief of the devices ($50 piece) as low as possible in order that the same may the more easily be brought up in coining.

Pollock replied on May 2:

> Sir, in compliance with your instructions of the 28th [sic] Ultimo, the Engraver will proceed to make a pair of dies for an experimental fifty-dollar gold coin; the devices to be identical with those on the obverse and reverse of the present double Eagle, and the dies to conform in other respects to the directions given in your letter.
> As suggested, I have conferred with the Assayer and the Engraver with regard to the thinness and concavity of the proposed new coin, and herewith transmit their views in writing. I entirely concur with the opinions they express.

The letter of the assayer, William DuBois, to Pollock is dated May 1, and reads:

> Sir, I have the following to offer in addition to what you will say, on the subject of the fifty-dollar gold coin.
> The double-concavity, on which the late Mr. Eckfeldt and myself spent much thought & made some experiments, was coupled with the idea of making thin coins, as a preventative of platinum-filling.[6] It would be of no use at all on a piece of higher value than ten dollars; and in fact is chiefly fitting for a five-dollar piece
> If a coin of fifty dollars is to be legalized, we must take the risk of fraudulent practices, for which it would offer a fine field.

Barber had written to Pollock the same day. He agreed with DuBois, adding that even the concavity would not prevent filling, but only vary the practice perhaps to "turning out the periphery or drilling the thicker parts, near the circumference, and then filling and gilding." He said it was a fixed rule that the

---

[5] They remained unknown until 1909, emerging in the collection of William Idler, one of th most favored individuals ever to have had dealings with the Mint.

[6] There was a widespread practice of splitting the edge of gold coins, hollowing out the middle and refilling it with platinum, which was then worth only six dollars an ounce. The double-con cavity mentioned by DuBois was caused by running the coin through the milling machine a secon time after striking. In 1878, the Mint experimented with quarter- and half-eagles of lesser thicknes and greater diameter than those in use.

larger and heavier the coin, the greater the temptation and facility offered to the counterfeiter.

Linderman seems nevertheless to have insisted on patterns, for on August 6, Pollock wrote to acting Director Preston: "The dies for the $50 gold coin are not yet completed. Will be able to send you specimens in copper, in a week or ten days." [7] These pieces were sent on the 30th.

An inventory of pattern and experimental dies in the Mint as of December 20, 1877, listed "3 obverse and 3 reverse dies for the $50 gold piece, plus 2 obverse dies for $50 gold piece with 'varied design.'" All of these were prepared by Barber.

1877 pattern for a quintuple eagle, or fifty-dollar piece, by William Barber.

In December 1876 and again in November 1877, the "friends of silver," led by Representatives Bland and Kelley, actually succeeded in passing through the House a free coinage bill restoring the old standard silver dollar. Although the bill was defeated in the Senate, Bland re-introduced it during the following year, when it again passed the House, this time by a vote of 163 to 34, with 92 abstaining. In the Senate, Mr. Allison modified the bill considerably before its passage. It was enacted on February 28, 1878 over the veto of President Hayes.

The Bland-Allison Act provided for the resumption of a 412½-grain silver dollar, of unlimited legal tender, to be issued in exchange for silver certificates of $10 or more. The Secretary of the Treasury was to purchase, at market price, between $2 and $4 million of silver bullion each month to be coined into dollars. At the deflated price of silver, each dollar was worth 9.2 per cent less than its face value. The coinage was to be used to purchase more bullion, and the seignorage paid into the Treasury. Thus, the more silver depreciated, the greater would be the Government's profit and the number of dollars coined.

The first patterns for the new dollar were struck in 1876, when Bland was menacing Congress with his free coinage bill. On August 1, 1876 Pollock wrote to Director Linderman:

Sir: I herewith send three impressions of the pattern dies prepared by Mr. Barber, for the proposed silver dollar. They were completed and handed to me this morning.

---

[7] Curiously, there is no record of the unique gold impressions now in the Smithsonian Institution.

The "Bland" dollar. **Top:** patterns by Barber; **bottom:** adopted design by Morgan.

Additional patterns for the dollar, the first two by Barber, the last two by Morgan.

No. 1. "Head of Liberty," without the motto "In God we trust" either on reverse or obverse. Reverse wreath etc.

No. 2. "Head of Liberty" on the obverse with motto "In God we trust" at the base of the Head. Reverse the same as No. 1.

No. 3. "Head of Liberty" on obverse, motto over the Head &c. Reverse the same as No. 1 and 2.

My preference would be for No. 3, with a slight alteration of the motto over the Head of Liberty. I will send you a specimen of the dollar with the alteration I have suggested, when completed by Mr. Barber, which will be in a few days.

These were the patterns with Barber's modified "sailor head" design.
On August 11, 1876 Pollock again wrote to Linderman:

Sir, When I sent you on the 1st inst. three impressions of the pattern dies for the proposed silver dollar, I then said I would send you when completed, a specimen with an alteration of No. 3 Motto (In God we trust) above the Head of Liberty. I now enclose the specimen referred to, and in my opinion, it is superior to those heretofore struck.

I herewith return the letter from Senator Sherman. I confess my surprise that No. 1 without the motto "In God we trust" was approved. I hope the day will never come when that motto will be omitted from our coins. In the hour of our nation's trial the Congress of the U. S. *unanimously*, authorized it.—the true patriotic and Christian sentiment of the country approved, and will approve, and may you never consent to its removal. Mr. Barber agrees with me in these opinions.

The Liberty Cap is jewelled (as such work is called) and the Head and arrangement of motto are artistic and appropriate. The 13 stars around the head improve the coin.

Linderman replied the following day that the alteration was a decided improvement and, "altogether this Head of Liberty may be regarded as equal if not superior to any heretofore prepared at the Mint." Despite this wholehearted endorsement, Barber furnished a new pair of pattern dies the following year.

In 1878, additional patterns of inferior style were submitted by Barber and Morgan. Both Liberty heads were massive, and classical in style. In Barber's design, the head is heavily-jowled, the eye stony, and the thyroid cartilage too prominent. Morgan's Liberty head is more feminine, but gives the impression of obesity. Barber's eagle is certainly the superior of the two; its head is reared, and every sinew expresses majesty and coiled power. By comparison, Morgan's bird is poorly drawn and uninspiring.

In a letter to Pollock on February 21, Linderman confided his choice of Morgan's design:

. . . The specimens struck from the dies prepared by Messrs. Morgan and Barber exhibit high skill as well as artistic taste and . . . there is little if any difference in their merits, but . . . since a choice has to be made, I have selected the one having the lowest relief and requiring the lightest power to bring up the devices and inscriptions. No mention however of my preference need be made until after the receipt of the specimens herein called for and notification to you of its adoption.

Linderman added that he had requested Morgan to make certain changes (i.e. in foliating the olive branch) in the reverse. Pollock submitted a revised pattern on the 25th, and the design was officially adopted on February 28. The Bland-Allison bill was enacted the same day, giving the Mint its busiest schedule since the early days of the flying eagle cent. On March 1, Pollock wrote to Linderman:

> Sir, Your telegram of today and your communication of yesterday, by mail, have been duly received.
>
> I had an immediate conference with Mr. Morgan who will proceed with all possible dispatch to complete the hubs for his design, which you inform me has been adopted. Our Engraver, Mr. Barber, has been instructed, and will proceed as soon as possible, to make the requisite collars and working dies.
>
> I have directed the Melter and Refiner to put his whole available force and furnaces to work immediately turning out ingots for the new silver dollars, and deliver to the Coiner daily, all the ingots that the latter can receive, and to store in his vaults any ingots that may be over from time to time, until the Coiner can take them.
>
> The Coiner has been instructed to roll the ingots, and cut, anneal, mill, and clean planchets to as large an amount daily as the facilities at his command will permit, and to accumulate as large a store of finished planchets as may be possible, so that when the working dies are ready we can proceed immediately to strike dollars to the full capacity of our coining presses, and maintain thereafter as continuous and large an outturn of these coins as the operative force and machinery of the Mint will permit.

The first "Bland" dollar was presented to President Hayes, who had vetoed the Act under which it was struck. Ultimately, in fact, the Bland-Allison Act satisfied no one. It subsidized the silver mining industry, but refused to allow it free coinage at a perverted ratio. The new dollars circulated widely in the West, and also in the South where the emancipated Negroes preferred silver to greenbacks, but only to a small extent in the North and the East. People in the latter areas seldom used the dollars except to pay taxes and customs duties, and the coins were immediately returned to the Government. In periods of increased prosperity and business activity, the "cartwheels" gained substantial circulation, but at other times the coins became superfluous and drove out gold in accordance with Gresham's law.

The second section of the Bland-Allison Act directed the President to initiate a new international monetary conference. Although the first conference had almost unanimously endorsed a single gold standard, Congress called the second "for the purpose of establishing, internationally, the use of bi-metallic money, and securing fixity of relative value between those metals." The members of twelve nations met at Paris on August 16, 1878. On behalf of the United States, Mr. Grosbeck introduced the following propositions: 1) that the unrestricted coinage of silver, and its use as unlimited legal tender, should be retained where it exists, and, as far as practicable, restored, where it has ceased to exist; and 2) that the use of both gold and silver as unlimited legal tender may be safely adopted; first by establishing an international ratio, and secondly by granting to each metal equal terms of coinage, making no discrimination between them.

These propositions were rejected by the European delegates who replied: 1) that while it is necessary to maintain in the world the monetary functions of silver as well as those of gold, the selection for use of one or the other or both simultaneously should be governed by the special position of each state or group of states; 2) that the question of restricting the coinage of silver also should be left to the discretion of each state or group of states; and 3) that the differences of opinion, even between states having the double standard, make it impossible to adopt an international ratio between the two metals. The conference adjourned on August 29.

In the meantime, another plan had been offered by inventor Wheeler H. Hubbell, the patentee of "goloid." Hubbell's goloid was a combination of gold and silver in equal amounts by value, and hence no different from the sym-metallic coinage proposed by Senator Hunter in 1851.

On November 5, 1877, a bill to authorize the coinage of goloid dollars and their fractions was introduced in the House, and referred to the committee on coinage, weights and measures.

The matter was duly taken up with the Mint, and on January 3, 1878 we find Pollock writing to Director Linderman:

> Sir, Your instructions of the 31st of December ultimo, based on a request, under date of Dec. 27th, from Hon. Alexander H. Stephens, Chairman of the Committee on Coinage of the House of Representatives, to have a pair of dies prepared from which to strike specimen dollars to illustrate the proposed "goloid" coin, were daily received, and have been communicated to our Engraver, who will set to work immediately to prepare the dies, with the inscriptions and designs suggested; but he cannot promise to have them ready under three weeks from this date. When completed the specimens of the required weight and composition, will be struck and forwarded, together with a bill for the value of the metal contained in them.

The first goloid dollars were struck on the 14th. The chief coiner, Oliver Bosbyshell, complained to Pollock that the color of the composition was no different from that of standard silver. He said a melter and refiner could slip him standard silver ingots, even by error, and that a "wicked coiner" would pawn off standard silver coins. On the following day, Bosbyshell sent Pollock specimen dollars of goloid and standard silver, both struck from the same dies. Only a defect in the letter "O" on the reverse of the silver dollar distinguished the two coins.

Linderman presented the specimens to the House committee on January 17 but if its members were convinced, Hubbell was not. The irate inventor accused the Mint of deliberately finishing the coins in a way to make them resemble standard silver.

On January 22, Linderman transmitted to Pollock a letter from the House committee, asking for new specimens of goloid coins "without an alloy dressing of metal placed upon the face of the coin but prepared and cleaned under the direction of Mr. Hubbell." Linderman enclosed Hubbell's directions, together with his own commentary thereon. He said that Hubbell apparently wanted to give a golden tinge to the coin by dissolving the copper, converting the silver into chloride, and dissolving the chloride by ammonia, which would leave film of gold upon the surface. Such a preparation, he added, would be useless since the film would disappear from the coin after a little wear.

While Congress was still toying with the goloid idea, Hubbell added variant sym-metallism which he called "metric-goloid."

A double eagle would contain 30 grams gold, 1.5 grams silver, and 3.5 gram copper. At the ratio of 16 : 1, the aggregate value of the metals was twenty dollars. Hubbell insisted that his composition would be lighter, richer in appearance, and more durable and sonorous than the present gold coinage.

On January 21, 1879 Representative Stephens introduced a bill to authorize

Experimental coinage: **Top:** 1878 goloid dollar by Barber, 1879 goloid metric dollar by Morgan, 1880 sym-metallic metric dollar by Morgan. **Bottom:** "stella," or four-dollar gold piece, by Barber, plus alternate obverse by Morgan.

metric-goloid coinage, and the Mint was asked to prepare a specimen double eagle. This time, Hubbell demanded three different impressions, the first finished as usual with sulphuric acid to give the gold a yellow color, the second with acid and alkali to give a purple-gold color, and the third with just alkali to give an orange color. Hubbell gave detailed directions for the last two processes. In a letter to acting Director Preston, Pollock said that he did not recommend such experiments, but that they would be done. The coins were struck on February 3.

In the same year, and again in 1880, the Mint struck two varieties each of metric dollars, goloid-metric dollars, and "stellas," or four-dollar gold coins. The stella was the brain-child of John Kasson, U.S. minister to Austria, and former chairman of the House coinage committee.[8] Kasson conceived the four-dollar piece as an approximate metrical equivalent to such European gold coins as the Austrian 8 florins and French 20 francs, though what international advantage coins of only approximate parity would enjoy is difficult to imagine.

By this time, the bi-metallic ratio had slipped to 18 : 1, and the gold reserves of most European nations were dwindling. A third international monetary con-

---

[8] J. Hewitt Judd, *United States Pattern, Experimental and Trial Pieces.*

ference met at Paris in April 1881, but for lack of agreement, adjourned without result. In the meantime, the vast majority of silver dollars issued under the Bland-Allison Act were flowing back to the Treasury as soon as they were issued. The coins could not be circulated, and their value as bullion was continually depreciating. Nevertheless, the Treasury was obliged to continue its purchases of silver, and coin additional dollars until Congress, in its wisdom, ordained otherwise. To prevent such an occurrence, the silver men loudly denounced the administration for "curtailing" the circulation of the coins.

By mid-1890, some 360 million silver dollars had been struck under the Bland-Allison Act, of which perhaps one sixth were in circulation. As the value of silver continued to decline, Congress was pressed from all sides for remedial legislation. In the House, a bill to restore the free coinage of silver was narrowly defeated. A similar bill was introduced in the Senate but, through the influence of Senator Sherman, replaced by a compromise bill providing for the monthly purchase of silver. This was enacted on July 14, 1890, and subsequently known as the Sherman Act.

The new law ordered the Treasury to purchase at market price 4½ million ounces of silver each month for the purpose of coining additional dollars. The Government was to pay for the bullion with Treasury notes which could be redeemed in gold or silver coin at the discretion of the Secretary of the Treasury. After the first year, the dollars were to be struck only as required for the redemption of the notes.

The Act declared that it was "the established policy of the U.S. to maintain the two metals on a parity with each other upon the present legal ratio or such ratio as may be provided by law." Secretary Windom reasoned that this could not be done except by submitting to public demand and redeeming the notes in gold. Otherwise, they would depreciate with the depreciation of silver, and destroy the parity between the two metals by creating a discrimination in favor of gold. A decision was thus made to pay out gold, and reissue the redeemed notes, together with the new issues. The result was a sudden rush on the gold reserves, particularly by European banks. Before long, the exportation and hoarding of gold had reached new peaks, and the nation found itself hurtling toward insolvency. A fourth international monetary conference met at Brussels in November 1892, but again adjourned without result. The following year brought a panic. More than three hundred banks suspended payment, and innumerable factories shut down. In answer to appeals from industrial and commercial organizations throughout the nation, President Cleveland, on August 8, 1893, urged Congress to repeal the purchase clause of the Sherman Act.

A bill for repeal was introduced by Representative William Wilson on August 11.

Bland then offered a series of amendments which he asked be considered in the following order:

> The vote shall be taken first on an amendment providing for the free coinage of silver at the present [Mint] ratio [16:1]. If that fails, then a separate vote to be had on a similar amendment proposing a ratio of 17 to 1; if that fails, on one proposing a ratio of 18 to 1; if that fails, on one proposing a ratio of 20 to 1. the above amendments fail, it shall be in order to offer an amendment reviving the act of the 28th of February 1878, restoring the standard silver dollar, commonly known as the Bland-Allison act; the vote then to be taken on the engrossed

ment and third reading of the bill as amended, or on the bill itself if all amendments shall have been voted down, and on the final passage of the bill without other intervening motions.

Bland called for a vote on the previous question which was carried by a vote of 219 to 99. The resolution was then adopted.

Maryland Representative Rayner spoke in favor of unqualified repeal, "without any conditions or provisos whatever." He explained his position at some length, exposing the sophistries of the silver men:

> I am not in favor of purchasing another ounce of silver, or of coining another dollar of it, either at the present ratio or at any other ratio that we can practically determine upon. Now, in saying this, I desire to add that I have no hostility whatever to the use of silver upon a proper basis as circulating medium; but with all the careful consideration I have been able to devote to this subject I am convinced beyond all doubt or question that its recognition by coinage, except upon international agreement, is a financial undertaking utterly impossible of accomplishment except at risk of ruin and disaster.
>
> The proposition that I had occasion to maintain in this House before, and that I again assert with all the emphasis I can, is that in my humble judgment the present ratio is unjust and arbitrary, rendered so by conditions that did not exist at the time of the demonetization of silver, in 1873; and that it lies not within the power of this Government, strong as it is, to corner the silver product of the mines to keep up the price upon a constantly declining market, to impress upon it a fictitious value, and by legislative decree compel the people to take it at a price in utter disproportion to the figure that it bears in every commercial center of the world. . .
>
> If this desperate system of finance, with nothing to justify it, with almost the whole intelligence of the country against it, with nothing in its track except disaster and ruin, is to prevail, then, in my opinion, until the day of a better judgment shall come, we might as well retreat from the lofty position we have occupied in the confidence of mankind, and descending, lock hands with every bankrupt government on earth that believes in the cheap manufacture of wealth at government mints, in cheap money, in broken contracts and in repudiated debts, and so believing have by reason of their faith been excommunicated as heretics from the roll of civilized communities and banished from the field of honor.
>
> I am aware of the fact that many of my colleagues, for whose opinions I entertain the greatest respect, assert, and it has been freely charged that the decline in the price of silver has been caused by its demonetization at the American mints and by what is constantly called "a conspiracy" to destroy it as a circulating medium among the governments of Europe. I deny this proposition, and the statistics will not sustain it. It may be true that the free coinage of silver at the mints would tend for a time to keep up the fictitious standard of the coin, but the value of the bullion would always be controlled by the market price; it would fluctuate.
>
> Like every other commodity, it would be governed by the laws of supply and demand, and eventually, according to every accepted axiom of political economy, the coinage price would become the bullion price; the unit of value would be the market value; the money basis would be the basis of the cheaper metal; the dearer metal would leave the avenues of trade; inflation would give way to panic; private obligations would be nullified; public obligations would be discredited, and the honor of the nation would be impaired.
>
> Now it is claimed that what we require in this country is a system of bimetallism, a bimetallic standard—that is to say the free use of both gold and silver at the Government mints. But Mr. Speaker, we will never have this until the commercial nations of the earth agree upon a proper ratio, and just so long as the Sherman act remains upon the statute book so long is an international ratio a financial impossibility. So long as we purchase silver and part with gold, so long will monetary conferences result in failure. When we cease purchasing silver and proclaim to the world that the gold dollar is the standard and the unit of American value, then

we can bring our rivals to terms, because in my opinion, there is not a sufficie amount of gold in existence to supply the demands of commerce and the necessit of the world's circulation. (Applause)

So long as the treasury continues to act as a pawn broker's shop for the bene of the Colorado and Nevada mines, so long will Great Britain and Germany refu to appreciate the collateral securities that we hold in our vaults; but when a silv certificate can be redeemed at par and a silver dollar is intrinsically worth t inscription that it bears, then we can proudly and defiantly meet them upon t field of finance without the slightest sacrifice of the stability of our currency or t slightest surrender of our honor as a nation. (Applause) . . .

Now let us look for a moment at the arguments that have been used upon t other side. . . First, it is claimed that the coinage of silver will make money mo abundant. How will it do this? Who will get this money? When a Colorado mi owner sends $600 worth of silver to the mint and the mint returns him a thousa: silver dollars for it, who gets a thousand silver dollars? Do the people get it? Do it increase the wages of the miner who has dug the silver from the earth? I expe not. I expect that the only persons who will profit by this iniquitous transacti will be those who sell the silver and control the product.

Now, I ask the Democracy of this House whether they are willing to stimul: an enterprise of this sort that deliberately robs the people to enrich a particu class who monopolize the mines. We who have never favored class legislation, a we prepared to lock hands with a few silver states to the utter ruin of the balan of the country? If more money is needed, can we not increase our currency up a legitimate basis? Is there no method known to the ingenuity of man besides device of this sort to enlarge the circulating medium of the country?

But it is said, if we do this, and coin silver at the present ratio, the price silver will be raised to the coinage value. What a shallow pretext that is! A scho boy would be ridiculed if he asserted any such proposition as this in any colle of the land. If the fiat of the Government can create values, what right have we select silver and convert it from a commodity into a coin? Well, it is claimed th this should be done because the Constitution says so. Now, we all have a Co stitution before us. Point to me the clause that says so. You cannot do it becau it is not there. Not a word about a ratio, not a word about the coinage of eith gold or silver for the Government of the United States. Yes, but it is said it w raise prices. I am not in favor of raising prices, on general principles. But how w cheap money raise prices? Is not the producer a consumer when he sells? Will not be compelled to buy?

No, Mr. Speaker, there is only one thing that it will do, and I admit that it w accomplish that. It will allow the debtor to scale his debts. It will be a weapon the hands of a dishonest borrower to break his contract and pay his creditor in coin different from the one that was impliedly contracted for. To such an arrang ment as this I am unalterably opposed, and I would stand here and let eve species of legislation go by default before I would favor any system that wou sow dishonor through the land, that would humiliate us in the eyes of mankind, a that would cover us with shame in every portion of the country where justice respected and honor prevails. . .

I ask what earthly right have the silver mine owners to haunt these halls d manding protection for their investment? Is the Government bound to guarant to them a profit upon their enterprise? Is the Government in partnership with t mine owners? I deny it. Does the statute bind the Government of the Unit States to maintain the ratio of 16 to 1 when it ought to be 28 to 1? I deny There is no contract which is binding or valid which is not based on considerati and founded on mutuality.

But if there is a partnership, let it be forthwith dissolved, and in the decree dissolution let there be a clause embodying the cardinal principle of government equity that we will never stamp a lie upon our coin to satisfy the greed or avari of any section of the country or any set of men, no matter what may be the influence or how potent or powerful they may be.

Rayner's speech was followed by those of Representatives Bland and William Jennings Bryan. The debate was partisan and bitter. It was charged that the panic had been deliberately precipitated by a conspiracy for the purpose of repealing the Sherman Act. At one point Bryan said:

> When a crisis like the present arose and the national bank of his day sought to control the politics of the nation, God raised up an Andrew Jackson, who had the courage to grapple with that great enemy, and, by overthrowing it, he made himself the idol of the people and reinstated the Democratic party in public confidence.[9]

The silver men admitted the "imperfections" of the Sherman Act but opposed its repeal until "something better" was adopted. The "something" was, of course, a bill for the free coinage of silver at a perverted ratio.

On August 28, the bill for repeal, together with Bland's amendments, was brought up for a vote in the House. The amendment for free coinage at a 16 : 1 ratio was defeated 226 to 125. Bland's other amendments were also lost, and the bill finally passed by a vote of 239 to 108.

In the Senate, the bill was vigorously debated, and finally passed in an amended form on October 29. It was agreed to by the House and signed by President Cleveland on November 2, 1893.[10]

The repeal of the silver purchase clause added new grist to the propaganda mill. The "friends of silver" bewailed the iniquities committed by Wall Street capitalists against the farmers, merchants, and laboring classes. These evils were enumerated and illustrated in a series of little pamphlets called *Coin's Financial School* (surnamed *Coin's Financial Fool*), which were distributed among persons ignorant of rudimentary economics. From 1876 to 1896, the silver interests steadily gained strength. The climax came in the latter year, when that magnificent bellwether William Jennings Bryan seized control of the Democratic party, emerging as presidential candidate.

Bryan, as a Representative from Nebraska, had risen to fame through his powerful advocacy of tariff reduction. By 1892, however, he found himself groping for a new platform, and seeing his district revamped to exclude Omaha, he aligned himself with the farming interests which favored the free coinage of silver. The farmers had been told that bi-metallism meant more and freer money and, consequently, higher prices for their goods. Bryan hadn't found time to study up on the question before he went barnstorming. He told the farmers: [11] "I don't know anything about free silver. The people of Nebraska are for free silver and I am for free silver. I will look up the arguments later."

Bryan is said to have finally "educated" himself with *Coin's Financial School*. For this reason, perhaps, his speeches seldom strayed from the moral issue:

> This is not a contest for the supremacy of one of two metals . . . If the gold standard advocates win, this country will be dominated by the financial harpies of Wall St. I am trying to save the American people from that disaster—which will mean the enslavement of the farmers, merchants, manufacturers and laboring classes to the most merciless and unscrupulous gang of speculators on earth—the money power.[12]

---

[9] Bryan did well to compare himself with Jackson who, in his own time, wrecked the Bank of the United States and caused a money panic.

[10] The Act, however, did not prohibit the coinage of silver dollars from bullion already at hand, and large quantities were struck through 1904.

[11] Paxton Hibbon, *Peerless Leader, William Jennings Bryan,* Farrar and Rinehart, Inc., 1929.

[12] Ibid.

In the Democratic convention of 1896, Bryan delivered his famous "Cross of gold" speech, sweeping aside the favorite "Silver Dick" Bland, and winning the nomination. He began, as always, with his irresistible appeal to self-righteousness.

> This is not a contest between persons. The humblest citizen in all the land, when clad in the armour of a righteous cause, is stronger than all the hosts of error . . .

Now he united the different strands of labor, exhalting their economic role:

> The man who is employed for wages is as much a businessman as his employers; the attorney in a country town is as much a businessman as the corporation counsel in a great metropolis; the merchant at the cross-roads store is as much a business-man as the merchant of New York; the farmer who goes forth in the morning and toils all day—who begins in the Spring and toils all Summer—and who by the application of brain and muscle to the natural resources of the country creates wealth, is as much a businessman as the man who goes upon the board of trade and bets upon the price of grain; the miners who go down a thousand feet into the earth, or climb two thousand feet upon the cliffs and bring forth from their hiding places the precious metals to be poured into the channels of trade are as much businessmen as the few financial magnates who, in a backroom, corner the money of the world. . .

Finally, Bryan persuaded his listeners of their plight, urging them to rise up and overcome the oppressor:

> It is for these that we speak. We do not come as aggressors . . . We have peti-tioned, and our petitions have been scorned; we have entreated and our entreaties have been disregarded; we have begged, and they have mocked when our calamity came. We beg no longer; we entreat no more; we petition no more. We defy them!
> Having behind us the producing masses of this nation and the world, supported by commercial interests, the laboring interests, and the toilers everywhere, we will answer their demand for a gold standard by saying to them: "You shall not press down upon the brow of labour this crown of thorns, you shall not crucify mankind upon a cross of gold."

It was a memorable night for Bryan. Men cheered, women wept, and far into the night one could hear the barbarous chant: "No crown of thorns, no cross of gold" and other disjointed phrases strung on the tunes of popular religious hymns.

Probably no candidate ever campaigned with Bryan's zeal. But if the young crusader poured in the sum of his personal energies, Republican William Mc-Kinley drew upon the united resources of big business everywhere. Moneyed institutions offered blandishments and exerted pressure. It was suggested that there would be five-year extensions on mortgages if Bryan lost. And so he did, by an electoral vote of 271 to 176, though the popular vote was uncomfortably close. Nominated for a second time in 1900, Bryan chose to run again on a free silver plank. This time he was decisively defeated, and Congress, as though to save face, declared gold the standard value. The nation heaved a sigh of relief, and large quantities of gold which had been hoarded for fear of Bryan's elec-tion returned to the market. As one newspaper summed it up, no one in history had ever filled so many people with such a prolonged fear without actually killing them.

The Trade Dollar

Since the history of this anomalous coin is to some extent independent of other Mint issues, it is given as an addendum to the present chapter.

The first patterns for a trade dollar (if we include the commercial dollars which differ only in name) were struck in 1871, using a left-over obverse die of J. B. Longacre. In the following year, Barber copied the Longacre design and added two trade dollar reverses, one with a wreath device, the other with a standing eagle.

On May 31, 1873, Pollock forwarded to Director Linderman seven different patterns and a plaster model for the trade dollar. Linderman replied on June 2 as follows:

> Sir: I have to acknowledge the receipt of your letter of the 31st ultimo, also seven pattern pieces of the trade-dollar. Having submitted all the specimens to the Secretary of the Treasury, and taken his instructions upon the subject I have to inform you that it is decided to adopt for the *obverse* and *reverse* of the new dollar the specimens returned herewith, and described briefly as follows:
>
> *Obverse.* A female figure seated upon bales of cotton (a sheaf of wheat in the rear) holding in her right hand, which is extended toward the open sea, an olive branch—date of coinage, thirteen stars surrounding the figure, and the motto "in God we Trust" at the base of the device.
>
> *Reverse.* The figure of an Eagle, and on a scroll in the open field above "E Pluribus Unum," and above that the inscription United States of America. Below the Eagle are the inscriptions 420 grains, 900 fine, and trade-dollar and a scroll bearing the motto "in God we Trust."
>
> The motto "in God we Trust" *on the reverse will be omitted,* it appearing on the obverse which has been selected.
>
> It is suggested that both the motto "in God we Trust" and the inscription "Liberty" be made to appear plainer than upon the specimen.
>
> The omission of the motto "in God we Trust" on the *reverse* will require a re-arrangement of the inscription of the weight and fineness.
>
> It is also suggested that the two stars on the reverse be omitted.
>
> With the foregoing suggestions as to minor details the completion of the matter is confided to yourself and your officers. The Secretary desires the coin issued as early as possible.
>
> It is but proper that I express my appreciation of the zeal and ability with which this work has been performed on the part of yourself and the officers of the Philadelphia Mint.
>
> Please return the specimens after comparing the same with my suggestions as to minor details in the final preparation of the dies. Very respectfully, etc.

Linderman evidently chose his obverse and reverse from two different patterns, as can be seen from the plate. In the modified design the lower motto was omitted and the eagle enlarged to fill the space.

On July 11, Pollock wrote to Linderman: [13] "I send you specimen of trade dollar in tin struck today. We will commence the regular coinage of trade dls. in a few hours."

When the first trade dollars reached Canton, an assay was immediately taken, and in October 1873, the following proclamation was published:[14]

---

[13] J. Hewitt Judd, *United States Pattern, Experimental and Trial Pieces.*

[14] *Bankers Magazine,* Nov. 1877; George G. Evans, *Illustrated History of the United States Mint,* 1885.

Patterns for the trade dollar. **Top:** 1871, Longacre's obverse design with Barber's commercial dollar reverse; 1873, Barber design; 1873, obverse by J. A. Bailly, reverse by Barber. **Bottom:** 1873, Barber design.

Trade dollar (continued). **Top:** 1873, the first two patterns by Barber, the third Bailly/Barber.
Bottom: adopted design by Barber.

There has lately come to Hong Kong a newly coined American Eagle Dollar, called the "Trade Dollar," and Sir Brooke Robinson, the British Consul, having requested that officers might be appointed to assay it, the Viceroy and Haikwan thereupon appointed officers to melt it down and assay it, (in concert with an officer from the British Consulate) . . . Taels 111.6 of this new Eagle Dollar are equal to 100 Haikwan Taels of pure silver. Minutes of the assay were drawn up in proof thereof . . .

This Proclamation, therefore, is for the information of you merchants, traders, soldiers, and people of every district. You must know that the "Eagle Trade Dollar" that has lately come to Hong Kong has been jointly assayed by officers specially appointed for the purpose, and it can be taken in payment of duties, and come into general circulation. *You must not look upon it with suspicion.* At the same time rogues, sharpers, and the like, are hereby strictly forbidden to fabricate spurious imitations of this new Eagle Dollar, with a view to their own profit.

And should they dare to set this prohibition at defiance, and fabricate false coin, they shall, upon discovery, most assuredly be arrested and punished. Let every one obey with trembling! Let there be no disobedience!

Although Chinese merchants greatly esteemed the trade dollar for its weight (it contained three quarters of a grain fine silver more than the Peso), they could seldom turn it to a profit since the coins were received at most Chinese ports at their assayed value and not by tale.

From a domestic view, the trade dollar was merely an overweight, subsidiary coin which could be purchased from the Mint for 378 grains of silver, plus the coining charge. Realizing that a continued depreciation would soon make this profitable, Representative Regan, in March 1875, introduced a bill to increase the legal tender of the coin from five to fifty dollars. The bill passed the House, and might have been enacted but for the fact that Senator Jones tried to tack on a free coinage provision for the standard silver dollar. By the following year, trade dollars could be purchased with advantage from the Mint, and millions of the coins suddenly appeared in California.

In an effort to drive the "trades" from circulation, Congress on July 22, 1876, revoked their legal tender status, and directed the Secretary of the Treasury to limit their coinage to the volume required for export.

A better solution would have been to suspend the coinage of trade dollars and permit their redemption. By continuing to issue the demonetized coin, the Treasury only worsened the situation. The trade dollars were now forced into circulation by brokers who manipulated the value of the coins, buying and selling them alternately at the expense of merchants and others.

In his report of June 1878, Secretary of the Treasury Sherman defended the demonetization of the trade dollar, saying that the "limited legal tender quality originally given to it was taken away before any of the coins were put into domestic circulation." He had apparently forgotten that, as a Senator, he championed the demonetization "to relieve a condition of embarrassment in California,"[15] where some two millions of the trade dollars were circulating.

In the same report Sherman stated that "there was no further export demand" for the trade dollar, and that "during the year 1877, and the first few months of the present year, trade dollars to the amount probably of four million pieces, were placed in circulation in the States east of the Rocky Mountains, with a full knowledge on the part of the parties engaged in the business that the coin was not a legal tender."

---

[15] *Congressional Globe;* Senate debates, June 21, 1876.

It was not, however, until October 15, 1877 that the Secretary actually directed the Philadelphia Mint and the New York Assay Office (and on October 19, the San Francisco and Carson City mints) "to discontinue until further order the receipt of deposits" for the coins.[16] Moreover, he was promptly gulled by a report that additional trade dollars were needed for the annual Chinese New Year's reckoning, and on November 5,[17] rescinded the order pertaining to the San Francisco Mint. Finally, on February 22, 1878, Sherman suspended the coinage of trade dollars for the second and last time.

It is curious that in his annual report, Sherman referred specifically to his October order which suspended the issue of the coins, but failed to mention that, less than a month later, he had ordered their resumption. Even stranger was his assurance to the Senate on February 26, 1885, that no trade dollars had been struck in 1878, when such pieces were circulating, and a total of 4,259,900 were recorded in the Mint Report of 1879. Sherman said:

> Sometimes tables are misleading, as was shown in the case of even my friend from Delaware [Mr. Bayard], who is usually so very accurate in his remarks. . . . he supposed that this [trade dollar] coinage was continued until 1878. It was continued into the fiscal year 1878, because the fiscal year 1878 commenced on the 1st of July, 1877; but the coinage of the trade dollar was discontinued on the 20th of October 1877, in Philadelphia, and three or four days afterward in California, as soon as by course of mail the order to discontinue might reach the mint at San Francisco.

By the time Sherman finally acted to suspend the coinage of trade dollars, enormous quantities were in domestic circulation, being used in a sordid traffic. This was described by members of the New York Mercantile Exchange, in a memorial to Congress, February 3, 1883:

> We are put to great inconvenience and pecuniary loss by a coin known as the trade dollar, which is not a legal tender in payment of debts, and which, notwithstanding, is so largely received and recognized as a dollar by the community that we cannot without loss of trade individually refuse to accept it in payment, and which, being not taken on deposit by the banks, and not accepted in payment of dues to the Government, we are compelled to sell at a discount.
>
> Some persons employing operatives make a practice of buying at a discount these coins and paying them at par value to their operatives, who again pay them to the retailers of goods, and these, again, pay them to us, and we, not being able to deposit them or pay them in large amounts to our creditors, are compelled to sell them to brokers at a discount for legal money. It results that there is a continual loss falling upon us, and a corresponding profit reaped by such unscrupulous persons.
>
> The United States Government coined and put into circulation said trade dollars, made them a limited legal tender, and subsequently repudiated them by taking away their legal-tender function and refusing to receive them for its own duties.
>
> The present status of this coin causes it to be a nuisance to us and disgrace to the nation. It seems to us absurd that a coin containing 420 grains of coin silver should be refused the legal-tender function as a dollar, and be forced thereby to a discount, while a coin containing 7½ grains less of coin silver should be given that function, and thereby kept at par.
>
> We respectfully urge upon Congress that it restore to the trade dollar its legal tender function, and that it receive it and issue silver certificates for it as it now receives and issues such certificates for the standard silver dollar.

---

[16] 45th Cong. 2nd Sess; Senate Exec. Doc. No. 80.
[17] Ibid.

Various other petitions urged Congress to reinstate the trade dollar, or at least to permit its redemption, and several bills were introduced for this purpose. In his annual report for 1883, Secretary of the Treasury Folger advised redemption, despite Sherman's earlier view. Folger wrote:

> The reading of the laws taught the people that the trade dollar was a coin of their sovereignty, and for the redemption of which, at an unabated value, their Government was bound . . . It is plain that a busy people, finding this coin afloat in the channels of business, styled a coin of the United States, would readily believe that it was an authentic issue of the Government and to be redeemed by the Government, the same as other money put out by it . . . It is best, once and for all, to call it in and put it out of possible use.

Most of the bills introduced for redeeming the trade dollars provided for their recoinage into standard dollars under the Bland-Allison Act. This measure, however, was vigorously resisted by the silver interests.

By the summer of 1883, most merchants had refused to accept any more trade dollars and some unloaded their accumulations on unwary producers. In its September issue, *Bankers Magazine* reported that "There seems to be a thorough determination in nearly all quarters in this country to get rid of the trade dollars now in existence, and to have no more of them coined."

In November, the same magazine stated:

> Inquiries in New York, in the region where the trade in butter, cheese, eggs vegetables, and fruit is the most active, showed that the success of the movement to banish trade dollars had been complete. Many of the persons had some of this money on hand when the refusal to take it became general, and lost on sums varying from five to a hundred dollars. They were well satisfied with the result of their experiment, however, and did not now have to resort to the brokers two or three times a week to sell what they had received . . .

Confectioners and liquor dealers, according to another part of the article were willing to receive trade dollars, but they would only give credit check and not coins in change.

By February 1887, when Congress, ostensibly to relieve the poor, passed a law redeeming trade dollars, most of the coins had passed into the hands of speculators. The silver interests were likewise appeased by an amendmen which counted the purchases of trade dollar bullion as distinct from those required by the Bland-Allison Act. In fact, the only virtue of the Act was that refused to redeem defaced or mutilated pieces. This disposed of the vast majority of the trade dollars, which had been "chop-marked" (i.e., punched with guarantees) by Chinese merchants.

The bill was ignored by President Cleveland, and became a law without his signature on February 19, 1887.

CHAPTER 21

The Barber Coinage

AS EARLY AS 1879, PUBLIC DISSATISFACTION with the "Bland" dollar led Barber and Morgan to submit new designs. William Barber died the same year, and was succeeded as chief engraver by his son Charles. The latter, who had almost been retired on Morgan's appointment, soon became an influential figure in the Mint. Morgan was reduced to assistant engraver, and William Key was given notice in 1885.

In 1881, Barber designed a uniform set of copper-nickel minor coins for Mint superintendent A. L. Snowden, who was attempting to revive interest in Wharton's plan. Although Snowden met with little success, patterns were struck during the same year and the following one, and Barber's Liberty head design was finally adopted on the five-cent piece in 1883.

It was the first time in twenty-four years that a change of devices had been authorized for an old coin. But Barber's triumph was short-lived. He had indiscreetly omitted the word "cents" from the legend, and the five-cent pieces were at once gilded and passed off as half eagles. A new hub was hastily prepared.

In 1882, while Barber was still preoccupied with his five-cent piece, Morgan designed an attractive set of patterns for the quarter, half dollar and dollar. Thereafter, for a number of years, the engravers produced little in the way of original work.[1]

---

[1] The few essays known for the period 1883-1890 were intended as experimental pieces rather than improvements in design. The most notable of these are the 1883 five-cent pieces with different proportions of copper and nickel, the 1884-85 annular silver cent and five-cent pieces, and the 1885 silver dollar with lettered edge.

In his annual report of 1887, Director Kimball called attention to the "popular desire for an improvement of the coinage in respect to the present designs." He said:

> The designs impressed upon the coins of any nation, ancient or modern, are accepted as an expression of the art of their time. But few citizens, who, with an artistic sense, have carefully scrutinized the current coins of this Republic, would consent to accept as a standard of excellence for their own day and generation almost any of the present compositions of statutory devices. The inferiority of our coinage to the same kind of work by almost every other advanced nation of the earth, as well as to the well-known work of numerous able designers in relief at home, seems to be perceived by all who have given attention to the subject, and to be keenly felt by many as unworthy of the development which the arts of sculpture and design have here attained. . .
>
> If new designs for present, or for statutory, devices be invited, the question naturally arises, how far competition shall be general or public.
>
> That a public competition for designs in relief would be productive of satisfactory results does not appear likely, and is certainly contrary to the experience of this Bureau in the way of suggestions from the public in such matters. It is believed, in agreement with section 3510, Revised Statutes, that desirable results are rather to be sought from the special engagement of the services of artists "distinguished in their respective departments of art."
>
> The question now arises who shall decide between the claims of artists more or less distinguished. This onerous responsibility falling, in terms of section 3510, upon the Director of the Mint, is virtually shared with the Secretary of the Treasury. Perhaps this is the only division of responsibility practicable under an official limitation.
>
> In the selection of designs, however, this responsibility might be further divided, not necessarily by law, so as to admit also of the services of judges distinguished for their discernment in matters of art and design, such judges, on the invitation of the Secretary of the Treasury, to act with the Director of the Mint, in the acceptance or rejection of designs submitted.
>
> The above suggestions are made not without full recognition of the fact that the voice of every citizen of the United States is heard upon a matter of art or aesthetics such as a design employed on a familiar coin of the Republic; or the fact that while distinguished artists stand ready to offer designs, no public officer could reasonably be called upon to pass upon the professional merit of artists or the art-value of their productions.

However, no immediate action was taken by Kimball, because of what he believed to be a limitation in the revised Mint statutes of 1873 and 1874. Section 3510 of the latter read:

> The engraver shall prepare from the original dies already authorized all the working-dies required for use in the coinage of the several mints, and, when new coins or devices are authorized, shall, if required by the Director of the Mint, prepare the devices, models, molds, and matrices, or original dies, for the same; but the Director of the Mint shall nevertheless have power, with the approval of the Secretary of the Treasury, to engage temporarily for this purpose the services of one or more artists, distinguished in their respective departments of art, who shall be paid for such service from the contingent appropriation for the mint at Philadelphia.

Kimball believed that the word "authorized" referred to Congress, and that no change of design could be legally undertaken without enactment. He specifically condemned the recent alterations in the dollar and five-cent piece. Whatever the merits of his argument, Kimball induced Senator Morill to present a bill amending the ambiguous section. The bill, which passed on September 26,

1890, authorized the Treasury Department to change the devices on the coins at any time after twenty-five years, and those currently on the silver dollar and five-cent piece "as soon as practicable after passage of this act."[2]

To secure the best possible designs, the Treasury Department decided to hold a competition among ten of the most distinguished artists in America. A letter of invitation was sent to Augustus Saint-Gaudens, J. Q. A. Ward, Daniel French, Olin Warner Herbert, Herbert Adams, Charles S. Niehaus, Miller Mac-Monies, Kenyon Cox, Will S. Low, and H. S. Mowbray. The artists, after a conference, jointly replied:

> The undersigned, having been invited to prepare designs for a new coinage for the United States, beg respectfully to state that the conditions of the competition as given in the circular letter of invitation are such as to preclude the possibility of any good result from it. The time given for the preparation of designs is too short and the compensation altogether insufficient, while no assurance is given as to who will make the awards.
>
> They beg to suggest the following terms of competition as such as they could accept:
>
> 1. The awards to be made by a jury of competent artists of standing in the profession, to be chosen by vote of the competitors, by presidents of the great art institutions or otherwise.
>
> 2. At least three months to be allowed for the production of sketch designs, and at least six months to be allowed for the production of completed models if these are to be insisted upon.
>
> 3. One hundred dollars to be paid out to each artist competing for each sketch design submitted, or $500 to be paid to each artist competing for each completed model accepted.
>
> 4. One thousand dollars in addition to the sum paid for competitive sketches or models finally accepted.
>
> 5. The obverse and reverse of any coin to be designed by the same artist and the reverse of the present half-dollar, quarter-dollar and dime to be abandoned.

On recovering from its initial shock, the Treasury Department gave up the idea of a serious contest. It arranged instead for a public competition to be judged by a committee consisting of Augustus Saint-Gaudens, the Boston gem and seal engraver Henry Mitchell, and the Mint's own engraver, Charles Barber.

The results were as discouraging as Kimball perdicted. At one point, Saint-Gaudens confided to Director Leech that there were only four men competent to do such designing, of which three were in France and he was the fourth. He could say this without egotism, he added, because of having made a special study of the subject before attaining celebrity as a sculptor.

Barber was willing to go a step further, especially after observing Saint-Gaudens' preference for high relief which was impossible to coin by modern machinery. In a conference with the Director, he said he knew of no one who could even assist him in preparing original designs.

On July 3, 1891 the committee submitted its results to Secretary of the Treasury Foster:

> Dear Sir: We would respectfully report, that in conformity with your written request, we have opened in the presence of the Director of the Mint, the new designs or models submitted for the silver coins of the United States, under the Department circular of April 4, 1891, and have carefully examined the same.

---

[2] Ironically, the designs on these two coins were the last to be changed.

We are of the opinion that none of the designs or models submitted are such a decided improvement upon the present designs of the silver coins of the United States as to be worthy of adoption by the Government.

We would respectfully recommend that the services of one or more artists distinguished for work in designing and relief, be engaged at a suitable compensation to prepare, for the consideration of the Department, new designs for the coins of the United States, Very respectfully etc.

Further gleanings on the competition are given in the *Boston Transcript* for July 31: [3]

"It is not likely that another competition will ever be tried for the production of designs for United States coins," said Mr. Leech, the Director of the Mint, yesterday. "The one just ended was too wretched a failure. Doubtless it was the first contest of the sort ever opened by any Government to the public at large.[4] The result is not very flattering to the boasted artistic development of this country, inasmuch as only two of the three hundred suggestions submitted were good enough to receive honorable mention. . . . No alteration is to be made in the gold coins, because they are really exquisite now and could hardly be improved upon. It is realized that the money of a nation is expressive of its art culture. Therefore, lest posterity imagine the present generation to have been barbarous, it is desirable that our silver pieces should be as handsome as may be.

"I have told our engraver," said Mr. Leech to another reporter a few days ago, "to prepare me a set of designs for the subsidiary coins to be submitted to Secretary Foster. I shall not do anything about the dollar for some time. There is no hurry about it, and the weather is too warm for us to worry ourselves about anything which does not require immediate attention. Our engraver at Philadelphia is the only competent person to prepare these designs, but it does not follow from the action I have taken that his work will be final. Of course, he receives no additional compensation for this. It is part of his regular work. I do not see any prospect of getting designs elsewhere in this country. We might get them in France. The French coin work is of the most artistic description. But the people of the United States would never forgive us if we went outside this country for our designs. To be sure, our designer is of an English family, but he is regularly in the employ of the Mint."

On August 8, 1891 Director Leech wrote to R. W. Gilder, art critic for *Century Magazine:*

Dear Sir: The cutting from the New York Tribune, containing your letter, in regard to coin designs, was received.

For your information I would say that the Engraver of the mint at Philadelphia has prepared some designs for the subsidiary coins, which he exhibited to me and to Mr. Henry Mitchell of Boston, and the latter gentleman was decidedly pleased with them. I suggested some modifications which the Engraver has endeavored to carry out in the models, but after an examination of the models on Monday of this week I was not entirely satisfied with them, and changes will be made which will occupy some weeks longer.

Mr. Barber comes from three generations of mint engravers and designers, and has done excellent work in coin designing, and is in every way equipped for this important duty.

Artistic designs for coins, which would meet the ideas of an art critic like yourself, and artists generally, are not always adapted for practical coinage.

When the designs are completed it is my intention to submit them to the Secretary and possibly the President, and I should be pleased to have you see them and I believe they will commend themselves to your judgment and taste.

If it should be decided to change the more important coins, that is, the gold

---

[3] "The New Designs for Our Coinage," *American Journal of Numismatics*, July, 1891.
[4] Evidently Leech did not know of Snowden's similar attempt in 1853.

coins and the silver dollar, I should consider the advisability of employing some skilled artist outside of the Mint service.

My only object is to improve the appearance of our coins, and if I find that this can be done satisfactorily within the mint service I see no good reason to go beyond it. Very respectfully etc.

By October, Barber had replaced his original standing Liberty design with an idealized head, and was at work simplifying the reverse model. A few late suggestions seem to have been offered by Director Leech, for on the 2nd we find the artist, with obvious irritation, writing to superintendent Bosbyshell:

Sir, Before passing upon the criticism of reverse for Half Dollar sent by the Director I would respectfully say that I am quite ready and willing to make any change in design, provided the suggestion in my judgment is a good one, but I must ask that criticism comes to an end before I am too far advanced with the die, as each suggestion involves going back to the starting point, and any and all labor that may have been put upon the work to advance the completion of the dies is absolutely lost. I mention this because when the Director was here, I was instructed to proceed with the dies which I did and now have the reverse considerably advanced.

The great seal is described as follows. An Eagle displayed, bearing on his breast a shield, in his dexter talon an olive branch, in his sinister talon a bundle of arrows. With his beak he holds a scroll bearing the motto E Pluribus Unum, above and around the head are thirteen stars, clouds and rays.

The Diplomatic medal engraved 1776, and the first Indian Peace medal engraved in this department in 1882 commemorating the centennial of the adoption of the Great Seal also has this same design, and was prepared at much trouble and research from the best data obtainable and I believe is correct as adopted 1782. From this material I formed my design adapting it to the requirement of a coin. In regard to the ribbon flowing over the neck of the Eagle being "contrary to artistic principles," I am sorry to say as an artist I beg to differ with the Director. The Diplomatic medal to which I refer was engraved by one of the best medallists who ever lived, Dupre, of Paris, one whose art knowledge cannot be questioned, and I call your attention to the fact that I have followed his arrangement of scroll very closely. If it is contrary to artistic principles to have the ribbon over the neck of the Eagle, it being wrong to have "One surface pass over another" is it not wrong to have the shield pass over the breast?

It must be remembered there is no law governing the manner displaying the design of the seal, each artist takes the description of seal and displays it to suit his taste and shape of article he wishes to decorate with it. Therefore you will find in the Diplomatic medal the olive branch contains about fifty leaves, while on the Indian Peace medal of 1792 the branch has but (15), and the seal of the U.S. on my commission has (17) leaves, showing that the Artist's taste governed this point. I have used thirteen leaves to conform to the thirteen stars and thirteen arrows believing there should be unity in these numbers, also significance.

I know of no authority for saying nine leaves are more used than any other number and very much question the correctness of the statement. In regard to increasing size of design with wreath omitted, I beg to say I had anticipated that requirement, knowing that the design must suit the area of the coin. Very respectfully, etc.

P.S. The Director will find both medals referred to (Diplomatic and first Indian Peace) in his copy of Loubat's Medallic History of the U.S.

But Leech, like Goldsmith's schoolmaster, "though vanquished, argued still." The trend of the Director's protest can be inferred from the reply of acting superintendent Cobb on October 6:

Sir, I transmit herewith a letter from Mr. Barber, our Engraver, more fully discussing matters unsettled in connection with new designs for coins. And I avail myself of this occasion to say, that Mr. Barber disclaims any intention to be captious, and certainly did not intend to question your prerogative as one of the officers designed by law to pass upon new designs for coinage.

As every essential change in design makes it necessary to remodel, and re-electrotype, I suppose Mr. Barber wished to avoid the inevitable delay thereby occasioned. Very respectfully etc.

The following letter from Barber to Bosbyshell was enclosed:

Sir: In answer to further remarks of the Director, in regard to olive branch and stars, I would respectfully say I had no intention of "brushing lightly aside" the criticism of the Director, and thought I had really gone into the consideration of his suggestions very fully, and fortified my own opinion with examples of some authority. I beg to say in relation to the number of leaves, that should or should not appear in an olive branch, I am after full examination of the subject unable to find any authority for saying what number of leaves constitutes the proper number for an olive branch. I would further add that it is the custom among artists of whom I have any knowledge to go to nature for examples of this character. I would be pleased to know the authority for saying nine is the proper number. In regard to ribbon passing over the Eagle's neck, I would call your attention to the fact that on the coins of the date 1799 to 1809, the reverse is made up of the great seal design, and the ribbon passes over the neck of the Eagle, only not in so graceful a manner as mine, and with my arrangement of clouds the ribbon would not, in my opinion, look as well if I should make the proposed change. The space being so limited it is only by the most careful arrangement that all the design can be displayed with distinctness. If the ribbon is carried up, as in the seal in present use, it would take the place of the clouds, which would then have to be raised higher in the design, and consequently increase the circle surrounding the design and at the same time decrease the interior of the design, making every part that much smaller. In regard to question of number of points to the stars, I beg to say in Clark Heraldry page 164 you will find he says "A star consists of six, eight, or more points." The same author quotes Mr. Nisbit, equally as good an authority, as follows: "Mullets or five points he takes as stars when surrounded by celestial figures," as is the case in my design. Six pointed stars are English, while five point are used by France, Holland and Germany, and also by the United States upon the flag. In the model prepared by Mr. Saint Gaudens for the Joseph Francis Medal, the stars on the obverse representing the 38 states, are five pointed while the star on the reverse is six. I prefer five points for use on present occasion for the following reason. The largest of the proposed coins is one-seventh the size of the model, and I think when you consider how small that would bring the stars, five points are more easily distinguished from a round dot, than six, but as I remarked to you I see no objection to using six if preferred, as either number is equally correct.

If the Director has any preference I would be glad to know it. Very respect fully, etc.

Having subdued the Director, Barber proceeded on his own to make the alterations. On October 23, he submitted to Bosbyshell three patterns for half dollar, the first modified only in the omission of rays from around the eagle; the second with six pointed stars on the obverse, a larger eagle and new wreath; and the third similar but with the ribbon passing behind the eagle head. Barber wrote to the superintendent:

Sir: I submit for your examination and criticism three impressions of experimental dies of the denomination of Half dollar. In doing so I wish to call your attention to some points. 1st. I have omitted the rays, finding they only confuse the design. 2nd. I have used a five pointed star on one obverse and a six on the other. I think with the two examples before one the six pointed star looks the richer of the two, and fills the coin better, and according to Clark's Heraldry is qua

Coins of Charles Barber. **Top:** 1883 five-cent piece; **bottom:** 1891 patterns for a half dollar.

Models for a silver dollar, by Charles Barber.

Models for a silver dollar, apparently by George Morgan.

correct, and as the six pointed star has always been used on our coins, it might call forth some adverse criticism if we should use the five pointed star.

I shall be glad to have your decision whether in preparing hubs I shall use the five or six pointed star.

The design of reverse with wreath omitted varies only in the ribbon from the design practically adopted. You can therefore form a very good idea of what the appearance of the new coins will be. Very respectfully, etc.

A still later alteration removed the clouds, and in this form the coins were issued from the first week of January 1892.

A movement to further improve the appearance of our coins was begun in October 1894 by the American Numismatic and Antiquarian Society, in conjunction with the National Sculpture Society, the Architectural League of New York, the Society of American Artists, the National Academy of Design, and the City College of New York. To give practical evidence of its interest, the National Sculpture Society offered a cash prize for the best design for a silver dollar.

Either from these submissions or from designs of their own, both Barber and Morgan sculptured models for a dollar in the following year. No patterns seem ever to have been struck, nor the models themselves considered by the Bureau. They are shown here for the first time.

In 1896, Barber made new dies for a cent and five-cent piece with the purpose of testing different coining alloys. The experiments proved a failure, artistically as well as metallurgically. Some years later Barber reworked his model for the five-cent piece, but by then the second Philadelphia Mint had passed into history.

PART IV

THE THIRD PHILADELPHIA MINT

CHAPTER 22

An Introduction to our Present Mint

IN JANUARY 1891, SECRETARY OF THE TREASURY Windom asked Congress to provide a new Mint building which could meet the increasing demands of our national coinage. A bill for this purpose was introduced in the Senate on February 19, and unanimously passed a week later. In the House, the bill was vigorously debated, first on the score of expense, and secondly because of the proposed site. An agitation developed for moving the Mint to either New York or St. Louis, but members developed second thoughts after Montana Senator Thomas Carter declared:

> On the occasion of a recent visit to Philadelphia in connection with the annual Assay Commission I was permitted to examine the various appliances and the rooms in which they were used at the Mint, and I want to add my testimony to the fact that there does not exist on this continent today an intelligent and prudent business-man who would ask free-born American citizens to spend their lives and perform their duties in the cold, damp, subterranean passages in which our fellow citizens are compelled to work in the Mint at Philadelphia.

The bill passed the House on March 2, and the following year an appropriation was made for a new site.

The third and present Mint, which was completed in mid 1901, stands between Sixteenth and Seventeenth Streets, Philadelphia, with its front on Spring Garden Street. During 1902, the first electrolytic refinery was installed, greatly reducing time and manpower. Today, the only government refineries are located at the Denver Mint and the New York Assay Office.

In 1907, the Hill reducing machine was replaced by the Janvier lathe, which not only cuts superior reductions, but can work in different heights of relief. The date and legend are now sculptured in the original model.

1

2

3

4

5

6

1. Former assistant engraver Engelhardus Von Hebel touching up his model for a Washington mint medal. 2. Operator adjusts Janvier machine which will make a hub from the large "galvano" or electroplate of the model.   3. Setting up hub and die blank for "hubbing" operation.

4. Turning the neck and body of finished coining die to proper shape and dimension. 5. Dies are packed in charcoal in nickel-chrome cup before hardening. 6. Matrices for Lincoln cent. **From left to right**: hub, die blank, die before turning, turned dies—the latter with base removed, dual dies in their holder. **Rear:** a box of working dies for obverse and reverse.

7

8

9

10

11

12

13

7. Casting silver ingots. 8. A ton of silver bullion being wheeled from the melting room. 9. First use of the larger alloying ingot mold. 10. Workman handling alloyed ingot; in the rear, an electric furnace. 11. Workman at left uses air-operated chisel to remove gate-line from ingot. His partner is removing scales with an electric wire brush. 12. Ingot emerges from rolling machine as a long ribbon of metal approximating the thickness of the planchet. 13. Coils of metal from which planchets will be punched.

14

15

16

17

18

19

14. Feeding a strip into the planchet cutter, or "blanking machine." 15. Workman collects perforated strips for remelting. 16. Planchets are poured onto riddle to remove clipped pieces and shruff. 17. Planchets receive their upset edge in the milling machine. 18. The planchets, which have just been annealed, are shown pouring out of the furnace. 19. The blank planchets are tumbled and cleaned.

20

21

22

20. Silver planchets are weighed on an electric scale before striking. 21. Press opera[t]
examines coins. 22. Visual inspection of the coins.

Third Philadelphia Mint, completed in June 1901. At the present time, a new structure is underway.

To change the date from year to year, the engraver grinds down the last numeral in the hub, sinks a new master die, and finally cuts in the correct figure. Date numerals are no longer punched, but carefully cut into the die with a fine engraving tool. Mintmarks are still punched, as required, into each working die.

Rolling mills, planchet cutters, milling machines and coining presses still operate on time-honored principles, though there have been a number of refinements. Gauging rollers are equipped with a micrometer, making it unnecessary to "draw" the strip. Planchet cutters punch out blanks in gangs, and coining presses, using dual dies, stamp the smaller coins two at a time.

❂   ❂   ❂

Except for the discontinuation of gold coins in 1933, and the ephemeral war issues of cents and five-cent pieces, there has been no major change in the composition of our coinage from the beginning of the third Mint until the present year (1965). Nevertheless, Congress, at various times, has considered the addition of other small denominations.

The most promising agitation began in 1911, after two Ohio mayors petitioned the legislature to reinstate the three-cent piece. On December 4, Representative Bulkley introduced a bill for this purpose. The new three-cent piece was to weigh 24 grains and consist of 95 per cent aluminum and five per cent copper. Mint Director Roberts and Secretary MacVeigh approved the idea, except for the alloy which superintendent Landis considered unsuitable for coining. It was finally decided to issue an annular coin of 75 per cent copper and 25 per cent nickel, the alloy used in the five-cent and earlier three-cent pieces. During March and April of 1912, a number of experimental planchets were made, to test not only different diameters of an annular coin, but also a square shape with round corners, and a scalloped edge.

Bulkley introduced a bill for an annular coin on April 13, and then, on the advice of Secretary MacVeigh, offered a substitute on the 20th, which also provided for a half cent. On May 1, the bill was reported to the House with an amendment which changed the composition of the cent to copper-nickel. The bill passed the House on May 6, but died in the Senate.

On April 7, 1913 Bulkley introduced two bills for a three-cent piece, one with, the other without, the half-cent. Neither bill emerged from committee.

*   *   *

The need for nickel and copper during World War II resulted in a change in composition of the minor coins. Title XII of the second War Powers Act, passed March 27, 1942, provided for a five-cent piece of 50 per cent silver, and 50 per cent copper, but authorized the Secretary of the Treasury, in conjunction with the chief of the War Production Board, to vary these proportions and add other metals if thought desirable. Accordingly, from October 1, 1942 through December 31, 1945 the five-cent piece was coined from an alloy of 56 per cent copper, 35 per cent silver, and 9 per cent manganese. To readily distinguish the emergency issue from the copper-nickel composition, a large mintmark was placed above the dome of Monticello. The Philadelphia Mint five-cent pieces for this period are the only coins ever struck at the principal Mint to bear an identifying initial.

On November 9, 1942 Senator Wagner introduced a bill "to further the war effort by authorizing the substitution of other materials for strategic metals used in minor coinage . . ." The act provided for coins of less value than ten cents, but was amended to read "not of other denominations than one cent, three cents and five cents." The reference to the five-cent piece was a formality, the denomination having already been altered by the War Powers Act. In the House this section was further amended to read: "Not of other denominations than 1-cent piece and 3-cent piece."

On December 10, 1942 Representative Somers explained the bill to the House as follows:

> The purpose of this bill is to conserve the metals required for war production purposes which are now used in minor coins. The bill will permit the minting of minor coins of 1 cent and 3 cents, which coins shall be of such metallic or other contents, weight, denominations, shape and limitations of form and design as the Secretary of the Treasury by regulation may prescribe. In determining those physical properties the Secretary of the Treasury is directed to take in consideration the use of these coins in coin-operated devices. The authority contained in this bill is limited to the period between the date of enactment and December 31, 1946.

There was a good reason for the bill's flexibility. When the shortage of copper first grew serious, the Mint experimented with zinc, which had been used by other countries in similar circumstances. But almost as soon as the metal had been approved, it was likewise added to the critical list. The Mint authorities then turned to plastics, but even these were found to be in short supply. Finally, they selected steel, which of all feasible materials seemed to be the most readily available. Even so, Congress provided that other substitutes might be used if necessary. The bill was enacted on December 18, 1942.

The three-cent pieces were never coined, their issue being discretionary with the Secretary of the Treasury. The steel cents (coated with zinc for protection and appearance) proved eminently unpopular. Not only were they confused with dimes, but their coating soon eroded, leaving a dingy, unattractive surface. They were replaced, in 1944, by cents of 95 per cent copper and five per cent zinc.

This composition was maintained through 1946, when authorization for an emergency issue expired. Tin was subsequently restored to the alloy, though only in trace amounts, and on September 5, 1962 the resumption of a copper-zinc cent was approved by Congress.

* * *

The Revised Mint statutes of 1874 permit the Treasury Department to engage outside artists when periodically redesigning its coins. This provision, together with the appointment of the Commission of Fine Arts as an advisory body, has generally enhanced the artistic merit of American coinage.[1]

The remaining chapters are devoted to each of the modern issues, from the Saint-Gaudens eagle and double eagle to the John F. Kennedy half dollar.

Particular attention has been given to the Saint-Gaudens coinage, not only because of the volume and significance of the letters that passed between the renowned artist and his executive patron, President Theodore Roosevelt, but because, in Roosevelt's words, " a great and permanent improvement was made in the beauty of the coinage."

The latter narratives are perforce a bit short, the only available source material (except for the chapter on the Kennedy half dollar) being the archives of the Commission of Fine Arts.

---

[1] Since President Harding's administration, the Treasury Department has been obliged to confer with the Commission of Fine Arts when bringing out a new coin. Nevertheless, the Secretary of the Treasury is not bound by the Commission's views, and may reject them if he desires.

CHAPTER 23

The Saint-Gaudens
and Bigelow-Pratt Coinage

SAINT-GAUDENS' FIRST CONTACT with the Mint developed during 1891, when he served on a committee to judge coin designs submitted through public competition. Subsequently, he was asked to design the 1892 Columbian Exposition medal. Saint-Gaudens accepted the commission with misgivings which, as it turned out, were fully justified; for after considerable delay, the artist was informed that his obverse had been combined with a reverse supplied by the Mint's own engraver, Charles Barber. Thereafter, Saint-Gaudens avoided the Mint — at least until 1905, when he was personally selected by President Theodore Roosevelt to execute his inauguration medal. Saint-Gaudens designed the medal and entrusted the modeling to the brilliant American sculptor Adolph Weinman. Roosevelt was immensely pleased with the result, and conferred with Saint-Gaudens on improving the appearance of our coinage. On November 6, 1905 he wrote to the artist:[1]

My dear Saint-Gaudens: How is the gold coinage design coming along? I want to make a suggestion. It seems to me worth while to try for a really good coinage; though I suppose there will be a revolt about it. I was looking at some gold coins of Alexander the Great today, and I was struck by their high relief. Would not it be well to have our coins in high relief, and also to have the rims raised? The point of having the rim raised would be, of course, to protect the figure of the coin; and if we have the figures in high relief, like the figures on the old Greek coins, they will surely last longer. What do you think of this? With warm regards etc.

[1] The Roosevelt-Saint-Gaudens correspondence was originally published in the April 1920 issue of *The Century* Magazine. Most of the originals (as well as the Roosevelt-Bigelow letters) are found in the Baker Library of Dartmouth College and the Library of Congress collection. Other letters reproduced here are in the Mint Director's file in the National Archives.

Saint-Gaudens replied on the 11th:

Dear Mr. President:— Your note of the 6th is at hand. You have hit the nail on the head with regard to the coinage. Of course the great coins (and you might say the only coins) are the Greek ones you speak of, just as the great medals are those of the fifteenth century by Pisani and Sperandie; Nothing would please me more than to make the attempt in the direction of the heads of Alexander, but the authorities on modern monetary requirements would I fear "throw fits" to speak emphatically if the thing were done now. It would be great if it could be accomplished and I do not see what the objection would be if the edges were high enough to prevent the rubbing. Perhaps an inquiry from you would not receive the antagonistic reply from those who have the say in such matters that would certainly be made to me.

Up to the present I have done no work on the actual models for the coins, but have made sketches, and the matter is constantly in my mind. I have about determined on the composition of one side, which would contain an eagle very much like the one I placed on your medal with a modification that would be advantageous; on the other side some kind of a (possibly winged) figure of Liberty striding forward as if on a mountain top, holding aloft on one arm a shield bearing the stars and stripes with the word Liberty marked across the field; in the other hand perhaps a flaming torch, the drapery would be flowing in the breeze. My idea is to make it a *living* thing and typical of progress.

Tell me frankly what you think of this and what your ideas may be. I remember you spoke of the head of an Indian; of course that is always a superb thing to do, but would it be a sufficiently clear emblem of Liberty as required by the law?

I send you an old book on coins, which I am certain you will find of interest, while waiting for a copy that I have ordered from Europe. Faithfully yours.

Three days later, Roosevelt wrote again:

My dear Saint-Gaudens: I have your letter of the 11th instant, and return herewith the book on coins which I think you should have until you get the other one. I have summoned all the mint people, and I am going to see if I cannot persuade them that coins of the Grecian type but with raised rims will meet the commercial needs of the day. Of course I want to avoid too heavy an outbreak of the mercantile classes, because after all it is they who do use the gold. If we can have an eagle like that on the inauguration medal, only raised, I should feel that we would be awfully fortunate. Don't you think that we might accomplish something by raising the figures more than at present but not so much as in the Greek coins? Probably the Greek coins would be so thick that modern banking houses, where they have to pile up gold, would simply be unable to do so. How would it be to have a design struck off in tentative fashion—that is, to have a Liberty with that Indian feather head-dress? The figure of Liberty as you suggest it would be beautiful. If we get down to bedrock facts, would the feather head-dress be any more out of keeping with the rest of Liberty than the canonical cap which never is worn and never has been worn by any free people in the world? Faithfully yours.

Saint-Gaudens replied on the 22nd:

Dear Mr. President: Thank you for your letter of the 14th and the return of the book on coins. I can perfectly well use the Indian head-dress on the figure of Liberty. It should be very handsome. I have been at work for the last two days on the coins and feel quite enthusiastic about it. I enclose a copy of a letter to Secretary Shaw which explains itself. If you are of my opinion and will help, I shall be greatly obliged. Faithfully yours etc.

[P.S.] I think something between the high relief of the Greek coins and the extreme low relief of the modern is possible and as you suggest I will make a model with that in mind.

The copy of Saint-Gaudens' letter to Secretary of the Treasury Shaw is dated November 22, and reads:

> Dear Sir: I am now engaged on the models for the coinage. The law calls for, viz., "On one side there shall be an impression emblematic of liberty, with an inscription of the word "Liberty" and the year of the coinage." It occurs to me that the addition on this side of the coins of the word "Justice" (or "Law," preferably the former) would add force as well as elevation to the meaning of the composition. At one time the words "In God we trust" were placed on the coins; I am not aware there was authorization for that, but I may be mistaken. Will you kindly inform me whether what I suggest is permissible. Yours very truly.

Roosevelt approved the addition, writing to Saint-Gaudens on the 24th:

> My dear Mr. Saint-Gaudens: This is first class. I have no doubt we can get permission to put on the word "Justice" and I firmly believe that you can evolve something that will not only be beautiful from the artistic standpoint, but that, between the high relief of the Greek and the very low relief of the modern coins, will be adapted both to the mechanical necessities of our mint production and the needs of modern commerce, and yet will be worthy of a civilized people—which is not true of our present coins. Faithfully yours.

In the end, however, Saint-Gaudens omitted the word "Justice" because of the encumbrance already presented by the required inscriptions.

Roosevelt wrote again on January 6, 1906:

> My dear Saint-Gaudens: I have seen Shaw about the coinage and told him that it was my pet baby. We will try it anyway, so you go ahead. Shaw was really very nice about it. Of course he thinks I am a mere crack-brained lunatic on the subject, but he said with great kindness that there was always a certain number of gold coins that had to be stored up in the vaults, and that there was no earthly objection to having those coins as artistic as the Greeks could desire. (I am paraphrasing his words, of course.) I think it will seriously increase mortality among the employees of the mint at seeing such a desecration, but they will perish in a good cause! Always Yours etc.

Roosevelt's letter must have greatly amused Saint-Gaudens who replied on January 9 with equal levity:

> Dear Mr. President: Your letter of January 6th is at hand. All right, I shall proceed on the lines we have agreed on. The models are both well in hand, but I assure you I feel mighty cheeky so to speak, in attempting to line up with the Greek things. Well! Whatever I produce cannot be worse than the inanities now displayed on our coins and we will at least have made an attempt in the right direction, and serve the country by increasing the mortality at the mint. There is one gentleman there,[2] however, who, when he sees what is coming, may have "the nervous prostitution" as termed by a native here, but killed, no. He has been in that institution since the foundation of the government and will be found standing in its ruins. Yours faithfully.

As the year wore on, Saint-Gaudens' health began to seriously decline. Consequently, the modeling, though continued under the artist's direction, devolved upon his worthy assistant, Henry Hering.[3] Liberty was personified as a winged figure with feathered head-dress, holding a torch and shield. Later on, the wings, shield and head-dress were omitted as unsuitable to the composition within a circle. From seventy different sketches of an eagle, Saint-Gaudens

---

[2] The engraver, Charles Barber.
[3] Henry Hering, "History of the $10 and $20 Gold Coins of 1907 Issue," *The Numismatist*, August 1949.

selected two for modeling. One depicted the eagle flying stiff-legged like a wading bird, the other standing as on his inaugural medal, and previously, his Shaw memorial and the shield of the Garfield monument.

On May 26, President Roosevelt wrote to Secretary Shaw:

> My dear Mr. Secretary: Referring to the Saint-Gaudens correspondence, there does not seem to be any reason for not putting the date on the coin in Roman numerals. Those numerals are Latin and our figures are Arabic. If Mr. Saint Gaudens is clear that the effect would be better if numerals should be used, I should give him his head about it. In such a case a V would have to be used and not a U because of the simple reason that it would actually be a V and not a U that he was trying to put on. V means 5; U is not a numeral at all.
>
> But under no circumstances should Mr. Saint Gaudens use the words "Aequum Cuique," which were used on the inauguration medal. The coin must have no reference either direct or indirect to the President.
>
> I suppose you have sent Mr. Saint Gaudens the permission to make a plaster cast of the present twenty-dollar gold piece. Sincerely yours.

Although Roosevelt was having his way with Secretary Shaw, Saint-Gaudens wasn't so sure the President would overcome the redoubtable Mint authorities. On May 29, the artist wrote:

> Dear Mr. President: I have your letter of May 26th enclosing a copy of your letter to Secretary Shaw of the same date.
>
> The reverse is done. But before showing it to you I wish you had the reductions made at the different reliefs. They will take some time. The obverse I am hard at work on. Its completion will not be delayed long and your "pet crime" as you call it will be perpetrated as far as I am concerned.
>
> I have sent a practical man to Philadelphia [4] to obtain all the details necessary for the carrying out of our scheme, but if you succeed in getting the best of the polite Mr. Barber down there, or the others in charge, you will have done a greater work than putting through the Panama Canal. Nevertheless, I shall stick at it, even unto death. Faithfully yours.

On June 22, Roosevelt wrote to Saint-Gaudens, encouraging him to complete the models. The artist replied on the 28th:

> Dear Mr. President: I thank you for your letter of June 22d. I will certainly inform you when your help will be needed with your friends in Philadelphia.
>
> I am here on the sick list, where I have to remain in the hands of the doctors until the first of August, but my mind is on the coins, which are in good hands at Windsor.
>
> The making of these designs is a great pleasure, but the job is even more serious than I anticipated. You may not recall that I told you I was "scared blue" at the thought of doing them; now that I have the opportunity, the responsibility looms up like a spectre.
>
> The eagle side of the gold piece is finished, and is undergoing the interminable experiments with reductions before I send it to you. The other side is well advanced.
>
> Now I am attacking the cent. It may interest you to know that on the "Liberty" side of the cent I am using a flying eagle, a modification of the device which was used on the cent of 1857. I had not seen that coin for many years, and was so impressed by it, that I thought if carried out with some modifications, nothing better could be done. It is by all odds the best design on any American coin. Yours sincerely.

---

[4] Henry Hering.

In a letter to Saint-Gaudens on July 30, Roosevelt inquired about the artist's progress. Homer Saint-Gaudens, the sculptor's son, replied on August 2. He said that his father was ill with sciatica, and feared the models would not be ready until after the summer. Secondary models had already been made and sent to Paris for reduction, and would be returned by the end of the month. Once these were approved, Saint-Gaudens would send the reductions back to Paris "where the die can be properly made." Apparently, the artist was determined to avoid Barber altogether.

On October 1, possibly after examining Saint-Gaudens' models for the cent, Roosevelt wrote to the artist:

> My dear Saint-Gaudens: The Mint people have come down as you can see from the enclosed letter which is in answer to a rather dictatorial one I sent to the Secretary of the Treasury. When can we get that design for the twenty-dollar gold piece? I hate to have to put on the lettering, but under the law, I have no alternative; but in spite of the lettering I think, my dear sir, that you have given us a coin as wonderful as any of the old Greek coins. I do not want to bother you, but do let me have it as quickly as possible. I would like to have the coin well on the way to completion by the time Congress meets.
>
> It was such a pleasure seeing your son the other day.
>
> Please return Director Roberts' letter to me when you have noted it. Sincerely Yours.

On October 8, Roosevelt instructed Mint Director Roberts to reduce Saint-Gaudens' models at the Mint. The President said that he wished to avoid another six months' delay.

In a letter of December 11, Roosevelt urged Saint-Gaudens to complete his models for the double eagle. The artist had, in fact, already finished except for shellacking, and the models were dispatched to the President three days later. On the 20th, Roosevelt gratefully acknowledged their receipt:

> My dear Saint-Gaudens: Those models are simply immense—if such a slang way of talking is permissible in reference to giving a modern nation one coinage at least which shall be as good as that of the ancient Greeks. I have instructed the Director of the Mint that these dies are to be reproduced just as quickly as possible and just as they are. It is simply splendid. I suppose I shall be impeached for it in Congress; but I shall regard that as a very cheap payment! With heartiest regards.

Apparently on the assumption that the Mint owned a Janvier reducing lathe, Hering had made the models in unusually high relief. His idea was to have experimental dies made, and then observe the number of strikes required to bring up a full impression. He thought that this would enable him to determine the highest relief feasible in the models.

Hering brought the models to the Mint where he was introduced to Barber.[5] The engraver rejected the work at a glance and only after considerable discussion agreed to experiment. Subsequently, the new double eagle dies were tried out in an hydraulic press, and with 172 tons pressure took nine blows to fully raise an impression.[6]

In the meantime, Saint-Gaudens had replaced the flying eagle on his cent

---

[5] Despite Saint-Gaudens' commission, Barber had made models and dies, and struck pattern double eagles of his own design. It is doubtful whether these were ever shown to the President.

[6] Some twenty-two or twenty-four pieces were allegedly made, several remaining with Barber. These are the so-called "exceedingly high-relief" patterns.

with a lovely profile head adapted from his Niké Eiréné (Victory and Peace) medal, and previously his unused bust for the Sherman monument. Roosevelt suggested the addition of an Indian head-dress to which the artist, on February 11, replied:

Dear Mr. President: I have received your letter of February the eighth regarding the Indian feather head-dress in its application to the one-cent piece.

I have already begun the trial in the way you suggest, so it should not be long before I will be able to tell you of the result. I shall endeavor to let you know with the utmost possible dispatch. Faithfully Yours.

On February 18, after receiving the new model, Roosevelt wrote again:

My dear Mr. Saint-Gaudens: I wonder if I am one of those people of low appreciation of artistic things, against whom I have been inveighing! I like that feather head-dress so much that I have accepted that design of yours. Of course all the designs are conventional when embodied in a woman's head; and I don't see why we should not have a conventional head-dress of purely American type for the Liberty figure.

I am returning to you today the model of the Liberty head. With hearty thanks etc.

Saint-Gaudens apparently did not agree with Roosevelt's modest self-appraisal, for on March 12, he wrote:

Dear Mr. President: I send today to the mint the models of the twenty Dollar gold piece with the alterations that were indispensable if the coin was to be struck with one blow. There has been no change whatever in the design. It was simply a question of the thickness of the gold in certain places, and the weight of the pressure when the blow was struck.

I like so much the head with the head-dress (and by the way, I am very glad you suggested doing the head in that manner) that I should like very much to see it tried not only on the one-cent piece, but also on the twenty-dollar gold piece, instead of the figure of Liberty. I am probably apprehensive and have lost sight of whatever are the merits or the demerits of the Liberty side of the coin as it is now. My fear is that it does not "tell" enough, in contrast with the eagle on the other side. There will be no difficulty of that kind with the head alone, of its effectiveness I am certain.

Of course there is complete justification for the small figure with the large object on the other side in a great number of the Greek coins, and it is with that authority that I have proceeded.

This all means that I would like to have the mint make a die of the head for the gold coin also, and then a choice can be made between the two when completed. If this meets with your approval, may I ask you to say so to Mr. Roberts, of the Mint? I have enclosed a copy of this letter to him. The only change necessary in the event of this being carried out will be the changing of the date from the Liberty side to the Eagle side of the coin. This is a small matter.

I enclose a copy of a letter I am sending today to Mr. Roberts. Yours faithfully.

Roosevelt's joy over the success of his Indian head-dress is obvious in his reply of the 14th:

My dear Saint-Gaudens: Many thanks for your letter of the 12th instant. Good! I have directed that be done at once. I am so glad you like the head of Liberty with the feather head-dress. Really, the feather head-dress can be treated as being the conventional cap of Liberty quite as much as if it was the Phrygian cap; and, after all, it is *our* Liberty—not what the ancient Greeks and Romans miscalled by that title—and we are entitled to a typically American head-dress for the lady. Faithfully yours.

In the meantime, work was progressing on the cent. On March 11, Saint-Gaudens had written to Director Roberts that he had "made the relief of the One Cent high, knowing from what Mr. Hering tells me that you have a Janvier Machine and can reduce it to the relief you wish."

The Janvier lathe had just been purchased at the instance of President Roosevelt. It seems that Hering had complained to Barber of the poor quality reductions made by the Mint's forty-year old Hill machine, and receiving no satisfaction, took up the matter with Saint-Gaudens. The latter informed Roosevelt with the result that a Janvier lathe was immediately installed.

The first reductions made on the new machine were from Saint-Gaudens' models for the eagle. The quality was apparently no better than before, a fact Barber pointed out with relish. Hering justly replied that a bad reduction could be made from a good machine, and that Barber was probably not well enough acquainted with the mechanism. Barber was not aware that Hering had procured from Mr. Janvier three superior reductions of the same models in different heights of relief.

By May, dies had been made from the second set of double eagle models. Once again, however, the relief proved to be too high for coining. Roosevelt conveyed the painful news to Saint-Gaudens in a letter of May 8:

> My dear Mr. Saint-Gaudens: I am sorry to say I am having some real difficulties in connection with the striking of those gold coins. It has proved hitherto impossible to strike them by one blow, which is necessary under the conditions of making coins at the present day. I send you a copy of letters from the head of the Department of Coins and Medals of the British Museum, and from Comparetti.[7] I am afraid it is not practicable to have coins made if they are struck with more than one blow. Of course I can have a few hundreds of these beautiful coins made, but they will be merely souvenirs and medals, and not part of the true coinage of the country. Would it be possible for you to come on to the mint? I am sure that the mint authorities now really desire to do whatever they can, and if it would be possible for you to go there I could arrange to have some of the Tiffany people there at the same time to see if there was anything practicable to be done. With regard, believe me, Sincerely yours.
>
> [Hand-written postscript] You notice what Comparetti says about our country leading the way. I know our people now earnestly desire to do all they can; and I believe that with a slightly altered and lowered relief (and *possibly* a profile figure of Liberty) we can yet do the trick.

With his strength failing and other commissions still to attend to, Saint-Gaudens was forced to decline the President's request. On May 11, he replied:

> Dear Mr. President: I am extremely sorry that it will be wholly impossible for me to leave Windsor at present, but I am sending to Mr. Roberts, and if you so desire, to you, my assistant Mr. Hering, who understands the mechanical requirements of the coin far better than I.
>
> After all the question is fairly simple, and I have not the slightest doubt that making the coins in low relief will settle the matter satisfactorily. Greatly as I should like to please you, I feel that I cannot now model another design in profile for the Twenty Dollar gold piece. Indeed, as far as I am concerned, I should prefer seeing the head of Liberty in place of any figure of Liberty on the Twenty Dollar coin as well as on the One cent. If the idea appeals to you, I would refine the modelling of the head now that I have seen it struck in the small, so as to bring it in scale with the eagle. I am grieved that the striking of the die did not bring better results. Evidently it is no trifling matter to make Greek art conform with modern numismatics. Faithfully yours.

---

[7] T. L. Comparette, the Curator of the Mint.

Roosevelt received this letter the following day, and immediately wrote:

> Dear Mr. Saint-Gaudens: All right. Your letter really makes me feel quite cheer-
> ful. I should be glad, if it is possible for you to do so if you would "refine" the
> head of Liberty; but I want to keep the figure of Liberty for at least one small
> issue of the coins. I look forward to seeing Mr. Hering. With hearty thanks, believe
> me, Sincerely yours.

In his last letter to Roosevelt, dated May 23, 1907, Saint-Gaudens expressed
his decided preference for the standing-eagle design:

> Dear Mr. President: Now that this business of the coinage is coming to an end
> and we understand how much relief can be practicably stamped, I have been
> looking over the other models that I have made and there is no question in my
> mind that the standing eagle is the best. You have seen only the large model,
> and probably on seeing it in the small will have a different impression. The
> artists all prefer it, as I do, to the flying eagle.
>
> First, in that it is more on the scale with the figure of Liberty on the other
> side.
>
> Second, it eliminates the sunburst which is on both sides of the coin as it will
> be if adopted as settled up to now.
>
> Third, it is more dignified and less inclined toward the sensational.
>
> Fourth, it will occupy no more time to use this model than it will to do the
> other work that will be necessary, and I think it is a little more favorable for
> stamping.
>
> The majority of the people that I show the work to evidently prefer with
> you the figure of Liberty to the head of Liberty and *that* I shall not consider any
> further on the Twenty Dollar gold coin.
>
> I write rather in haste as Mr. Hering leaves in a very little while. Faithfully
> yours.

When Saint-Gaudens died in early August, Hering had not yet furnished
the Mint with a new set of models for the double eagle. The confusion that
followed is evident from Roosevelt's letter of August 7 to Secretary of the
Treasury Cortelyou:

> Dear Sir: I return Mr. Roberts' letter which accompanied your note of the 3rd.
>
> I do not want to wait about those new coins. I would like the Director of the
> Mint to go ahead with the dies of the coins as they now are, and then if experience
> shows that the clear cut finish must be obtained make the change in the original
> die after submitting it to me. Mr. Saint Gaudens is dead. I do not know whether
> there is any man associated with him to whom we can refer. One of his
> assistants has been in communication with the mint authorities about this matter.
> Why don't they get in touch with him again? I am sure there has been good-will
> upon the part of the mint authorities, but I cannot help feeling that there has
> been a certain cumbersomeness of mind and inability to do the speediest modern
> work, as shown by these delays. There must be no further delays. Let the two
> coins be finished and put into circulation at once; by September first. Then if
> experience shows, or even if experience does not show, that there should be a
> sharper outline, let the mint authorities consult with the late Saint Gaudens'
> assistant and prepare dies of a sharper cutting. There has been altogether too
> much delay about this matter and I want it finished immediately.

The order was duly transmitted to Barber who, on August 14, replied to
superintendent Landis:

> Sir:— I beg to state that the dies for the Eagle coin, new design, have been
> ready and awaiting approval since July 22nd., when some of the coins and plaster
> casts were submitted to the Director and also to Mr. Saint Gaudens as he requested.

Since that date there have been no instructions received regarding these coins. With the instructions just received "to go ahead with the dies as they now are" I beg to state that the dies are now ready for the Eagle coin.

In regards to the Double Eagle, you will remember that dies have been made from models furnished by Mr. Saint Gaudens and coins struck as medals and submitted to the Director with a full statement of the impossibility of using dies for coinage made from the models in their present state on account of the high relief.

The last this department heard on this subject was that Mr. Saint Gaudens had seen the impossibility of coining high relief and had determined upon reducing the relief to within the requirements of modern coinage.

I have no model for the Double Eagle that can be used, for the reason above stated namely, the relief being entirely too high.

I have been anticipating a new model that would not have this objectionable feature, but have not received such an one, therefore it is not in any sense the fault of this department that dies are not ready.

The appliances in this department for doing die work are of the most improved and have been used in every possible way even to working day and night and Sundays to expedite this new coinage, and in the case of making the first reduction Mr. Saint Gaudens reported that it would take six months to get it made in Paris, while I made it in one month.

I think this statement is necessary to clear up the idea that the Mint has caused any delay in the production of the new dies, as from the first I have had to wait upon Mr. Saint Gaudens for models as I am now doing in the case of the Double Eagle.

Mr. Saint Gaudens asked for samples of the models when reduced to the size of the Double Eagle and they were furnished, since that time I have heard nothing more of them and do not know whether he left other models or any one to take up his work, and until the new and suitable models are sent, I am powerless to produce Double Eagle dies of the Saint Gaudens model that can be used for coinage.

In the case of the Eagle Mr. Saint Gaudens reduced the model until with the aid of the new French reducing machine it was possible to make a die that would produce a coin, this has not been done with the Double Eagle models and until it is done my hands are tied.

I furnish you with this full statement of the present condition of the new designs and models and respectfully await your instructions as to who will supply the models for the Double Eagle, and also advise you that if the models were here now, it would be utterly impossible to get ready to coin the Double Eagle by September 1st. Respectfully etc.

On September 25, superintendent Landis submitted new impressions of the eagle to Mint Director Frank Leach:

Sir: I beg to enclose herewith for approval specimen of new eagle struck from the dies reduced from Saint Gaudens' last model.[8] I also enclose for comparison a specimen taken from the $315,000 in eagles now on hand of the first Saint Gaudens' model as modified by Mr. Barber.[9]

You will notice that the eagle from the last model is a great improvement over those of the first model. The latter are indefinite in detail and outline, not being at all sharp and look like imperfect coins or coins that have been sweated, while the former is sharp in outline, the detail shows up well, the border is broad and prominent and the coins will stack perfectly.

We have on hand $315,000 of the first model, struck on the coining press, and $500, struck on the medal press. If this last model meets with your approval, I would strongly urge upon you the expediency of immediately replacing the

---

[8] The regular issue, without periods before and after the legends.
[9] The second variety, with periods and rolled edge.

$315,000, now on hand, of the first model with eagles of the last model. We have $100,000 in eagle blanks ready for coinage and a larger amount in strips and unadjusted blanks and are therefore ready to proceed with this coinage at short notice.

I think we will be severely criticized, and certainly deserve to be, if the eagles already struck should be allowed to go into circulation. Please acknowledge receipt of these two pieces. Respectfully etc.

Three days later, Hering arrived at the Mint with the long-awaited third pair of double-eagle models. These were immediately rejected by Barber who, to Hering's surprise, insisted that the relief was still too high for coining. On October 10, the engraver wrote a long letter of complaint to superintendent Landis:

Sir: Replying to the letter of inquiry regarding the double-eagle, new designs, I beg to say that the models arrived at this mint September 28th. Upon examination it was found that the relief of the models was so great that it would be a waste of time to make reductions for coinage, as it would be quite impossible to coin when these were made. I say impossible, because the relief does not conform to the mechanical requirement of modern coinage, namely, that the relief shall be no more than can be made perfect with one operation of the press, and here we have an inflexible law which governs the movement of metal under pressure.

The son of Mr. Saint-Gaudens wrote the mint concerning the models for eagle and double-eagle, and promised to send models of the same relief as those made by the French Medallist, M. Chaplain, for the gold coins of France, but when the models arrived it was very evident that there was a mistake in the relief, and while it was possible to use the models for the eagle, the models for the double-eagle instead of being in lower relief, were actually higher. The relief of the design for the double-eagle must be lower than the eagle, because it is larger, with greatly increased area and, therefore, more difficult to make.

With these conditions before us there was nothing to do but try to reduce the relief mechanically with the aid of the Janvier reducing lathe, but as the models were plaster and too large to be reduced to the size of the double-eagle, I had to make paraffine intermediate reductions, which I have done and sent to New York on the 5th instant to be cast into bronze, from which I can make steel reductions. These bronze castings were returned to the mint today, the 10th instant; you will see, therefore, that out of ten days we have had but five for our work. I have started the steel reduction today.

In answer to the question, "What are the prospects that the new double-eagle will be satisfactory?" I beg to remind you of our experience with the eagle, which had to be treated in the manner already described. You will remember that it was very unsatisfactory to both yourself and the Ex-Director, as the coin had a worn out, dull, or as we term it, blind look; no sharpness of detail. This is quite unavoidable when the relief is reduced mechanically, and not until the low relief model for the eagle was sent us was it possible to make a partially satisfactory coin.

In regard to the double-eagle, my fear now is that before I can reduce the relief on many sudden high points of the design sufficiently to coin, the portions that are already low will be lost and all detail will have disappeared.

That it will ever be satisfactory I cannot say, though I have very grave doubts. From the first time that this change of design in our gold coins was proposed I have tried to impress upon the mind of Mr. Saint Gaudens' representative, the absolute necessity of low relief models for coinage, and until proper suitable models are furnished, there can be no certainty that there will be any satisfactory results.

What we are now doing is in the line of experiment, as it is a departure from all well established methods of making coinage dies, which methods are to prepare the model for the intended purpose with a full knowledge of the process and requirements of modern coinage. This has not been done up to the present time, but, on the contrary, models have been furnished, made without the least knowledge of the minting of coins or the preparation of dies, and, consequently, the result has been simply failure, and accounts for the unparalleled waste of time.

Dies enough have been made to have coined millions had the models been made with the least rudimentary knowledge of the subject of coinage. Nevertheless, we have done and are doing all that we can to solve what Mr. Roberts, the Ex-Director, called the problem, to which I add, of making coinage dies from models devoid of the first requisite.

I beg to remind you that each time one of these high relief models have been sent, I have pointed out to the Director of the Mint the impossibility of making coins from such high relief models, and when the dies were made, they confirmed my statement. This condition being brought to the notice of the late Mr. Saint-Gaudens, he made some slight modification and returned the models, until we now have three sets of models, all of different relief, from which dies have been or are being made, but in no case has there been sufficient change in the models to guarantee success.

As soon as I can see the effect of the reducing lathe, I will report what prospect there may be of using the dies. Respectfully etc.

By this time Treasury officials were harried enough to suggest striking the whole issue of double eagles on the Mint's hydraulic medal presses. In a letter to Landis on October 25, Barber vehemently opposed the idea:

Sir: The following questions are asked by Hon. J. H. Edwards, acting Secretary of the Treasury. I therefore give you the answers for transmission by special delivery as requested:

First—How many (double eagles, new design) per day can be coined from medal presses now in the mint with three operations of the press?

Second—Cost, as compared to present coinage?

Third—How long before additional presses can be built?

In answer to the first question—with the present medal presses now in mint four hundred pieces per day can be struck. Second, as to cost, six dollars per hundred, or six cents each, while if struck on the automatic coining press now in use, the cost is one-twentieth of a mill each. To recapitulate, for six dollars and fifty cents you can strike 130,000 pieces with one coining press, while with medal presses you use two presses and strike but 200 pieces for twelve dollars.

As it is desired by Assistant Secretary Edwards to have this letter today, I beg to say that the only solution of this gold coinage is to have a model prepared of a relief that when dies are made coins can be struck as is being done by all the civilized countries of the world, namely, with automatic presses with one operation and a perfect impression of the dies.

To show the fallacy of making coins with medal presses and with more than one operation, allow me to state that to coin the number of pieces required, that is, the volume of coinage, the equipment would have to be enormous. For example —to coin the same number of pieces per day on the medal press, as suggested, with three operations each, would require 144 presses and 288 men.

The cost of the presses would be about $450,000, and if they were given us we have not enough room in the mint to store them to say nothing about operating, nor one foot of ground upon which an enlargement of the mint could be built— and all this for no purpose, as if a proper model is furnished, the difficulty is solved and any amount of coinage may be struck. Respectfully etc.

It is said that Roosevelt finally grew so impatient he ordered the Mint to begin the new issue even if it took an entire day to strike one impression. The story must contain at least a germ of truth, for nothing less would explain what followed. On November 22, when Barber was in the process of making low relief dies from Hering's third models, the Mint was instructed to furnish about six thousand high relief double eagles within ten days. Barber wrote to superintendent Landis the following day:

Sir:- Replying to the letter of the Director of the 22nd instant I beg to say that I have made arrangements with my people to work all day and all night and Sunday, and while I cannot promise any specific number of the double eagle pieces, all that is possible will be done.

We are making most strenuous efforts to get another pair of dies so that I can start up another press and Mr. Hart is working up an attachment that we hope to use on the press to put the inscription on the periphery.[10] If this works, as we anticipate, it will save much time in giving the last blow, as it will save the operation of taking the collars out of the press and knocking the coin out by hand and then placing the sectional collar back in position, which is a slow process.

We want to make these coins in one thousand lots, working with a plain collar for the first blows, using the inscription collar for the last blow only; we are doing this because if one die should break before the pieces were finished it would be almost impossible to turn another die so precisely that it would follow without causing a double in the impression, which, if it did occur, would involve delay in forging it out in the press. Therefore, I will report as soon as the first thousand pieces are made and then estimate how many pieces I can deliver daily.

In regard to the low relief upon which we are working I beg to state that this new order to make dies for the high relief coin will cause some interference with the completion of the hubs, as the high relief dies are so difficult to hub that we cannot make them in the ordinary way, but have to cut out and hammer in order to get the steel to follow into all the difficult and high points, therefore, Mr. Morgan and myself have to do this work.

I hope to be able to report early in the coming week the day we will be in shape to test the low relief dies for the double eagle, and will advise you in time to notify the Director that he may be present, as he desires. Respectfully etc.

In addition to their fatal high relief, the double-eagle models had no border, or determinate edge. The result was that in striking the coins (with several blows) on an hydraulic press, the metal which would normally flow into the borders was forced between the die and the collar, creating a high-wire edge. When the new double eagles were issued in mid-December they were immediately criticised by banks for not stacking properly.

In a letter of the 20th, Barber wrote to Director Leach that the mill of the coin had been altered to avoid a wire edge. He added:

I send you two pieces showing the result, these are not selected as all the coins now made are the same as these two, which gives me alarm, as they are so well made that I fear the President may demand the continuance of this particular coin, and while the effect of the mill is good it does not increase the output.

In the meantime, Barber had revised Hering's third pair of models, replacing the Roman date with Arabic numerals, and greatly reducing the relief. Much of the beauty and detail were lost during this operation, but the new models were finally adopted, Congress refusing to permit the expense of striking coins on an hydraulic press.

So far as Roosevelt was concerned, the artistic success of the high-relief

---

[10] This was a three-piece segment collar, based on the same principle invented by Droz more than a century before.

Models for a standing Liberty figure by Augustus Saint-Gaudens. *Whitman Publishing Co.*

Top: Bronze head of Victory by Saint-Gaudens, originally intended for Sherman monument. *Whitman Publishing Co.* **Bottom:** Head adapted for Niké Eiréné medal. *National Archives.*

Top: Model of Victory head as intended for the cent. **Bottom:** Model similar to last but with Indian headdress added. This was finally reproduced without the legend on the ten-dollar piece. *Whitman Publishing Co.*

Top: Saint-Gaudens' flying eagle model, the design originally intended for the cent, but adopted on the twenty-dollar piece. **Bottom:** Standing eagle model, intended for twenty-dollar coin, but adopted on the ten-dollar piece. *Whitman Publishing Co.*

From top down: Barber's pattern for a double eagle; Saint Gaudens' double eagle as finally issued by the Mint in low relief and with Arabic date; Saint-Gaudens' eagle as finally issued; Bigelow-Pratt half eagle.

coins more than compensated for their ephemeral issue. On January 10, 1908 he wrote to his friend William Sturgis Bigelow:

> Dear Sturgis: I am very much pleased that you like that coin. I shall have all kinds of trouble over it; but I do feel that what you say is true, that is, that it is the best coin that has been struck for two thousand years, and that no matter what is its temporary fate it will serve as a model for future coin makers, and that eventually the difficulties in connection with making such coins will be surmounted. I had a hundred thousand of them struck before Congress could get to me, which they did on the score of expense, and the subsequent coins are not as good as the first issue . . .

Hering, for his part, refused to approve the revised models. This created a new difficulty since Mrs. Saint-Gaudens could not be paid until such approval was given. The affair dragged on until spring, when Hering, accompanied by Homer Saint-Gaudens and Mrs. Saint-Gaudens' lawyer, visited the Mint. Hering cited the poor quality of the Mint's reductions, and produced as evidence the superior reductions he had obtained from France. This settled the argument, and payment was made without the approval.

The story of the Saint-Gaudens' coinage would not be complete without some reference to the mysterious small and extra-thick 1907 double eagle. The following letter of January 8, 1908 from Mint Curator T. L. Comparette to Director Leach should suffice:

> Sir: Among the numerous dies made from the Saint-Gaudens designs for the Double Eagle was one having the diameter of the Eagle, a very thick piece. There are several of them yet in existence and I beg leave to request that you give authority to place a specimen in the Cabinet of the Mint.
>
> My reasons for this request are purely practical. While it is an entirely illegal "coin" and for that reason should not I believe be put into a collection of historical coins, yet it was produced by the government and for that reason the few specimens will in after years command enormous prices, easily $3,000 each. Dealers are now offering large prices for them. Now it is very likely that in years to come the administration of the Mint and Cabinet will fall into hands that take a different view of its purpose than the one now held and in that case the purchase of one of these rare specimens at two or three thousand dollars is almost sure to follow.
>
> To prevent such a possible waste of funds in the future is the reason for making this request. An even exchange of but $20 will render that impossible. Very respectfully.[11]

❖   ❖   ❖

In October 1792 Matthew Carey, writing in the *American Museum*, had urged the Mint to strike intaglio coins. The optical effect, he said, would be normal at a distance, and the designs would not become abraded by circulation. A similar though not quite identical idea occurred to Dr. William Sturgis Bigelow in 1908. Bigelow wished to retain a relievo design, but depress it below the field of the coin. As an intimate friend of President Roosevelt, it was not difficult for Bigelow to advance his idea, particularly as new designs were still lacking for the quarter and half eagle.

On January 17, 1908 Bigelow wrote to Roosevelt:

---

[11] According to a letter from superintendent Landis to Director Leach on February 3, 1908, two of the small double eagles had been placed in the coin cabinet, eight had been defaced, and one still remained with Barber "who states that he will return it when the other [experimental] pieces are received from you for destruction." There is also a reference by Mint Curator T. L. Comparette to one specimen in the hands of the New York Numismatic Society. Perhaps this is the piece that was sold some years ago by a New York dealer.

. . . The coin is progressing finely. Will send you something soon to beat the one-hoss-shay both for style and wear.

Is is true that you are going to meet the criticisms on taking— "In God we Trust"— off the coins by putting "I know that my Redeemer liveth" on the Treasury notes?[12]

Bigelow entrusted the preparation of models to the well known Boston sculptor Bela Lyon Pratt. The latter completed his work on June 29, writing that day to Director Leach:

Dear Sir: I am sending to the mint at Philadelphia, the model of the coin which I have prepared and I hope same will prove satisfactory. I wish that those in charge of making the die would follow the models absolutely or at least would make no changes without consulting me.

I shall be exceedingly interested in seeing the finished coin. Will you kindly let me know when we may hope to see the coins. Yours etc.

The issue seems to have gone without a hitch, for on September 26, Roosevelt wrote to Bigelow:

Dear Sturgis: I enclose you the visible proof of a great service you have rendered the country—and I am speaking with scientific accuracy. Here you will see the five dollar gold piece, the copy of the models you have prepared, and a month hence our five dollar gold pieces that are issued from the mint will all be of this type. This one I send you as the first one struck. It therefore has a peculiar interest and I feel you are peculiarly entitled to have it; so please accept it with the compliments of Director Leach and myself. Ever yours, etc.[13]

Despite Pratt's request, Barber now proceeded to retouch the obverse model. With this done, Landis wrote to Director Leach on October 9:

As requested in your letter of the 26th ultimo, Mr. Barber has made a new die of the Indian head for the half eagle and quarter eagle, having worked up the detail and given the design the appearance of bold relief.

I have forwarded you today by United States Express, for approval or rejection two half eagles and two quarter eagles struck from the new die.

When the Bigelow-Pratt coins were issued in early November, there was a great deal of unfavorable comment. A famous pro and con correspondence between the numismatist and antiquarian S. H. Chapman and Dr. William Sturgis Bigelow was published in *The Numismatist*, and is quoted here.[14] On December 7, 1908 Chapman wrote to President Roosevelt:

To Theodore Roosevelt, President of the United States: It was the hope of every one that when our new coinage appeared we would have one of great beauty and artistic merit. But the new $5 and $2.50 gold pieces just issued totally lack these qualities, and not only those of beauty, but actually miss the practicability to which every effect of beauty in relief has been sacrificed.

The idea of Dr. William S. Bigelow, of Boston, to sink the whole relief below the flat surface of the coin causes it to appear like a design merely incised in the blank, and precludes entirely the effect of miniature bas-relief.

The head of the Indian is without artistic merit, and portrays an Indian who is emaciated, totally unlike the big, strong Indian chiefs as seen in real life. The

---

[12] Roosevelt considered it a sacrilege to use a religious motto on the coinage, and finding that it was unauthorized by law, prohibited its use. This raised a great hue and cry, and in 1908 Congress passed a bill restoring the motto on the gold and silver coins.

[13] Unfortunately, the coin was stolen before the letter reached Bigelow.

[14] "New U.S. Gold Series Criticized and Defended," *The Numismatist*, Feb. 1909.

treatment of the head is crude and hard, with sharp, abrupt outlines, as if carved by a mere metal chaser; and on the reverse is a reproduction of the Saint-Gaudens' eagle, which represents not our national bird (the white-headed eagle—commonly but erroneously called the bald headed eagle—which has no feathers on its feet), but resembles more closely the golden eagle, which is also indigenous to Europe.

The placing of the design below the surface of the flan, with deeply incised outlines, gives the effect of having been engraved into the metal, and can, therefore, be closely imitated by any metal chaser with the graver, without dies or moulds. And I am certain that if this had been suggested to the secret service officials it would never have been issued by the Treasury Department, and the issuance ought to be immediately stopped and the coins recalled, for every one will be in danger of the imitations.

The sunken design, especially the deeply sunken portion of the neck of the Indian, will be a great receptacle for dirt and conveyor of disease, and the coin will be the most unhygienic ever issued.

The principal claim put out for this coin, and which, according to the claim, would appear to be the most important any design can have, is that it will stack. But, alas! even this is not obtained by this means, for I have before me a stack of twenty pieces—$100—the stack used by cashiers, and it is the most tottering stack of modern coins, rocking to a great degree, and when the table is jarred about four times the upper coins slide off.

They will fall when carried on a bank tray. It is well known that you cannot strike a lot of flat blanks and get them perfectly true. As a connoisseur remarked to me: "Coins should be like a table, which we do not make with a flat bottom, but with feet to stand upon, and this result in coins can and has always been obtained by a flat rim."

And then the new coins, being thinner, as the metal is taken up by the full field, they do not make stacks equal in height to the old, and when mixed with the other issue cause the piles to be of unequal height, and the cashier cannot use the height of a stack as a test of count, but must sort this issue out.

The criticism from the bankers that the first model of the $20 and $10 pieces did not stack firmly should not cause the mint officials to throw all other considerations to the winds, for the firmness in stacking a coin, as stated above, could be obtained by the use of a sufficiently wide and high rim.

These coins will be a disgrace to our country as a monument of our present ideas of art as applied to coinage.

As compared with those of recent issues of European countries, not to mention the beautiful works of the ancient Greek coin engravers, it is an utterly miserable, hideous production, and let us hope that its issue will not be continued and that it will be recalled and remelted.

I would summarize the above objections as follows:

First—Lack of beauty. The coinage of our country should be an example of beauty and art to all its citizens. Second—Ease with which it may be counterfeited. Third—Unhygienic. Its filth-bearing capacities. Fourth—Not forming stacks of equal height.

I would suggest as a means of obtaining a competent committee to pass upon designs for coinage, that in future all designs for coinage be submitted to the American numismatic societies. For instance: The American Numismatic Society of New York, President Archer M. Huntington, and the American Numismatic Association, President Farran Zerbe.

The matter would then be weighed by men who have devoted their lives or leisure to the study of the art of coinage from the earliest period to the present time, and thus, having a complete purview of the subject, they would be able to judge of the merits of designs offered, and if such course were adopted we would be saved the mortification of seeing generally the worst designs accepted and the taste of our people degraded, instead of elevated, by the coinage passing through their hands.

Bigelow, on receiving a copy of the letter, wrote to Roosevelt:

Dear Mr. President: I have a line from Mr. Loeb dated December 8th enclosing an interesting letter from Mr. Samuel Hudson Chapman concerning the new gold coins. Some of Mr. Chapman's criticisms are well founded, others less so. He says that "sinking the relief below the surface makes it look like an incised design and precludes the effect of a bas-relief." This is hardly correct, as Mr. Chapman can readily see for himself in photographs of the Egyptian sculptures. There may be at the Museum at Philadelphia some casts or originals of Egyptian wall-carvings which will illustrate the principle. The bas-relief effect is accentuated and not diminished by the shadow of the sharp outline.

He says the head of the Indian is "without artistic merit and portrays an Indian who is emaciated, totally unlike the big, strong Indian chiefs as seen in real life." The answer to this is that the head was taken from a recent photograph of an Indian whose health was excellent. Perhaps Mr. Chapman has in mind the fatter but less characteristic type of Indian sometimes seen on the reservations.

"The treatment of the head is crude and hard, with sharp, abrupt outlines, as if carved by a mere metal chaser." This doubtless refers to the feathers of the head-dress which were retouched in the die, the modeling of Mr. Pratt's design having been a little too delicate to hold its own in the reducing machine. I enclose a photograph from a plaster cast of Mr. Pratt's clay, which illustrates this point.

The matter of the eagle was thoroughly threshed out at the time of the issue of the Saint-Gaudens' coin. That design proved to be an absolutely correct representation of the white-headed American eagle, except that the head was, perhaps intentionally, a little small and the leg feathers a little heavy. Both these criticisms Mr. Pratt has met in the present design. Mr. Chapman says that the American eagle has no feathers on its feet. This statement is true, but not exactly new.

"The placing of the design below the surface of the flan with deeply incised outlines gives the effect of having been engraved into the metal (sic), and can, therefore, be closely imitated by any metal chaser by the graver without dies or moulds." This criticism can hardly be taken seriously. If a forger were going to engrave anything he would not waste his labor on a single coin. It would be as easy to engrave a die as a coin of any issue.

"The sunken design will be a great receptacle for dirt and conveyor of disease, and the coin will be the most unhygienic ever issued." This remains to be seen. The question of hygiene has more relation to silver coins than gold, as they find their way into dirtier pockets. A dirty gold coin would be an anomaly. I have never happened to see one.

What Mr. Chapman says in regard to the fact of the coins not stacking is perfectly true. I noticed it as soon as they were issued and called Mr. Leach's attention to it. It proved to be due to an accidental warping of the steel die in hardening. Mr. Leach tells me that it can and will be avoided in future.

"Coins should be like a table, which we do not make with a flat bottom, but with feet to stand upon, and this result in coins can and always has been obtained by a flat rim." This is true, and it is exactly the principle on which the present issue is made. The flat rim extends from the edge of the coin to the edge of the design.

The thickness of the coins after striking depends on the amount of metal displaced by the die. A stronger relief would give greater thickness. I agree with Mr. Chapman that it would be well if all the coins in circulation were of the same thickness. . . .

Not to be outdone, Chapman wrote again to Roosevelt:

To his Excellency THEODORE ROOSEVELT, President of the United States.

Honored Sir: I am in receipt of your letter of December 16th, enclosing copy of a letter from Dr. Bigelow, dated December 10th, in which he reviews the criticisms I expressed in regard to the new half and quarter eagles.

Dr. Bigelow practically admits the principal points in my letter.

I cannot agree with him that the bas-relief effect is accentuated by the shade of the sharp outline, as it is really the shadow of the surrounding blank plane left standing at level with it or above the design proper, and which prevents top high light.

The Egyptian wall-reliefs, from which, of course, I recognized Dr. Bigelow obtained his idea, do not equal in effect bas-reliefs where the surrounding surface is cut away to the level of the lowest part of the design. The first or general effect of the Egyptian wall-reliefs is simply that they are wall-paintings with incised lines and slight modeling to help out or accentuate, and give the effect of shade on mural paintings; and when viewed at an oblique angle are invisible.

Egyptian art, unlike the Greek, remained frozen in conventionalism and did not progress to the full free rendering of the round.

I am glad to hear from Dr. Bigelow on one phase of the subject, on which he has expert knowledge, that the health of the Indian is excellent. But, to me his shrunken mouth and nostrils indicate a man below par in his physical condition.

He admits crude treatment in regard to head and eagle.

He thinks that the coin could not be easily imitated by incision, as a "man would make a die instead of a single piece." With this, I would beg to differ on account of actual experience, as I have met with several incised counterfeits. Recently I saw as small a denomination as a dime, which had been made by engraving on the piece of metal. The effect was that of a very much worn example. To make dies requires more time, mechanical appliances to use them, or, if moulds be used, furnaces to melt the metal, whereas a skillful engraver can make a copy rapidly on inferior alloy and without having the evidence against him of dies or moulds in his possession.

Anyone can see that this coin will be more dirt-bearing than previous types, on account of the extreme depressions.

When Dr. Bigelow says "a dirty gold coin would be an anomaly," he is evidently thinking only of the gold coins he sees in the East, which are from reserves in the banks, as gold is not used in circulation here; but I have seen many filthy gold coins and am advised that in the West poor and dirty people, when their little hoards amount to enough to convert them into gold, usually do so, and gold coins in the filthiest condition are often seen in California.

He fully admits the coins do not stack, but he misunderstands the quotation I made, "that coins be like a table . . . with a rim." That means a rim or foot near the circumference, but these coins are a plane, lacking only the surface around the design.

Chapman's diatribe was in vain. Protected by their twenty-five year statutory lease, the Bigelow-Pratt designs continued to be struck so long as the Mint issued quarter- and half-eagle coins.

CHAPTER 24

The Lincoln Cent

DURING THE SUMMER OF 1908, while President Roosevelt was posing for Victor D. Brenner's Panama Canal Service medal, the artist suggested the issue of a Lincoln coin. Brenner had already modeled a plaque and medal for Lincoln's birth centenary and, as he later remarked, his mind was "full of Lincoln." Roosevelt approved the idea, and invited him to submit designs.

The new portrait was at once similar to, and distinct from, that on the medal. The March 1909 issue of *The Numismatist* quotes Brenner as saying:

> "The other, yes, it is good, but this one is more intimate, deeper, more kind and personal. It is closer to the man; it makes you feel that you are sitting with him in his library. When it is finished I shall be nearly satisfied with it."

By January 18, 1909 the artist had submitted models for a Lincoln cent using a reverse design similar to that on the French two-francs. Under separate cover, he wrote to Director Leach: "If it please you and the President as it is, or with some changes it would be ready for a formal acceptance for the '22 of Feb. the date of Mr. Lincoln's birth. I am working on the other models and improving them and they will be posted very soon."

One of the new models showed an eagle which (Brenner thought) might be used in making a Lincoln half dollar. Another, with a standing figure of Liberty, was brazenly copied from the obverse of the two-franc piece. On February 1, Brenner wrote to Leach:

> . . . I have Ex. to you four plaster casts today; one is a new Lincoln head just finished resembling the one you have only in the mask.

The model of this Eagle is improved by the engraving you gave me, and if my last Lincoln head is adopted, the Eagle could well [be] made for the other side. I think that a half dollar would be more suitable for the Lincoln coin than a penny. In a day or so I shall send on to you a helmeted head of Liberty for one side of the cent or nickel, so that with the head I am to send, I think the models for the three coins would be accomplished, except the changing of the denominations and final finishing of detail in face and otherwise. I would also finish the Hubs so as to get all I want in the ultimate size . . .

I should consider it a privilege to have the cent and nickel adopted during the president's administration whose time expires but too soon.

If the Lincoln half dollar could be adopted I might be able to get photographs ready by the 12th. The head naturally would have to be reduced in relief so as to bring it up with the pressure . . .

Leach replied on February 2:

Your letter of the first instant just received. It is useless at this time to make any attempt to change the designs of the subsidiary coins, as no changes in these coins can be made for seven years without permission of Congress. We have only two coins on which we can make a change now, the penny and the nickel. For one of these coins I had already requested Mr. Barber to submit a design, and therefore I can only use your design, if it [is] accepted, on the penny or the nickel. . . . All engraving must be done by the engravers at the Philadelphia Mint. I think we all prefer the second model of Lincoln which you sent.

By February 9, things were still up in the air. Leach had discovered the origin of Brenner's branch design, but not of his standing Liberty which was stolen from the other side of the same coin. Somewhat distressed, the Director wrote to Secretary of the Treasury MacVeigh:

In the matter of furnishing the designs for the proposed new one cent coinage, Mr. Victor Brenner is insistent upon introducing another design for the reverse side in place of the one first offered. It is necessary that we should have some other design than the one first submitted by him, for I have discovered that it is an exact copy of the design used by the Government of France on its two franc piece, the only difference being in the inscriptions. We should also refuse to adopt the second design offered, embracing a female figure, first, for the reason that there is a question as to its legality. This figure is supposed to symbolize Liberty, and to use it, it seems to me, would destroy our license to use the Lincoln head, so much desired, on the obverse side. The law does not provide for two impressions or figures emblematic of Liberty. Then, as this is the simplest coin we have it seems to me it should call for the plainest and most distinct design.

Another objection, which is not so serious, being only a mechanical one, is that a figure on the reverse side of the coin, unless of the lowest possible relief, would interfere with securing the best results in producing the Lincoln portrait on the obverse side.

Later in the day Leach wrote to Brenner:

The subject of the design for the reverse of the penny has been discussed by the President and the Secretary and myself, and it was decided that owing to the law permitting of only one figure emblematic of Liberty to be on the coin, and the desire that the coin should be plain and simple, your suggestion of the female figure, left with me yesterday, is rejected; and you are requested to submit another design which shall be in compliance with the memorandum furnished you yesterday.

Brenner replied the following day:

. . . I beg also to acknowledge receipt of your letter dated Feb. 9th [?] fixing the designs for the cent piece—for the obverse to have the portrait of Mr. Lincoln

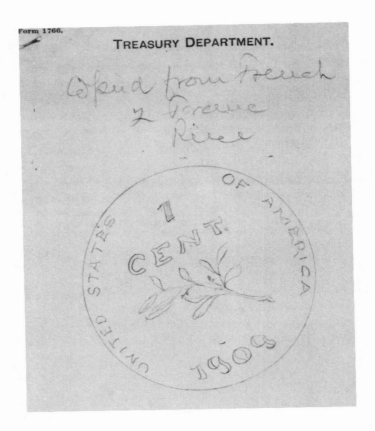

Early sketches by Victor D. Brenner for the reverse of the cent. Both were copied from the French two-franc piece. *National Archives.*

Top: model by Brenner based on obverse of French two francs, and intended for cent. **Bottom:** Medallic representation of Lincoln head by the artist. *National Archives.*

with the word Liberty and the date of the coinage, for the Reverse to have United States of America, One Cent and E Pluribus Unum. I shall submit my arrangement of the design to you shortly.

Lastly, Barber wrote a long letter to the artist, explaining the technical requirements of coinage dies.

Dear Mr. Brenner:— Your letter of the 10th inst., received and the contents have been discussed with the Director who I understand has given you certain instructions regarding the design.

Mr. Leach tells me that he has explained to you that he desired the field of coin to be finished with a fixed radius or curve, therefore the model must be made with a fixed radius.

I find in you[r] Lincoln medal that the field in front of the face is one plane while the field at the back of the head is an entirely different plane. This you will see will never do as we have to finish the field of the dies mechanically in order to comply with the wish of the Director, namely to have the field finished smooth and one radius.

In making your design you must avoid as much as possible one bold part of your design coming opposite another on the other side of the coin, as that would be fatal to the coining of the piece.

In regard to what relief you had better adopt I am sorry to say that I cannot give you any fixed instructions as so much depends upon the design of both sides and the particular metal the design is for, also the area of the coin.

You can look at the cent, judge from that, and that is the extent of the relief that can be successfully used for the one cent coin, and you will also see that from the point of utility, that the design is good, as it is so arranged that no one point comes in opposition to another, and as these coins are struck by tons every year, not thousands, but millions and if the usual average per pair of dies was not produced, the Coiner would condemn the dies at once.

In designing for a coin you must give due weight to the mechanical requirements of coinage and remember that great quantities of coin are demanded against time, and therefore, everything that can be done to simplify both the making of the dies and the production of the coin, must be considered.

You also know that the coins drop from the press at the rate of 120 per minute and that unlike a medal there is no bronzing or finishing of any description, no chance to bring out the design by coloring. It comes from the press one color and that [is] the color of the metal whatever that may be.

On February 17, Brenner brought the completed models to Washington. The reverse was entirely new, showing a single wheat leaf on either side of the denomination. On the following day, Leach conferred with the President who approved the designs except for the latinized V-shaped U's in the legends. The models were thus returned to Brenner for alteration. On February 26, he wrote to the Director:

I have the honor to inform you that I have today Expressed to you the completed models of the Lincoln penny, also the moulds of same. I trust you will find them satisfactory. I will appreciate the permission of examining the Hubs before they are hardened, and should any retouching be necessary, to do so under the supervision of Mr. Barber.

When the models arrived in Washington the following day, Leach immediately wrote to the superintendent of the Philadelphia Mint:

I send you by express today the models adopted by the President of the design for the proposed new issue of the one cent piece. I notice that Mr. Brenner insists upon putting his name in full on the obverse side. I am sorry to have to disappoint him in this matter, but after consultation with the Secretary of the Treasury upon the subject it was decided that only his initials could be permitted, and that in an unobtrusive way.

Mr. Brenner writes me that he desires to see the hub in time to have touched up any imperfections that he might notice. I wish you would advise me whether or not his request is practicable.

As soon as the dies are ready and proof pieces struck I shall be pleased to be advised of the fact.

On March 4, Brenner visited the Philadelphia Mint, returning home with the plaster models. He wrote to Leach: "I fully agree with you that my name on the Obverse looks obtrusive and thanks for calling my attention to it. I shall take it out, and put it in small letters on the reverse near the rim."

Brenner re-shipped the models a few days later, and on March 23, acting superintendent Norris wrote to Leach:

Mr. Barber, the Engraver, informs me that he has the reductions from the models for the one cent Lincoln piece finished. Mr. Brenner has requested that the reductions be forwarded to him for his alterations or approval. I beg to be informed whether I am authorized to ship these reductions to Mr. Brenner.

The request was denied by acting Director Robert Preston, to whom Barber replied on the 25th:

Mr. Landis has just shown me your letter regarding the request of Mr. Brenner to have the reductions from his models sent him for approval and any retouching that he may consider necessary for the proper representation of his work.

I hope you will reconsider your refusal to comply with Brenner's request as I think it only a reasonable one and most desirable and perfectly safe, as no doubt Brenner only wants to look the reductions over and sharpen up some points that he may think have lost distinctness in the process of reducing. This he ought to be allowed to do, and I know of no other way of his doing this, than sending him the reductions.

There can be no extra risk in doing this, as Mr. Brenner will have no advantage over the Mint that he does not already possess, as he has the model and also some medals having the Lincoln head and therefore, has all the opportunity to play crooked if he wanted, which I do not think he has any disposition to do, his request being only natural, that before making this coin he should be allowed to see that the reductions properly represent his work, and if not, that he should be allowed to touch up any parts that he may think ought to be improved.

I do not want to be in the position where Brenner can say that he was not allowed to do his best.

You know the St. Gaudens' people have appeared in print asserting that the Mint would not execute St. Gaudens' work as he desired, and now Mr. Bigelow in his reply to Chapman regarding the half and quarter eagle makes the statement, that the remark of Chapman that the treatment of the head being hard and crude, refers to the retouching done at the Mint.

I want to be spared this humiliation and therefore ask that Mr. Brenner be allowed to do his own retouching as he requests, and [which] I could not think of undertaking.

The reductions I have made from the Brenner model are good, but he may want to go over them in some points to satisfy himself and from the peculiar style of the modelling it would be impossible for anyone else to retouch his work in a satisfactory manner to him.

I therefore see no alternative but to let him have the reductions and return them as soon as he has passed upon them, which I am quite sure will be very soon, as he appears most anxious to have the coin brought out.

Barber's appeal would come with better grace if he hadn't subsequently altered Brenner's design without the artist's knowledge. At any rate, Preston relented and on March 27, Brenner wrote to Barber:

> I am sending back the hubs, having retouched the reverse. The obverse has been rubbed, and is too indistinct, so it will have to be recut. If it pleases you, you need not send me the die for the reverse for retouching, as there need only be a few lines rectified. Please suit yourself about that.
>
> It appears to me that something has happened to the model of the portrait side, as the whole neck looks rather fallen in.
>
> In the next reduction please use no brush over it, and send it on as it leaves the reducing machine.
>
> In case you shall finish up the die for the reverse of the cent, I would thank you to let me see an impression before its being hardened.

Barber transmitted the letter to superintendent Landis, commenting:

> In view of the fact that everything has been done to make this work entirely satisfactory to Mr. Brenner and we have failed, I beg to ask that Mr. Brenner be allowed to furnish a steel hub of his model, that is, that he be allowed to furnish the reduction, having it done in New York, under his own supervision, the same as he is doing with his medals.
>
> I make this request as I am quite sure we cannot satisfy Mr. Brenner. He does not appear to understand that when he asks to have the relief of the models reduced mechanically, some detail must necessarily be sacrificed and, therefore, he must prepare his models accordingly, which he has not done.
>
> The model furnished is of soft impressionistic character and when reduced to one tenth of the size of the model, and especially reduced in relief, the natural result is a want of detail, which Mr. Brenner complains of. It will facilitate the matter if Mr. Brenner be allowed to do as I suggest, but, if the Director positively objects, I can think of no way out of this difficulty, except to ask that we be furnished with a bronze casting of the model from which to make the reduction.
>
> I sincerely trust that the Director will grant this request to let Mr. Brenner furnish the reduction, as it will save much time and avoid friction of a most unpleasant character.

After some hesitation Brenner agreed to have hubs prepared by the Medallic Art Company of New York. Barber then sunk a master die of the obverse which he forwarded to Brenner for retouching.

On May 22, Director Leach wrote to Brenner:

> I have to inform you that I was not satisfied with the first proof of the Lincoln cent. I found that you had not dropped the Lincoln portrait down so that the head would come nearer the center of the coin, a matter I called your attention to when we were discussing your model. This is necessary to get the best result in bringing out the features in striking the coin. Therefore I had Mr. Barber make me a proof of this change, and as this left so much blank space over the top we concluded that it would be better in putting on the motto "In God We Trust." [1] This change has made a marked improvement in the appearance of the coin. I cannot send you a sample but if you feel enough interest in the matter it would be better for you to go down to Philadelphia where Mr. Barber can explain and show you what has been done.

Since no reply to this letter can be found, it seems probable that Brenner made the trip to Philadelphia and approved the change. The coin was finally authorized on July 14 by Secretary MacVeigh, and its issue set for August 2.

---

[1] This is said to have been done at the request of President Taft.

But the difficulties were far from over. When the new coins reached Washington, MacVeigh protested against the tiny V.D.B. at the bottom of the reverse, although he himself had approved the final design. On August 5, the mints were asked to suspend the coinage of cents, and Barber was ordered to Washington "to arrange to have the initial 'B' placed upon the new one-cent pieces in an inconspicuous manner."

The engraver was interviewed the following day by assistant Secretary Norton, who then wrote to MacVeigh:

> The letter B could be engraved in the mother die easily but the letters V.D.B. cannot be erased from the mother die because it is intaglio. To make a new mother die with an inconspicuous B and without the V.D.B. would take at least fourteen days.
>
> This delay can be avoided by simply erasing the V.D.B. from the "hub" and having no B whatever on the coin. From this amended "hub" the coinage dies can be rapidly and promptly struck off within three days and the mint can continue the coinage of the pennies for which there is a great demand (and in which there is a great profit to the government).
>
> Mr. Barber favors cutting off the initials and leaving them off the coin entirely. This is not unusual as there are no initials on the five-cent piece and formerly there were no initials on the Eagle, Half-Eagle or Quarter-Eagle. On the other hand it is not unusual to have an initial show on a coin. St. Gaudens' initials appear on the gold pieces, Pratt's on the Half-Eagle and Quarter-Eagle, etc. I have before me a French five-franc piece coined in 1870 on which Barre's full name appears. On another piece coined in 1831, the name E. A. Oudine appears. An Italian 20 centime piece bears the full name of both the Engraver and Designer.
>
> There are two reasons why Mr. Barber favors erasing the initials from the new penny; first, because it involves a delay of only three days in coining operations instead of a delay of about fourteen days. Second, because if the B is placed in an inconspicuous place, he fears that it may be confused with the B which now appears on the half-dollar which was engraved by himself. He is not willing to be held personally responsible for the Lincoln penny which he has always opposed and does not regard as a successful coin.
>
> Shall we take fourteen days and insert a small B in an inconspicuous place, or three days and elide the initials entirely? If the former, what is the inconspicuous place? Mr. Barber states that it is very difficult to place it on the Lincoln shoulder inconspicuously because the bust comes to the edge of the coin. On the reverse side he thought that he had found the least conspicuous place for the initials which he regarded as very small, but the American newspaper reporters have made it very clear that the place was by no means inconspicuous and the initials were by no means small.

Later in the day, Norton transmitted a copy of the letter to the acting Mint Director, adding: "I have just shown the above to Secretary MacVeigh and he authorizes me to direct you to erase the initials V.D.B. as above indicated."

Barber's explanation of the difficulty in placing Brenner's initial on the shoulder was an obvious subterfuge. On the very day he told Norton that "the bust comes to the edge of the coin," Brenner wrote to superintendent Landis:

> Much has been said for and against my initials on the Lincoln cent, and as the designer of same, it was natural for me to express indignation to their being taken off. In reality there is a feature in the new cent which was brought in without my knowledge, and which concerns me most. Lincoln's bust in my design was to *touch* the *edge of the coin*—in the minted cents, the bust is separated from the border. This feature makes my coin lose much of its artistic beauty.
>
> I beg you Sir—before more cents are minted, and before new dies are made, to kindly consider, and advise.

Although no reply can be found to this interesting letter, it is clear from the coin itself that Brenner's appeal was ignored. The alteration was apparently made to "bring up" the reverse motto, but the clandestine manner in which it was done belies Barber's pose as the much-maligned Mint artist.

Another objection to the Lincoln cent was the fact that it was too thick to use in vending machines. Leach, apparently frightened by press comments that the coin would never circulate, ordered new hubs and dies to reduce its thickness to that of the earlier cent. Barber was summoned back from Cape May, New Jersey, and on August 13, he wrote to Landis:

> In compliance with your request to make the new one cent the same thickness as the old I beg to state that I have made such changes as can be readily made without an entire reconstruction of the model.
>
> If it was desired that the new coin was to conform to all the conditions of the old coin it should have been so arranged and stipulated with the designer, as it is placing this department to great disadvantage to accept a model from an artist who never has modelled for coinage and knows absolutely nothing of the process of coinage and then insist that this department shall make dies that shall answer all Mint conditions, even to the thickness of the pieces when struck.
>
> Independent of the fact that the model was made without any thought of this requirement, the change that takes place in hardening may be sufficient to create a difference in the convexity of the die which will show when the pieces are gauged in slot machines, or piled fifteen or twenty high, and are we to sacrifice the appearance of the coin or limit our production to satisfy the manufacturers and venders of slot machines? I think not, although if the change I have already made does not conform to these machines, the only possible thing to do is to remodel the design and alter it, that it will at least satisfy the slot machine manufacturers, although it may not be satisfactory to anyone else.
>
> The change I have made may interfere with the average number of pieces per pair of dies that the Coiner expects and is almost necessary when the demand for one cent pieces is great, but it is the only change that can be made without as I have already said an entire reconstruction of the model.
>
> The relief of the Lincoln head is so great that in order to protect it from abrasion the border must be higher than the highest point of the head and consequently to make both sides of the coin alike the reverse border must be high also and these two borders regulate the thickness of the coin. You will therefore see the difficulty is two fold, first if the borders are not the same height the two sides of the coin will differ, one from the other and the mechanical difficulty is, that the borders not being equal the strain on the lowest border is too great and the die cracks before a proper average of pieces is obtained. The change I have made does not reduce the thickness of the piece to the same thickness of the old coin which I do not hesitate to say cannot be done without new models. And even then it will be only experiment as the designs are so entirely different that it is impossible for any one to say how the metal will be swallowed up by the design, and as the law regulates the diameter and weight of the piece we have no remedy in that direction and therefore I earnestly advise that the change I have made be accepted as fina' unless, it proves to reduce our production in which case there is nothing to do but return to our present hub.

In the end Leach relented, and the coin machine interests modified the dies in their detectors. Barber died in February 1917, and the following year the initials V.D.B. were added to Lincoln's shoulder where the engraver had found it too difficult to place a single letter. The coin was thus issued until 1959, when the reverse was redesigned to show the Lincoln memorial. The new design, which was prepared by the present Mint engraver (then assistant engraver) Frank Gasparro, copies the reverse of the five-dollar bill. Unfor

Lincoln cent, with original reverse and Lincoln Memorial reverse by Frank Gasparro.

tunately, the conception is ill-suited to a small coin. On the bill, the regularity of the outlines is broken up by a chiaroscuro within and surrounding the building. There are no shadows on the coin, and there is no feeling of depth. The details are lost, and what remains looks at a glance more like a trolley car. It is a poor memorial to Lincoln, to Brenner, and to the Commission of Fine Arts which opposed its adoption.

CHAPTER 25

The Indian Head, or Buffalo,
Five-Cent Piece

IN A LETTER TO SUPERINTENDENT LANDIS on March 26, 1910 Barber described several patterns he had prepared for a five-cent piece. The work was undertaken at the verbal request of Director Leach who, unfortunately for Barber, had since retired. One of the pieces resembled the engraver's 1896 shield design, while the others depicted a head of Washington.[1] Interest in a new five-cent coinage was not revived for over a year, and then under surprising circumstances.

On May 4, 1911 Eames MacVeigh wrote to his father, Secretary of the Treasury Franklin MacVeigh:

> A little matter that seems to have been overlooked by all of you is the opportunity to beautify the design of the nickel or five cent piece during your administration, and it seems to me it would be a permanent souvenir of the most attractive sort. As possibly you are aware, it is the only coin the design of which you can change during your administration, as I believe there is a law to the effect that the designs must not be changed oftener than every twenty-five years. I should think also it might be the coin of which the greatest numbers are in circulation . . .

Not long afterwards, assistant Secretary Andrew announced that the Department was considering new coinage designs.

The news soon reached James Earle Fraser, a world-renowned sculptor and student of Saint-Gaudens. After Fraser's initial meeting with the Mint au-

---

[1] These pieces are illustrated by Judd as numbers 1781-1788. Barber said that thirty-nine pieces had been struck of which twenty-six were destroyed. The remaining thirteen were accounted for as follows (we adopt Judd numbers for convenience): J-1781 to 1786, unique; J-1787, 2 pieces; J-1788, 5 pieces.

340

Indian head, or Buffalo, five-cent piece (enlarged) by James E. Fraser; **at left,** pattern for five-cent piece by Charles Barber.

thorities, Director Roberts wasted several weeks by asking the artist to design a new Lincoln head. On June 13, 1911 Fraser wrote to the Director:

> I think your idea of the Lincoln head is a splendid one and I shall be very glad to make you some sketches as soon as possible and let you see them. I think they should be reduced to the actual size of the coin; otherwise we will not be really able to judge them, even in the sketch period. I will have that done here, where I can watch the process.
>
> I have numerous sketches underway, some of which I hope may be of value.

Before long, Fraser had developed some definite ideas of his own. The artist prepared several small wax models of an Indian head and a buffalo, devices he considered characteristically American. These were eventually adopted, in lower relief, on the five-cent coin.[2]

Both assistant Secretary Andrew and Director Roberts were pleased with Fraser's designs, and introduced the artist to Secretary MacVeigh. Although MacVeigh frankly admired the work, he was reluctant to commit himself before seeing the results of a competition. The Secretary finally gave in, however, after Fraser wrote to Andrew on July 20:

> In reference to the competition, I think the great trouble is that you may have numbers of sketches in the competition one of which you choose and, if I'm not mistaken, you will be forced to stick very closely to that design, even though it might not be quite up to what you would want. Whereas, working with a competent man, there would be no doubt that a great many designs would be made, in fact, you would go on working til something of real merit was produced. You may say, if you like, that I would be perfectly willing to satisfy the Art Commission Mr. Mac Veigh spoke of.
>
> I will send you a few photographs of my work provided you wish to use them for reference.

On September 19, the artist, feeling perhaps more confident, wrote to MacVeigh:

> Although I realize that no definite commission has been given me in regard to the designs for the new coins, I have become so much interested in the sketches that I have pushed them a little further and now they are in the shape of electrotypes which I should like to submit for your consideration. Of course, this means that they are still merely sketches and not finished products, but I have had them reduced and made into their present form for the purpose of showing exactly what I would wish done, provided I furnished them.
>
> At present, they are the size of the penny but they could easily be enlarged to any size desired. The idea of the Indian and the buffalo on the same coin is without doubt, purely American and seems to be singularly appropriate to have on one of our national coins. You will see that the Indian is entirely different than any that has ever been used on a coin. Most of the heads have been caucasians with an Indian head-dress; in this case I have avoided using the war-bonnet and have made a purely Indian type. Therefore, I should like to ask whether or not you would consider placing these designs on the new model.
>
> I have also carried the Lincoln head further, not only because I was personally interested in it, but because Mr. Roberts has rather encouraged the idea of my doing so.

---

[2] In an undated letter in the archives, Fraser wrote that the Indian Head was a "type rather than a portrait." He went on to explain that prior to undertaking the five-cent design, he had made several portraits of Indians including Iron Tail, the famous chief who fought General Custer at Little Big Horn. Although Fraser failed to name his other Indians, they have since been identified as Two Moons and Chief John Tree. The buffalo (or rather bison) was modeled after Black Diamond, a resident of Central Park Zoo in New York. See Leonard J. Ratzman, "The Buffalo Nickel, A 50-Year-Old Mystery," *Whitman Numismatic Journal*, May-June 1964.

Possibly you will be interested in knowing that the Italian Government has purchased a collection of my models for its National Museum in Rome. The Belgian government obtained a somewhat similar collection of my work last year.

On January 13, 1912 MacVeigh wrote to Fraser, apologizing for the delay in reaching a decision. The Secretary also wrote to Director Roberts, asking him to inform Fraser that his designs had been adopted.

On January 20, McVeigh again wrote to Roberts:

Did you see Mr. Fraser, the medallist, when you were in New York, and if so, did he throw you out bodily into McDougall's Alley [the street on which Fraser lived], as a result of the neglectful treatment he had received, or did he invite you in to talk the matter over?

If you can find the time, would you drop me a line and let me know how the matter now stands; or would you ask Miss Kelly to do so?

Was any conclusion reached between you and Mr. Fraser as to what he would do with the inscriptions?

Fraser's ideas on the latter are given in a letter to Roberts, dated January 27.

. . . I believe in placing as little lettering as possible on the coins, since the design will be just so much better for the fewer things it contains. I am very anxious to go on with the designs and make them reduced to the nickel size, after which I believe it would be wise to confer with the Mint in Philadelphia. Possibly it would be better for me, before going to Washington, to complete the coins and have the reductions to bring with me. . . .

Fraser did not complete his work until midyear. On June 26, he wrote to Roberts that "the models for the five cent piece have been finished and reduced in several heights of relief." In early July, Fraser presented the reductions to Secretary MacVeigh who approved them, requesting only that the artist lower the relief still further and, if practicable, increase the size of the lettering in the denomination. MacVeigh then submitted the designs to the Commission of Fine Arts where they were highly praised by Cass Gilbert, Daniel French, and Edwin Howland Blashfield.

So far, things were going smoothly enough, but there was one factor that neither the artist nor the Mint had counted on. Fraser later described it in a letter to Secretary MacVeigh:[3]

In the latter part of July, Mr. Roberts, during one or two of my numerous trips to Washington at your request, told me that there was some company which manufactured coin detecting machines and that they had made inquiries about the new coin, and in the latter part of August or the early part of September, 1912, Mr. Roberts informed me specifically that the Hobbs Manufacturing Co., had raised with him or in the Department a question as to whether or not a machine which had been patented by the Hobbs Co. would act satisfactorily with the coins struck from the dies made from my designs, that is, the question they raised was whether their machine, which they claim discriminates automatically against counterfeit coinage, would work satisfactorily with the new nickel, and Mr. Roberts then requested me to meet Mr. Hobbs here in New York . . .

Hobbs together with a Mr. Reith, the inventor of the machine, called at the artist's studio around November 7, "to see what was the results of the efforts that I had agreed to make." Fraser said that the pair seemed dissatisfied with the result, and that for his part he found it "impossible . . . to understand from their conversation . . . the matter involving measurements of one thousandth of an inch."

---

[3] February 8, 1913.

"What I was expected to do," Fraser said on another occasion, "was to make a large model so perfect that when it was reduced five times it would open a combination lock on being run through it." Fraser furnished Hobbs with electrotype shells of the two models, and on November 22, the latter returned the shells, sweated together, and showing what he considered necessary changes in the designs. Director Roberts was impressed by the "public utility" of the machine, and suggested to Fraser that the artist and the company "work together."

Fraser, possibly recalling the "togetherness" clause, wrote to Roberts on December 1, 1912:

> I am in receipt of a letter from Mr. Hobbs—which I am enclosing—in reference to the five cent piece.
>
> I notice that there is no concession whatever on his part; he asks me to reduce the size of the buffalo, inscription, etc., eight-one-hundredths of an inch which, practically is one-tenth of an inch. I have carefully considered every space surrounding the buffalo and have changed them all back and forth many times, arriving at this design only after the utmost care. So you see how radical any change approximating one tenth of an inch would be in the relation of the spacing in a coin of this size.
>
> Not only that but it is no sure thing that the coin-detector will be a practical success. I suggested that the first rim of the nickel be used instead of a circle inside the fretwork and also to bring the second circle nearer the stars.[4] This I am sure can be done.
>
> . . . I hardly think that the Government should be forced to accept a design which is inferior to the present one when the machine could be changed without altering to any great degree its effectiveness, thus leaving the coin nearly in its present state. There would have to be a slight reduction even in the event of using the first rim of the nickel. In the future, this would eliminate the wide rim which, on the present coin, is wholly out of proportion to its size thereby adding to the difficulty in making the design. I called on Mr. French and he thinks it would be nearly out of the question to make so great a change in my design.
>
> I only received the coins from Mr. Hobbs last Saturday so have had little time to work on them. I am perfectly willing to do anything to help them without making the design bad . . .

Roberts replied on December 3, asking Fraser to "perfect the design going as far in the matter as you think you can without impairing its artistic effectiveness." The Director said that he neither wanted to spoil the design nor block development of an improved automatic machine.

On December 15, Fraser took the deformed electrotype to Washington to show to MacVeigh and Roberts. The Secretary was distressed by Hobbs' alterations, and flatly rejected them. Roberts, however, still hoped for a working compromise between the artist and the machine.

On the 19th, the Director, with Secretary MacVeigh's approval, authorized Fraser to perfect the designs already submitted and approved by the Department. Fraser at once complied, sending a pair of dies to the Philadelphia Mint[5] where, on December 26, they were received by Barber. The engraver prepared hubs and dies, and on January 7, 1913 experimental pieces were struck "with great success." The workmen said that the coins required even less pressure to bring up than the old Liberty head design.

---

[4] This would seem to indicate that Fraser's original design had a starred border though, curiously, it is not found on the 1912-dated plaster model in the engraver's office at the Philadelphia Mint.

[5] The master hubs and dies had been made by the Medallic Art Company of New York.

On January 11, Mint superintendent John Landis wrote to Roberts that he "intended to harden the hubs today" and would "be ready to begin manufacture of the working dies on Monday."

But Fraser's joy was shortlived. After examining the new coins, Hobbs demanded further changes, and the vacillating Director asked the artist to revise his models.

Fraser, with admirable patience, complied, and on January 20, he cabled Roberts: "Dies are finished and will be in Philadelphia tomorrow, delay caused by working with inventor until he was satisfied. The coin is practically the same."

Fraser, the inventor Mr. Reith, and a Mr. Henson of the Hobbs Company, arrived at the Mint the same day. Reith, on examining the new dies with a micrometer, discovered one small point still misaligned, but said he could make the necessary modification in his machine. He then allowed Barber to proceed with the coinage.

On returning home, however, Reith informed Hobbs that the promised changes had not been made. Hobbs dashed off a frantic letter to Roberts, and Barber, incredulous, contacted Henson who explained that Reith was sometimes inclined to be "over sanguine."

On January 24, after nine impressions had been taken from the controversial dies, one was forwarded to Hobbs.

On February 3, Hobbs sent Roberts a long list of changes which, he insisted, would be necessary to satisfy the coin detector. The bewildered Fraser was thereupon called to a new conference, this time with Hobbs and Reith. The latter had brought a new machine which he said would not work properly unless the changes were make.

Fraser, at his wits' end, appealed to Secretary MacVeigh. In a letter of February 8, the artist complained of "being used as a means to bring the new five cent piece back to the low artistic standard of the old nickel."

MacVeigh forwarded the letter to Roberts, adding that he hesitated "to cause Fraser more trouble and loss of time."

Roberts was less sympathetic. On February 10, after advising MacVeigh to interview Hobbs "and be fully informed before final action is taken," he said:

> . . . The importance of the automatic vending machine has grown upon me during the negotiations and I think the question of whether it shall be ignored or not should be decided now upon broad grounds of public policy without regard to the history of the negotiations with Mr. Fraser up to this time. That the latter has done his work well cannot be questioned but we can better pay him and throw his work away than adopt it if to do so is contrary to sound public policy . . .

A final meeting took place on February 15. Attending were Secretary Mac-Veigh, Director Roberts, Barber, Hobbs, his vice-president and their attorneys, Mr. Reith, Mr. Henson, and Mr. Fraser and his attorney. Writing to Roberts a few hours later, MacVeigh declared "that it would be injudicious to make any further changes in the coin." He added:

> The effort to make satisfactory changes has been continuous for more than two months; and it is evident to me that Mr. Fraser, to meet the requirements of the Astumco people,[6] had done everything he could without sacrificing the essentials

---

[6] The Hobbs Co.

of the designs. On the other hand, the requirements specified by the Astumco representatives, to wit, a clear space between the rim and the rest of the design and a radical change in the cheek of the Indian are, in my judgment, impossible to concede without the practical abandonment of the artistic qualities of the design. This is not simply my opinion, but is the opinion of the sculptor, who has shown himself a man of great personal tolerance, and of various high authorities who have written me within a day or two.

But even these concessions the representatives of the slot machine were not able to assure us would be sufficient. They said frankly that the solution would still depend upon trials and tests after these changes had been made.

At the same time it was a fact that changes in the machine—in the effort to accommodate it to the new coin—had already been made; and I was impressed with the fact that the inventors were not at all at the end of their possibilities— so that a solution may be found in further changes in the machine rather than in further changes in the coin.

Other slot machines would probably not be affected by a new coin as the Astumco would be; and this would seem to be the reason why no other has been heard from. It was stated in the Conference that seventy machines had been entered in competition at the Post Office Department, indicating a far larger number of slot machines than I had supposed existed. None, however, as I have said, of these machines has entered any objections to the new coin. The Astumco machine alone makes any suggestions. And in this connection it is necessary to call attention to the fact that the Astumco Nickel slot machine is a new one, not yet introduced—scarcely at all introduced. It still has its way to make; and it is still a question whether it will acquire a wide field. Altogether, therefore, the commercial interests involved in this case are not relatively important. They are but a very small fraction of the slot machine interests.

I am definitely impressed by the fact that the design as it now has become under Mr. Fraser's efforts to adjust it, should stand.

It is fortunate that the commercial interests involved are relatively slight; for one must always be impressed in such a case by the claims of business. It is of course true that only the most serious business considerations should stand in the way of an improvement of the coinage; and this particular coin has great claims of its own because of its special quality. If we should stop new coinage—which is always allowed every twenty-five years—for any commercial obstacles less than imperative we should have to abandon a worthy coinage altogether. This would be a most serious handicap to the art of the Nation; for scarcely any form of art is more influential than an artistic coin, where the coin is widely circulated.

You will please, therefore, proceed with the coinage of the new nickel.[7]

---

[7] By March 1913, it had become obvious that the letters in the denomination were too thin and would rapidly wear away. Barber strengthened the area in one of the working dies, and on April 21, sent Roberts a nickel of revised design together with a standard piece for comparison. Fraser, on receiving the samples, approved the change but declined MacVeigh's invitation to another conference.

In 1916, a new Indian portrait, with longer nose and higher relieved LIBERTY, replaced the 1913 design. This obverse seems to have been continued through 1938 when the Fraser design was abandoned.

The archives reveal the following record of patterns for the Indian head five-cent piece:

January 13, 1913. Seventeen impressions taken from the first pair of dies (0.839" diameter, no initial F below date), of which six were destroyed and the remainder given to the Mint collection, Mint officers and the designer, Mr. Fraser.

January 21. Nine impressions taken from the adopted dies, of which five were destroyed.

February 13. Four impressions taken from dies with the diameter slightly greater than adopted (0.869" diameter, no initial F below date), of which one was destroyed. These were made to show the effect of a small space between the design and the border in case it was decided to slightly reduce the size of the Indian head.

The unique copper trial piece of type 2 design (i.e. with modified FIVE CENTS) is neither a trial piece nor made of copper. It was struck from an experimental alloy of ninety-five per cent copper, five per cent nickel and zinc, and "issued" in the original presentation case which held the five 1913 Liberty head nickels.

CHAPTER 26

The Weinman and MacNeil Coinage

BY 1916, TIME HAD RUN OUT on the Barber coins, and the Treasury Department arranged a competition to provide new designs. After considering all the submissions, the Department, with the approval of the Commission of Fine Arts, awarded contracts to Adolph Weinman and Hermon MacNeil. On March 3, Mint Director Woolley notified Barber of the results:

> Dear Mr. Barber: I beg to advise you that selections have been made from a large number of designs submitted for the proposed new subsidiary silver coins. The models submitted by Mr. Adolph Weinman have been chosen for the Half Dollar and the Dime, and the designs submitted by Mr. Hermon MacNeil have been determined upon for the Quarter Dollar.
>
> It is understood that satisfactory working models are to be delivered to the Mint not later than May 1st, 1916, and they are to conform in all respects to the requirements of the Mint.
>
> In advising you of the decisions reached I beg to express the appreciation of the Secretary of the Treasury and myself of the very beautiful designs submitted by you, and to thank you for your deep interest in the matter. With kindest regards etc.

Accordingly, arrangements were made for the artists to visit the Mint and confer with Barber on the mechanical requirements of the coinage. Weinman, on his first trip, found Barber absent, but held a lengthy conversation with his almost forgotten assistant George Morgan. Other meetings followed, with Barber apparently as sullen as ever. On March 29, Director Woolley wrote to superintendent Joyce:

347

Dear Mr. Joyce: I beg to enclose a letter to Mr. Barber. Confidentially, the sculptors designing the new coins felt that on their last trip Mr. Morgan was much more cordial and cooperative than Mr. Barber was. I realize I am dealing with artistic temperaments at both ends. Cordially etc.

In as much as it was Barber's designs that were being replaced, Morgan could afford to be cordial! The enclosed letter announced that the artists would again visit the Mint.

On April 25, Weinman wrote to Director Woolley:

Dear Mr. Woolley: Since your visit to my studio on Friday last I have had the model for the reverse of the Half Dollar cast in hard bronze and have yesterday forwarded it to Mr. Barber at the Philadelphia Mint.

I have worked steadily upon the obverse of the Half Dollar and of the Dime but they will not be in shape for your final inspection tomorrow. Though I am pushing the work as rapidly as possible, it becomes quite apparent that the four models for the Half Dollar and the Dime cannot be completed for the date at which I promised them and I would therefore request an extension of ten days or two weeks.[1] Trusting this will not cause any embarrassment, I am etc.

In a letter of June 22, Weinman wrote to the Director:

Dear Mr. Woolley: Your letter dated May 29, 1916 informing me that the designs submitted by me for the proposed new Half Dollar and Dime have been accepted has just been received.

I was at the Philadelphia Mint yesterday and Mr. Barber showed me two new Half Dollars, one with modelled background, the other with burnished background. I discovered that the word "Liberty" inscribed in field above walking figure is rather too pale and somewhat thin and I am convinced that this should be remedied before the final dies are made. If agreeable to you, I will make the change immediately. In order to help in this, I would request the loan of the two examples of the new Half Dollar, above mentioned. The making of the proposed change should not require more than ten days at most and I am sure will help the coin very much. If you approve of my request, will you kindly instruct Mr. Barber or the Superintendent of the Mint to forward the coins to me, with the understanding that I will guard them closely and return them safely to the Mint. Very sincerely yours.

Progress and problems are revealed in Woolley's letter of June 24 to superintendent Joyce:

Dear Mr. Joyce: The dime is all right. Please see that working dies for the three mints are made as rapidly as possible, in order that the coinage of the new dimes may be begun quickly. The demand for these coins is exceedingly great.

The model of the obverse of the half dollar will have to be made over and Mr. Weinman informs me he is now at work on it. The same is true of the quarter dollar. The reverse of both the quarter dollar and half dollar, as shown on the coins struck from the polished dies, are satisfactory. I can see no good end to be accomplished by having the models remade on plate bases.

Everyone to whom the coins have been shown here thinks they are beautiful.

I beg to enjoin you not to pay out any of the new dimes until you have received special instructions from this office . . .

During the next few months a number of unexpected difficulties cropped up. A letter from Woolley to Joyce on August 15, mentioned an "alteration of the designs of the ten cent piece" required by some fault in the striking.

On September 7, Weinman's half dollar design was said by Joyce to be "pro-

---

[1] Weinman had fallen behind schedule due to a severe attack of tonsilitis.

ducing an obvious unevenness of thickness in the edge of the coin." The Director added that the design would have to be further modified.[2]

Although the new coins had entered circulation by December, MacNeil wrote to Mint Director von Engelken on January 11, 1917 asking permission to alter the design on the quarter. This interesting letter cannot now be located, but its general content is clear from the Director's reply on the 13th:

> Dear Mr. MacNeil: I have your letter of the 11th instant relative to the design of the Quarter Dollar.
>
> The changes you propose have been read with interest, and it may be practicable to conform to your wishes to some extent. However, as the coins have gone into circulation, no marked changes could be undertaken.
>
> If you care to have prepared and sent to the Mint a bronze cast carrying the changes you suggest, and will do this with the understanding that the Government is not to be involved in any expense whatever, I will have dies made at the Mint and have specimen coins struck for submission to the Secretary of the Treasury. No radical changes would be considered, and I would reserve the right to decline to execute dies if the model submitted showed a departure from the accepted design.
>
> I am most anxious to do anything I can to meet your wishes. Very truly yours etc.

On January 19, Director von Engelken wrote to superintendent Joyce that the new quarters and dimes had been criticized for "having a fin and being coined with a dirty die." He added that he had examined specimens of both coins under a lens and verified the charges.

Three days later, von Engelken wrote again to Joyce:

> Sir: This letter will be handed to you by Mr. Hermon A. MacNeil whom you already know.
>
> At my suggestion Mr. MacNeil has had a conference with Secretary McAdoo relative to some modifications in the design of the 25 cent piece that Mr. MacNeil wishes to carry out.
>
> It is the Secretary's request that Mr. MacNeil be granted every facility in your institution in connection with your Engraving Department to have his modifications embodied in coin size to be submitted to the Secretary.
>
> You will please instruct your Engraving Department to cooperate with Mr. MacNeil to the end that he may have entire freedom and liberty in incorporating any changes and alterations that he may desire.
>
> Whenever the changes may have been made satisfactory to Mr. MacNeil have them struck off in the customary lead discs and notify me. Respectfully etc.

The changes were subsequently approved by Secretary McAdoo who, on April 16, wrote to Representative William Ashbrook, chairman of the House committee on coinage, weights and measures:

> My dear Congressman: I have the honor to submit for your consideration a draft of an act to authorize the modification of the design of the current quarter dollar in accordance with a specimen submitted by Mr. Hermon A. MacNeil, the sculptor whose designs were accepted on May 23, 1916 for the quarter dollar now being issued.
>
> The modifications proposed are slight, the principal one being that the eagle has been raised and three of the stars placed beneath the eagle. On the reverse the lettering has been rearranged and the collision with the pinions of the wings obviated. These changes together with a slight concavity will produce a coin

---

[2] The number of variant patterns known for the half dollar reflects many experiments which are only hinted at in Mint correspondence.

Sketches by Hermon MacNeil for reverse of the quarter dollar. The lower right is inscribed "O.K. for model [Director] Woolley."

Top: 1916 "Mercury dime" by Adolph Weinman; **center:** 1916 and 1917 quarters by Hermon MacNeil; **bottom:** 1916 half dollar by Weinman.

materially improved in artistic merit and not interfere in any way with its practical use.

I am sorry to have to ask for this change, but since the original dies were made the artist has found that they are not true to the original design and that a great improvement can be made in the artistic value and appearance of the coin by making the slight changes the act contemplates. Sincerely yours etc.

Curiously, when Ashbrook introduced McAdoo's bill on April 30, he said only that the alterations were required to make the coin stack properly. This provoked some criticism of the Mint, and on June 25, when the subject was resumed, Ashbrook admitted that the Secretary did not like the old designs. McAdoo's letter to the chairman was read into the Congressional Record.

The bill, as passed July 9, 1917, specified that "No changes shall be made in the emblems or devices used. The modifications shall consist of the changing of the position of the eagle, the re-arrangement of the stars and lettering, and a slight concavity given to the surface."

Considering that McAdoo himself had framed the bill it is difficult to explain the further alteration which garbed the beautiful but bold Liberty figure in a mailed vest. The Secretary may have wished to avoid a provocative discussion, but in doing so he caused the issue of an obviously illegal quarter from 1917 to 1930.

Legalities apart, it would be captious to deny the outstanding merit of the Weinman and MacNeil designs. An excellent description of these designs, based on the artists' own interpretations, is given in the annual Mint Director's report for 1916:

By far the most notable achievement of the mint service during the fiscal year 1916 was the selection, with your approval, of new designs for the dime, quarter-dollar, and half-dollar pieces. For the first time in the history of our coinage there are separate designs for each of the three denominations, and their beauty and quality, from a numismatic standpoint, have been highly praised by all having expert knowledge of such matters to whom they have been shown. The striking of these coins for general circulation will doubtless be well underway by the coming of the Christmas holiday season.

The process of selecting the new designs (authority under sec. 3510 of the U.S. Rev. Stats., approved Sept. 26, 1890) began in January last, when, with your permission, I conferred with the members of the Commission of Fine Arts. Noted sculptors were commissioned to prepare a number of sketch models, and from more than 50 submitted 3 sets were chosen. It is a pleasure to note that the models which you and I selected were also the choice of the members of the Commission of Fine Arts.

The dime and half dollar are the work of Mr. Adolph A. Weinman. The design of the half dollar bears a full-length figure of Liberty, the folds of the Stars and Stripes flying to the breeze as a background,[3] progressing in full stride toward the dawn of a new day, carrying branches of laurel and oak, symbolical of civil and military glory. The hand of the figure is outstretched in bestowal of the spirit of liberty.

The reverse of the half dollar shows an eagle perched high upon a mountain crag, his wings unfolded, fearless in spirit and conscious of his power. Springing from a rift in the rock is a sapling of mountain pine, symbolical of America.

The design of the 25-cent piece is intended to typify in a measure the awakening interest of the country to its own protection.

---

[3] Actually, Miss Liberty wears the flag as a dress—a heraldically unorthodox conception. Most specimens issued prior to World War II are too weak to show the striated (for red) stripes, the branch hand, or Miss Liberty's headgear.

The law specifies that on the obverse of the coin not only the word "Liberty" but a representation of Liberty shall be shown. In the new design Liberty is shown as a full-length figure, front view, with head turned toward the left, stepping forward to the gateway of the country, and on the wall are inscribed the words "In God We Trust," which words also appear on the new half dollar, mentioned above. The left arm of the figure of Liberty is upraised, bearing the shield in the attitude of protection, from which the covering is being drawn. The right hand bears the olive branch of peace. On the field above the head is inscribed the word "Liberty," and on the step under her feet "1916." The reverse of this coin necessitates by law a representation of the American eagle, and is here shown in full flight, with wings extended, sweeping across the coin. Inscription: "United States of America" and "E Pluribus Unum" and "Quarter Dollar" below. Connecting the lettering above on outer circle are thirteen stars.

The design of the dime, owing to the smallness of the coin, has been held quite simple. The obverse shows a head of Liberty with winged cap. The head is firm and simple in form the profile forceful. The reverse shows a design of the bundle of rods, with battle-ax, known as "Fasces," and symbolical of unity, wherein lies the Nation's strength. Surrounding the fasces is a full-foliaged branch of olive, symbolical of peace.

CHAPTER 27

The Peace Dollar

THE ORIGIN OF THE PEACE DOLLAR can be traced to a paper prepared by Farran Zerbe, and read before the 1920 convention of the American Numismatic Association. At Zerbe's recommendation, a committee headed by Judson Brenner was appointed to introduce the subject to Congress, and in December a meeting was arranged with Representative Vestal, chairman of the House committee on coinage, weights and measures.

The proposal was forwarded to Mint Director Baker who consulted Charles Moore, chairman of the Commission of Fine Arts. Moore recommended special legislation to waive the requirements of law regarding designs. Thus, on May 9, 1921 Vestal introduced a bill to provide for a silver dollar "of an appropriate design commemorative of the termination of the war between the Imperial German Government and the Government and people of the United States." The design was to be selected by the Director of the Mint with the approval of the Secretary of the Treasury. The new dollar would be known as the "Peace dollar."

For some reason (allegedly on Baker's advice) the bill was never acted upon, and the Peace dollar emerged with traditional devices and superscriptions.

To obtain the best possible designs, the Commission of Fine Arts arranged a competition among the nation's leading medallists, inviting Victor D. Brenner, Adolph Weinman, Hermon MacNeil, Chester Beach, John Flanagan, Henry Hering, Robert Aitken, Robert Tait McKenzie, and Anthony De Francisci.[1]

---

[1] Apparently one of these artists failed to participate since later records of the Commission and the Treasury Department refer to only eight contestants. Fraser was at this time the sculptor member of the Commission, and thus could not compete.

The models of De Francisci were selected by the Commission and finally approved by President Harding.

For the young artist and his wife it was the realization of a childhood dream. In fact, it was from the classical features of Teresa Cafarelli (Mrs. De Francisci) that her husband derived his ideal Liberty head. The choice was appropriate, for Teresa, who had come from Naples at the age of five, was passionately fond of art and loved the American ideal of liberty as native Americans seldom do.

Teresa recalled how, as her Italian steamer plowed into New York harbor, she caught sight of the Statue of Liberty and eagerly called her family over to see it. Then she struck a pose imitating Bartholdi's great lady, holding her torch aloft. Such was the impression that the statue made on her youthful mind. Later, when the first Peace dollars were struck, she wrote to her brother Rocco:

> You remember how I was always posing as Liberty, and how brokenhearted I was when some other little girl was selected to play the role in the patriotic exercises in school? I thought of those days often while sitting as a model for Tony's design, and now seeing myself as Miss Liberty on the new coin, it seems like the realization of my fondest childhood dream.

De Francisci himself has described how he set about to create his famous Liberty head:

> I opened the window of my studio and let the wind blow on her hair while she was posing for me. . . . The nose, the fullness of the eye and the mouth are much like my wife's, although the whole face has been elongated.

To columnist Hannah Mitchell,[2] De Francisci said:

> You will see that the Liberty is not a photograph of Mrs. De Francisci. It is a composite face and in that way typifies something of America. I did not try to execute an "American type" or a picture of any woman. I wanted the Liberty to express something of the spirit of the country—the intellectual speed and vigour and virility America has, as well as its youth. I had nothing of the magazine-cover idea.

The artists had not been invited to compete until November 19, 1921, leaving them but three weeks to submit sketches to the Commission of Fine Arts, and after the sketches were approved, only four days to complete models for each side of the coin. De Francisci prepared two different models for the reverse, each showing a broken sword to symbolize disarmament. In the first, the eagle rent the sword as he stood upon it. The second was similar to the adopted design except that the eagle clutched a broken sword instead of the olive branch, which was thus placed above his head. The jury of the Commission of Fine Arts originally preferred the first design, but later chose the second. On December 17, sculptor member James Fraser wrote to chairman Charles Moore:

> Dear Mr. Moore: You will be interested to know what Mr. Adams had to say about the new dollar. His opinion was very much like our own in regard to the design, and he said that, left to himself, he probably would have chosen the seated eagle rather than the other one.
> I have given the Saint-Gaudens head to De Francisci as an example of what

---

[2] *Duluth Minneapolis Tribune,* January 12, 1922.

we consider a beautiful type, and he is working to complete it by Sunday night. He will leave two models with me, and take two to Washington with him, after which, if the Secretary approves, De Francisci will telephone me, and I will have them put into bronze at once.

It is necessary, I believe, to have the artist approve a bronze cast of his model, instead of plaster, if a reduction is to be made. This can be sent to the Mint, and will obviate bad electrotypes, bad bronze casts, and so forth, and, I feel, will be of great aid in obtaining good results. A plaster cast is so very easily changed and marred, and an electroplate bent,—which is really a very serious matter, and, I feel sure, makes it practically impossible to get it back to the original form, all of which so easily ruins a work of art.

I was glad that Mr. Adams so quickly approved our thought on the subject. Very truly yours.

De Francisci's models were finally approved by President Harding on the 19th. Teresa, in describing to her parents the President's reaction, wrote:

> . . . All the designs submitted were carefully gone over by President Harding himself, who took a great interest in the work. Last Saturday he was about to approve Anthony's design, when he noticed an extra dimple in the chin of Liberty. "It is not exactly a dimple" he explained to the President, "but only an extra artistic touch, which seems to indicate the presence of one."
>
> The President, however, maintained that he preferred a dimpleless Liberty, because the dimpled variety did not exactly express peace, so Anthony resubmitted the design, minus the dimple. The new coin is symbolic of peace, liberty and the Disarmament conference. On one side of the coin is the well known profile of Liberty, together with the numerals 1921 and "E Pluribus Unum" in the usual position. On the reverse side is an eagle, with folded wings, perched upon the top of a mountain, with the rising sun in the distance. Above the eagle's head are the olive branches of peace, while a broken sword, symbolic of the end of the war, is clutched in its talons. Just beneath the eagle is the word "Peace," while caroling the top of the coin are the words "United States of America."

Recalling his own experience as well as that of Saint-Gaudens, Fraser suggested that the Commission of Fine Arts keep close check on the coin while reductions and dies were being made. Moore conveyed this idea to Director Baker, and on December 20, wrote to Fraser:

> Dear Mr. Fraser: Everybody beginning with the Director of the Mint and going up to the under Secretary and Secretary of the Treasury is pleased with the Peace Dollar, in fact they are quite enthusiastic over it.
>
> I met the delightful little midgets at the office of the Director of the Mint. They were beaming all over with fun and it was very good to see them. Unfortunately I was called away after a few words of greeting and congratulations.
>
> I reinforced what you had to say about following the coin through the Mint.
>
> Mr. Baker was very glad to have the support of the Commission in this particular, and he is really depending upon you and Mr. Francisci to get a perfect coin. He will back you up to the very last in the struggle to obtain the highest possible degree of excellence at the Mint, and he will be seriously disappointed if this result is not attained. I know the difficulties as to time, and of course the impossible cannot be accomplished excepting on such extraordinary occasions as this. I am particularly happy over the head which is exactly what I have been longing for and expecting some day to see realized. I feel that through your good offices the Commission has been able to make another real contribution to the coinage of the country. Cordially etc.

When the President's choice became known, the "broken sword" was widely criticized as a symbol of defeat. De Francisci replied:

Top: Teresa Cafarelli (Mrs. De Francisci), the model for Miss Liberty on the Peace dollar. **Bottom:** 1922 Peace dollar (type of '21) and De Francisci's alternate model showing controversial "broken sword." *Courtesy of the artist.*

Also with the sword there is the olive branch of peace, and the combination of the two renders it impossible to conceive of the sword as a symbolization of defeat. It does not seem credible that any one would place such an interpretation on my design, as the Washington conference must be first in the public mind, and America has never suffered defeat.

The broken sword was nevertheless discarded, and on December 25, 1921, the *New York Telegram* reported:

> The design of the new silver dollar, known as the Peace dollar, has been changed according to announcement just made by the Treasury Department. The broken sword, grasped in the hands of the American Eagle, has been obliterated. As finally minted, the Peace dollar will show no sword at all. The talons of the American eagle will be empty, and, as it were, at rest.

As finally issued, the eagle held an olive branch in its talons. One can hardly find a more beautiful rendering of an eagle though it is different from that on the MacNeil or Weinman coins. De Francisci's eagle perches on a mountain peak, gazing into an infinite expanse of blue. His majesty is born of repose, not movement. He leans forward ever so slightly and his strength, though poised, is easily perceptible. It is De Francisci's conception of America, and it is a beautiful conception. In the east, the sun's rays burst forth, heralding a new era.

It is difficult to understand the criticism that greeted the Peace dollar, particularly when its designs are compared to the massive head and amateurishly executed eagle on the Morgan coin. Of course, attacks by the press on new coins are a tradition, and like the rain, fall on the good and the bad alike. Some critics charged that Liberty looked like a modern flapper, despite her distinctly old fashioned hair-do. Others protested because her mouth was open. Even the eagle was abused. On January 30, 1922, the *Syracuse Herald* commented:

> The old dollar had a solemn and serious look. The new one seems sissified by comparison. One has dignity, the other has prettiness, and if one wanted to be critical it might be added that while the old dollar had sentiment the new one has sentimentality.
> The two leading differences are in the eagle, and the Goddess of Liberty [a brilliant comment!]. The old eagle was a scrapper. He looked as if he were on the alert to start something any time, and between whiles, to scream to his heart's content. The 1922 version of the American bird of freedom looks anything but free. He looks out of luck. He has wings furled and is sitting, gazing into vacancy with the cheerless and pepless attitude of a wet barnyard fowl waiting for the weather to clear. There are some who say that he even wears pants, but that is an illusion. The real eagle does have thick foliage on his legs, all the way to his claws, which, when in a standing position gives something of a trousered effect.

On January 8, the *Albany-New York Telegram* complained that the coins were thinner on top than at the sides and would not stack. The critic did not realize that the diameter of the edge varies on every coin because more metal is absorbed between the dies where the relief is highest. Nevertheless, the charge that the coins would not stack was immediately echoed by papers across the country. It was untrue.

One of the ugliest attacks appeared in the *Wall Street Journal*. The article does not merit acknowledgment, except for its closing suggestion that new designs be chosen from a national competition, judged by a committee including artists of national repute. The writer did not know that this was exactly what had been done.

In the February 1922 issue of *The Numismatist,* Judson Brenner elaborated on the *Journal's* article, but his pique at the Mint is apparent throughout.[3] Brenner's remark that "The coin is only attractive to those to whom all dollars look alike" is amusing in the light of the high praise given the designs by his committee members Farran Zerbe and Howland Wood.

There was, however, one genuine difficulty in that the coins could not be perfectly struck up by the ordinary means.

On January 3, the Mint's engraver George Morgan[4] wrote to De Francisci:[5]

> Dear Mr. Francisci: Today by American Express I send to you 50 of the Peace Dollars. I know you will be disappointed, but the pressure necessary to bring up the work was so destructive to the dies that we got tired of putting new dies in.
>
> In changing the date to 1922 I took the opportunity of making a slight change in the curvature of the ground. I anticipate at least 20 tons less pressure will be required to bring up the design. This could double the life of the die. I send you an early strike of the 1922. Yours very truly.

Apparently, Morgan wrote again to De Francisci a day or so later, for on January 6, the sculptor complained to Mr. Caemmerer, Secretary of the Commission of Fine Arts:

> My dear Mr. Caemmerer: I have received a few of the Peace Dollars from the Philadelphia Mint and although the rush in which this coin had to be produced was too great to give a very perfect result, either artistically or mechanically, I feel now that something must be done since we will have more time for the 1922 issue. Primarily, I would suggest and with emphasis, that if possible, to forbid the mint engravers from touching in anyway the dies or hubs of said coins.
>
> A letter from Mr. Morgan which I enclose herewith states his intentions to do more changes small in mechanical gain but very damaging to artistic values. That is regrettable because unnecessary. The Mint's chief complaint is the height of the relief of the liberty head. Mr. Fraser and I have agreed that in order to overcome that mechanical hindrance to reduce the general relief of the coins by machine—a very simple process—a new hub would have to be made but the result, surely pleasing, would justify my work and the ideals and prestige of the American Fine Arts Commission.

Neither the Commission of Fine Arts nor Director Baker seem to have prevailed upon the self-willed Mr. Morgan. Not only did the engraver make numerous minor changes in De Francisci's models,[6] but (according to Fraser), he lowered the relief by hammering the surfaces of the electroplate with a flat board! Consequently, one should not judge De Francisci's designs except on the basis of the few proof impressions made prior to Morgan's "retouching." The 1922 "type of 21," of which three pieces are known, most faithfully represents the artist's conception, and is thus shown on the plate.

---

[3] Although the American Numismatic Association had first suggested the idea of a Peace dollar, Mint Director Baker ignored the association's auspices, failed to push legislation for original designs, and finally took full credit for the coin.

[4] Morgan had succeeded Barber on his death in 1917.

[5] Correspondence of the Commission of Fine Arts, National Archives.

[6] Walter Breen, "The 1922 Type of 1921 Peace Dollar," *The Numismatic Scrapbook,* July 1961.

CHAPTER 28

The Washington Quarter

IN HONOR OF GEORGE WASHINGTON'S BIRTH BI-
CENTENNIAL, the Treasury Department, together with the Commission
of Fine Arts and the Washington Bicentennial Commission, proposed the
issue of a medal and new coin of commemorative design. The program of
competition read:

> That, subject to the approval of Congress, the coinage of the United States
> silver half-dollars during the calendar year 1932 shall have a commemorative
> character. That the obverse shall bear a head of Washington based on the Houdon
> bust at Mt. Vernon.
> That the design of the reverse is left to the sculptor, with the proviso that it
> shall be national in conception.
> That one sculptor be selected to design both the coin (If Congress shall so
> provide) and the medal (already provided for).
> That each competitor shall submit in plastic form one design for each the
> obverse and reverse of the medal. The designs for the Coin will be considered
> when and if Congress shall so provide.[1]

The winner of the competition for the medal was Laura Gardin Fraser,
distinguished wife of sculptor James Earle Fraser. Mrs. Fraser had previously
furnished models for several commemorative half dollars, including the magnificent Oregon Trail Memorial.

Congress subsequently decided upon a Washington quarter, authorizing
the issue by the Act of March 4, 1931.

In a letter of July 14, 1931, assistant Mint Director Mary O'Reilly asked the

---

[1] An Act of Congress was required since the subsidiary coin designs were less than twenty-five
years old.

Commission of Fine Arts to furnish names of sculptors for a new competition. Chairman Moore replied that this would be contrary to the original program which provided for one artist to execute both the medal and coin. He therefore urged the selection of Mrs. Fraser.

Moore's letter was forwarded to Secretary of the Treasury Andrew Mellon who politely but firmly rejected its proposal. Mellon said that the Treasury Department had not been a party to the Commission's agreement and would not abide by it. A second program was thus arranged for October 27, 1931. A memorandum of that date by the Secretary of the Commission reads:

> Mr. Moore, Mr. Weinman [2] and I visited the office of the Mint this morning to inspect models that had been submitted for the George Washington Bicentennial 25 cent piece that has been authorized by Congress. There were over 100 models from some 98 competitors. The models had been arranged in Mr. Grant's office for inspection.
>
> The models showed the head of George Washington on the obverse, which was prescribed. For the reverse an optional design by the artist was shown but in over 75 per cent of the models an eagle had been portrayed. Mr. Weinman gave the models particular attention and after consideration eliminated all excepting Nos. 21, 22, 28, 56, 58, 72, and 90. It was finally agreed that Secretary Mellon should inspect all the models by Monday afternoon, at which time Mr. Weinman in company with members of the Commission would make the final selection.

The Commission eventually selected the models bearing the number 56, with the proviso that certain alterations be made. The models had been sculptured by Mrs. Fraser.[3] Secretary Mellon conferred with the Commission on November 2, and then selected a different model. On the 4th, he wrote to Moore:

> Dear Mr. Moore: Following the conference which we had with the members of the Fine Arts Commission two days ago, I inspected the models of the design for the new quarter dollar selected by the Commission as the one most nearly meeting with their approval. I understand that you wish the sculptor given an opportunity to restudy this design in order to make certain changes which would meet with my own and your wishes in this matter.
>
> I am very glad to accede to your request for a restudy of the design but, as the one selected was not my first choice and as it might be construed as showing discrimination if we give this opportunity to one sculptor and not extend it to others whose designs have equal merit in my eyes, I have designated the designs of three other sculptors and shall be glad to have a restudy made by these sculptors and by the one designated by the Commission.
>
> I am enclosing photographs of the designs to be submitted for restudy and will be grateful if you will forward them to Mr. Weinman, the sculptor member of the Commission, and ask if he will be kind enough to suggest the changes which he feels are necessary in order that the designs shall conform with the views of the Commission and with my own.
>
> Upon receipt of Mr. Weinman's suggestions, I shall ask the Director of the Mint to transmit them to the various sculptors who will be given an opportunity to make a restudy of their designs. Sincerely yours.

On November 10, Moore informed Mellon that the Commission had carefully considered his submissions, but definitely favored models No. 56. He added:

---

[2] Adolph Weinman was at this time the sculptor member of the Commission.

[3] This is disclosed in a letter of November 17, 1931 from Moore to Weinman. According to a statement made by Miss O'Reilly to Mrs. Fraser, Secretary Mellon also knew the identity of the Fraser models.

The Commission feel that this design would result in a very excellent coin. They quite agree with the Secretary's criticism that the eagle should be strengthened by a more vigorous treatment of head and body and a modification of the movement of the wings.

The treatment and size of the head of Washington and its arrangement within the circle are admirable. There might be further study as to contour.

From the point of general design this model seems to the Commission easily the best of the four under consideration. Therefore, they respectfully advise that it be accepted and that the sculptor be required to modify his existing model in the particulars stated above.

If the Commission were pulling for Mrs. Fraser, Mellon had other plans. Still, trying to convince the Secretary, Moore wrote on January 20:

Dear Mr. Mellon: In accordance with your request, the Commission of Fine Arts on January 19, 1932, considered the models selected from the number submitted in the original competition for re-study and re-submission.

The Commission selected from among the models an obverse and reverse which they marked. These selected models in the judgment of the Commission, adequately and in a distinguished manner meet what the Commission believe to be requirements for the design of the most used and so the most representative coin of the United States. The models were numbered 56.

For the head of Washington the standard naturally is the life-mask made by Houdon at Mount Vernon in 1785, and used by him as the basis of his statue at Richmond. This bust is regarded by artists who have studied it as the most authentic likeness of Washington. Such was the skill of the artist in making this life-mask that it embodies those high qualities of the man's character which have given him a place among the great of the world.

Judged by this high standard the model selected for recommendation to you is distinguished above those submitted by other sculptors. Simplicity, directness, and nobility characterize it. The design has style and elegance. The composition, from the medalist's point of view of spacing and balance, is entirely satisfactory. The Commission believe that this design would present to the people of this country the Washington whom they revere.

The selection of the model for the reverse was based on its universality as an emblem of the United States. The general conception is the one universally accepted by the people of this country. This fundamental conception has been worked out by the artist in a truly heraldic fashion. The eagle is exceptionally well rendered. It has vigor. It has sculptural quality. The emblematic characteristics get proper emphasis.

The Commission considered the alternative designs submitted by the above artist above recommended to you as in a class by themselves. Which of the alternatives is the best was the question. . . . This decision was based on a combination of elements in the design which seemed to the Commission to be the most artistic one.

While it is satisfactory to point out excellence in a recommended design, the Commission naturally hesitate to criticize the work of other artists beyond the point that the commendation of the one for specific qualities is in itself a criticism of the competitors.

The Commission, however, found in a design which called for detailed examination a lack of simplicity and vigor in the head, and an artistically unfortunate and also an unnatural arrangement of the hair which became conspicuous in the reduced size representing the actual coin. The reverse was pictorial rather than medallic in character. For these reasons the Commission felt that the design lacked these very elements of universality and permanence which the quarter-dollar should embody.

The Commission also considered a suggestion that the Saint-Gaudens eagle on the twenty-dollar gold piece be used for the reverse. They considered that to use a design that had been used on another coin would be unfortunate and sure to provoke criticism. Moreover, the eagle as it now appears on the coin has lost that essential quality which Saint-Gaudens gave to it. In reducing the relief vigor has been lost. Now the eagle has the quality of an engraving: It has become a picture instead of an emblem.

In submitting for your consideration advice as to the selection of designs for the new quarter-dollar, the Commission have been guided by the experience of its members in the art of the medal and also with the art of coinage. They have given to this particular recommendation most careful consideration, based on such experience. Also they have felt the responsibility laid upon them both toward the Government which they serve and to the Fine Arts which they are appointed to represent.

Within a few weeks, Mellon was succeeded by Ogden L. Mills, and the Commission issued a new protest. On March 31, Moore wrote to Secretary Mills:

Dear Sir: The Commission of Fine Arts return herewith the models of the proposed twenty-five cent piece, submitted with your letter of March 23, with the advice that they be not executed. This is the unanimous decision of the Commission reached after a careful examination of the models at their meeting on March 25, 1932. The suggestion in your letter that the models be restudied in order to meet the criticisms made by the Commission in their letter of January 20, 1932, is not practicable, in the judgement of the Commission, since these objections are fundamental.

The face of Washington is weak. It should be strong, as shown in the Houdon life mask at Mount Vernon. The arrangement of the hair is not only unnatural but also it detracts from the strength of the head.

The eagle on the reverse is not a good eagle in itself, and it is lacking symbolic quality. It does not represent the dignity and power which an emblem of the United States should have. Moreover, the balance is not good. The model shows emphasis on nonessentials and subordinates essentials.

The Commission has in mind that in reducing these models to the actual size of the coin, some details now visible will be lost, and, on the other hand, other details will be increased. Emphasis, balance, simplicity and dignity are essential in medallic art, and the Commission are confident that in the coin itself these essentials would be lacking.

For these reasons the Commission find the models submitted unacceptable and advise their rejection. They do not reach the standard of design which should characterize the coinage of the United States. It is these standards which the Commission is solicitous that the national coinage should attain.

In this connection, this Commission respectfully calls attention to these pertinent facts: On the completion of legislation by Congress authorizing a new quarter-dollar, the Treasury Department instituted a wide open competition, which resulted in the submission of about one hundred models, the great majority of which were sent in by persons unskilled in medallic art and were easily rejected. Among the number, however, were designs for an obverse and reverse which were highly acceptable, subject to slight modifications easily made by the medalist. The Commission recommended that these models be restudied and resubmitted. The Department then selected five models for resubmission, and one of the number was approved as entirely acceptable. The reasons for the rejection of the others were given. Then one of the unacceptable sets of models was sent to the Commission with the suggestion that it be again restudied. It is this set that the Commission now returns with the advice that the objections are too serious to be overcome.

It is respectfully submitted that in instituting competitions it is only just to all the competitors that their work should be judged by the recognized rules of their profession and that the decision shall be made accordingly. Otherwise artists of reputation cannot afford to enter competitions. In calling attention to those considerations this Commission feel that they are working in the best interests of the Government, as well as in the interests of the artists who have

Models for a Washington head quarter by Laura Gardin Fraser—the choice of the Commission of Fine Arts. *Courtesy of the artist.*

Models for a Washington head quarter by John Flanagan—the choice of Secretary Mellon.
National Archives.

accepted the invitation of the Government, with the understanding that the work to which they devoted their skill and time shall receive corresponding consideration. Very respectfully yours.

Mills replied on April 11:

Dear Mr. Moore: I have before me your letter of March 31, referring to my letter of March 23, setting forth the recommendation of the Commission that the restudied model for the new quarter dollar referred to in my letter, be not accepted.

As you state, the model in question was one submitted in the competition for the proposed new design of the twenty-five cent piece, and it was clear to all that this model was one of the more interesting and meritorious. My predecessor in office, Honorable A. W. Mellon, gave thought and attention to the models submitted in the competition and finally selected the particular model in question. In the light of your suggestions, I gave further thought to the matter and certain changes have been made by the artist, prompted by these considerations. I have given further consideration to the subject and am constrained to adhere to the decision of my predecessor, and I select that model.

You will realize, of course, that the duty of making the selection falls upon the Secretary of the Treasury and not upon the Commission of Fine Arts, the function of that body being purely advisory.

I appreciate the thought which the Commission has given to this matter and its full expression in your letter. As I have said, my own choice is the same as that of my predecessor, and it is my belief that the interests of the Government and of the artists concerned in such competition will be served by adherence to that choice. Sincerely yours.

In a letter to Moore dated April 16, the Secretary named John Flanagan as the sculptor whose models had been selected for the new quarter dollar.[4]

---

[4] The approved models, used from 1932 through the beginning of 1934, proved unsatisfactory in that the motto "In God We Trust" was all but illegible, even in newly minted specimens. Since then, not less than seven different obverses have been prepared.

CHAPTER 29

The Jefferson Five-Cent Piece

WITH THE SILVER ANNIVERSARY of the buffalo five-cent piece, Treasury officials lost little time in supplanting the famous coin. The story is told in part by the following announcement:

NATIONAL COMPETITION FOR NEW DESIGN FOR FIVE CENT COIN

OPEN TO ALL AMERICAN SCULPTORS

The Treasury Department, Procurement Division, Section of Painting and Sculpture invites competition for designs for a new five cent coin to be known as the "Jefferson Nickel." This competition is open to all American sculptors.

The competition requirements are that a sculptor entering the competition must submit two plaster models, one representing the obverse and one the reverse of the coin.

The sum of $1,000 is to be paid to the winner. The sculptor whose designs win the competition will be required to execute a formal contract with the Treasury Department, agreeing to make any revisions required by the Secretary of the Treasury.

All designs will be judged by the following Advisory Committee who have kindly consented to act with the Section of Painting and Sculpture in judging the competition:

Mrs. Nellie Tayloe Ross, Director of the Mint

Mrs. Sidney Waugh, Sculptor

Mr. Albert Stewart, Sculptor

Mr. Heins Warneke, Sculptor

The models should not be signed. They should be accompanied by a plain, sealed envelope, enclosing the sculptor's name and address. These envelopes will be carefully numbered when received with the same number as the designs they accompany and will remain unopened unless they conform strictly with the foregoing conditions.

Any sculptor may submit as many designs as he desires. Should he submit more than one set of designs he should remember to send a sealed envelope with his address with each entry.

The subject matter must contain on the obverse of the coin an authentic portrait of Thomas Jefferson. On the reverse side the subject matter will be a representation of Monticello, Jefferson's historic home near Charlottesville. In addition to the words required by law to appear on the coin, the coin may contain the inscription "MONTICELLO," in order to identify the architecture. The coinage laws require that there shall appear upon the obverse side of the coin the word "LIBERTY" and the date "1938," and "UNITED STATES OF AMERICA," and the denomination "FIVE CENTS." The coin should also contain the motto "IN GOD WE TRUST." None of the legends are to be abbreviated and should be all in capital letters.

Neither the United States of America nor any officer, agency, agents, or employee thereof shall be liable to the sculptor for the use by any person of any idea, plan, or design, expressed or executed by the sculptor in connection with the work.

Competitors are invited to participate in this competition subject to the condition, in view of the provisions of the laws of the United States, that any and all sketches, designs, molds, models, and the like, made by them in connection with such competition, whether or not submitted, be delivered to the committee by not later than April 15, 1938 so that they may be ultimately delivered to a representative of the Treasury Department for destruction or such other disposition as the Department may see fit to make of them.

The Treasury Department shall be under no obligation to show, exhibit, or preserve the work of any sculptor.

The models in order to be acceptable to the Treasury Department must be of plaster and should not exceed 8½ inches in diameter and should be executed in such a manner as to be suitable for coinage purposes. The background or field should have a slight radius, that is, the background must curve slightly from the center to meet the edge of the coin or border. A model with an absolutely flat background would be practically impossible to coin. The extreme depth of relief from the border to the deepest part should not exceed 5⁄32 of an inch and the highest part of the design should be kept slightly under the level of the border.

The competition will terminate April 15th, on which date the models should have been delivered, carrying charges prepaid, to the Section of Painting and Sculpture, Procurement Division, Treasury Department, Washington, D.C.

If no designs are submitted which are of sufficient merit to justify an acceptance, no contract will be awarded as a result of this competition.

Photographs of a front and side view of Monticello are available and may be obtained by writing to the Section of Painting & Sculpture.

A colorful description of the contest is given in the April 21 edition of the *Washington Post*:

A new nickel was born yesterday. Art judges peered at 390 plaster models, showing Thomas Jefferson on one side and his Monticello home on the other, and picked a winner to supplant the Indian-buffalo design. It may be a day or two until the winning artist is disclosed, however.

Jefferson, third President and author of the Declaration of Independence, never looked like so many different people as he did yesterday. The models depicted him as everything from a coarse barbarian to a royal dandy. The facial features varied from skinney to the triple-chin type. On a few casts, Jefferson scowled. He smiled on none, usually wearing a calm expression.

On some models, Jefferson wore his hair in a typical colonial pigtail. On others he had bobbed and even marcelled hair.

The classic Monticello fared little better, the competitors, in some instances, perching eagles on its roof.

In violation of rules for the contest, some artists substituted the Liberty Bell and even an ear of corn for the house.

The new Jefferson nickel will enter circulation some time this fall, the present buffalo nickel having served its minimum statutory life of 25 years.

On April 24, the winner was announced to be Felix Schlag, a Chicagoan of German birth who had come to the U.S. only nine years before. It was soon discovered, however, that the models had to undergo minor changes to meet the requirements of coinage. On May 11, the Hollywood *Citizen News* reported:

The Treasury today said that news isn't worth a nickel, but—the design for the Thomas Jefferson five-cent piece has gone back to artist Felix Schlag for a few changes.

What was the trouble?

Was Jefferson's face going to be lifted?

Was his jaw too lantern-like?

The Treasury said, "no." There are a few minor revisions, like angles and curves.

Further investigation disclosed the nickel won't be ready for the public for a couple of months. It still has to be approved by a lot of people.

The Fine Arts Commission must say it is O.K. The Director of the Mint, Mrs. Nellie Tayloe Ross, must nod and tell Secretary Morgenthau it's all right.

When and if the Secretary says all's well, the design goes to the Philadelphia Mint, which will then begin to stamp out the new coins.

The Commission of Fine Arts was not altogether pleased with the designs, particularly the modernistic reverse. Schlag thus revised his models, refining the "lantern jaw" and substituting a more traditional version of Monticello.

On July 17, Commission chairman Charles Moore noted:

The Treasury being anxious for a report as soon as possible, the photographs were submitted to Mr. Lawrie, who reported as follows:

"The models are of good workmanship. I feel that the main lettering on the United States side should be as bold or bolder than the lettering on the Jefferson side; also I feel that UNITED STATES OF AMERICA should be at the top of the coin, thus reversing the position of that and E PLURIBUS UNUM. In looking through a reducing glass at the photograph, which brings the image down to the size of a nickel, the letters FIVE CENTS seem to me too small."

The Commission concurred in Mr. Lawrie's criticism. It was noted that the sculptor had considerably improved his model of Monticello. The Commission concurred in this and a report was sent to the Director of the Mint, approving the model subject to Mr. Lawrie's criticisms.

The alterations required by the Commission of Fine Arts met with various reactions from the press.

On August 21, the *Anderson Indiana Herald* said:

The prize winning design for the new Jeffersonian nickel has been altered by order of the Federal Fine Arts Commission. They didn't like the view of Thomas Jefferson's home, Monticello, so they required the artist to do another picture of the front of the home. They did not like the lettering on the coin. It wasn't in keeping, but they forgot to say what it wasn't in keeping with.

The Commission compelled the artist to use the classical Roman letters that have been used on coins for decades. They are more familiar and perhaps easier to read, but who reads the lettering on a five cent piece, anyway?

Originally the letters were akin to the slim, graceful type without serifs (those curley-cues at the top or bottom of a letter) that are seen in up-to-date newspapers today. The letters on coins, as on public buildings, are purely decorative and should express the contemporary American spirit. There is no more reason for imitating the Romans in this respect than there would be for modeling our automobiles after the chariot of Ben Hur's day.

Jefferson five-cent piece by Felix Schlag, including alternate reverse (lower left) rejected by the Commission of Fine Arts. *National Archives.*

In its September 12 edition, the *St. Louis Globe Democrat* expressed a more sympathetic view:

> The new Jefferson nickel which will be in initial production at the Philadelphia Mint this week, will present a kindlier likeness than the original design on which it was based. Original lines by Felix Schlag, who won a $1000 prize contest over 400 competitors, have been softened and the pictured face of the author of the Declaration of Independence lifted. That is, on order of the Federal Fine Arts Commission, Mr. Felix Schlag removed the hollow from the great Democrat's cheek, smoothed hard lines around the mouth into a pleasant smile and even cut down the size of Jefferson's collar. And the original side view of Monticello, which is for the obverse [?] side of the coin, has been changed somewhat. Under orders of the Commission, Monticello was twisted around to a front view and a modernistic tree, which was shown in the foreground, was chopped down.
>
> So it will be a handsome and somewhat pleasing coin that, starting production this week, will begin trickling into circulation from Federal Reserve banks the first week in November, when supplies will be of circulating stature.

As this book goes to press, a movement is being sponsored by *Coin World* for the addition of Felix Schlag's initials to the Jefferson five-cent piece. The writer hopes that a resolution to this effect will be adopted by the Mint thus giving to Mr. Schlag the recognition so long due him.

CHAPTER 30

The Roosevelt Dime

IN BRINGING OUT THE ROOSEVELT DIME, the Mint broke a tradition of nearly four decades by assigning the modeling to its own engraver. The work thus devolved upon John R. Sinnock who had quietly replaced George Morgan in 1925.

In early October 1945, Sinnock submitted models of the obverse and sketches of the reverse to acting Director Leland Howard, who sent them on the 12th to the Commission of Fine Arts. Ten days later, chairman of the Commission, Gilmore Clarke, replied:

> In the opinion of the Commission, the head of the late President Roosevelt, as portrayed by the models, is not good.[1] It needs more dignity. It may be that the position of the head—the angle at which it is placed on the background—and the shape and ending of the neck are at fault.
>
> Also, the small letter R in the word Trust is too small. It would be better to reduce the phrase that the letters will be of one size.
>
> The design for the reverse having the branches on each side of the torch without the hand, and ONE DIME in large lettering at the bottom, is excellent.[2] Our only suggestion would be that the flame of the torch have a more classical form. A model for the reverse should be submitted.

A conference was arranged between Lee Lawrie, the sculptor member of the Commission, and Sinnock who, with members of the Treasury Department, met at Lawrie's home. Subsequently, Sinnock completed a new obverse model embodying Lawrie's suggestion. The change was more in execution than con-

---

[1] Two models were submitted which were identical except for the date, the latter having been altered to 1946.

[2] Sinnock's alternate reverse showed a hand holding the torch, together with two olive branches.

371

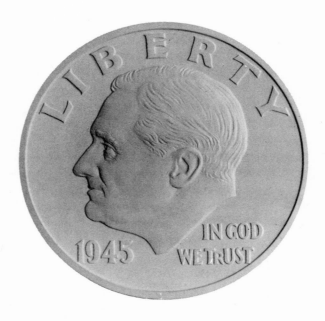

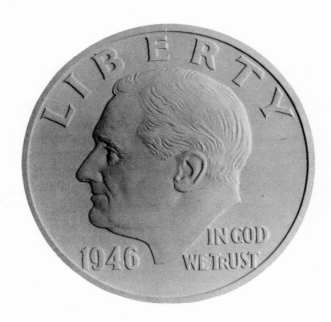

Early models for the Roosevelt dime by John R. Sinnock. *National Archives.*

Intermediate and adopted models for Roosevelt dime by Sinnock. *National Archives.*

Rejected and adopted sketches for reverse of the Roosevelt dime by Sinnock.
National Archives.

ception. In the first model, the modeling of the head was exceedingly soft and undetailed, a weakness that reduction would have intensified. In the second, the relief was bolder and more varied, giving life to the portrait. Otherwise, the heads were the same.

Director of the Mint Nellie Tayloe Ross transmitted photos of the new models to the Commission which again rejected the obverse. The Commission suggested that a competition be held among five artists—Edward McCartan, James E. Fraser, Paul Manship, A. A. Weinman, and Jo Davidson—in order to secure a more satisfactory design. The Director rejected this proposal on the ground that the coins had to be ready for the March of Dimes program, in January 1946.

During the last week of December, the models were shown to Secretary of the Treasury Vinson who also rejected the obverse. Sinnock again conferred with Lawrie who conveyed the suggestions of the Commission. Sinnock's third model was completed soon afterwards, resulting in a great improvement. The word LIBERTY had been moved to the left, permitting enlargement and in particular a lengthening of the head. Wrinkles were softened, the neck was refined, and a hollowness in the cheek filled. Roosevelt had never looked better!

Sinnock finished just under the wire. On January 7, F.D.R. Jr. gave a broadcast from the White House about the March of Dimes, and the Mint was asked to complete the new dies. The following day, Mrs. Ross telephoned the Commission to say that Lawrie and the Secretary of the Treasury had approved the models and that production of the coinage must quickly begin.

This conversation touched off an unpleasant interlude between the Mint and the Commission of Fine Arts. Lawrie had approved the model subject to the concurrence of the whole Commission, but its members could not possibly convene within the allotted period. Sinnock himself was ill and unable to visit Lawrie's studio. Mrs. Ross, however, believed she had fulfilled her obligation to the Commission, and ordered the coinage to proceed.

When the first Roosevelt dimes entered circulation, there were widespread rumors that Sinnock's initials (J.S.) stood for Joseph Stalin. Ridiculous as this seems, the Mint was finally required to issue an official denial of the charge.

CHAPTER 31

The Franklin Half Dollar

IT IS SAID THAT MINT DIRECTOR Nellie Tayloe Ross envisioned a Benjamin Franklin coin after the issue of Sinnock's Franklin medal in 1933. It was not, however, until 1947, after four presidential portraits had been adopted on the coinage, that the Director asked Sinnock to design a Franklin half dollar. Sinnock modified his earlier profile, and adopted for the reverse of the coin the Liberty bell device on his 1926 U.S.A. sesquicentennial half dollar. To meet legal requirements, a diminutive eagle was placed to the right of the bell.[1]

A lead impression of the obverse (complete except for the date which was represented by four X's) was sent by acting Director Leland Howard to the

The Benjamin Franklin half dollar by John R. Sinnock.

[1] Sinnock died in May 1947 and was succeeded as chief engraver by Gilroy Roberts.

Commission of Fine Arts on November 17, 1947. Apparently the Commission had already seen obverse and reverse models, for the trial piece was struck from a re-engraved master die. Chairman of the Commission Gilmore Clarke wrote to Mrs. Ross on December 1, expressing dissatisfaction with the reverse design.

> Dear Mrs. Ross: The Commission of Fine Arts, at their meeting on November 25, 1947, gave careful consideration to your letter of November 17th [2] and to the designs submitted therewith for the proposed new fifty-cent piece which, as you state, is to be minted in the near future. The designs received the particular attention of the Honorable Lee Lawrie, sculptor member.
>
> The Commission recognized good workmanship in the head of Benjamin Franklin, as portrayed on the medal by the late Mr. Sinnock.
>
> However, the Commission are not satisfied with the model of the reverse. The eagle shown on the model is so small as to be insignificant and hardly discernible when the model is reduced to the size of a coin. The Commission hesitate to approve the Liberty Bell as shown with the crack in the bell visible; to show this might lead to puns and to statements derogatory to United States coinage.
>
> The Commission disapprove the designs.
>
> For a coin as important as the fifty-cent piece, the Commission recommend a limited competition, in which some of the ablest medallists of the country would be invited to participate. What St. Gaudens, Fraser, Weinman, and MacNeil have accomplished in producing notable designs for coins that are acknowledged as works of art, could be repeated in this instance. For the Commission of Fine Arts: Sincerely yours, etc.

Possibly in deference to Sinnock the Commission's ideas were rejected, and their records show nothing further concerning the Franklin half dollar.

---

[2] i.e., Dr. Howard's letter.

CHAPTER 32

The Kennedy Half Dollar

THE FOLLOWING IS A REMINISCENCE of Gilroy Roberts, retired chief engraver of the Mint.[1] Mr. Roberts modeled the obverse of the Kennedy half dollar; the reverse was modeled by the then assistant engraver Frank Gasparro. This article originally appeared in the April 21, 1965 issue of *Coin World*.[2]

Shortly after the tragedy of President Kennedy's death, November 22, 1963, Miss Eva Adams, the Director of the Mint, telephoned me at the Philadelphia Mint and explained that serious consideration was being given to placing President Kennedy's portrait on a new design U.S. silver coin and that the quarter dollar, half dollar or the one dollar were under discussion. For the design, they were weighing the merits of either a front view or a profile for the obverse and the possibility of using the President's Seal of Office for the reverse.

From the standpoint of good composition and elegance of design the profile is much superior to any other view for the presentation of a portrait in bas-relief on a circular medal or coin. This is almost a universally held opinion among designers and artists and it was strongly recommended here that a profile be used.

A day or so later, about November 27, Miss Adams called again and informed me that the half dollar had been chosen for the new design, that Mrs. Kennedy did not want to replace Washington's portrait on the quarter dollar. Also it had been decided to use the profile portrait that appears on our Mint list medal for President Kennedy and the President's Seal that has been used on the reverse of this and other Mint medals.

---

[1] Mr. Roberts resigned from the Mint on October 8, 1964 having served as chief engraver for sixteen years. He is not only a splendid sculptor and engraver, but an astronomer, precision instrument maker, and inventor. Mr. Roberts is now chairman of the board of General Numismatics Corporation. He has been succeeded as chief engraver of the Mint by Mr. Gasparro.

[2] Reproduced by permission of *Coin World*.

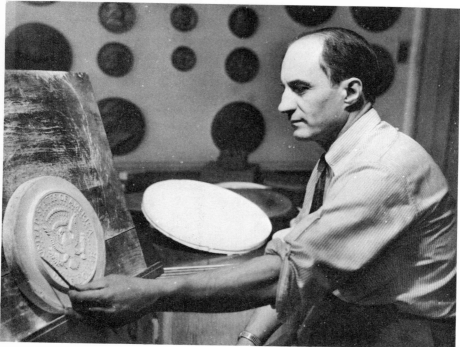

Top: Gilroy Roberts touches up intermediate reduction for obverse of Kennedy half dollar.
Bottom: Frank Gasparro examines reverse model. *Courtesy of "Coin World."*

Since the Franklin Half Dollar had not been issued for the statutory 25-year period, new legislative authority would be required. However, we were to begin immediately because they wanted to start striking the new half dollar in January, 1964, only about four weeks away. This seemed almost an impossibility, but the fact that we had, on hand, large models for both sides made the problem less insurmountable. There was still a great amount of work to be done, all stops were out. Mr. Frank Gasparro tackled the reverse and the obverse became my problem.

Starting back with the original plastilene model of President Kennedy's portrait, which he had approved, the coat was deleted, the periphery was changed to bring the head nearer center and to decrease the size of the circle in relation to the portrait. The background was reshaped to provide the required depressed field necessary for proper coinage. The inscription and date required by law were established.

On December 10, White House press releases were issued by President Johnson stating the reasons and the steps required to establish the new coin.

Work on the processing to the die stage continued. An intermediate reduction was made, approximately five inches in diameter, drastically reducing the relief and from this intermediate, preliminary trial dies with further reduction in relief were made. On December 13th, trial strikes were produced and these were immediately delivered to Miss Adams in Washington.

The following week, December 15, Miss Adams requested my presence in Washington to discuss the new half dollar with her and with other Treasury Department officials.

Both sides of the trial strikes received very favorable comment; however, Secretary of the Treasury Dillon wished to have Mrs. Kennedy's opinion and wanted me to accompany him at that time. On December 17, we met Mrs. Kennedy and Attorney General Robert Kennedy.

Mrs. Kennedy was favorably impressed with the design on both sides of the coin but felt it would be an improvement if the part in the hair, on the portrait was less pronounced and more accents were added. They also had in mind a design showing a full figure or half figure of the late President.

There was simply not enough time to create new designs and models, get approvals, etc. and have the new coin in production by January, 1964. I strongly advocated the simplicity and directness of a profile portrait as being the best possible arrangement for a handsome, outstanding coin whose beauty would endure and there could be no doubt as to the identity of the subject.

Mrs. Kennedy's suggestions were carried out on the intermediate size and another trial die was made for the obverse. New trial strikes were prepared. Secretary of the Treasury Dillon wanted to see this second trial piece and on December 27, I flew to West Palm Beach where the Secretary and Mrs. Dillon inspected the strikes. They both felt that Mrs. Kennedy's wishes had been complied with and in their opinion the coin was very handsome. It was decided to proceed with tooling up for production. The Congressional Act authorizing the Kennedy half dollar was approved December 30, 1963.

Time was fast running out and if we did not have working dies for Proof half dollars, the coiner would be unable to start Proof coin production which meant that up until the time dies were available some 30 or 50 employees would be without work . . . Extreme pressure was exerted to push this program through and by January 2, 1964, Kennedy half dollar Proof dies were delivered and our tremendous Proof coin production could get started. Some minor problems still had to be ironed out for regular production but by January 30, 1964, Denver had started production of regular half dollar coinage using the new design. Sometime during the following week, the Philadelphia Mint started regular half dollar coinage.

On February 11, 1964, Assistant Secretary of the Treasury Robert Wallace, Director of the Mint Eva Adams, Assistant Director of the Mint Fred Tate, Superintendent of the Mint Michael Sura, and other Treasury and Mint officials held ceremonies concurrently at the Denver and Philadelphia Mints to commemorate the striking of the new U.S. Half Dollar bearing the late President's portrait and

Adopted models for the John F. Kennedy half dollar, reduced to coin size.

issued by a sorrowing nation as a fitting and enduring memorial honoring our former President John F. Kennedy.

On March 5, 1964, an initial delivery of some 26 million of the new Kennedy Half Dollars was made to the Federal Reserve banks for eventual issue to the local banks and to the people of our country.[3]

---

[3] Just as certain perverted minds translated the J.S. on the Roosevelt dime as Joseph Stalin, there were some who saw in the G.R. (Gilroy Roberts) monogram of the Kennedy half dollar a Russian hammer and sickle. The rumor was quickly spread by over-zealous newspaper columnists until officially refuted by the Treasury Department.

Epilogue

AS THESE WORDS are being written, the Mint is busily preparing for its most important changeover since 1792. The standard silver coin has passed into history, replaced (for the time at least) by laminated base metal issues.[1]

Such was the decision of Congress on July 23, 1965, after considering the growing silver shortage, the demands of private industries, and the requirements of our modern, sophisticated vending machines.

The silver producers, who had enjoyed a Government subsidy from 1934 to 1955 are "sorely vexed." So vehement, in fact, was their opposition that only two months before President Johnson recommended legislation for a near-silverless coinage he was persuaded to order the resumption of silver dollars. Mercifully, this order was rescinded, scaling our support of the mining interests to only a certain proportion of silver in the half dollar. Yet, even this is unnecessary liberality. Nevada Senator Cannon's remark that a silverless coinage would damage "confidence in our coinage" has about as much merit as Representative Jensen's proposal, in 1942, to put a little "gold or silver" into the zinc cents "to satisfy the American people."

Moreover, unless the mining industry is greatly revitalized, the increasing shortage of silver and dwindling Government reserves will eventually compel its elimination from our coinage. With this expectation before us, it is clear that the last chapter of our story has yet to be written.

---

[1] See Appendix B

APPENDIX A

U. S. Mints and Mint Directors

(Reproduced, with additions and revisions, from the Report of the Director of the Mint)

Location of Mints	Acts establishing the Mints	Distinguishing Mint marks	Period covered in coinage data
Philadelphia, Pennsylvania	April 2, 1792	None, except letter P on copper-silver-manganese 5 cents	1793–196–
Denver, Colorado	April 21, 1862	D	1906–196–
San Francisco, California	July 3, 1852	S	1854–Mar. 31, 1955
New Orleans, Louisiana	March 3, 1835	O	1838–1861 1879–1909
Carson City, Nevada	March 3, 1863	CC	1870–1893
Charlotte, North Carolina	March 3, 1835	C	1838–1861
Dahlonega, Georgia	do.	D	1838–1861

#	Director of the Mint	Appointment by President	Date of Senate confirmation	Term of Service [1] From	To
1	David Rittenhouse	George Washington	Apr. 14, 1792 [2]	Apr. 1792	June 1795
2	Henry William de Saussure	Do.		July 1795	Oct. 1795
3	Elias Boudinot	Do.	Dec. 15, 1795	Oct. 1795	July 1805
4	Robert Patterson	Thomas Jefferson	Dec. 23, 1805	Jan. 1806	July 1824
5	Samuel Moore	James Monroe	Jan. 3, 1825	July 1824	1835
6	Robert Maskell Patterson [3]	Andrew Jackson	Jan. 5, 1835	May 1835	July 1851
7	George N. Eckert	Millard Fillmore	Aug. 30, 1852	July 1851	Apr. 1853
8	Thomas M. Pettit	Franklin Pierce	Mar. 31, 1853	Apr. 1853	June 1853 [4]
9	James Ross Snowden	Do.	Feb. 4, 1854	June 1853	1861
10	James Pollock	Abraham Lincoln	July 15, 1861 [5]	Spring 1861	Fall 1866
11	William Millward	Andrew Johnson		Fall 1866	Apr. 1867
12	Henry Richard Linderman	Do.	Apr. 2, 1867	Apr. 1867	May 1869
13	James Pollock [6]	Ulysses S. Grant	Apr. 20, 1869	Spring 1869	Spring 1873
14	Henry Richard Linderman [6]	Do.	Dec. 8, 1873	Apr. 1873	Dec. 1878
15	Horatio C. Burchard	Rutherford B. Hayes	Feb. 19, 1879	Feb. 1879	1885
16	James P. Kimball	Grover Cleveland	May 6, 1886	Dec. 1885	1889
17	Edward O. Leech	Benjamin Harrison	Dec. 19, 1889	Oct. 1889	1893
18	Robert E. Preston	Grover Cleveland	Jan. 12, 1894	Nov. 1893	Feb. 1898
19	George E. Roberts	William McKinley	Jan. 26, 1898	Feb. 1898	July 1907
20	Frank A. Leach	Theodore Roosevelt	Feb. 12, 1908	Sept. 1907	Nov. 1909
21	A. Piatt Andrew	William H. Taft	Aug. 5, 1909	Nov. 1909	June 1910 [7]
22	George E. Roberts [6]	Do.	Dec. 14, 1910	July 1910	Nov. 1914
23	Robert W. Woolley	Woodrow Wilson	Mar. 3 (legislative day of Feb. 19), 1915	Mar. 1915	July 1916
24	F. J. H. von Engelken	Do.	Aug. 17 (legislative day of Aug. 16), 1916	Sept. 1916	Feb. 1917
25	Raymond T. Baker	Do.	Mar. 15, 1917	Mar. 1917	Mar. 1922
26	F. E. Scobey	Warren G. Harding	Mar. 7, 1922	Mar. 1922	Sept. 1923
27	Robert J. Grant	Calvin Coolidge	Dec. 18, 1923	Nov. 1923	May 1933
28	Nellie Tayloe Ross	Franklin D. Roosevelt	Apr. 28 (legislative day of Apr. 17), 1933	May 1933	Apr. 1953
29	William H. Brett	Dwight D. Eisenhower	July 1, 1954	July 1954	Jan. 1961
30	Eva Adams	John F. Kennedy	Sept. 23, 1961	Oct. 1961	——

[1] If the beginning date of service precedes date of confirmation, this generally indicates that the Senate was in recess.
[2] The Senate was in recess during the entire term of service.
[3] Son of fourth Director.
[4] Deceased.
[5] Appointment not confirmed by Senate. For some unknown reason Millward's appointment is omitted from the official roster of Mint Directors.
[6] Former Director (see above).
[7] Became Assistant Secretary of the Treasury on June 8, 1910.

APPENDIX B

Tables of U.S. Coinage

GOLD COINAGE [1]

Denomination	Authorizing act	Standard weight	Standard fineness
		Grains	Thousandths
Double eagle ($20)	Mar. 3, 1849	516	900
Eagle ($10)	Apr. 2, 1792	270	916⅔
Do.	June 28, 1834	258	899.225
Do.	Jan. 18, 1837	258	900
Half eagle ($5)	Apr. 2, 1792	135	916⅔
Do.	June 28, 1834	129	899.225
Do.	Jan. 18, 1837	129	900
3 dollars [2]	Feb. 21, 1853	77.4	900
Quarter eagle ($2.50) [3]	Apr. 2, 1792	67.5	916⅔
Do. [3]	June 28, 1834	64.5	899.225
Do. [3]	Jan. 18, 1837	64.5	900
1 dollar [2]	Mar. 3, 1849	25.8	900

[1] Sec. 5 of the Gold Reserve Act of Jan. 30, 1934 provides as follows: "No gold shall hereafter be coined, and no gold coin shall hereafter be paid out or delivered by the United States * * *. All gold coin of the United States shall be withdrawn from circulation, and, together with all other gold owned by the United States, shall be formed into bars of such weights and degrees of fineness as the Secretary of the Treasury may direct."

[2] Discontinued by act of Sept. 26, 1890.

[3] Discontinued by act of Apr. 11, 1930.

387

SILVER (and other subsidiary) COINAGE

Denomination	Authorizing act	Standard weight	Standard fineness
		Grains	Thousandths
Dollar	Apr. 2, 1792	416	892.4+
Do. [1]	Jan. 18, 1837	412½	900
Trade dollar [2]	Feb. 12, 1873	420	900
Half dollar	Apr. 2, 1792	208	892.4+
Do.	Jan. 18, 1837	206¼	900
Do.	Feb. 21, 1853	192	900
Do.	Feb. 12, 1873	192.9	900
Do.	July 23, 1965	177.5	400 [3]
Quarter dollar	Apr. 2, 1792	104	892.4+
Do.	Jan. 18, 1837	103⅛	900
Do.	Feb. 21, 1853	96	900
Do.	Feb. 12, 1873	96.45	900
Do.	July 23, 1965	87.5	[4]
20 cents [5]	Mar. 3, 1875	77.16	900
Dime	Apr. 2, 1792	41.6	892.4+
Do.	Jan. 18, 1837	41¼	900
Do.	Feb. 21, 1853	38.4	900
Do.	Feb. 12, 1873	38.58	900
Do.	July 23, 1965	35	[4]
Half dime	Apr. 2, 1792	20.8	892.4+
Do.	Jan. 18, 1837	20⅝	900
Do. [6]	Feb. 21, 1853	19.2	900
3 cents	Mar. 3, 1851	12⅜	750
Do. [6]	Mar. 3, 1853	11.52	900

---

[1] Dollar of 1792 discontinued by Act of Jan. 18, 1837; dollar of 1837 discontinued by Act of Feb. 12, 1873, but resumed under the following acts:
    Feb. 28, 1878 (Bland-Allison Act)
    July 14, 1890 (Sherman Act)
    Nov. 1, 1893, to June 12, 1898
    June 13, 1898, war revenue bill
    Mar. 3, 1887 and 1891, trade-dollar conversion
    Apr. 23, 1918, Pittman Act replacement
    May 12, 1933 (sec. 43), Executive proclamation, Dec. 21, 1933
    June 19, 1934 (sec. 7), Executive proclamation, Aug. 9, 1934
[2] Discontinued by act of Mar. 3, 1887.
[3] Has surfaces of .800 fine silver clad to .210 fine core.
[4] Has surfaces of copper-nickel (75:25%) clad to pure copper core.
[5] Discontinued by act of May 2, 1878.
[6] Discontinued by act of Feb. 12, 1873.

MINOR COINAGE

(Minor coinage was confined by law to the Philadelphia Mint until the act of April 24, 1906. Minor coins were first manufactured at the mint at Philadelphia in 1793, at San Francisco in 1908, and at Denver in 1911.)

Denomination	Authorizing act	Standard weight	Standard composition
		Grains	
5 cents (copper-nickel)	May 16, 1866	77.16	copper, 75%; nickel, 25%
5 cents (silver)	[1]	77.16	copper, 56%; silver, 35%; manganese, 9%
3 cents (copper-nickel) [2]	Mar. 3, 1865	30	copper, 75%; nickel, 25%
2 cents (bronze) [3]	Apr. 22, 1864	96	copper, 95%; tin and zinc, 5%
Cent (copper)	Apr. 2, 1792	264	pure copper
Do.	Jan. 14, 1793	208	pure copper
Do.	Dec. 27, 1795 [4]	168	pure copper
Cent (nickel) [5]	Feb. 21, 1857	72	copper, 88%; nickel, 12%
Cent (bronze)	Apr. 22, 1864	48	copper, 95%; tin and zinc, 5%
Cent (steel)	[6]	41.5	steel with zinc coating not exceeding .001 inch.
Do.	[6]	42.5	Do.
Cent (copper-zinc)	[7]	48	copper, 95%; zinc, 5%
Half cent (copper)	Apr. 2, 1792	132	pure copper
Do.	Jan. 14, 1793	104	pure copper
Do.	Dec. 27, 1795 [4]	84	pure copper

[1] 5 cents (silver) coined, under provisions of act of Mar. 27, 1942, as amended by act of Dec. 28, 1945 from Oct. 1, 1942 until expiration of authority Dec. 31, 1945.

[2] 3-cents (nickel) discontinued by act of Sept. 26, 1890.

[3] 2-cents (bronze) discontinued by act of Feb. 12, 1873.

[4] Authority of the President in conformity with act of Mar. 3, 1795. The proclamation was not issued until Jan. 26, 1796. The annual reports of the Director of the Mint continue to list a fictitious weight of 186 grains for the cent as above authorized.

[5] Nickel cent discontinued by act of Apr. 22, 1864.

[6] Zinc-steel cent coined, by orders of Secretary of the Treasury dated Dec. 23, 1942, and May 15, 1943, pursuant to act of Dec. 18, 1942, during calendar year 1943.

[7] Copper-zinc cent coined, by order of Secretary of the Treasury of Dec. 16, 1943, pursuant to act of Dec. 18, 1942, from Jan. 1944 until expiration of authority Dec. 31, 1946. Resumed by Act of Sept. 5, 1962.

Index